EUROCOMMUNISM
BETWEEN
EAST AND WEST

JUL 1 0 1985

9.45

D1443959

EUROCOMMUNISM
BETWEEN
EAST AND WEST

Edited by
VERNON V. ASPATURIAN
JIRI VALENTA
DAVID P. BURKE

With my Warmest Compliments

[signature] Aspaturian
9/22/83

INDIANA UNIVERSITY PRESS
Bloomington

To our students at the Naval Postgraduate School

First Midland Book Edition 1980

Copyright © 1980 Indiana University Press

All rights reserved

No part of this book may be reproduced or utilized in any form
or by any means, electronic or mechanical, including photocopying
and recording, or by any information storage and retrieval system,
without permission in writing from the publisher. The Association
of American University Presses' Resolution on Permissions constitutes
the only exception to this prohibition.

Manufactured in the United States of America

Library of Congress Cataloging in Publication Data
Main entry under title:

Eurocommunism between East and West.

Includes bibliographical references.
1. Communism—Europe—Addresses, essays, lectures.
I. Aspaturian, Vernon V. II. Valenta, Jiri. III. Burke, David P.
HX238.5.E762   1980   335.43'094   80-7489
ISBN 0-253-32346-0   1   2   3   4   5   84   83   82   81   80
ISBN 0-253-20248-5 (pbk.)

Contents

Preface   vii

Part One • Origins and Evolution of Eurocommunism

  I. *Vernon V. Aspaturian* Conceptualizing
      Eurocommunism: Some Preliminary
      Observations   3
 II. *Herbert S. Dinerstein* Communism in Europe,
      1944–1949: The Historical Antecedents
      of Eurocommunism   24
III. *Stephen F. Cohen* Bukharin and the
      Eurocommunist Idea   56
 IV. *Jan F. Triska* Eurocommunism and the Decline of
      Proletarian Internationalism   72

Part Two • Eurocommunism and Eastern Europe

  V. *Jiri Valenta* Eurocommunism and the USSR   103
 VI. *Andrzej Korbonski* Eurocommunism and
      Poland   124
VII. *Melvin Croan* Eurocommunism and
      East Germany   140
VIII. *Jiri Valenta* Eurocommunism and
      Czechoslovakia   157
 IX. *Trond Gilberg* Eurocommunism and Romania   181
  X. *Robin Alison Remington* Eurocommunism and
      Yugoslavia   202
 XI. *Paul R. Milch* Eurocommunism and Hungary   223
XII. *Eric Willenz* Eurocommunist Perceptions of
      Eastern Europe: Ally or Adversary?   254

Part Three • Eurocommunism and the World

XIII. *Robert E. Osgood* The Effects of
Eurocommunism on NATO 272
XIV. *Parris H. Chang* Chinese Perceptions and
Relations with Eurocommunism 296
XV. *Peter Berton* Japan: Euro-Nippo-Communism 326

Contributors 363
Index 365

Preface

This, we believe, is a different book on Eurocommunism. Different in that it does not focus on the internal affairs of the West European Communist parties or on the domestic politics of the countries where the main Eurocommunist parties exist. Instead, it concentrates on some of the broader and more neglected questions of Eurocommunism viewed as part of the worldwide Communist movement: Eurocommunism as a concept; its evolution and its precursors; the complex and varied connections between Eurocommunism and the politics of Eastern Europe and the USSR; and the significance of Eurocommunism to China, the Japanese Communist party, and NATO.

The contributors to this volume address these questions in different ways. They were not held to a rigid frame of reference, nor do they represent a single point of view. With free rein to express their own judgments, they were invited to contribute and to share their ideas as authoritative analysts of the politics of particular countries or of particular aspects of the Communist movement. Their only common starting point was an invitation to consider some questions regarding Eurocommunism that had been raised in articles by Charles Gati and Jiri Valenta.[1]

The following chapters are the result. They vary widely in style, approach, and conclusions, and raising perhaps as many questions as they answer. Both questions and answers cluster around three main issues: the significance of Eurocommunism to the Communist movement, the implications of the appearance of Eurocommunist parties for pluralistic Western political systems, and the policy implications of Eurocommunism for the United States and the other liberal democracies.

This book has its roots in the seminar on Soviet-European relations conducted since the spring of 1977 at the Naval Postgraduate School by two of the editors, David Burke and Jiri Valenta. In its first term the seminar dealt specifically with Eurocommunism, and though it later covered many topics, Eurocommunism was a recurrent theme. This continuing interest inspired the Naval Postgraduate School Conference on Eurocommunism, Eastern Europe, and the USSR, which was organized by Valenta and Burke and conducted under the chairmanship of Vernon Aspaturian in August 1978. Generous sponsorship by the Naval Postgraduate School Foundation permitted a group of prominent scholars from throughout the United States to attend the conference. Their presentations and the lively exchange of ideas among them generated ten of the fifteen contributions to this book.[2] In addition Lieutenant Paul Dahlquist, USN; David Albright, the editor of *Problems of Communism;* and Captain David Helms, USAF, of the American Embassy in Bonn, addressed the conference and served as discussants. Their comments helped to form and to hone many of the ideas that appear below.

In addition to the authors and conference participants, the editors would like to express their thanks to several others who made this book possible. First among these are our students, especially the remarkable group of officers of all US military services who have pursued studies in Soviet and European affairs at the Naval Postgraduate School during the book's gestation. Among them, two Air Force specialists, Captains Mary Walsh and Craig McElroy, deserve special mention. Their ideas on various aspects of Eurocommunism and the European Left had an important, if indirect, effect on discussion at the conference, and thus on the content of this book.

For their material aid and their encouragement of this project we are particularly grateful to Dean David Schrady and Professor Patrick Parker of the Naval Postgraduate School. To William Tolles, the School's Dean of Research, and to his staff we owe special thanks for their aid in arranging financial support for the conference and for leading us through the exotic red tape that flourishes where academia and the US Navy overlap. We owe a particular debt of gratitude to Heidi Aspaturian whose fine editorial hand is apparent throughout this book. For help in preparation of the manuscript our thanks go to Pat Crabb of the Department of National Security Affairs of the Naval Postgraduate School and to Connie Boob, Secretary of the Slavic and Soviet Language and Area Center at the Pennsylvania State University. Finally, we are especially grateful to Anna Burke and Virginia Valenta for their support of their husbands throughout this project and for their hospitality to the editors' colleagues.

Any credit for editing this volume belongs as much to those we have mentioned as to us. The editorial imperfections are ours alone.

V.V.A

J.V.

D.P.B.

NOTES

1. Charles Gati, "The 'Europeanization' of Communism?" *Foreign Affairs* (April 1977), pp. 539–553; and Jiri Valenta, "Eurocommunism and Eastern Europe," *Problems of Communism* (March-April 1978), pp. 41–54. The latter article has also been published in revised form in Teresa Rakowska-Harmstone and Andrew Gyorgy, *Communism in Eastern Europe* (Bloomington: Indiana University Press, 1979).

2. Contributors to this volume who participated in the conference are Vernon Aspaturian (Chapter 1), Herbert Dinerstein (Chapter 2), Jiri Valenta (Chapters 5 and 8), Andrzej Korbonski (Chapter 6), Melvin Croan (Chapter 7), Trond Gilberg (Chapter 9), Robin Remington (Chapter 10), Paul Milch (Chapter 11), and Robert Osgood (Chapter 13). The five remaining contributions were commissioned after the conference to round out the book.

Part One •

ORIGINS AND EVOLUTION
OF EUROCOMMUNISM

CHAPTER I

Conceptualizing Eurocommunism: Some Preliminary Observations

Vernon V. Aspaturian

Introduction

It is a universal but predictable lament that Eurocommunism as a concept—and at this point it should be pointed out that almost all writers call it a concept, although it is more appropriately a label or perhaps an *appellation controllé*—is ambiguous, amorphous, elastic, and elusive. This is true whether the analysts are proponents, opponents, or neutral in their approach. Like many terms and concepts in political discourse and political science, Eurocommunism was not the product of a systematic empirical investigation of political phenomena that revealed certain regularities and uniformities sufficient to conceptualize it into an analytical or hypothetical construct that could then be further tested. Rather, Eurocommunism suddenly appeared out of the blue as a convenient impressionistic label for describing certain common tendencies in the Communist parties of Italy, France, and Spain, which distinguished them sharply from the Communisms in Eastern Europe, East Asia, Africa, and Latin America. Only after the *a priori, ad hoc*, and adventitious appearance of the label did a veritable army of would-be conceptualizers materialize to gratuitously characterize the term as imprecise, ambiguous, and without fixed meaning, but nevertheless ready to domesticate it and give it systematic form.

It must be stated at the outset that the calculated attempt to convert an impressionistic label burdened with inevitable polemical and normative baggage into an analytical concept is a hazardous business. Such a concept can never completely escape its origins, and its semantic ancestry will inevitably continue to cast a shadow over its analytical functionality. Like Impressionism in the field of modern art, Eurocommunism is not a self-designated label but originated with critics of Communism rather than proponents. Unlike Impressionism, however, the term was not conceived initially as one of derision, but, like Impressionism, it has been eagerly embraced by its victims as an entirely appropriate designation. In the words of the Spanish Communist leader Santiago Carrillo:

> The reader may perhaps be surprised at the frequency with which in the following pages I use the term 'Eurocommunism.' It is very fashionable, and though it was not coined by the Communists and its scientific value may be doubtful, it has acquired a meaning among the public and, in general terms, serves to designate one of the current Communist trends. If it is still rather imprecise, a part of this imprecision corresponds to what is still undecided, exploratory, in this trend which has up till now manifested itself more as a serious, self-critical rectification of policy than in theoretical elaboration. This demonstrates once again that practice is usually ahead of theory, that theory is a generalization of practice, though practice gains solidity and basic content when theory confirms it, gives it scientific precision and extends and clarifies its influence.[1]

As Carrillo strongly suggests, Eurocommunism is still more a tendency, an ongoing, evolving process, at this point more self-critical than substantively innovative, and hence not a completed, mature, political phenomenon that can be systematically conceptualized with precision as an analytical tool or integrated into a coherent normative ideological or political doctrine. Like many terms in political science, Eurocommunism as a concept is destined to have both an analytical and a normative existence. Whatever confusion and misdirected controversy this will inevitably produce can only be compounded if Eurocommunism is prematurely conceptualized in either its normative or analytical mode or both. Hence all attempts at conceptualization will necessarily be tentative, provisional, exploratory, elastic, and even transient. Any attempt at this point to give Eurocommunism precise, fixed meanings, with the full panoply of criteria, indices, and testing procedures, can only produce results that are likely to be obsolete and overtaken by events soon after their appearance.

I

All useful concepts and labels are likely to have claimants for their coinage, origination, or first-usage. Remarkably, no one has really come forward to claim paternity, maternity, or parentage in any form, although the term is only a few years old and one can hardly blame the proverbial mists of time for the obscurity of its origins. Obscure they appear to be nevertheless. Parentage has been ascribed but, as noted above, appears never to have been claimed. It is universally agreed that the term did not originate within the world of Communist parties, but where outside the world of Communism remains somewhat clouded. The favorite Soviet explanation of its origins is that "the term first cropped up comparatively recently . . . was originally coined by bourgeois political theorists and since has been bandied about in one form or another depending on who uses it and what interpretation is placed on it."[2] More specifically, Vadim Zagladin asserted in December 1976 that the term was "invented by the Americans, particularly Zbigniew Brzezinski," a remarkable, if inadvertent, tribute to the power of President Jimmy Carter's National Security Advisor to influence ideological development in the Communist world.[3]

The perceptive French critic Jean-François Revel writes that "one of the favorite amusements of 'political scientists' is to search for the author of the term 'Eurocommunism.'" He also notes that some attribute coinage to Brzezinski, others to Arrigo Levi of *La Stampa* (Turin), who, it appears, actually coined the transitional term "neocommunism" rather than Eurocommunism. It was, however, German pedantry that unearthed the unromantic information that the term was first used in the summer of 1975 by the Yugoslav journalist Frane Barbieri, former editor of the Belgrade weekly *N.I.N.* who now contributes to *Il Giornale* (Milan).[4]

The fact that such a widely used term is still a semantic orphan indicates the extent to which Eurocommunism still lacks substantive value beyond its existence as a clever neologism. Once Eurocommunism firmly establishes itself as both a movement and a concept there will be no shortage of claimants to parentage.

When the Eurocommunists themselves adopted the term as an appropriate label is also somewhat obscure. The introduction to Carrillo's book *Eurocommunism and the State* is dated December 1976, which suggests that Carrillo must have accepted it sometime between July and December 1976. Moscow feigned both surprise and dismay at its adoption by Carrillo so soon after the Berlin Conference:

> To begin with, it should be noted that in the matter of 'Eurocommunism' . . . Carrillo has undergone a truly staggering metamorphosis. Only a year ago, at the Berlin Conference [June 29–30, 1976], he said that there is no such thing as "Eurocommunism." Today he proclaims himself not simply a Eurocommunist, but some-

thing of an apostle of this new concept and sets out to formulate its basic dogmas for the benefit of the whole world.[5]

The Madrid meeting of three major Western Communist parties, held in March 1977 after the publication of Carrillo's book but before its condemnation by Moscow in *New Times* (June 1977), appears to be the definitive point and locale of general adoption. In any event, the participants of the Madrid Conference, in the words of James Goldsborough, "came away calling themselves Eurocommunists."[6] The French Communist leader Georges Marchais was reported to have been converted by his discovery that the term Eurocommunist had positive symbolism. "I was struck," he said, "by the headline in a reactionary French newspaper yesterday that said, 'Eurocommunism is a farce.' I say no, it is not a farce. It is something serious."[7]

Soviet leaders, viewing with concern and apprehension the possibility that developments within the Italian, French, and Spanish Communist parties were threatening to create yet a third major schism in the Communist movement, attempted to deal with the situation through rhetorical cooptation. Repeatedly Soviet leaders insisted that differences between Moscow and West European Communist parties were natural and simply reflected the democratic and participatory nature of the Communist movement. Simultaneously, Moscow rejected various terms and concepts, such as "national communism," as unnecessary, inaccurate, or mischievous inventions of Western psychological warriors intent on introducing conflict and controversy within a movement that, in spite of its internal differences, operated within a common set of doctrinal parameters encompassing the Leninist component of Marxism-Leninism.

The Soviet leadership recognized that two major schisms, the denunciation of Stalin and the repudiation of Stalinism, and the growing autonomy and indigenization of major nonruling Communist parties, particularly in France, Italy, and Japan, made it impossible for Moscow to deal with the situation through excommunication, subversion, or intimidation. As a result, it adopted a more flexible approach to the threat of Eurocommunism, neither repudiating it nor accepting it, but simply criticizing it, hoping to domesticate and assimilate it in form if not in substance. The major approach to the problem, which must be adjudged a failure, was to endow Eurocommunism with a purely geographical significance and to invent something called the European Communist movement (encompassing all Europe) as a counterpoise to Eurocommunism (including only Western Europe). This, for example, was the major thrust of the Soviet compendium *Europe and the Communists*, written in 1976 by a team of writers including Vadim

Zagladin. The book is essentially the Soviet version of the proceedings of the 1976 Berlin Conference of European Communist parties.[8] It stresses the unity of Europe and dismisses the distinction between Western and Eastern Europe as artificial and mischievous. The term European Communist movement appears repeatedly in the Soviet commentary, but nowhere is there even the slightest hint of something called "Eurocommunism."

A major Soviet purpose of the Berlin Conference was to elicit a *de facto* charter for a European Communist movement in the form of a document, but although Moscow accepted important emendations insisted upon by Western Communist parties, not a single party signed the document.[9] In spite of this, Moscow and some East European Communist parties proclaimed that it was a document "unanimously adopted" by the conference, a distortion that impelled Western Communists to publicly dispute the contention. They virtually repudiated the document and publicly suggested that another such all-European conference of Communist parties was neither desirable nor likely.[10] It was obvious that Moscow had overplayed its handling of the Berlin Conference, and the Moscow-envisioned European Communist movement did not enjoy even a lingering death.

Moscow's dismay was amply demonstrated in its intemperate attack upon Carrillo's book in *New Times,* which it sought to mitigate defensively and even apologetically in subsequent issues after widespread negative reaction among both West and East European Communist leaders. In its attack upon Carrillo, *New Times* again attempted to counterpoise the idea of a European Communist movement as opposed to a Eurocommunist one. Interestingly enough, *New Times,* like virtually all observers, started out initially by referring to Eurocommunism as a term but quickly shifted to calling it a concept. Thus, in recognizing the underlying political and social realities of Eurocommunism, *New Times* observed:

> One interpretation originates among the Left, including the Communist Parties. Some, while pointing out as a rule that the term is not a Communist one, that it was not thought up by the Communists, use it in reference to the common features characteristic of the present strategy of the Communist Parties of the developed capitalist countries. . . . True enough, the strategies of a number of West European parties, and on a broader plane, of the parties of the capitalist countries at a high level of socio-economic development, do have common basic premises. This is a widely known fact that was recognized long ago. . . . The Communist parties of the developed capitalist countries, as all other Communist parties for that matter, naturally seek to take account of the national and historical context in their countries.[11]

Continuing to examine Eurocommunism as an *analytical* concept, *New Times* went on to make a number of points with which the Eurocommunists would agree and that strengthened their position rather than Moscow's. First, the article correctly noted that "Eurocommunist" characteristics applied also to the United States, Japan, Canada, and Australia, "which means from this standpoint 'Eurocommunism' is too narrow a concept."[12] The article thus inadvertently shifted from a geographical definition of Eurocommunist to a cultural/civilizational/developmental one that served to separate West European Communism from that of Eastern Europe, and to unite it with Europe and Europe *outre mer*, as it were.

Second, the article gratuitously noted that lumping *all* West European parties together "is an oversimplification," which is a homogenization no Eurocommunist has advanced. Finally, "the concept is erroneous also because it affords grounds for assuming that what is in question . . . is not some specific features of the strategy of the Communist parties in some countries, but some sort of specific brand of Communism."[13] Then in a few ill-chosen words, *New Times* effectively nullified its discussion about variety, diversity, different roads, and so forth, by reaffirming its traditional dogmatic notion that, in spite of everything, there is only one true Communism:

> Yet there is only one Communism—if we speak of true, scientific Communism—namely, that whose foundations were laid by Marx, Engels, and Lenin, and whose principles are adhered to by the present-day Communist movement.[14]

It was quite evident to the Soviet leadership that, unless Eurocommunism as a "specific brand of Communism" could be assimilated, it would be on a collision course with the Leninist brand of Communism and would inexorably result in the de-universalization of Leninism, reducing it to little more than a Russian brand of Marxism originating in "the specific conditions in which a party functions." Indeed, Carrillo launched a frontal attack upon both Lenin and Leninism. In the introduction to his book, Carrillo bluntly notes:

> It must be recognized, however, that the approach to the problem of the state in the following pages involves a difference from Lenin's theses of 1917 and 1918. These were applicable to Russia and theoretically to the rest of the world at that time. They are not applicable today because they have been overtaken in the circumstances of the developed capitalist countries of Western Europe. . . .
> It may strike some people as blasphemous to read that some of Lenin's theses are out of date; there are those who are unaware that Lenin said the same thing about Marx, and that the Soviet successors to Lenin openly revised some of his theses.[15]

Recent Soviet ideological literature is obsessed with maintaining the integrity of Leninism as an inseparable component of Marxism-Leninism, whose principles are enduring in time and universal in scope. Thus, Soviet writers continue to maintain the fiction that, in spite of internal differences among parties on strategy and tactics due to various circumstances, events, and other variable objective conditions, all Communist parties operate within a common set of doctrinal parameters embracing the five fundamental principles of Leninism: (1) democratic centralism; (2) monolithic unity; (3) proletarian revolution; (4) dictatorship of the proletariat; and (5) proletarian internationalism. All are simultaneously Communist code-words, whose operational definitions until about 1956 were determined solely and arbitrarily by Moscow. Whereas the content and precise execution of these principles varied considerably in response to a number of conditions, the variations and reasons were originated and approved in Moscow. One of the problems Moscow has in communicating, not only with the outside world but also with other Communist parties, is that in spite of the often convulsive changes in the operational meaning of these principles, the Soviet Union invariably acts as if *any current* application of the principle has been continuous and unchanging throughout. This has required a form of self-deception increasingly difficult for foreign Communist leaders to accept. One of the truly innovative behavioral characteristics of the Eurocommunists is their refusal to engage in this bizarre charade of retaining rhetorical loyalty to principles whose content and context has radically changed. Instead, they have resorted to the more honest approach of repudiating outright certain "durable" principles whose durability was in semantic form only. The words remained the same, but the meaning and content changed. Instead of engaging in the scholastic and ideological gymnastics of redefining in acceptable operational terms concepts like "dictatorship of the proletariat," "monolithic unity," and "proletarian internationalism," the Eurocommunists are calling them inapplicable or obsolete as principles. Thus, with respect to the unchanging content and changing forms of the "dictatorship of the proletariat," Carrillo forthrightly observes:

> In this sphere, and at the risk of being accused of heresy, I am convinced that Lenin was no more than half right when he said: "The transition from capitalism to Communism, naturally, cannot fail to provide an immense abundance and diversity of political forms, but the essence of all of them will necessarily be a single one: *the dictatorship of the proletariat.* . . . "As we can judge today . . . *the diversity and abundance of political forms* likewise entails the possibility of *the dictatorship of the proletariat not being necessary.*[16]

Since the publication of his book, Carrillo has carried his assault against Leninism to its ultimate conclusion. The Spanish Communist party under his direction has formally renounced Leninism, becoming the first Eurocommunist party that no longer refers to itself as a Marxist-Leninist party. Aside from being viewed as a serious provocation by Moscow, the renunciation may be premature for purely tactical reasons. The renunciation of Leninism may even endanger Carrillo's position within his own party, since it heightens Moscow's incentive to do something about the Spanish Communist leader. On the other hand, the longer Moscow delays taking action—either excommunication or subversion of Carillo—the more likely that other Western parties will follow in Carillo's footsteps, since Eurocommunism, if it means anything, means stripping away the Leninist component of Marxism-Leninism, and more importantly, the residual Stalinist elements that had been inextricably co-mingled with Leninism over the years. Already a number of other Eurocommunist parties have followed Carillo's example.

II

It is useful to summarize attempts to conceptualize Eurocommunism despite the hazards of dealing with the term at a time when it is more a tendency or a process without a firm future. Such an examination must, of course, deal with the various approaches, perspectives, and perceptions that have been offered. Even more importantly it must recognize that essentially three different dimensions of conceptualization are involved, and these are often inadvertently confused and interchanged with one another. Commentators who attempt to discuss Eurocommunism are frequently talking on different wavelengths and speak past, rather than to, each other. Furthermore, depending upon the observer, one dimension of Eurocommunism as a concept may have greater saliency than another.

Three distinctive conceptual dimensions of Eurocommunism based upon function can be isolated: (1) Eurocommunism as an analytical concept; (2) Eurocommunism as a normative concept; and (3) Eurocommunism as a polemical concept. Soviet commentators on Eurocommunism clearly recognize these conceptual dimensions of Eurocommunism and, since each presents special dangers for Moscow, they attack all three dimensions. The review of Carrillo's book in *New Times* carefully and systematically segregated these three conceptual dimensions, isolating and defining the specific dangers each posed for the USSR and the CPSU. Eurocommunism as an analytical concept attacks the basic Leninist cognitive and epistemological tools of analysis; as a normative concept, it rejects Leninist models and solutions; and as a polemical concept, it drives a wedge between "Soviet" Communism and West European Communism, and in fact attacks the "Communist" credentials of the Soviet Union, but from directions different from that of Peking.

Most commentators on Eurocommunism appear to agree that Eurocommunism as a distinctive analytical concept is marked by four principal characteristics. One can certainly agree with Charles Gati's observation that "despite its imprecision, the term 'Eurocommunism' has gained wide currency as a convenient designation for a more tolerant, moderate, and democratic tendency in world communism,"[17] while at the same time noting that this general description has been applied to other earlier and unsuccessful brands of Communism. More specifically, Eurocommunism is characterized by the following:

1. The organizational, tactical, and ideological autonomy and independence of each Communist party in applying the principles of Marxism-Leninism.[18]

2. The renunciation of violent revolution, the dictatorship of the proletariat, and the irreversibility of Communist power as necessary elements in the creation of a socialist society. These are retrograded to optional, rather than inevitable or necessary, modes.[19]

3. Permanent commitment to the values of Western humanism, democratic values, and pluralism, that is, a pledge to honor the institutions of free and universal suffrage, the freedoms of opinion, expression, press, and association; the right to strike, the free movements of people, and so forth.[20]

4. The alteration of the balance between internal and external commitments in the search for a socialist and Communist society, that is, giving higher priority to finding common ground with domestic kindred anticapitalist political and social forces than to the preservation of common ground with the USSR. This shift to giving increasingly greater priority to the interests of domestic constituencies than to external constituencies or higher ideological abstractions represents a general trend in world Communism, whether in the USSR, Yugoslavia, or China, and in ruling and nonruling parties alike.

What makes these four characteristics "Eurocommunist" rather than a new universal model of Communism in opposition to the Soviet and Chinese "universal" models is that whatever "universalism" exists would be in form rather than in substance, because point one emphasizes autonomy, individuality, and diversity, while point three is historically, culturally, and developmentally—not necessarily geographically—specific. As Carrillo himself recognizes, Communist parties cannot promise to preserve democratic and pluralistic values and institutions where they never existed. He continues to defend Lenin and the Russian revolution precisely on these grounds.

The conceptual impact of Eurocommunism is not that it simply rejects the idea of universal models or universal processes of revolution, but that it threatens to demolish the residual vestiges of Soviet preeminence, if not primacy, in the world Communist movement. Lenin is desanctified from a demigod to a national Communist leader; demoted from universal philosopher on the level of Marx and Engels to a Russian revolutionary and political leader on a par with Mao Tse-tung, Josip Tito, Carrillo, Palmiro Togliatti, and Maurice Thorez. The Russian Revolution is demythologized from a "historic" event to a mere historical event, without any particular lessons of a universal character, except perhaps negative ones. Leninism is retrograded from doctrinal and even strategic significance to the purely local and tactical in a manner really not much different from the Maoist conception:

> The combination of Marxist theories with the practice of the . . . Russian revolution gave rise to Russian Bolshevism-Leninism-Stalinism. . . . What Mao Tse-tung has done as a disciple of Marx, Engels, Lenin and Stalin is precisely to unite the theories of Marxism with the actual practice of the Chinese revolution, thus giving rise to Chinese Communism—the thought of Mao Tse-tung . . . [which] is Marxism applied to China.[21]

Unlike Maoism and Titoism, however, Eurocommunism is untested. No ruling Communist party calls itself Eurocommunist, although the Prague Spring came close to establishing at least a proto-Eurocommunist regime. Thus Eurocommunism as an analytical concept is still relegated to the realm of theory and potential, rather than practice, and this creates no little confusion when referring to the reality of Eurocommunism. It is this notion of Eurocommunism as a "reality" that focuses the concern of non-Communist critics of Eurocommunism such as Henry Kissinger and Jean-François Revel. Kissinger stresses the untested character of Eurocommunism, while Revel refers to it as a "myth," and both emphasize the sad history of the prewar popular fronts in Western Europe and the tragic fate of the postwar popular and national fronts in Eastern Europe. The concern of the critics is not mitigated, but exacerbated, when proponents of Eurocommunism and neutral observers cite both prewar and postwar popular fronts as historical antecedents of Eurocommunism.

In seeking to conceptualize Eurocommunism, some attention must be paid to the etymological construction of the word itself. At first glance it gives the impression of being regional and geographical in conception. The word is actually an acronym for European Communism, which Moscow seized upon in its effort to create a "European Communist movement" including both Western and Eastern Europe. The Berlin Conference of 1976 was to be the organizational expression of the movement's unity. The West European parties convened their own conference in Brussels before the Berlin Conference, however, as a sort of Eurocommunist "caucus," while the Warsaw Pact parties met in counterpart separate sessions. As a result, the Berlin Conference was more like the meeting of two organizational branches of Communism rather than as a single organization. This was reflected in the post-Berlin bickering between Moscow and the Eurocommunists over the meaning and significance of the conference itself. Moscow emphasized the common areas of agreement and inartfully suppressed differences, while the Eurocommunists stressed the ideological distance between them and the CPSU.[22]

Virtually all observers agree that Eurocommunism as a concept is applicable or potentially applicable to all highly developed capitalist countries. All but Japan are European geographically or culturally. The universal recognition that the Japanese Communist party is a Eurocommunist-type party—even a prototype of Eurocommunism—renders it difficult to conceptualize Eurocommunism even in cultural/civilizational terms, unless modernization is defined as a European cultural/civilizational creation. Since all agree that it is precisely the adopted European characteristics of the Japanese polity, and not the indigenous Japanese culture, which makes the Japanese Communist party a Eurocommunist-type party, it would be accurate to say that Eurocommunism is essentially a phenomenon of geographical Western Europe and its demographic and cultural offshoots—the United States, Canada, Australia, New Zealand, and Japan. Alternatively, Eurocommunism can be conceptualized in developmental terms as the adaptation of Communism to highly developed capitalist states in Western Europe, North America, Australasia, and Japan.

While Eurocommunism currently is restricted in its application to cultural, developed, and capitalist Western Europe, it does have potential recruits in Eastern Europe, particularly in places like Hungary, Czechoslovakia, East Germany, Poland, and northern Yugoslavia, where Western traditions have penetrated to a considerable degree. Alternatively, in order to overcome the current artificial distinctions between Eastern and Western Europe, defined essentially in terms of Communist and non-Communist Europe, one can even make a case that the developing schism between Western and Soviet Communism corresponds closely with the historic division between the Western and Eastern Roman Empires, which gave rise to Western and

Eastern Christianity, and now threatens to create Western and Eastern Communism. An examination of the potential application of
Eurocommunist ideas in Eastern Europe shows that it is precisely
those areas of Eastern Europe that were not part of the Byzantine
tradition (East Germany, Czechoslovakia, Poland, Hungary, and
northern Yugoslavia) that are most susceptible. Conversely, in
"Western" Europe it is precisely Greece and Turkey that are least
likely to be infected with Eurocommunism, and which coincidentally
are within the realm of the Byzantine tradition. (In fact peninsular
Greece, European Turkey, and Anatolia constituted the core of
Byzantium.) The appeal of Eurocommunism, as distinguished from
independent/national Communism, apparently is minimal in Albania,
Bulgaria, Romania, and southern Yugoslavia. In fact, whatever
"Eurocommunization" has been taking place in Yugoslavia as an
input into Titoism largely originates and is most widely practiced in
Slovenia and Croatia.

III.

Any conceptualization of Eurocommunism must take into consideration the intellectual origins, ideological precursors, and historical
precedents of the phenomenon. Indeed, one of the intriguing issues
that may attract a phalanx of investigators will be the search for the
forerunner of Eurocommunism. There are numerous possible candidates: Karl Kautsky, Rosa Luxembourg, Nikolai Bukharin, Earl
Browder, Milovan Djilas, and Alexander Dubcek, all of whom gave
expression to ideas that resemble those of Eurocommunism. The
Japanese Communist party as a whole can also be considered in this
regard. In fact, the reluctance of the Soviet leadership to publicly rehabilitate Bukharin may be due to fear that such a rehabilitation might
serve to legitimize Eurocommunism as an alternative for the Soviet
Union itself. The correspondence between Bukharinist Communism
(right-wing Bolshevism in general) and the core ideas of Eurocommunism are much too close for comfort.

Santiago Carrillo notes that the prewar views of Harry Pollitt and
John Gollan in Great Britain were what might be called proto-
Eurocommunist, but he gives the preeminent role to Palmiro Togliatti,
who in this analogue would be the main candidate for Messiah rather
than forerunner. Carrillo characterizes, perhaps inadvertently,
Kautsky as a powerful expositor of proto-Eurocommunist ideas, although he sharply criticizes Kautsky's opposition to Lenin. Nevertheless, Carrillo observes:

It cannot be denied that in Kautsky's work there are certain abstract, general arguments which, if considered apart from the context in which this work [*The Dictatorship of the Proletariat*] was written, might seem reasonable; they relate to the value of democracy for the proletariat and to the importance of capitalist development for the creation of a socialist economy.[23]

Carrillo objects to Kautsky's views mainly because Kautsky appeared to be trying to apply proto-Eurocommunism to an inappropriate country and within an international context that was inapplicable:

In the Russia of 1917 the choice between proletarian dictatorship and democracy did not present itself; the choice was between a return to autocratic military dictatorship . . . or the dictatorship of the proletariat. . . . Nevertheless Kautsky shut his eyes to that reality and presented the democracy-dictatorship contradiction as if he had been on another planet.[24]

Carrillo, however, cites the experience of the prewar popular fronts in France and especially Spain as important historical antecedents of Eurocommunism. As noted earlier, both proponents and opponents of Eurocommunism agree that the prewar and postwar popular fronts in Western and Eastern Europe were important organizational and intellectual antecedents. But the legacy is ambiguous at best, and thus both sides arrive at different conclusions. For proponents, the popular fronts were innovative non-Soviet creations that failed because of Soviet domination of the Communist movement. Nevertheless, they reflected the intellectual individuality of local Communist leaders that persisted until opportunities were created for their materialization as Eurocommunism.

Those who recognize Eurocommunism as a distinct variant—a Western form—agree that the Western parties were under Moscow's control and that the prewar popular fronts and the postwar coalition governments may indeed have been tactical moves by the Soviet leaders to deceive Western publics and thus facilitate the Communization of Eastern and Western Europe. At the same time they emphasize that substantial numbers of the Western Communists, including some leaders, exhibited more than mere tactical enthusiasm in their support of coalitions with bourgeois parties, and that it is this residual legacy that serves as a foundation for Eurocommunism.

Opponents like Revel, on the other hand, maintain that there is little in the record to justify that local Communist leaders will not use popular fronts as a cover for establishing Communist dictatorships, irrespective of whether they are controlled by the Soviet Union or are independent. Popular fronts can be employed to serve the interests of local Communists or Moscow. As far as many critics are concerned, a Communist dictatorship remains a dictatorship whether or not it is controlled by Moscow. Albania, Romania, China and others can be cited as examples. For Revel, Eurocommunism is not a variant of Communism, but on the basis of the record so far, simply a variant of Communist duplicity.[25]

There is, of course, sufficient evidence to support both positions, for both tendencies obviously existed. The evidence is, however, insufficient to prove the argument of either side or in fact to determine the relative strength of various factions that may have existed within the Communist parties themselves. Carrillo, for example, urges that these divergent tendencies within prewar Western parties be thoroughly researched and investigated in an endeavor to disaggregate what might be called the Stalinist tactical component of the popular front and the indigenous "democratic" substantive component. He goes so far as to suggest that someone should "make a thorough study of the extent to which the line of the Popular Front, sanctified in 1935, was the independent creation of certain parties, such as the French and Spanish, and to what extent it was a Soviet contribution bound up with the need to stand up to Fascist aggression against the USSR."[26] He further maintains that in the prewar period important differences existed between Thorez and the Comintern over participation in the French popular front, to which the Comintern was allegedly opposed:

> The official historians may reflect a tendency to gild the lily and present an idyllic picture of the Popular Front. But today we do know, for instance, that between the French Communists and the Comintern there were at that time important differences regarding it. The confrontation with Maurice Thorez (who was in favour of taking part in the Popular Front government after its victory in Paris), and the Comintern (which was against this)—even though we have no detailed knowledge of the discussions to which it gave rise and even though the question was settled through the authority of the Communist International—was not, if viewed correctly, a difference of secondary importance. It was not just a question of having or not having ministerial portfolios. It was a basic question; it concerned the content and the scope of the Popular Front. A Popular Front without the Communists taking part in the government was one thing; with them, it was another. In different conditions, within the framework of a war, this was confirmed in Spain.[27]

The prewar popular fronts were never much more than partially and erratically implemented in any event, and died a sudden death with the advent of the Nazi-Soviet Pact. The postwar coalition governments in Western Europe never metamorphosed into Communist regimes as did those in Eastern Europe. Thus, the overwhelming burden of proof would still seem to remain with those who argue that Eurocommunism is essentially a new variation of Communism, rather than a new variation on a previous tactical theme.

Since no prewar popular fronts were transformed into Communist systems of any variety and all postwar East European popular fronts were converted into authoritarian Communist regimes, and contemporary Eurocommunism has never been tested, the views of critics like Revel and Henry Kissinger must be given the most serious consideration. Nevertheless, one can still discern significant variations in the fate of two marginal states, Finland and Greece, and the unique circumstances surrounding the establishment of a Communist authoritarian regime in Czechoslovakia. What emerges are three possible reference points against which to measure the possible impact of pre-Communist political culture and traditions upon the behavior of Communist parties in Western Europe. It is true that no precise historical precedent exists for the hypothetical model that the Eurocommunists, particularly Carrillo, brandish. This hypothetical model would be a West European industrialized, pluralistic, democratic state in which a coalition government metamorphosed into a Communist controlled regime without a corresponding Communist transformation of society, and continued operating within the context of a democratic multiparty system. This is the missing historical model.[28]

The contrasting behavior of the Communist parties in Finland, Czechoslovakia, and Greece in the postwar years may provide us with a kind of historical triangulation that can aid in assessing the validity or workability of the missing historical model. We can summarize the behavior of the Communist parties in Czechoslovakia, Finland, and Greece as follows:

1. In Czechoslovakia, an industrialized country with democratic traditions and institutions, the Communist party successfully established its hegemonic control without resorting to direct insurrectionary violence.

2. In Finland, a relatively industrialized country with democratic traditions and institutions, the Communist party failed to seize power, but resisted resorting to insurrectionary means after it was ousted from the coalition and behaved more or less like a West European Communist party, but within a special context, given Finland's size and proximity to the USSR.[29]

3. In Greece, a nonindustrialized country with a feeble modern democratic tradition and a strong prewar quasi-Fascist authoritarian background, the Communist party attempted to seize power, even re-

sorting to guerrilla warfare, but failed and was reduced to semi-illegal status.

The two East European models that most closely approximate the postwar situation in Western Europe are Finland and Czechoslovakia. The geographic and strategic variables are central in both instances. Since the results were different, however, the contrasting experiences raise just enough doubt to admit the possibility that the hypothetical missing model may have been viable in postwar Western Europe, and thus even more viable now. In most respects Czechoslovakia is the key case, since it most closely resembled the states of Western Europe. But it constitutes a negative precedent: instead of ruling through existing democratic institutions, a dominant Communist party in a coalition government disestablished the pluralistic order in favor of a dictatorship of the proletariat. Thus, the Czechoslovak case would not seem to support the Eurocommunist contention that the democratic tradition would act as a shield against Leninism and subdue it. On the other hand, it must be noted that it was in Czechoslovakia that a proto-Eurocommunist order appeared to be taking shape in 1968. This would seem to support the view that even the Czechoslovak Communist party was unable to shed its democratic baggage completely and that a version of Eurocommunism might have triumphed in Czechoslovakia were it not for Soviet military intervention. Although the proximity of Soviet power was the crucial variable in the various postwar outcomes in Eastern and Western Europe, the results even in Eastern Europe were sufficiently mixed as to leave no absolute certainty. Thus, recognizing that special circumstances were involved in both cases, the proximity of Soviet power did not result in Communists coming to power in either Finland or Greece. Nevertheless, Stalin's caveat to Tito in 1948 should be kept in mind. The Soviet leader informed Tito that the Yugoslav party came to power because the Soviet army "created the conditions that were necessary for the CPY to achieve power" and that "unfortunately the Soviet Army did not and could not render such assistance to the French and Italian CPs." This strongly suggests a Czech rather than Finnish outcome had Soviet power been in the vicinity, or a Greek outcome had the Western parties resorted to insurrection.[30]

Clearly, pre-Communist political culture serves to condition the behavior of Communist parties, whether they be in or out of power, and represents a significant, if precisely unmeasurable, input. It would be premature to conclude that the influence is decisive or determinative, but it is certainly critical and its saliency may be sufficient to decide outcomes in marginal cases. Just as most East European Communist parties functioned within the context of prewar authoritarian political cultures, Western parties have been obliged to function within democratic political systems. Whatever compromises and adjustments to reality that had to be made (institutional or political socialization in effect) in the interests of survival and political viability were made within the context of an authoritarian or democratic milieu, respectively. If one can argue that the Tsarist political system conditioned Marxism and deformed it into Leninism, one might argue that to a certain degree the Western political system within which Western Communist parties function tends to recondition Leninism back to Western Marxism. A thorough historical examination of the period might thus illuminate more clearly the covert, and perhaps often unconscious, resocialization of Leninism into Marxism. The fact that one spreading tendency of Eurocommunism is something akin to de-Leninization would tend to support this hypothesis.[31]

It has been observed that neither the French nor Italian Communist parties have had an insurrectionary tradition, nor have they resorted to revolutionary violence in their behavior. This cannot be dismissed simply as tactics deriving from prudence. Certainly the various avenues of political action open to Western Communist parties played some conditioning role. The different outcomes in Finland and Greece also serve to illuminate this important variable in another way. The Communist parties in Finland and Greece were unable to seize power. The Finnish Communist party, however, rather than resort to insurrection or revolutionary violence, adjusted to the Western political process much like the Western parties after they were expelled from the coalition. The Greek Communist party, on the other hand, resorted to insurrection and revolutionary violence rather than adjust to the prevailing political culture. The following question naturally arises: to what extent were the differential behavioral responses of the Finnish and Greek parties shaped by the different political cultures within which each had evolved—pluralistic and democratic in Finland's case, authoritarian and quasi-Fascist in the Greek instance? In the absence of Soviet encouragement and very possibly in the face of Soviet displeasure, the Greek Communists resorted to insurrection, which suggests very strongly that its prior political conditioning and institutional socialization rendered it difficult for the Greek party to behave like a Western Communist party. Two collateral questions also emerge: To what extent did the insurrectionary behavior of the Greek Communist party reinforce the authoritarian traditions of Greece and undermine its feeble democratic heritage? Would the political evolution of Greece have been different and more in the direction of democracy had the Greek Communist party behaved like a West European party? The contrasting evolutions in Italy and Greece could be instructive in this connection. One can make a strong argument that the noninsurrectionary behavior of the Italian Communist party served to assist powerfully the revival of Italy's feeble pre-Mussolini democratic heritage, and had the Italian party behaved like the Greek party, the political development of Italy might have more closely resembled that of postwar Greece. This point is also particularly pertinent to the evolution of the political system in the Iberian peninsula since the deaths of Francisco Franco and Antonio de Oliveira Salazar.

IV

Eurocommunism exists as a label, but whether the label represents farce, myth, deception, or reality remains an open question. After all, the critics argue, *in words,* all of those so-called characteristics of Eurocommunism have been articulated even by Lenin and Stalin: independence, separate roads to socialism, national peculiarities, parliamentary democracy, freedom, and so on. Even today, Moscow continues to subscribe verbally to many of these ideas. Protestations of sincerity to the popular fronts by East European leaders were at their most vocal just prior to Communist takeovers. So, the critics argue, what is particularly new about Eurocommunism? They cite one powerful index: no Eurocommunist leader has seriously criticized Soviet foreign policy.[32] On the other hand, they appear to ignore substantial differences in the speech and behavior of current Eurocommunist leaders as opposed to those in the prewar and the immediate postwar period. The latter, after all, were under Soviet control and their "moderation" was approved and encouraged by Moscow. By the 1970s, in contrast, Eurocommunist leaders severely criticized internal Soviet practices and relationships with other Communist parties and states. Carrillo, in particular, expresses fundamental anti-Soviet views that attack the basic nature and character of the Soviet system. Furthermore, in light of Tito, the Twentieth CPSU Congress, polycentrism, and the Sino-Soviet schism, the belated independence of West European Communist leaders is to be framed within a broader context. While it may be possible that Eurocommunists are engaging in deception and chicanery, they are more likely doing so on their own behalf and not on behalf of the Soviet Union.

The independence of the Eurocommunists from Soviet control is far more credible than their independence from their own traditions and behavioral reflexes. Among the Leninist principles that have not been abandoned is "democratic centralism." How, critics like Revel query, can one accept the sincerity of Eurocommunist commitment to pluralism and democratic values and institutions when Eurocommunists retain Leninist principles in the organization and procedures of their own party? This is a powerful point for which the Eurocommunists have as yet no satisfactory answer. Can a party that is anti-democratically organized function credibly within a pluralistic democratic coalition with parties organized along different lines over an extended period of time, without either subverting their coalition partners or abandoning the final vestiges of Leninist principles? Of course that is the supreme conundrum and it can go either way. No one can foretell.[33]

Carrillo has made a heroic and remarkable effort to disassociate himself from Soviet Communism and Soviet behavior. Nevertheless, in his endeavor to preserve his Communist credentials and meet the obvious necessity of distinguishing his brand of Eurocommunism from social democracy, he casts doubt not so much upon his sincerity, but upon the validity of his political analysis and prognosis:

> On the other hand, there, *cannot be any confusion* between 'Eurocommunism' and social democracy in the ideological sphere . . . as it has manifested itself up to now. What is commonly called 'Eurocommunism' proposes to *transform* capitalist society, not to *administer* it; to work out a socialist alternative to the system of state monopoly capitalism, not to integrate in it and become one of its governmental variants. . . . At the same time, the "Eurocommunist" strategy aims to bring about a convergence with the socialist and social democratic parties, with the progressive Christian forces, with all the democratic groups that are not henchmen of monopoly-type property. These aims are not contradictory, if social development is seen as a fluid and changing process and not as something static.[34]

The precise sticking point in Carrillo's exposition is that the "strategy" of the Eurocommunists is contradictory. Aside from being free from Soviet control and domination, but not necessarily input and influence, the strategy outlined by Carrillo is still based upon the *inevitability* of Communism rather than its "optionability." If the Communists have no intention of simply *administering* capitalism, what are the non-Communist parties to administer once the Communists have been elected to power and then voted out? Can non-Communist constituencies and the parties that represent them survive a transformation of society, and if they do, will they be content to merely administer socialism or will they, too, seek to transform it back to capitalism?

NOTES

1. Santiago Carrillo, *Eurocommunism and the State* (Westport, Conn.: Lawrence Hall and Co., 1978), p. 8.

2. "Contrary to the Interests of Peace and Socialism in Europe," *New Times* (Moscow), 26 (June 1977), p. 10.

3. *L'Espresso* (Rome), December 26, 1976.

4. Jean-François Revel, "The Myths of Eurocommunism," *Foreign Affairs* (January 1978), p. 295. See also "Ursprung und Konzept des Eurocommunismus," *Deutschland-Archiv* (April 1977).

5. "Contrary to the Interests of Peace," p. 9.

6. James O. Goldsborough, "Eurocommunism after Madrid," *Foreign Affairs* (July 1977), p. 800.

7. Ibid.

8. G. Shakhnazarov et al., *Europe and the Communists* (Moscow: Progress Publishers, 1977).

9. This, incidentally, is not mentioned in the book. The text of the document can be found in ibid., pp. 159–195.

10. See Georges Marchais in *L'Humanité*, July 2, 1976, and in *Morning Star* (London), July 12, 1976.

11. "Contrary to the Interests of Peace," p. 10.

12. Ibid.

13. Ibid.

14. Ibid.

15. Carrillo, *Eurocommunism and the State*, pp. 9–10.

16. Ibid., p. 154.

17. Charles Gati, "The 'Europeanization' of Communism?" *Foreign Affairs* (April 1977), p. 541.

18. See ibid., and "Contrary to the Interests of Peace," p. 12.

19. Ibid., and Carrillo, *Eurocommunism and the State*, ch. 6.

20. See Jean Kanapa, "A 'New Policy' of the French Communists?" *Foreign Policy* (January 1977), pp. 281–284.

21. Liu Shao-chi, *On the Party* (Peking: Foreign Languages Press, 1950), pp. 33–34. The since discredited Liu further wrote: "Mao Tse-tung . . . in the theoretical field . . . was boldly creative, discarded certain specific Marxist principles and conclusions that were obsolete and incompatible with the concrete conditions in China, and replaced them with new principles and new conclusions that are compatible with China's new historical conditions." Ibid., p. 35.

22. Thus in Shakhnazarov et al., *Europe and the Communists*, Soviet writers attempted to minimize the differences between the Brussels Declaration (Conference of West European Communist Parties held in January 1974) and documents issued by the Warsaw Political Consultative Committee in April of the same year, although the differences were substantial. Carrillo, *Eurocommunism and the State*, p. 9.

23. Carrillo, *Eurocommunism and the State*, p. 151.

24. Ibid., pp. 151–152.

25. Revel, "Myths of Eurocommunism," pp. 295ff. For a rebuttal to this view by an Italian non-Communist, see Ugo La Malfa, "Communism and Democracy in Italy," *Foreign Affairs* (April 1978), pp. 476–488.

26. Carrillo, *Eurocommunism and the State*, p. 113.

27. Ibid., pp. 113–114.

28. San Marino should be ruled out as an authentic historically tested model even though it meets the technical specifications of the hypothetical model. The "Most Serene Republic of San Marino" is a completely land-locked "sovereign" micro-state located in north central Italy, completely surrounded by Italian territory. Essentially a tiny city-state with a population estimated at 70,000 in 1977, it is 92 percent urban, ethnically Italian, with a territory of about 23.5 square miles. It was governed by a Communist-led coalition from 1947 to 1957, when the coalition was voted out of office, although a similar coalition assumed power again in 1978.

29. It is, of course, precisely this "special context," which has given rise to the notion of Finlandization.

30. *The Soviet-Yugoslav Dispute* (London: Royal Institute of International Affairs, 1948), p. 51.

31. This holds not only among Eurocommunists. To date, the Japanese, Spanish, and Romanian Communist parties have formally dropped the use of "Leninism" in favor of less culturally-loaded terms like "scientific socialism."

32. It should be noted, however, that some West European Communist parties have adopted positions on the foreign policies of their own countries that are at variance with those of Moscow. Thus, Carrillo's views on U.S. bases in Spain, the French party's position on the French nuclear force, the Italian party's position on Italy's membership in NATO, are all at variance with Soviet positions, as is support for strengthening the EEC and Spain's inclusion within it. The Soviet invasion of Afghanistan, it should be noted, was denounced by a number of European Communist parties.

33. Every Western Communist party is gripped by factional conflict and within almost every party a more-or-less pro-Soviet faction, whose strength may wax and wane, exists. There is, of course, no guarantee that Eurocommunist-oriented factions may always be in control, and thus it is not even a question of the "sincerity" of leaders like Carrillo, but rather that the internal factional balance might shift to pro-Soviet factions once Communist parties come to power.

34. Carrillo, *Eurocommunism and the State*, pp. 103–104.

CHAPTER II

Communism in Europe, 1944–1949: The Historical Antecedents of Eurocommunism

Herbert S. Dinerstein

Introduction

The emergence of Eurocommunism in the 1970s as a possibly distinct brand of Communism, native to Western Europe in particular and to advanced capitalist democratic states in general, has provoked a lively controversy over its bonafides. Both those who perceive Eurocommunism as a fundamental transformation of Communism shaped by its incubation in a Western pluralistic political culture and those who brand it a sham reach back to the periods of the prewar popular fronts and the postwar coalition governments in Western and Eastern Europe to support their views. Thus, a reexamination of European Communism in the immediate postwar period, together with an episodic reexamination of the prewar popular front period, might serve to establish with greater clarity the historical precedents for Eurocommunism. It may also serve to illuminate the extent to which the differential outcomes in postwar Western and Eastern Europe derived from the differing political cultures of the two parts of Europe.

A reexamination of the period may also throw additional light on the issue of whether those who condemn Eurocommunism as a transitory tactic, and thus a substantive fraud, underestimate the impact of Western pluralistic political culture upon the conditioning of West European Communism. Needless to say, such a reexamination of the immediate prewar and postwar history of European Communism at this point is designed more to rephrase old issues and questions and raise new ones rather than to provide definitive answers.

Many of the salient features of Communism in Europe from 1944 to 1949 were manifest in 1949. In that year the following generalizations could have been made:

1. The ruling and nonruling parties were essentially different: the nonruling parties could participate in the governments of parliamentary systems; the ruling parties managed all the important affairs of state.

2. By 1949 no Communist party participated in any parliamentary government; only vestigial non-Communist parties remained in the socialist states.

3. The policies of ruling and nonruling parties were coordinated through the Cominform. The Soviet Union set the limits of national individuality, especially in the ruling parties.

4. Yugoslavia claimed to represent a legitimate variant of Communism, a claim not accepted by other socialist states.

5. The Soviet Union set its own state and party interests (termed internationalism) above the national interests of other parties.

6. The nonruling parties accepted Soviet guidance, but their policies more or less reflected national necessities.

Only the sixth feature has been appreciably modified. In 1949 nonruling parties publicly supported and followed the Soviet line. Now they frame their policies in response to national necessities, one of which is to make repeated declarations of ideological independence. This paper shall seek to see how these relationships developed through four periods: (1) the war years; (2) liberation to the peace treaties; (3) peace treaties to the founding of the Cominform; and (4) Cominform to the establishment of the German Federal Republic.

Fighting for Victory in War

Winning the war was everything for the Soviet Union, and the Communist parties of Europe were expected to help in every way. In Germany and in the countries of its allies (Italy excepted) the Communist parties played a very minor and, to the Soviets, disappointing role. In none of these countries did the Communist party amount to much, and in every case the government pursued what were accepted as national aims in the war. The Communist parties were too insignificant to mount a fight alone against their respective governments and could not find allies in other parties, nor support in the population at large. In Yugoslavia, Poland, Czechoslovakia, France, and Italy (after the defection of the king and part of the army) at least some elements of the population (and the proportion grew as German defeat approached) were willing to resist or to help the resistance movement against the government. The Soviet Union urged the Communists to form or join national fronts that included anyone willing to turn against the Germans and their allies. Whether it was King Michael of Romania or King Victor Emmanuel of Italy, their political past was to be forgotten if they were willing to change sides.

From the Soviet point of view, and Stalin was explicit on the subject in private, the resistance movement could make only a very modest military contribution to the war. The Soviet Union preferred that entire state armies switch sides. The Soviets were able to arrange this in Romania, Bulgaria, and even in Finland, where, the Finns disarmed the remaining German troops according to the terms of the armistice. By comparison, the Communist resistance groups in the occupied countries offered only an anti-Fascist resistance front, which the Soviet Union urged them to make as broad as possible. They succeeded when other parties were willing to work with them, as in Italy; they failed when no important parties would join them, as in Poland.

Consistent with their low estimate of the military potential of the Communists, the Soviets did not expect that they would acquire much power. In a conversation with Stanislow Mikolajczyk in 1944 Stalin deprecated the role of the whole Polish underground using standards that relegated all the resistance movements to minor importance. He boasted that when underground, the Bolsheviks had organized six party congresses, six conferences, twelve meetings, and twenty to twenty-five conferences of the Central Committee.[1] The comparison was not fair: the Okhrana hardly matched the efficiency of the Sicherheitsdienst. But Stalin, who despised his closest associates, had even less regard for the leaders of the European parties. Not believing that these parties would play much of a role, much less come to power, Stalin sought to make postwar arrangements with the governments-in-exile resident in London. Thus until late in the war he believed that Draza Mihailovic, not Josip Tito, would prevail. *Mutatis mutandis* he followed the same policy everywhere else, from China to France. Stalin preferred to come to terms with a strong opponent rather than to prop up a weak ally.

Nevertheless, the Communist leaders were able to lay a basis for greatly expanded postwar activity in most occupied countries. In Europe people generally joined the resistance movements out of necessity rather than preference. Few Communists had any choice. In France and Yugoslavia, most importantly, but elsewhere too, the police turned over their files on Communists to the occupation authorities. The Nazis were consistent all over Europe, including the USSR, in rejecting the services of those Communists who were willing to turn their coats. One can surmise that, since some socialists and labor leaders collaborated, some Communists would have also.

The Nazi refusal to recruit them gave them an automatic solid core and permitted them to claim, with justice, that they were free of the taint of collaboration—at least after June 22, 1941.

The fragmentary evidence available indicates that non-Communists who joined the resistance movements were also people without a choice. The Jews, Spanish loyalist refugees in France, and the Serbs in Croatia found more security in the resistance and in the underground than in acceptance of the fate the governing authorities had in store for them. Many became Communists and others developed respect and sympathy for them. Compliance with the Soviet directive to create the broadest possible front varied from country to country.

In Italy the directive was executed most successfully. The leader of the Italian Communist party, Palmiro Togliatti, was a major figure in the Comintern and, according to Paolo Spriano's persuasive account, had preferred popular front policies long before they became official Comintern policy in 1935.[2] He had learned in the early years of the party's existence that it prospered in class alliances and came close to destruction in isolation. The Communists played a minor role in the plot to overthrow Benito Mussolini, but they played a major role in the remarkable strike movement in German-occupied Italy. Nowhere else in Europe did workers mount such a successful strike, gaining significant economic concessions before returning to work. In the armed resistance that drew heavily upon young men unwilling to be drafted into the armed forces or for work in Germany, the Communists too played a major, if not the largest, role. Overnight, a handful of illegals had become the leaders of a mass movement. Six anti-Fascist parties formed the Committee of National Liberation for all of German-occupied Italy. The committee operated on the unanimity policy, so that the Communists from the beginning were committed to a minimal policy. Locally the individual parties operated separately, so that the Italian Communist Party (PCI) could put pressure on the others to follow their example of successful resistance. Nevertheless, the principle was clearly established: the PCI was to work with, and not against, the other parties. In Communist language, it pursued a policy of unity from above, not unity from below.

In the south of Italy, occupied by the Anglo-American forces, the same policy was followed. Although the USSR theoretically participated in the surrender of the king and Pietro Badoglio, it was effectively excluded from any but the most formal role. Nevertheless, the PCI took the lead in supporting Anglo-American occupation policy. The other parties initially refused to serve in a government headed by men who had been Fascist leaders only the day before. Togliatti, whose return to Italy had been negotiated by the Soviet authorities with the Anglo-American authorities (as had Maurice Thorez's with Charles De Gaulle),[3] agreed to serve the king and Badoglio in his famous *svolta di Salerno,* the policy shift of Salerno.[4] Thus he forced the other parties to follow his suit. The Americans and the British made little use of the Italian armies who had deserted Mussolini, an example the Russians were not to follow when they managed affairs.

For a long time the Russian authorities, probably influenced by Italian events, hoped for a revolt against Hitler, and they prepared an embryonic anti-Hitler German army from prisoners of war in the Free Germany Committee. German Communist exiles in Russia played a major role in the recruitment of this body.[5] On the assumption that an uprising would precede the defeat of Germany, the German Communists prepared detailed plans for bourgeois-democratic reforms in the new Germany. When the revolt against Hitler failed, a new set of plans was prepared with much more modest goals. This was an early indication that the Russians wanted to rule Germany with the support of a coalition, rather than through the Communist party alone, and would adjust the pace of social transformation to the stage of political development in the society.

The modification of Soviet plans for Germany, about which we have more evidence than the plans for Germany's allies, reveals the guiding principle of Soviet policy. It had its roots in Soviet experience in the Revolution and the Civil War. A small party cannot make a revolution or begin to govern by excluding all other groups. Rather, the Communists try to induce groups of the enemy camp to change sides or, at least, to remain neutral. To accomplish this in Germany, the Communists had to advance minimal goals or risk isolation. The Americans and British, by contrast, had no policy but unconditional surrender and never even hinted that the German state could be preserved as Stalin insisted it would be. To them "working in isolation" had different overtones than for the Soviet leaders because they never tried to make a revolution or govern from a narrow base.

In Poland the directive to the Polish Communists was to coordinate action with other parties. But the others (save some insignificant groups) were unwilling to cooperate with the Communists despite repeated invitations. The whole course of Polish history, particularly recent Polish history, had made association with the Russians and with a political party beholden to them obnoxious. The PZPR now claims and adduces documentation to show that it advocated resistance and an aggressive policy against the Germans, while the non-Communist groups, particularly the Armija Krajowa—the agent of the London government—preferred to conserve their strength for the day when they could use it most effectively, rather than be destroyed

by the Germans in a badly timed, futile rebellion.[6] The Warsaw uprising capped this policy. Had it been successful, the Armija Krajowa
and the London government would have been in a better position to
claim a large share of power, or all of it, in the new state. (Small
wonder that the Russians permitted the Germans to destroy them, as
they allowed the Germans to destroy the Slovak partisans and their
own partisans in western Russia.) Nevertheless, as soon-to-be-
published documents of the Polish Communist party Politburo reveal,
Stalin stubbornly sought to enlist non-Communist elements into the
Lublin government. A broad front failed in Poland. This was not because the Soviets and the PPR (much less enthusiastically) did not
try, but because hardly any partners could be found.

In Yugoslavia, as the voluminous documents published by the
Yugoslavs indicate, the Soviets persisted in the belief that Tito was
not likely to prevail and kept urging him to find common ground with
Mihailovic.[7] Even if the Yugoslav partisans had wanted to join forces
with Mihailovic, the latter would have refused.

The partisan movement in Yugoslavia was much less important
militarily than politically. The military situation resembled that in
many other countries. The partisans hampered the Germans, but the
latter were able to reduce them to a mere remnant when they decided
to commit the necessary forces to comb-through and encircling operations. The great "victories" of the Yugoslav partisans reflected the
underlying reality of this balance of military force. The partisans were
able to survive, much reduced in numbers, by withdrawing to, and
over, difficult terrain where superior German equipment could find
less employment. Late in the war Tito had to be evacuated by British
aircraft from the mainland to the island of Vis. But survival was political victory. Many thousands with little prior political experience had
come to be in the partisan forces, sometimes voluntarily, sometimes
under heavy pressure. In the process they became politicized and saw
their future prospects lying in cooperation with the Communists, who
presented themselves as Yugoslav rather than Serb, Croat, or Slovene
leaders, and gained some acceptance of that claim. The Soviets failed
to realize until very late how solid a political base Tito had forged.
Although Tito had failed to effect, or had avoided, a policy of unity
from above, he had succeeded, as no other Communist leader in
Europe had, in establishing a policy of unity from below, especially
among the Serbs and Slovenes. Although the majority of his forces
were wiped out or dispersed in a series of battles, the travail gave the
Communists a mass base—in striking contrast to the interwar period.
When the Soviet armies, together with the newly allied Bulgarian
army, swept through northern Yugoslavia toward Austria, they incor-

porated whatever armed forces they could into their own armies. By contrast with the Anglo-Americans, who accepted De Gaulle's participation in the final battle reluctantly and kept the forces of the resistance at arms' length, Tito's partisans were armed and employed, providing Tito with an instrument of compulsion against the many elements of Yugoslav society hostile to him. During most of the war the Soviet Union refused to recognize the accomplishments of the partisans, but at war's end and in pursuit of immediate military goals, the USSR very much enhanced their power.

In Western Europe the Allied armies disarmed the forces of the resistance as soon as they could. Although some militants balked, Communist party policy accepted the decision on the ground that winning the war came first. Stalin had publicly voiced his suspicions that the Anglo-Americans might make a separate peace with the Germans and thus snatch the spoils of victory from his hands. A Communist uprising in the rear of the Anglo-American armies in France or Italy would have only increased that dread possibility. On the other hand, the Communist parties of Italy and France found the prospect of being part of the new governments appealing. The latter joined the French Committee of National Liberation and its successor, the provisional government. It was accepted as no more than a second-class party, however, and received only minor portfolios. In Italy the Communists were in a somewhat better position because Togliatti took the initiative at Salerno and because no dominating figure of De Gaulle's stature put them in the shadow. The political tradition of these countries, in contrast to that of Greece, made it quite reasonable for the French and Italian Communists to calculate that they would survive after giving up their weapons. Ever since the end of the religious wars of the sixteenth century, the French had given up the practice of massacring their defeated enemies, the major exception, of course, was the brief but traumatic experience of the French Revolution. Primarily from a desire never to repeat that bloody period, the French had since followed a tradition of forming new regimes without proscribing and killing the leading officials of the defeated regime. The efficient bureaucracy survived more or less intact from regime to regime, as the Vichy bureaucracy ultimately did. The very tradition that protected the majority of the Vichy officials and, of course, the population that had obeyed their orders, served the Communists.

In Italy the tradition of tenure in office through changes in regime had not been established. Although Mussolini jailed and mistreated his beaten enemies, he killed very few. The murder of Giacomo Matteotti caused such an enormous scandal that it remained an exception. Most of the Communists survived the Fascist prisons, and there was no likelihood that they would now lose their lives if they laid down their arms.

In Greece the situation was quite different.[8] No significant force loyal to the government-in-exile took the field against the Germans. The Greek Communist party had suffered mistreatment and demoralization at the hands of the security forces. The latter, using various forms of pressure, caused many to recant their Communist beliefs; others, confused by the pronouncements of a sham Communist party, left the KKE. Nevertheless, small forces led by the Communists organized small scale resistance in the mountains. The British succeeded by blackmail and threats in getting some non-Communist leaders into the field and forcing cooperation between them and the Communists in one spectacular sabotage operation against the railroad system. Even so, the united front among them was precarious, punctuated by fighting and always marked by the most deep seated suspicions. By the time the Germans withdrew from the Balkans to avoid being cut off by the Soviet armies advancing into Romania, the British had patched up an uneasy agreement among the Communists and the non-Communist leaders in Greece, and among the leaders of the exile groups. The Soviet ambassador to the Greek government in exile, then resident in Cairo, quietly but effectively urged the Communists to join this broad front. The Communists agreed to lay down their arms and join the forces of a new Greek provisional government, but fighting broke out before they did so.

The Greek population was deeply divided about the future. By the end of the war, a large fraction wanted to eliminate the royal family from political life, or at least prevent their return until a plebescite was taken to decide the matter. The British pressed hard for the retention of the monarchy, and since they supplied and controlled the Greek forces abroad, they had their way. Even during the war, a quarrel over this issue occasioned a mutiny of the republicans in the Greek armies in Egypt. They were put down by force of arms and lodged in concentration camps. This was only the latest in a series of violent conclusions to political quarrels. In every change of the Greek regime since independence the victors had proscribed and executed some of the defeated. Laying down one's arms had a very different significance in Greece than in France or Italy. In any case, soon after a small British force had landed in Piraeus and moved up to Athens, a riot, sparked by the police shooting at a crowd demonstrating in the main square of Athens, became an insurrection. It was put down by the British troops. A truce was arranged, and the Communists and their allies left Athens armed, with a host of hostages in their train who were atrociously treated. Only a few weeks after liberation the second round of the civil war had been fought, and all was readied for the third round. The United States officially protested the British action and leaked to the press Winston Churchill's order to treat Athens as a conquered city, but the Soviet press reported the events without criticizing the British and sent an ambassador to the Papandreou government. A month later at Yalta Stalin courteously asked Churchill about the situation in Greece—merely as a matter of information.

In Finland, although the civil war following independence had been bloody and terrible, the Communists had been allowed to exist in front parties. Very little violence had been visited upon them in the interwar period and even during the war with Russia. Very few Finnish Communists had committed treason during the war, so there was no need to proscribe and punish them as a class. By the same token, they could feel secure as long as they were loyal to the state.

In Czechoslovakia, Edward Benes had, without previously securing the consent of his cabinet colleagues, agreed to give the Czechoslovak Communist leaders resident in Moscow important portfolios in the new government. Thus, the only mass Communist party in Eastern Europe was assured of an enhanced position within the government.

On the continent, mass Communist parties had existed only in Rechtsstaater, and they reappeared with the restoration of the prewar or the pre-Fascist order. Thus large Communist parties were "natural" in France, Italy, and Czechoslovakia, and "artificial" in Poland, Hungary, Romania, and Bulgaria. Yugoslavia was the exception. The end of the war saw the collapse of the Serbian-dominated state, and Croatian nationalism had been discredited by the Ante Pavelic policy of attempting to convert the Serbs in Croatia to Roman Catholicism or of exterminating them. Restoration of interwar Yugoslavia was out of the question, and separatism was very much associated with the Italian and German occupiers. Thus, the idea of a multinational Yugoslav state had great appeal after the terrible atrocities committed by the nationalities of the state against each other. Perhaps even more important, Tito alone among the Communists in Europe led an army that, whatever its military contribution to the outcome of the war, had fought bravely and stubbornly against great odds and had earned the loyalty of many of its members and the admiration of large elements of the population. Had the peoples of Yugoslavia had free choice, they might or might not have chosen to be ruled by the Communists, but no one consulted them.

From Liberation to the Signature of the Peace Treaties, January 1947: The Bright Future Becomes Dimmer

The needs of the Soviet Union (termed internationalism in Communist parlance) changed immediately upon the conclusion of the war. Now the first two priorities of the state were to restore its devastated areas and to prevent Germany from ever again having the opportunity to invade the USSR. These "international goals" were not necessarily identical with the national goals of the several European Communist parties. For reconstruction of war damage, the Soviet Union expected reparations from Germany and its allies. The victorious powers had reached agreement on the main feature of that part of the peace settlement during the war. In addition, the Soviet Union expected large loans from the United States.

In the last years of the war preparations had been made to satisfy these needs, and a theoretical underpinning had been established. Eugene Varga, a Hungarian Communist domiciled in the USSR after the success of the counterrevolution in Hungary in 1919, had earned a great reputation as an economist and guided the activities of a research institute. In articles that he combined into a book published early in 1946,[9] Varga developed his view of the nature of the postwar economic situation. The United States had multiplied its productive capacity several times during the war; it had very greatly expanded its labor force and had thus emerged from the war, unlike any other great power, with its economic strength greatly enhanced. Europe, by contrast, had suffered enormous destruction of industrial and agricultural capital, and consumption was often below subsistence levels. From Russia to the channel, he could have said, many millions were starving or near starvation. For the United States to avoid the depression that would be the inevitable consequence of a greatly expanded economy whose internal and external markets were not large enough to absorb production, exports would have to expand many fold. If the United States furnished credits to the shattered economies of Europe (including the USSR), the next depression in the capitalist economic system could be postponed for ten or fifteen years. (It should be noted that many American economists who had not yet adopted John Maynard Keynes' theories shared Varga's prognosis for the United States economy.) The United States then would be compelled to export capital and goods, unless those capitalists who preferred a depression and unemployment in order to break the unions and to gobble up their weaker fellows prevailed. But, argued Varga, the capitalist states would probably continue the wartime practice of directed economies.

Driven by economic self-interest and the need to gain and keep Soviet cooperation in keeping Germany down, the United States would have to maintain the wartime alliance against Germany. To avoid a new Dawes Plan, which might restore beaten Germany, Germany would pay reparations in the form of dismantled industrial plants and goods from current production. As an indication of the great importance Stalin attached to reparations, he recalled his highly successful ambassador to Britain, Ivan Maisky, and put him in charge of the Soviet reparations commission. During the war Maisky had been able to extract deliveries of war goods from Churchill when Britain itself was in desperate straits.

Despite the abrupt cancellation of Lend-Lease, the Russians continued to hope, despite obvious American reluctance, that they would receive large loans from the United States. As for Germany, they wanted to reduce its size rather than to divide it up, but the reductions were to be made only in the East to the aggrandizement of Polish and Soviet territory. The remainder of Germany was to remain a single economic and political unit—a solution that promised greater reparations than a dismembered Germany administered by several Allies in their own zones.

There were several impediments to the Russian scheme for Germany. First, the French felt that the key to their future security was the separation of the Rhineland, the Ruhr, and the Saar and their incorporation into, or domination by, France. Whereas the French were clear in their purposes, the United States at first worked to punish Germany and then to reshape it through reeducation in proper principles. Britain feared that Germany might become an economic competitor and was reluctant to reindustrialize it, but increasingly it began to suffer the strain of keeping its zone of Germany fed without restoring its economy. In the first year of occupation the United States and the USSR both professed a desire to convert the occupation zones into a single economic and administrative unit. The United States felt that the French veto prevented this highly desirable arrangement, and the Soviets suspected that the French were behaving according to the secret prompting of the United States.

In Germany all political and economic life seemed to be at the zero level, and, as the Germans were all too keenly aware, they were the object of the politics of others and not the initiators of anything. The revival of political life would be within the limits prescribed by the conquerors. Before any elections were held, the German Communist party (KPD) rejected the social democratic proposal to restore the unity of the German working class by a merger, fearing that they would be submerged in a new party. Later, when they could arrange the merger to assure their dominance, they reversed their policy and forced a merger with the more numerous social democrats in the Soviet zone of occupation. This newly created workers' party, the

Socialist Unity Party (SED), was permitted, in order to bolster its position, to preserve silence on the question of a border at the Eastern Neisse. As Stalin said in Moscow on July 14, 1947, to Otto Grotewohl, a socialist member of the SED, it was understandable that the German and Polish parties (and he might have added the Soviet party as well) took different positions on border questions in dispute between their countries.[10]

The day of decision on all border questions had to come, and when it did, the KPD suffered from the truncation of Germany's eastern marches; the French Communist party (PCF) suffered when the Russians finally made clear that they would not support French control or ownership of the Rhineland and the Ruhr; and the PCI lost prestige when the Soviets supported the Yugoslav claims to Venezia Giulia. As long as it seemed possible that the Soviet Union might support French and Italian territorial aspirations, the Communist parties were valued by the other parties as influential with the USSR. Thus Soviet interests and the interests of the national parties coincided until the Soviet Union had to make its choice on disputed border questions, and the final choice served "international," that is, Soviet interests.

Communist mass parties in states with a genuine parliamentary tradition found that the united front from above policy furthered their cause. The idea of an alliance from above dated from the 1935 meeting of the Comintern, where the popular front strategy replaced the class against class policy. After June 22, 1941, the popular front policy became a national front policy, that is, a fighting alliance that included anyone willing to join the struggle against Hitler. In the post-liberation period the popular fronts did not stretch as far to the right, but they encompassed socialist and bourgeois parties; in Germany, a Christian but not a Catholic party, and in Italy, a Catholic but not a clerical party. How did the continuation of this broad class alliance benefit Soviet interests?

First, it gave the Communists in each country a voice in the determination of foreign policy. Because of their poverty and weakness, neither France nor Italy swung much weight in foreign policy, but France, at least, could employ its power to obstruct. Second, it would threaten the wartime alliance if American vital interests were jeopardized. If the PCI and the PCF could have been moved to a revolutionary or an insurrectionary policy after the defeat of Germany, and that hardly seemed promising with Allied armies of occupation in Italy and across the Rhine, the United States would not have cooperated with the Soviet Union on reparations or loans. Thus from the Soviet point of view the USSR sacrificed little, if anything, of the French and Italian Communists' prospects to avoid ruffling the United

States. The Communist parties were urged to cooperate loyally within the governments in which their ministers were members and to join in a program of economic restoration. This policy had its limits. The Communist parties were to cooperate as long as the governments of which they were a part were friendly to the Soviet Union and created a political and economic climate that promised them a better future. But if the situation changed—for example, if the United States withdrew from Europe, as many thought likely, or if Communist electoral strength swelled for one reason or another—the Communist party should be able to follow whatever tactic suited it best. Cooperation with the bourgeois parties was not an end in itself, but a stepping stone to an eventual expansion of power. If, however, the Communist party dissolved itself because of some supposed identity of interests with capitalism, no matter how reformed that capitalism might be, the future was foreclosed. It is this extreme case that explains the Jacques Duclos letter to the American Communists that severely criticized the position of its leader, Earl Browder, who had expressed his conviction that the New Deal represented a reform movement within which the Communist party could work.

Duclos had been the chief parliamentarian in the PCF and felt his career in the party would flourish best in a popular front matrix. In France he was a strong proponent of cooperation with the bourgeoisie and the economic reconstruction of France, often at the cost of postponing workers' demands. He was selected by the Epigones of the Comintern to set the limit of Communist party cooperation with the bourgeoisie.[11]

The French and Italian party leadership, with perhaps greater internal opposition in the former case, had embraced the strategy of cooperation with the bourgeois parties. In France, especially, where the devastation of war was not as great as in Italy, liberation had created great expectations in all the left and even beyond it. The feeling was strong that the rotten Third Republic was gone and buried, that Vichy was in the past, and that a new reborn France was in the offing. This remarkable faith in a totally changed future also guided the policies of the Christian parties that had participated in the resistance. Immediately after liberation, stories circulated about Communist atrocities and murders of political enemies in the first vigilante days of the punishment of collaborators. Whatever the extent of these actions, they served to frighten and silence the right wing.

In addition to this drumhead kind of punishment for collaboration, a regular procedure was set up for punishment of war criminals and collaborators. Since the judges trying these cases had served Vichy, it was not surprising that they found very few guilty of collaboration.[12]

A few great industrial establishments were nationalized (for example, Renault), a few prominent men were punished, and then life returned to normal. For a combination of reasons, the wartime currency was retained, thus preserving the old class and economic structure. (Some charge that the PCF favored this policy because its commandos had stolen a great deal of money in raids on banks. In any case, the PCF financed an enormous publications and newspaper program as soon as the war ended.) The rightist forces in the country had lain low until it became clear that those who had obeyed the orders of, and perhaps prospered in, the Vichy government would not suffer if they raised their heads. It turned out that France was not so radical after all.

Although the Third Republic was consigned to the dustbin of history, the French public rejected in a referendum a plenipotentiary constituent assembly of the kind the PCF preferred. Such an assembly would have been able to enact social reforms that would have altered the class structure while preparing a new constitution. The public rejected a strong president and created a powerful parliament whose divisions meant that France would move slowly, regardless of the direction it took. A mood of Thermidor prevailed, and many in the working classes felt that the Communists had betrayed them. The PCF in Parlement and in the unions cooperated in the restoration of France with a will and faithfully prevented strikes, while prices rose faster than wages. The electoral base that gave the Communists a position in the government was eroding because they loyally, too loyally, some charged, served the purposes of that government.

Events in Italy followed much the same pattern. The right was more sheltered because of the presence of the Anglo-American troops until the signature of the peace treaties in 1947. The plebescite on whether the king should be retained revealed how deep the regional divisions in the country still were. The vote of the southern regions, the northeast, and the islands for the king was interpreted not so much as a preference for royalty but as a vote against the dominance of the industrializing north and all its ways. Even if the Committees of National Liberation had stayed outside the governmental system and had promoted radical social change, the conservatives, whose power was centered in the south and the northeast, would have resisted, and Italy might have faced a civil war as Togliatti feared. Much of the old social order was restored. In the Constituent Assembly the Communists favored the retention of the Lateran Pact, which gave the Catholic Church a special position in Italian society. The PCI-dominated unions prevented strikes under the same sort of agreement that the French Communists had, and they too found their electoral base eroding. The Christian Democrats were originally a nonclerical party in the tradition of Don Sturzo. Events in Italy, however, closely resembled in many respects those that had occurred in France. When former Fascists realized they were not to be punished for supporting the regime of another time and prospering under it, they joined the Christian Democrats, making it ever more conservative and clerical in its outlook.

In Greece, after the withdrawal of the EAM (the front dominated by the Communists) from Athens and the negotiation of an armistice agreement at Varkiza in early 1945 (urged on the Communists by the Soviet Union), the situation deteriorated rapidly. Greek collaborators with the Germans did not even undergo a token purge. They were immediately set to the performance of their old tasks, along with the Greek forces employed by the Germans against the guerillas. Both sides engaged in shocking barbarities as Greece became engaged in a terrible civil war from which it has still not completely recovered. The Soviets advised the Communists, as their recent histories of the events maintain, to participate in elections and to try to establish at least the verisimilitude of a working government so that the British troops could be put under pressure to withdraw. But that advice was easier to give than to take, because the Communists and their sus-pected sympathizers were being killed by anti-Communist bands, sometimes with, and sometimes without, the approval of the many Greek governments that followed in quick succession. It was not merely that the Soviets were loyal to the agreement that they had made with Churchill in October 1944 stipulating that Romania was to be in the Soviet sphere and Greece in the British sphere. They thought that the rebellion was doomed. The Soviets have not been known for their support of lost causes when the cost goes beyond faint praise.

In contrast, the Bulgarians and the Yugoslavs had different pur-poses. For both, Macedonia was a burning issue. Each claimed the area and joined in denying Greek rights to it. The Greek Communist party (KKE) had suffered in the past from endorsing the Slavic claims in a formula favoring national self-determination for the area. In Greece, the royalist and conservative sentiment was centered in the Pelopenessus and the Communist forces in the civil war found refuge in the northern mountains and found themselves pushed into Greek Macedonia and the areas bordering Bulgaria and Yugoslavia. In their dependence on these two states for sanctuary and supplies, the KKE had to yield increasingly on the Macedonian issue, giving credence to the charge that they were agents of the Bulgarians and the Yugoslavs.

The national interests of the Bulgarian, Soviet, Greek, and Yugo-slav Communists diverged on the Macedonian question. It is not clear whether the Bulgarians and the Yugoslavs openly defied the Russians in supporting the Communist side in the civil war, or whether the Russians disapproved but kept their options open, ready to repudiate the Yugoslavs and Bulgarians if the venture soured.

The Soviet Union in the immediate postwar period had severe security problems in the newly reannexed Baltic states and the Ukrainian areas transferred from the eastern part of interwar Poland. Its immediate goal was to pacify these regions, and its long term goal was to establish governments on its western borders that would be friendly to the Soviet Union, that is, have no alliances with countries other than the USSR. Of all the countries on the western borders of the Soviet Union, only Finland was able to meet the Soviet criteria for a friendly country and yet keep its internal independence almost intact. This exceptional outcome owed something to the circumstances of the outcome of the war and to the nature of the Finnish political system.

Of all the countries bordering on the Soviet Union in Europe, only Finland had not been occupied by the USSR. In exchange for armistice terms by which Finland lost important territories, paid heavy reparations, accepted a Soviet naval base in Porkkala with transit rights through Helsinki, and disarmed the remaining German troops, the Finns were spared occupation, and the Russians were spared the trouble of diverting troops from the Central Front to occupy Finland. A coalition government, in which conservative leaders played a prominent role, signed the armistice and prepared to sign the peace treaty carrying out its terms. The Finnish arrangements suited the Russians because they had a guarantee of the foreign policy they considered necessary for their security from a legitimate government with strong popular support. The hopes of Finnish emigrés in the Soviet Union, like Otto Kuusinen, that the Communist party could capitalize on war with Russia had been dashed twice since 1940. An agreement of all the Finns to submit to the Russian demands was preferable to a minority government of Communists that would have to coerce the Finns into a foreign policy satisfactory to the Russians.

The Finnish non-Communist parties had to take the Communists into the government, not only because they had gained the votes that entitled them to it, but because it seemed like an earnest of their good faith in meeting the Soviet demand that they limit their freedom of independence in foreign policy. Only in 1948 did it become possible to dispense with the Communist presence in the government without frightening the Russians. The tacit understanding between Russians and Finns on the foreign policy question seemed to have been almost complete. Only once was there a flurry of conflict when the Finns raised the question of borders at the peace conference, only to be firmly put down by the Russians.

Domestically, the Finnish Communists in the government shared much of the experience of their French and Italian comrades. The economic situation was very bad. Heavy reparations due the Soviet Union aggravated inflation. In executing a policy of wage controls, the Finnish Communists were not only restoring the capitalistic economy of the country but assuring the payment of reparations to the USSR. The Finnish Communists also agreed with their partners in the government on a common program for nationalization and social reform, but very little was accomplished in this regard before the Communists were dropped from the government in 1948.

The Finnish Communists had enjoyed only a shadow political life in the interwar period, and the two wars were a difficult time for them. They enjoyed coming out into the light of day and their acceptance as fully equal citizens. They had no great desire to return to their old illegal status, and there is no evidence that, like their Bulgarian, Polish, and Hungarian comrades, they pressed the Russians to gain for them a greater say in the government than their electoral successes had earned. They were neither as experienced as the French Communists in the parliamentary game, nor did they seem to have any leaders of the intelligence and acumen of the Italians. It is not surprising that the other parties made use of them as long as they were needed and then got rid of them.

In Czechoslovakia, the Communists put to good use the agreements reached among Benes, Stalin, and the Czechoslovak Communists. The expulsion of the Sudeten and other Germans and the Hungarians meant that much good agricultural land with its inventory had become available for redistribution. The farmers who received this land believed that the continued presence of the Communists in the government and the connection with Russia was the best guarantee for continued possession of their new property. A program of extensive nationalization of industry and business was undertaken, made easier by the circumstance that the most recent owners had been Germans. As in France and Italy, however, the initial electoral gains of the Communists seemed to be slipping, and the future looked worse than the present.

In Poland, Bulgaria, Romania, and Hungary the situation strikingly contrasted with that in Finland. The right wing parties either refused to work with the Communists, or the Communists persuaded themselves and the Russians that the right was not to be trusted. The integration of different classes of society into a nation with a strong sense of common purpose was not nearly as complete as in Finland, and no consensus could be reached on a common policy toward the Soviet Union that commanded general support. In Poland, the non-Communist underground now fought the Russians instead of the Germans, and the Provisional Polish Government could not, in its own judgment, assure its own security without the presence of Soviet troops. In Hungary, Romania, and Bulgaria, many of the non-Communist political figures entertained quite unrealistic hopes that the Western powers might actively support their anti-Communist activity. There is some evidence that these hopes were nourished by Western intelligence agents. Whatever the extent and importance of these activities, the Soviets saw them magnified through the glass of their weakness and in particular the disorder in the new western regions of the USSR.

Land reforms did not contribute to the electoral successes of the Communist parties in Hungary, Poland, and Romania as they did in Czechoslovakia. In fact, the dislocation of the land reforms aggravated the already scarce food supply. The reparations to the Soviet Union and the countless irregular levies weakened the position of the Communist party. Where genuine elections took place, as in Hungary, Austria, and Berlin, the Communist parties fared very badly, and where elections were rigged, the Communist leaders knew how weak their electoral base was.

Paradoxically, in the former Fascist or semi-Fascist countries where the bourgeoisie was still weak, the Communists fared badly, partially because they had never had a mass base and partially because the behavior of Russian troops and administrators did not cast a favorable light on Communism. It was precisely because these parties were so weak that Stalin urged them to gain allies, and only when they failed did he agree to the basically unitary rule of the Communist parties. The international goals of the Soviet Union would have favored broadly based governments like the Finnish. With the Finnish right wing in the government there were no Finnish guerrillas in the forests. Stalin would have preferred to spare American sensibilities without giving up the substance of security, as he did in Finland. However, the right would not cooperate and could not be trusted. Stalin then had to fall back on countries ruled, in some cases, by Communists too insignificant to have been purged and killed in 1938. Varga was very clear in stating that the countries of the new democracies were not to be socialist countries and would remain in the capitalist sphere of economic relationships, where they would be eligible for capitalist aid and investment. Only when that preferred Soviet policy failed did the national Communist leadership become the beneficiaries of their own weakness and gain a role in the management of the affairs of their respective countries that their popular support could not have justified.

The Peace Treaties to the Founding of the Cominform:
The Cloth is Cut to Fit the Lean Communist Purse

The Cominform was founded when the Soviet Union relinquished its major hope: that resources from conquered Germany and allied America would be available for the reconstruction of Russia. Once it was clear that little help could be expected from the United States, the Soviet leaders reduced their goals to preventing the United States from jeopardizing the positions they held. Now it was no longer appropriate to avoid irritating the United States. On the contrary, it was necessary to thwart its purposes. This could be accomplished by impugning its motives, attacking its policies, and stirring up opposition wherever possible. The Americans in increasing numbers had come to fear Communist expansion and had hardened their policy toward the USSR. This, in turn, caused the latter to move from a policy of soliciting cooperation to confrontation. Germany was at the heart of the difference between the two.

In the United States itself, as John Gimbel has so convincingly demonstrated, the War Department and the State Department were sharply divided on European policy.[13] The American army was increasingly nervous about administering an occupation in which strikes and hunger demonstrations had appeared, and it wanted to restore German economic production. The State Department felt that Germany's standard of living could not be permitted to rise above that of its wartime victims. The impasse was broken by the Marshall Plan, whose true purpose and instrumentalities were discussed and elaborated only after its announcement. Under terms worked out by the summer of 1947, all Europe, including the Soviet Union, would be eligible for its benefits. How generous the US Congress would be with grants and loans for Europe was an open question, and the Marshall Plan was presented as perhaps the last chance to save Western Europe from chaos and Communism. Although the presentation served the political interests of its proponents, it did no violence to their true sentiments.

The first meeting of the future recipients of the Marshall Plan, held in Paris in 1947, made clear that the United States would require information about the economies of the countries the plan was intended to rescue and continuing information on the employment of the grants. Given the narrow base of the Communist parties in Eastern Europe, it is not surprising that the Soviet Union vetoed the quite natural desire of the Poles, the Czechoslovaks, the East Germans, and perhaps others to benefit from American largesse. At the founding meeting of the Cominform in the fall of 1947, Georgi Malenkov revealed that Soviet economic plans had been predicated on economic aid from the West and that these plans had been revised when it was realized that the assistance would not be forthcoming. Malenkov did not say so, but it was obvious that he meant that economic aid would only be accepted on Soviet terms that did not encompass American control of the way in which the aid was to be used in Eastern Europe and perhaps in the Soviet Union.

Since the Soviet Union was compelled to give up reparations from all Germany and direct assistance from the United States, Soviet interests were no longer served by cooperation with the United States. On the contrary, the second line of defense was to prevent the restoration of the West European economies, which could be expected to bring in its train American political hegemony in the area. Since the reluctance of the American Congress to provide relief for Europe had been well advertised, and its approval of funding for that purpose was in doubt, the Soviets adopted the strategy of trying to defeat the Marshall Plan by ranging the Communist parties of Europe against it. This policy helped bring about what it was meant to prevent.

Moreover, events elsewhere had changed the international political climate and the political situation in the key countries of Italy and France. In the winter of 1946–47 the British were no longer willing, or able, to support the Greek government in the civil war. The Americans could only gamble that the Greek government could survive on its own or assume the burden. In retrospect, it is difficult to judge whether the KKE could have succeeded had the United States not intervened. Since they had achieved independence from the Ottoman Empire more than a century before, the Greeks had never believed themselves strong enough to maintain it without the support of a great power and had never achieved that broad consensus on the nature of their state and its preservation that characterized Western Europe. The legacy of five centuries of Ottoman rule was not easy to throw off.

Whatever the case, the Truman administration was unwilling to take the chance that the Greeks could defeat the Communists by themselves. The Truman Doctrine justified American intervention in Greece in broad ideological terms by presenting the Soviet Union as a state intent on expansion. The American appreciation of the situation, it is easy to say from hindsight, greatly exaggerated the Soviet willingness to take risks at that juncture, but very likely finished off the Soviet hope, as expressed by Varga, that a ten or fifteen year period of stabilization and American aid could be expected.

Almost simultaneously the position of the PCI and PCF altered. The PCF had been increasingly uncomfortable within the tripartite government. To be a member of the parliamentary coalition, the PCF had to support its foreign and domestic policies. The first was easier than the second because the members of the PCF wanted to punish Germany and to preserve the French Union, that is, hold onto Indo-China, Madagascar, and Algeria. To support wage controls while prices mounted, however, meant facing the bitter complaints of the rank-and-file workers.

We know from Vincent Auriol's diaries that the French government had almost immediate access to the meetings of the PCF politburo and that the party was sharply divided on how many concessions it should make to preserve its position in the government.[14] As long as Moscow favored the coalition policy, Thorez and Duclos overawed their party opponents. (The PCF was far less than an equal member of the tripartite government. This is indicated by the activities of the French intelligence agencies, which conducted espionage against the party and made its findings available to other members of the coalition.)

In May 1947 the position of the PCF was made impossible by a wildcat strike in the Renault plant in Paris. At first the PCF denounced the strike as a Hitlerite-Trotskyite conspiracy, but as it spread the party approved it and assumed its leadership. After all, it presumed to lead the working class and so had to follow where it went. Alexandre Auguste Ledru-Rollin, one hundred years earlier, had gone along with a radical policy initiated from below that he opposed, saying: "Je suis leur chef; il faut que je les suive" (I'm their chief, I have to follow them).[15] The PCF could not remain in the government when it broke the three party agreement on wages and price control. In his farewell interview with Auriol, Thorez protested that the socialists had betrayed him by provoking the strike and had put the PCF in an untenable position and forced it much against its wishes to leave the government. Although the interview was friendly, Thorez maintained with tears in his eyes that the Communists would soon return to the government, and Auriol agreed that it would and should happen. After all, with the Communists effectively excluded as a possible member of the government, the ability of the socialists to negotiate with parties to their right disappeared. Nor was it certain that the United States would remain in Europe. Duclos stated publicly that the Communists' departure from the government was only temporary and that they would soon return.

In Italy, Togliatti, who was perhaps shrewder and more farsighted than his French counterparts, foresaw that the PCI would no longer be needed, and he adopted a lower profile within the government, but maintained a policy of conditional support for it. His purpose apparently was to preserve the role of the PCI within the Constituent Assembly and to create institutional safeguards for the future.

At the Cominform meeting in September 1947, the departure of the Italian and French Communist parties from their respective governments was presented as part of an orchestrated American plan to achieve hegemony in Europe. This view has persisted, but it is not entirely accurate. The position of the Communist parties in the government had become increasingly less viable. In May 1947 Georges Bidault, the foreign minister, returned from the Moscow Conference where he had failed to get Soviet support for French claims against the Rhineland but received a consolation prize of coal deliveries and control of the Saar from the Anglo-Americans. He became very anti-Soviet and by reflex much less willing to continue the presence of the Communists in his own government. In Italy, after the very disappointing peace treaty was signed, Alcide De Gasperi had nothing to gain from Russian benevolence and therefore no stake in the possible intervention of the PCI with the Soviet Union.

On the contrary, although no formal American commitments on this point seem to have been offered, it should have been obvious to even a moderately attentive reader of the American press that American aid and assistance would be much more likely if the Communists were no longer in the government. Very likely both Leon Blum and De Gasperi, who visited the United States in the early part of 1947, realized this political fact of life.

As the wartime allies found they no longer had any common purposes in postwar political arrangements, the United States and the Soviet Union each moved to consolidate its position in what it deemed to be a threatened sphere of action. The Communists disappeared from their official positions in the West, and the non-Communist parties disappeared to all intents and purposes from the people's democracies in the East.

The founding meeting of the Cominform in Poland signaled the Soviet realization that the new political situation in Europe required new policies.[16] Held in great secrecy and attended by the second and third men of the parties of the USSR and the peoples democracies plus the PCI and the PCF, the Cominform enunciated a new line. (The absence of the KKE perhaps reflected the low Soviet estimate of its likely success.) The theme of the meeting was that the Communist parties of Europe had in some cases been pursuing mistaken policies and that greater coordination was required to harmonize their action. Here the customary Soviet practice of denouncing as error what had been approved the day before was followed. The Soviet organizers of the conference, without informing the PCF and the PCI, determined that these parties were not to try to reenter their governments but to work against them to thwart the success of the Marshall Plan. In the style so familiar in Soviet society, the managers of the old policy were to be given a chance to become the managers of the new policy if they abjectly confessed that they (and not the Soviet leadership) had been mistaken and were now prepared to do the right thing.

The opening speeches were ominous enough. Milovan Djilas, speaking for the Yugoslavs, attributed their success to the timely purge in 1938 that enabled them to enter the war with solid ranks. (This implicitly approved the Soviet Great Purge—the Yezhovshchina—an obscene act in Poland, where almost every Polish representative had close friends and associates who had perished at the hands of Stalin's officials.) Djilas went on to excoriate the French and Italians for not having seized power at the end of the war as the Yugoslavs had. It is difficult now after the series of sophisticated writings that have come from Djilas's pen to conceive he could have been so provincial as to think that the Yugoslav situation was comparable to the French and Italian. But one must not forget the isolation in which the Yugoslavs had operated and the intoxication of a victory that could only have seemed like a wild dream less than ten years earlier.

Later the Yugoslavs maintained that the Russians had put them up to attacking the Western political parties within the Cominform as a precedent for doing the same thing to the Communist League of Yugoslavia later. But that explanation smacks somewhat of hindsight. It is perhaps sufficient to conclude that the Soviet Union wanted to maximize control of the East European Communist parties in order to preserve hegemony in that area and to exploit the strength of the Western Communist parties in order to frustrate American plans to establish hegemony in the West.

Duclos's speech revealed that the change in the Soviet line had been very recent or withheld from the French and Italians.[17] The second explanation seems unlikely, since the Soviet leaders were never chary of communicating their wishes to other parties once they had made up their minds. Duclos's speech was full of statistics about the increase in French production and gave the PCF credit for this great accomplishment. He sounded like a Soviet oblast secretary boasting that he had overfulfilled the plan. He was forced to confess error—to recognize that the PCF had been mistaken in viewing its departure from the government as temporary. If we follow the account of Eugenio Reale, one of the Italian representatives to the founding

meeting of the Cominform who later left the PCI, the Italians sus-
pected what would happen at the meeting. Reale wrote that Togliatti
had been invited but refused to go on the grounds of illness. The strict
adherence of the Russians to protocol in party matters, however,
makes it seem unlikely that only one head of party would have been
invited.

Ex-Communists have argued that the PCI and the PCF were forced
to adopt policies against their own interests, but this seems a little
overdrawn. Elements in both parties were unhappy about the principles they felt they had compromised to stay in their governments. It is
interesting that in 1950 and 1951 Thorez had these people, notably
André Marty and Charles Tillon, expelled from the party on the
ground that they had mistakenly advocated an uprising in 1944. The
PCI, always more flexible and independent, did not organize a treason
trial *à la Russe*. The whole argument seems to be a little beside the
point because the other parties in Italy and France preferred to govern without the Communists and could do so now that American economic aid was assured.

If one could stretch one's imagination sufficiently to conceive a
situation in which the Soviet Union, not the United States, was able
and willing to provide large scale economic assistance to France and
Italy, and the United States then withdrew from Europe, one would
also have to imagine a very different status for the Communist parties
of Western Europe during the late 1940s and early 1950s. The same
applies to Germany. Had the SED been the channel for large injec-
tions of Soviet aid rather than the instrument for extraction of goods
and services for the Soviet Union, the position of the KPD in West
Germany would have been quite different too. This is not merely to
suggest that if things had been different they would have been different. In the contest between the USSR and the United States for
influence in Europe, the former was desperately poor and the latter
unprecedentedly rich. This was not the only critical element in the
outcome of the contest, but it does point to the limited instrumentalities at the disposal of the Soviet authorities, which in turn automatically limited their options.

**From the Founding of the Cominform, September
1947, to the Establishment of the West German
Republic: Consolidation in the East—Retrenchment
in the West**

Soviet policy in this period was to consolidate the positions the
Russians occupied in their own sphere and where possible to prevent

the United States from doing the same in its sphere. Let us consider
the great strikes in France and Italy, the decision to liquidate the
KKE uprising in Greece, the Prague events of February 1948, the
Berlin blockade, the expulsion of the Yugoslavs from the Cominform,
and the departure of the Finnish Communists from the government
coalition.

Organized labor in France, Italy, and Finland suffered great difficulties until the economic effects of the Marshall Plan were felt.
Once the Communist parties left the government and the wage price
squeeze got worse, strikes broke out spontaneously and, in accordance with the new Cominform directive, the PCF and the PCI supported and led them. The strikes were more serious in France, and
our information on them is better. They were widespread, general,
and attended by considerable violence. The PCF led the strikes
through the unions it dominated. The government, in the person of a
socialist minister of interior, responded vigorously and paid little attention to legal niceties. The strikes failed when the workers started
to return to their jobs and the unions had to follow them and sanction
their actions. What attracted most attention was the temporary occupation of the Hotel de Ville in Marseilles—an action incorrectly but
widely put at the door of the Communists serving in the Marseilles
riot police.[18] The impression was widespread that the PCF was trying
to start a revolution. French intelligence reported communications between the Soviet embassy in Paris and Moscow, and if the information was authentic, the Soviet ambassador in Paris was constantly
pressing the PCF to be more aggressive. It is not possible with the
information available to judge the validity of this report, but it is certainly within the realm of possibility. Whatever the facts may have
been, once the crisis was over, the French political class was not
ready to consider the PCF as a possible member of the government
for many years.

The strikes were not as violent in Italy. Nevertheless, they were
also put down firmly, and the PCI, too, was not perceived as a possible member of the government for a long time afterwards.

These parties had already passed their electoral peak, the right was
more self-confident, American economic assistance was in the offing,
and the economic reconstruction of these countries could go forward
without the Communists. It is important to note, however, that these
Communist parties never became insurrectionary parties and therefore avoided being proscribed. As some French writers have explained, it was not possible to proscribe one Frenchman in four or five
and retain the essence of the French political system. But if the
Communists had been a revolutionary party, civil war might have

ensued. Neither the Communist leaders nor the French and Italian political class wanted a civil war, and that was the basis of the tacit bargain. With the benefit of hindsight it does not seem possible to say that the Soviet Union forced upon the PCF and the PCI a course that led to their exclusion from government. It was inherent in the political situation within these countries and in the willingness of the United States to offer effective economic assistance to its clients.

The civil war was going badly in Greece for the KKE. The failure to invite it to the founding meeting of the Cominform and the faint support it received from the Soviet press indicated that Djilas's call to militance was not meant to apply to all parties everywhere. The KKE leader, Nikos Zakharaidis, believed that if only he could capture one city, the people's democracies and the Soviet Union would have to recognize the government he had proclaimed, but neither event ever came to pass. In pursuit of his goal he forced the guerrillas to fight set battles against the wishes of guerrilla leaders, who wanted to follow the traditional strategy of hit and run. The improved equipment, especially air power furnished by the United States, was quite effective against such a faulty strategy. When Georgi Dimitrov made a public statement about a possible Balkan confederation of states of the people's democracies and named Greece as a possible member, Stalin exploded in rage and ordered the Greek adventure liquidated. One can presume that he felt the Greek uprising had no prospects and that he feared a continuation of that war with the presence of American troops could threaten Bulgaria and perhaps Yugoslavia. According to one persuasive account, an uprising in Albania was planned in the West and revealed to the USSR by Kim Philby.[19] The Yugoslavs apparently did not agree that it was dangerous to provoke the West further in Greece. After they were expelled from the Cominform, they continued to provide sanctuary and logistic assistance to the Greek rebels.

The assumption of power by the Communists in Prague in February 1948 was perhaps the most important event in convincing the West that the Soviet Union was embarked on an aggressive course whose goal was to Communize Europe. An examination of the course of events in Czechoslovakia, however, offers a more complex picture. At the fall 1947 Cominform meeting, the Czech Communist leader Rudolf Slansky interpreted the departure of the PCF and the PCI from their respective governments as part of an overall imperialist offensive and pointed out that the Communist party of Czechoslovakia faced a similar fate unless it was vigilant. As in France, Italy, and Finland, the Communists in Czechoslovakia were slipping electorally, and their position was especially precarious in Slovakia. They took advantage of a governmental crisis, unwisely precipitated by their opponents, to extend the political contest to the streets, exploiting their places in the police, the unions, and the workers' militia. Although violence and illegal actions were limited, the threat of civil war was posed. President Benes, ailing and broken in spirit, agreed to the formation of a new government in which the Communists enjoyed positions of power not justified by their electoral strength. Once ensconced in these positions, the Communists proceeded to consolidate their power by extralegal measures. The extent of the Soviet role in the instigation of the crisis has been much discussed on the basis of very slender evidence. The discussion is largely off the mark. The Communist party in Czechoslovakia was eager to secure its position and afraid that not to advance meant to retreat. In all likelihood the Soviet Union approved the action, but it was indigenous in inspiration.

The minor role the Soviet Union played in Czechoslovakia can be even more confidently applied to Finland. For a long time the accepted version in the West was that the Finnish Communists planned a coup d'etat, but that the Communist Oiva Leino, in a spasm of patriotism, tipped off the Finnish authorities who foiled the plot. According to A. F. Upton's convincing account, the other parties in the governmental coalition invented the plot as a pretext to drop the Communists from the government.[20] In any case, Leino had long been excluded from the inner councils of the party and would not have known of a plot if there had been one. Correcting the facts about the plot is of considerable importance in explaining the Soviet general plan for Communist parties in Europe. If there was no plot, the Soviet Union could not have approved it in advance. What the Soviets had to deal with, then, was "bourgeois trickery" to exclude a Communist party from the government and not the disappointment of a Soviet hope. Stalin seems to have considered for a while the imposition of a treaty on the Finns that would have even further limited their freedom of action, but when the Finns objected he thought better of it. The Soviets had achieved their original objective of establishing control over foreign policy in Finland. Imposition of Finnish Communist domination risked a second Finnish civil war, and without Soviet intervention, the Finnish Communists would have been defeated again. With Tito still successful in his defiance and with the Marshall Plan underway, the people's democracies and East Germany were threatened. The Soviet decision seems to have been to leave well enough alone in Finland. What is striking in retrospect is how closely events in Finland fit into the Italian and French pattern. An important difference was that the non-Communist parties in Finland could not expect American economic aid because its rejection was the condition of Finnish independence in internal affairs.

The quarrel with the Yugoslavs was fateful for the future of all the Communists of Eastern Europe. The events are well known, and it is only necessary to remark that the tactics the Comintern had earlier employed in dealing with recalcitrant Communist parties failed in Yugoslavia. Soviet officials charged with the affairs of Communist parties had long pursued a policy of maintaining their contacts with the opposition within each party and would threaten to throw support to it if the ruling group resisted Soviet directives. Once the anathema pronounced by the Cominform proved to be without force, a search for Titoists, starting with Hungary, was set in motion all over Eastern Europe, ending in what has properly been called the Stalinization of these parties. The imminent consolidation of the American position in Western Europe made the consolidation of the Soviet position in Eastern Europe all the more urgent, but the fear that others might emulate Tito was the driving force. Because the Communist parties of Eastern Europe were too weak and discredited to pursue a successful popular front policy, they had no alternative but to go it alone, thus becoming the creatures, not the associates, of the CSPU. Once they became part of the Soviet political self, their capture or defection became a loss to the Soviet state itself—a feature of European Communism that still persists.

The last remnant of Allied cooperation was the joint occupation of Germany. With the failure to reach agreement on reparations and the establishment of a single German government, the Soviet Union and the United States had to determine how far to go in making their respective zones autonomous or even new states. The United States took the lead because it had long given up the expectation of reparations from Germany and because it wanted to restore the West German economy to provide an essential element for the recovery of Western Europe. The American predilection for a free enterprise economic system meant that this could be done only with German cooperation. As a result, the United States moved rapidly to transfer economic and political control to the Germans themselves. For the Soviet Union the division of Germany and the economic recovery of the Western zones meant no reparations for them and a satisfied client for the United States.

The initial step in the American scheme for economic advance was a currency reform in Western Germany—thus eliminating one of the last two Soviet-American institutions for all Germany. The Soviets attempted to use the only other Allied institution—the government of Berlin—as a bargaining lever. When the Berlin blockade failed, largely as a result of the successful improvisation of the Berlin airlift, the division of Germany was completed, save for the anomaly of a Berlin divided among four powers within the territory of East Germany. With the lifting of the blockade in 1949, the Soviet Union accepted the division of Germany—permanently as it turned out. Although in imposing the blockade the Soviet Union was employing the only instrumentality it possessed to keep the German situation fluid, the results were counter-productive. The Soviets were cast in the role of the brutal power that tried to starve and freeze the population of Berlin to put pressure on the United States. It should be remembered that West German Socialists and Christian Democrats, too, had initially hung back from full cooperation with the United States for fear of being tainted by collaboration with a failed enterprise. They now entered into an alliance with the Americans with a will. Of the non-Communist members of the SED in East Germany and the leaders of the other parties, only a few puppets remained, and the Communists of East Germany assumed the formal as well as the actual governance of affairs. The circumstances of the division of Germany discredited the KPD in West Germany and created a seige mentality in the SED from the very beginning. Another Germany, larger, better endowed naturally, and generously supported by the United States, refused to recognize the legitimacy of East Germany and announced as its goal the adherence of East Germany to West Germany. No information on resistance to SED rule has come to light, but the mutual claim of each of the Germanies to be Germany created the sense of precariousness for the East German Communists that armed resistance created in Poland.

By 1949 the main features of the landscape of European Communism were discernible. The mass parties of Western Europe and Finland, embedded as they were in a parliamentary system, could survive and work for a better day. The political decision to keep them out of the government did not compromise their juridical position: they were eligible to participate in a governing coalition, or if they could gather the votes, to be the governing party. The other parties in these states could not deny this legal opportunity to the Communists without violating the democratic system that served their own interests so well. The future was always open to the Communists—if they accepted that system. But if they became revolutionary parties or seemed likely to win a majority of the vote—only a theoretical possibility in this period—then they might be suppressed and declared outlaws. Experience had shown in the Soviet sphere that free voting would have unseated the Communist parties and surely would have meant the loss of these areas.

In the years since Tito's expulsion, the Communist parties of Eastern Europe have exercised different degrees of authority over their own affairs. But in the last analysis, the CPSU has set the limits of permissible variation in their policies.

Whatever Eurocommunism might mean, since 1949 the Communist parties of all Europe have had less, rather than more, in common. The differences between ruling and nonruling parties were and are differences in kind and not of degree. For a brief period in 1944 and 1945 it might have seemed as if there was a continuum between people's democracies in Eastern Europe and popular front governments in Western Europe, but since then the two branches of European Communism have remained distinct.

In the 1960s and 1970s the Communist parties of Western (and sometimes Eastern) Europe began to insist on their differences with the CPSU. In the process they hearkened back to the popular fronts of the 1930s as the golden age rather than to the period just described. They claimed the credit for the shift in Soviet policy from the class-against-class policy to the popular front policy. The practice of treating the social democrats as the main enemy, which had been so disastrous in Germany, was replaced, they maintained, by a popular front against Fascism because of the success and the influence of the West European Communist parties. They had served the CPSU well by serving themselves, argued the historical reconstruction, implying that they could do so again. The Soviet literature on the subject, citing the minutes of Politburo meetings and internal Comintern documents, seeks to show that the initiative came from the Russian leaders of the Comintern, or at least that the Russians and the non-Russian Communists saw eye to eye. As is often the case in the Communist world, the purpose of historical writing is to influence the present-day struggle among different Communist political parties or factions.[21] Since the goal of the Eurocommunists today is to pursue independent internal political policies in their own countries without interference from the Soviet Union and without the embarrassment of their repressive behavior in Eastern Europe, the popular front period is more suitable as a model than the period of the people's democracies and Communist participation in coalition government. If the present day Communist leaders agree with the assessment that in this period they conformed (largely willingly) to Soviet wishes, that they accepted treatment as a second-class party from the bourgeois parties, and that they were dismissed to live in a political ghetto when they had served their purpose, it is understandable that they do not care to recall that period of failure when they seek once again to participate in the government as a partner with other parties.

NOTES

1. Edward J. Rozek, *Allied Wartime Diplomacy: A Pattern in Poland* (New York: John Wiley & Sons, 1958), p. 269.

2. Paolo Spriano, *Storio del Partito Comunista Italiano* (5 vols., Turin: Guilo Einaudi, 1967–).

3. Raimondo Luraghi, "Sui rapporti diplomatici tra l'Italia e l'Unione Sovietica agli inizi dell'anno 1944," *Il Moviemento di Liberazione in Italia*, nos. 52–53, (July-December 1958), pp. 113–118; Geraud Jouve, "Le retour de Maurice Thorez en France," *Le Monde*, November 28, 1969.

4. Aurelio Lepre, *La svolta di Salerno* (Rome: Editori Riuniti, 1966).

5. K. L. Selesnjow, "Reise mit deutschen Antifaschisten in ein Kriegsgefangenenlager bei Karaganda (Dezember, 1941)" *Beiträge zur Geschichte der Arbeiterbewegung* (1970), pp. 278–290; Michail Iwanowitsch Burzew, "Mit Wilhelm Pieck in den Tagen des zweiten Weltkriegs," *Zeitschrift für Militärgeschichte* ([East] Berlin) (No. 3, 1971), pp. 339–348.

6. Ryszard Halaba and Wladyslaw Waziewski, *Polska Partia Robotnicza 1942–1948* (Warsaw: Ministerstwo oborny Narodowej 1971), pp. 22–23, passim.

7. Stephen Clissold, *Yugoslavia and the Soviet Union* (London: Oxford University Press, 1975).

8. The best three books on the Greek civil war are: C. M. Woodhouse, *The Struggle for Greece: 1941–1949* (London: Hart Davis, MacGibbon, 1976); G. D. Kir'iakidis, *Grazhdanskaia voina v Gretsii, 1946–1949* (Moscow: Izdatel'stvo Nauka, 1972); and Heinz Richter, *Griechenland zwischen Revolution und Konterrevolution (1936–1949)* (Frankfurt am Main: Europaische Verlaganstalt, 1973).

9. Eugen Varga, *Izmeniia v ekonomiki kapitalizma v itoge vtoroi mirovoi voine* (Moscow: Gosizd-vo polit. literatury, 1946).

10. Erich W. Gniffke, *Jahre mit Ulbricht* (Cologne: Wissenschaft und Politik, 1966), pp. 249–250.

11. See Philip J. Jaffe, "The Rise and Fall of Earl Browder," *Survey* (Spring 1972), pp. 14–65.

12. Peter Novick, *The Resistance Versus Vichy: The Purge of Collaborators in Liberated France* (London: Chatto and Windus, 1968).

13. John Gimbel, *The Origins of the Marshall Plan* (Stanford: Stanford University Press, 1976).

14. Vincent Auriol, *Journal du Septennat 1947–1954*. Vol. I:*1947, Version Integrale* (Paris: Librarie Armand Colin, 1970), especially pp. 139–141.

15. E. L. Woodward, *War and Peace in Europe 1815–1870* (Hamden, Conn.: Archon Books, 1963), p. 136.

16. Eugenio Reale, *Nascità del Cominform. Documenti e testamonianze sulla conferenza. . . . tenuta . . .dal 22 al 27 settembre 1947* (N.P.: Arnoldo Editore, 1958); Eugenio Reale, "The Founding of the Cominform," in M. Drachkovich and B. Lazitch, eds., *The Comintern: Historical Highlights* (New York: Frederick A. Praeger, 1966); Lilly Marcou, *Le Kominform: Le Communisme de guerre froide* (Paris: Presses de fondation nationale des sciences politiques, 1977).

17. The most complete text is to be found in Jacques Duclos, "The French Communist Party in the Struggle for the Independence of the Country, against

American Expansionism,'' *For a Lasting Peace, For a People's Democracy* (December 1, 1947).

18. Maurice Agulhon and Fernand Barrat, *CRS* [Compaignies républicaines de sécurité] *à Marseilles, la police au service du peuple 1944–1947* (Paris: Armand Colin, 1971).

19. Bruce Page, David Leitch, and Phillip Knightley, *The Philby Conspiracy* (New York: Signet Books, 1969), pp. 181–182.

20. A. F. Upton, *Communism in Scandanavia and Finland, Politics of Opportunity* (Garden City, N.Y.: Anchor Press, 1973), pp. 262–298.

21. A whole literature on this subject appeared in Eastern and Western Europe. Some of the major works are: B. M. Leibzon and K. K. Shirina, *Povorot v politike Kominterna, istoricheskoe znachenie VII kongressa Kominterna* (Moscow: Mysl', 1975); Giorgio Bocca, *Palmiro Togliatti* (Rome: Editori Laterza, 1973); Dobrin Michev, ''Georgi Dimitov i podgotovkata na Sedmiia kongres Komunistichekiia internatsional (mart-iuli 1934-g),'' *Vekove* (Sofia), 2 (1972), pp. 30–42; Akademia Nauk, ed., *Sedmoi kongress Kominterna i bor'ba za sozdanie narodnogo fronta v stranakh Tsentralnoi i Iugo-Vostochnoi Evropy* (Moscow: Izdatel'stvo nauka, 1977), pp. 75–77; Milos Hajek, *Storia dell'Internazionale comunista (1921–1935). La politica del fronte unico* (Rome: Editori Riuniti, 1975), pp. 204–249; Dieter Wolf, *Die Doriot-Bewegung. Ein Beitrag zur Geschichte des Französischen Faschismus* (Stuttgart: Deutsche Verlags Anstalt, 1967), pp. 77–98; Ernesto Ragioneri, *Palmiro Togliatti. Per una biografia politica e intellectuale* (Rome: Editori Riuniti, 1976), pp. 568–598; Branko Lazitch, ''Le Comintern et le Front Populaire,'' *Contre-point*, 3 (1971), pp. 83–94; Celie Vassart and Albert Vassart, ''The Moscow Origins of the Popular Front,'' in Milorad M. Drachkovitch and Branko Lazitch, eds., *The Comintern: Historical Highlights* (New York: Frederick A. Praeger, 1966); Santiago Carillo, *Eurocomunismo y Estado* (Barcelona: Editorial Crítica, 1977), pp. 143–146.

CHAPTER III

Bukharin and the Eurocommunist Idea

Stephen F. Cohen

The past is never dead. It's not even past.
WILLIAM FAULKNER

The idea of a Communist alternative to Stalinism has a long history, inside and outside the Soviet Union. It stretches from the early years of the Bolshevik Revolution through the search for different roads to socialism in Eastern Europe after Stalin's death in 1953. Today it is embodied most fully in the idea of Eurocommunism. Through all of its stages, the history of the anti-Stalinist idea has been reflected in the historical fate of the Bolshevik leader Nikolai Ivanovich Bukharin.

Bukharin, whom Lenin had called the "favorite of the whole party,"[1] was condemned to death by Stalin at the Moscow purge trial of March 1938. Falsely accused of being the archcriminal behind a vast anti-Soviet conspiracy of treason, sabotage, and assassination, his illustrious career as a Soviet founding father was transformed into the biography of a "rabid enemy of the people." His name, along with Lev Trotsky's, became synonymous in Stalinist demonology with the treacherous and murderously repressed idea of an anti-Stalinist alternative, anathema inside the Soviet Union and throughout the Communist movement. Even in the West the once renowned Bukharin was half-forgotten, remembered mainly and unfairly as the morally bankrupt old Bolshevik Rubashov of Arthur Koestler's novel *Darkness at Noon.*

Forty years later, in the wake of de-Stalinization, Bukharin's reputation outside the Soviet Union had revived spectacularly, and in 1978, which marked both the ninetieth anniversary of his birth and the fortieth anniversary of his execution, his fate inspired an international campaign by Eurocommunists and Western socialists for his exoneration and political rehabilitation. The campaign grew out of an array of personal and political factors, including the efforts of his widow and son to gain justice for Bukharin and the relations between Soviet and Western Communists. It demonstrated that Bukharin and what he represented in Soviet history had become an important symbol in the struggle between Communist reformers and Communist conservatives—anti-Stalinists and neo-Stalinists—from Moscow to the capitals of Eurocommunism.

The Bukharin affair is rooted in the intensely historical nature of Communist politics, in which the past continues to collide with the present. The traumatic events of Stalin's long rule from 1929 to 1953—forcible collectivization, mass terror, the Gulag system, 20 million deaths in World War II, twenty-five years of despot worship, and Moscow's fateful domination over the international Communist movement—live on as festering controversies between Stalinists and anti-Stalinists in the various Communist parties. They underlie current struggles over policy that will influence the future of Communism as a system and as a movement.

Conservative Communists, who control the Soviet party and dominate most of its East European allies, must defend, even sanctify, the Stalinist past, which shaped so many of their repressive policies, institutions, attitudes, and careers. Reformers inside the parties, if they are to set Communism on an innovative and less authoritarian course, must repudiate large parts of the Stalinist past. But to demonstrate the different non-Stalinist potential of Communism today, reformers must show also that it had a different historical potential. In addition to Lenin, they must find in Soviet history before the onset of Stalinism in 1929 programmatic ideas and leaders who represented an authentic Communist alternative to Stalin. The search has led reform Communists, covertly in the Soviet Union and openly elsewhere, to Bukharin.

I.

Bukharin's appeal as an ancestral symbol of contemporary anti-Stalinism begins with his importance as a Soviet leader during his years in power. Although he was only twenty-nine years old when the Bolshevik party came to power in 1917, he stood high among the small group of men who ruled the first socialist state during the ensuing twelve years—a leading member of the Politburo and the Central Committee, editor of *Pravda,* head of the Communist International from 1926 to 1928, and coleader with Stalin of the ruling Soviet party from shortly after Lenin's death in 1924 to his political defeat in

1928–29. He was also, in Lenin's words, the "biggest theoretician" of Soviet Marxism. His books—among them *Imperialism and World Economy, The ABC of Communism,* and *Historical Materialism*— were published in dozens of Russian and foreign editions, becoming standard reading for Communists and sympathizers around the world. By the mid-1920s his political stature was second to none in the Soviet leadership.[2]

After decades of Eastern-style despotism and Stalinist bureaucracy, Bukharin's attraction derives also from his international outlook and his appealing personality. Steeped in Western culture and speaking its languages (he lived as an émigré in Europe and the United States between 1911 and 1917), he, like Trotsky, embodied the internationalist traditions of Soviet Communism before its descent into Stalinist chauvinism. Though he was the original theorist of "socialism in one country," Bukharin warned against the tendency, already evident in the 1920s, "'to spit' on the international revolution; such a tendency could give rise to its own peculiar ideology, a peculiar 'national Bolshevism.' . . . From here it is a few steps to a number of even more harmful ideas." Anticipating Communists of contemporary Eastern and Western Europe, from Josip Tito to the Eurocommunists, he assumed the validity, even the necessity, of different roads to socialism. As a result of Russian conditions, he said, the Soviet model could be only a "backward socialism."[3]

Bukharin's popularity acquired the proportions of a legend passed on by generations of Soviet and foreign Communists. A small zestful man with boyish charm and a puckish humor, his assorted enthusiasms for ideas, sports, animals, scientific discoveries, and painting were the subject of much discussion and admiration. He was, as Lenin wrote in his last testament, the best-liked leader of the Bolshevik revolution. It was characteristic that despite his relentless defense of the party's dictatorship, he developed warm friendships with people of opposing views. They included the septuagenarian physiologist Ivan Pavlov, whom he impressed, the doomed poet Osip Mandelstam, whom he protected for more than a decade, and Boris Pasternak, who dedicated a poem to him.[4]

These qualities enhance but do not truly explain Bukharin's contemporary importance, which is essentially programmatic and tied to an equally dramatic revival of interest in the Soviet 1920s. Known as the period of the New Economic Policy (NEP), the years between the end of the Russian Civil War in 1921 and the coming of Stalin's revolution from above in 1929 represent the first and still most far-reaching liberalization in Soviet political history—a kind of Moscow Spring.[5]

The policies introduced by Lenin in 1921 were new in that they broke sharply with the extremist measures and coercive ideas of the

Civil War. They gave birth to the first dual economy in the history of Communist movements, combining a public and a private sector, socialist aspirations and capitalist practices, plan and market. The Soviet state retained control of heavy industry, foreign trade, banking, and transportation. Lesser enterprises were denationalized, the principle of private peasant farming reaffirmed, and market relations, which had been suppressed during the Civil War, restored.

NEP brought also new, more conciliatory politics. The party maintained its dictatorship, but the Soviet party-state of the 1920s was limited and relatively tolerant, allowing a greater degree of social, cultural, and intellectual pluralism than has ever existed since in that country. As in economic life, the excesses of statism and coercion were deplored. Social harmony and class collaboration, rather than strife and terror, became the principles of NEP. The Soviet 1920s were neither democratic nor, in our sense, liberal. But when Stalin unleashed a virtual civil war against the peasantry and the private sector in 1929, repudiating NEP as "rotten liberalism," he destroyed a model of Communist politics and economics that many citizens would remember as the "golden era" in Soviet history, and in which, three decades later, Communist reformers in the USSR and Eastern Europe would find a lost alternative to Stalinism.[6]

Lenin created the NEP, but with his death in 1924 and the splitting of his heirs into warring factions, Bukharin became its interpreter and greatest defender, first in alliance with Stalin against the Trotskyist left and then against Stalin in 1928–29. (One opponent dubbed him, contemptuously, the "Pushkin of NEP.")[7] While the Bolshevik left spoke theoretically and apocalyptically of exploiting the country's 25 million peasant households as an "internal colony" of state industry, an idea later carried out by Stalin in a ruthlessly different way, Bukharin insisted that the gradualist, conciliatory measures of NEP were the only road to industrialization and socialism in peasant Russia.

The defense of NEP led Bukharin to a whole system of ideas and policies in the 1920s radically unlike what became known as Stalinism and which anticipated the criticisms and proposals of anti-Stalinist reformers in the USSR and Europe after 1953. Or as Czech reformers, in search of "lost" ideas, said during the Prague Spring (which can be viewed as a "forerunner of Eurocommunism"),[8] Bukharin's ideas "make themselves heard, so to speak, in the language of the contemporary era."[9] He became the great critic of the willful temptations of monopolistic state power incited by ideological zealotry—the opponent of warfare measures and great leaps; administrative caprice and lawlessness; overcentralization and parasitic bureaucratism; and gigantomania and systematic inefficiency.

Instead, Bukharin advocated evolutionary policies that would allow the peasant majority and private sector to prosper and "to grow into socialism" through market relations. He wanted a pattern of development based on what he called "socialist humanism" and on the principle that "our economy exists for the consumer, not the consumer for the economy." Rejecting "Genghis Khan" schemes, he proposed a form of economic planning that combined rational goals set at the top with the "initiative of lower agencies, which act in accordance with the actual conditions of life." He told Soviet industrial managers, "We shall conquer with scientific economic leadership or we shall not conquer at all." He eulogized the party's dictatorship, but he insisted upon the role of "Soviet law, and not Soviet arbitrariness, moderated by a 'bureau of complaints' whose whereabouts is unknown." In other areas, he defended a cultural-intellectual life based on the "principle of free, anarchistic competition," rather than "squeezing everybody into one fist."[10]

In these and other ways Bukharinism was both an alternative to and premonition of Stalinism. When Stalin broke with NEP and drifted toward Draconian industrialization and forcible collectivization in 1928–29, Bukharin's protests put him at the head of the so-called right opposition inside the party. Even before Stalin's policies culminated in the rural holocaust of 1929–33, Bukharin saw their "monstrously one-sided" nature—the "military-feudal exploitation of the peasantry"—and their consequence. "Stalin's policy is leading to civil war. He will have to drown the revolts in blood." The result, he warned, "will be a police state."[11]

These prophetic objections, on the eve of the coming of Stalinism, sealed Bukharin's fate. Ousted from the Politburo in November 1929, his evolutionary programs were anathemized as a "right deviation" and a betrayal of socialism. He remained a nominal member of the Central Committee until his arrest in February 1937. During the short-lived thaw of 1934–35, he played significant roles as editor of *Izvestiia*, author of the civil rights sections of the 1936 constitution, and advocate of anti-Fascist alliances against Nazi Germany. But these last years were really a prelude to becoming the most representative victim of Stalin's terror against the old Bolshevik party during 1936–39.

The catastrophe of collectivization, with its terrible toll in millions of peasant lives and the ruination of Soviet agriculture in the 1930s, only redoubled Stalin's claim that his policies alone were the rightful outcome of the Bolshevik Revolution. Rival programs were no longer mere "deviations," but counterrevolutionary crimes. The show trial of Bukharin in 1938 was therefore designed to deny the Bukharinist alternative by criminalizing his entire political biography. All of Stalin's rivals were condemned during the purges as "nothing other than a gang of murderers, spies, diversionists, and wreckers, without any principles or ideals."[12] Stalin, speaking through the prosecutor Andrei Vyshinsky, attached a special epithet to Bukharin, who represented the most appealing and thus most threatening alternative: "The hypocrisy and perfidy of this man exceed the most perfidious and monstrous crimes known to the history of mankind."[13] The charge prevailed throughout the Communist world for almost twenty years.

II.

In 1956, shortly after Nikita Khrushchev denounced Stalin's "mass repressions" before a closed session of the Twentieth Congress of the Communist Party of the Soviet Union, a family reunion took place in a remote Siberian town. A twenty-year-old youth, Yuri, raised in orphanages and foster homes and living an ordinary life in central Russia, learned that his real mother was alive and in Siberian exile. He traveled to her and discovered that he was the only son of Nikolai Bukharin. Anna Mikhailovna Larina had married the forty-five-year-old Bukharin in 1934 at the age of nineteen. Arrested four months after Bukharin, in June 1937, and torn from her infant son, she spent the next two decades in jail cells, labor camps, and exile as a "wife of an enemy of the people." By 1961 Bukharin's widow and son had managed to resettle in Moscow, where they began to petition for his exoneration.

The only thing extraordinary about this event was the family name. Countless similar reunions—personal sagas that soon began to influence public affairs—were under way throughout the Soviet Union. The early stages of de-Stalinization—the pivot of Khrushchev's reformism of 1956–64—freed perhaps 7 million to 8 million people who had somehow survived in the murderous labor camps and exonerated, or "posthumously rehabilitated," another 5 million to 6 million who had died during Stalin's twenty-five-year terror.[14]

These acts of partial justice—millions more had perished since 1929—were traumatic and divisive. Revelations about the past threatened elites with vested interest in Stalinist policies, offended intransigent nostalgia for the Stalin years, and confronted millions who had directly abetted or profited from the terror with the memory, and even the presence, of their victims. On the other side, returnees from the camps and other relatives of the dead demanded fuller revelations and more rehabilitations. They became a constituency pressing for de-Stalinization. For them it was a duty to the dead but also a practical necessity: only legal rehabilitation of a husband or father could remove the official stigma of criminal guilt. It could mean permission to return to a native city, a flat, a widow's pension, or a child's education and career.

The fate of prominent officials who had perished was a particularly divisive issue inside the post-Stalin leadership. In the years before his overthrow in 1964, and against strong opposition, Khrushchev presided over the full rehabilitation—both juridical exoneration and restoration to political honor—of thousands of party, state, military, and cultural figures. They did not, however, include the highest leaders of the original Bolshevik party—most notably, Bukharin, Trotsky, Grigory Zinoviev, and Lev Kamenev. Because it raised the question of an alternative to Stalinism in 1929, the Bukharin case turned out to be the most important. It was linked inextricably to the Stalin question, and it was a kind of barometer of the rise, limits, and demise of Khrushchev's reformism.

Later, in forced retirement, a pensive Khrushchev would privately admire Bukharin and regret the decision not to rehabilitate him.[15] But Khrushchev himself formulated the new and still prevailing official position on Bukharin in his Secret Speech of 1956. It derived from his initial effort to limit de-Stalinization by combining a denunciation of Stalin's terror against the party in the late 1930s with a fervent defense of the dictator's peasant and industrial policies of 1929–33, which created the foundations of the modern-day Soviet system. Thus, while virtually acknowledging the fraudulent nature of Bukharin's trial, Khrushchev pointedly endorsed his political defeat in 1928–29.[16] As a result, references to Bukharin as a criminal were replaced in the Soviet press by political characterizations of his policies as "anti-Leninist" and "objectively a capitulation to capitalism."

Even this half-step, which raised the possibility of juridical (though not political) rehabilitation, was strongly resisted. Sometime between 1956 and 1958, after a secret commission confirmed the baselessness of the criminal charges, the Soviet leadership debated and rejected a proposal to announce publicly the legal exoneration of Bukharin and other defendants in the Stalinist trials. Khrushchev later blamed the decision on the intervention of Western Communist leaders who warned that another major revelation about the past would damage their own parties. His explanation seems implausible and self-serving. Though recent sources confirm that the French and British Communist leaders, Maurice Thorez and Harry Pollitt, protested in Moscow, it is unlikely that their voices were decisive.[17] Khrushchev himself probably lacked resolve, or his Soviet opponents were too strong

But the episode did illustrate that the Bukharin question had ramifications beyond the Soviet Union, especially for those European
Communists who had loudly applauded Stalin's terror and who remained, in fundamental ways, Stalinists.

Here matters stood until an embattled Khrushchev, seeking to
break conservative opposition, launched the first public attack on
Stalin's crimes at the Twenty-second Party Congress in October 1961.
A sporadic wave of anti-Stalinism swept the country during the next
two and a half years. Stalin's body was unceremoniously removed
from the Lenin Mausoleum. His name was stripped from hundreds of
cities and institutions. Personal tales of the terror and of prison camps
appeared in the Soviet press. And of great political importance,
Soviet historians began investigating previously sacrosanct events,
including Stalin's conduct of collectivization and industrialization,
thereby raising implicitly the idea of an alternative to the Stalinist
experience.[18]

Reflecting the connection between past and current politics, this
new de-Stalinization campaign was part of an increasingly radical reformism, especially in economics. Khrushchev's initiatives in the
early 1960s encouraged Soviet economic reformers to develop far-
reaching criticisms of the hypercentralized planning and administrative system inherited from the Stalin years. Their own proposals, re-
volving around a greater role for the market, echoed long forbidden
NEP ideas of the 1920s and thus, unavoidably, Bukharin's famous
admonitions against the excesses of centralization, bureaucratism,
and willful state intervention. In a study of these Soviet reformers,
whose proposals were closely related to economic reforms already
under way in Eastern Europe, a Western scholar has written: "It was
astonishing to discover how many ideas of Bukharin . . . were
adopted by current reformers as their own and how much of their
critique of past practices followed his strictures and prophecies even
in their expression."[19]

An official ban on a historical figure such as Bukharin was, however, also a constraint on the whole range of ideas and policies associated with his name. Although they never mentioned Bukharin publicly, many of the Soviet reformers were certainly aware that their
proposals opened them to political charges of repeating his "right deviation." This circumstance, along with Khrushchev's renewed assault on the Stalin cult, brought the Bukharin question to the fore
once again.

In March 1961 Bukharin's widow was summoned to the Central
Control Commission, the party judiciary body in charge of rehabilitations, and asked for testimony in connection with a dossier being pre-

pared on the Bukharin question. In addition to other personal information, Anna Larina revealed Bukharin's "last testament," a letter
written only days before his arrest. He had instructed her to
memorize it for a "future generation of party leaders" and then to
destroy it. In the letter, Bukharin expressed his "helplessness" before "the hellish machine" and "organized slander" of Stalin's terror
and his complete innocence. "In these days, perhaps the last of my
life," he appealed to future leaders to "sweep the filth from my head
. . . to exonerate me. . . . Know, comrades, that on the banner which
you will carry in your victorious march to communism there is a drop
of my blood."[20]

Encouraged by this development and the Twenty-second Party
Congress seven months later, Anna Larina sent a personal appeal for
Bukharin's rehabilitation to Khrushchev and the Politburo. The fam-
ily's situation improved somewhat. Larina received a pension, and
Bukharin's son Yuri began a career as an art teacher. But
Khrushchev's de-Stalinization campaign, including the Bukharin ini-
tiative, was now under intense fire from party conservatives. No pub-
lic comment on Bukharin's status appeared for more than a year.

It came, finally, on December 22, 1962, in an odd form, evidently
Khrushchev's only way of circumventing his opponents in the leader-
ship. Speaking to a national conference of historians, Petr Pospelov, a
Khrushchev ally on the Central Committee, read a prearranged ques-
tion from the audience. "Students are asking: were Bukharin and the
others spies of foreign states?" Pospelov's reply was unequivocal.
"Neither Bukharin nor Rykov [Soviet premier in the 1920s and
Bukharin's estwhile ally] was, of course, a spy or a terrorist."[21]

Pospelov's informal remark remains the only public exoneration of
Bukharin ever to appear in the Soviet Union. It was never followed
by a formal announcement. Nor did it have political force. Despite a
temporary softening of anti-Bukharin invective in official publications,
his name was still excluded even from encyclopedias, his status fro-
zen by the struggle inside the leadership. In the end, Bukharin's rehabilitation became a casualty of Khrushchev's overthrow in October
1964. Further petitions by Bukharin's family and others went unanswered. By the late 1960s, the Brezhnev administration had grown
into a broad conservative reaction to Khrushchev's reformism, embracing different historical attitudes and symbols.[22] De-Stalinization
was ended, and Stalin himself partially rehabilitated.

Any lingering hope that Bukharin's case might be reconsidered
ended with the Soviet invasion of Czechoslovakia in 1968. The reform
policies of the Prague Spring, animated by the dream of a "socialism
with a human face," were the culmination of anti-Stalinist ideas that

had circulated in various forms and had threatened neo-Stalinist conservatives in the Soviet Union and Eastern Europe since the 1950s. Since 1968 the policies and ideas associated with the Prague Spring, whose relationship to what became known as Eurocommunism is clear to Soviet conservatives, have become in official Soviet propaganda the epitome of the "anti-socialist and counterrevolutionary" outcome of "right opportunism." In the large Soviet literature "exposing" this "danger," a lineal connection between Bukharin's "right deviation" and the Czech reformers, as well as other anti-Stalinists, is suggested repeatedly. The pivot of this hardline view is Stalin's own axiom, first set out against Bukharin in 1928–29, that the "right deviation" is the "main danger" in the Communist movement.[23]

The neo-Stalinist approach to Bukharin that became perceptible in Soviet literature after 1968 was made explicit on June 9, 1977. A high official of the same party judiciary body that had raised Anna Larina's hopes in 1961, G. S. Klimov, telephoned her apartment and spoke with her son Yuri. "I am instructed," said Klimov, "to inform you that your request that Bukharin be reinstated in the party . . . cannot be satisfied since the criminal charges on the basis of which he was convicted have not been removed."[24] The significance of this announcement, which quickly became known through *samizdat* sources, lay in the astonishing assertion that criminal charges against Bukharin were still in force. It amounted to a reversal of decisions taken during the Khrushchev years (at least seven of Bukharin's codefendants had been fully exonerated by 1964). Instead of exonerating Bukharin, Klimov's announcement in effect rehabilitated the notorious purge trials of the 1930s and, indirectly, the Stalinist terror.[25]

III.

Just as Moscow can no longer monopolize the Communist idea, official Soviet attitudes toward Bukharin no longer reflect the actual status of his reputation in the world or even inside the Soviet Union. The end of de-Stalinization from above triggered a flood of *samizdat* writings about the Stalinist past and historical alternatives. In these uncensored writings, circulating from hand to hand, Bukharin is already rehabilitated. In addition to being portrayed favorably in a variety of *samizdat* memoirs, Bukharin's policies are treated with undisguised approval by nonconformist historians. One places him "first after Lenin in the revolutionary annals of the 20th century." Another finds that his ideas "have not lost their pertinence to this day."[26] Roy Medvedev, who represents a kind of Eurocommunist trend among Soviet dissidents, has written a moving book, *Bukharin's*

Last Years, that describes his execution as "one of Stalin's most terrible crimes before the Soviet people, the party, and the world communist movement."[27] Even a non-Marxist dissident, Boris Shragin, agrees. Emphasizing Bukharin's opposition to Stalin's collectivization drive, Shragin calls his defeat "Russia's greatest tragedy."[28]

Outside the Soviet Union two parallel developments produced the major rediscovery of Bukharin in recent years and led up to the campaign around his name in 1978. One is, of course, the unfinished advent of international Communist reformism—beginning in Belgrade, gaining strong adherents in the Polish and Hungarian parties after 1956, flourishing briefly in Prague, and now called Eurocommunism—that led party anti-Stalinists to the "lost" antecedents of the Soviet 1920s and thus to Bukharin. Meanwhile, non-Communist scholars in the West began correcting historical injustices in their own treatment of Bukharin. The mainstream view of Stalinism's inevitability after the Bolshevik Revolution, axiomatic during the Cold War, gave way in the 1960s and 1970s to a more problematic approach and thus to a new interest in the Bukharinist alternative.[29]

By the beginning of 1978, the historical rediscovery of Bukharin, expressed in a growing volume of scholarly studies, was virtually complete in the West, even becoming something of a popular fashion in left circles. Nonetheless, it appeared that the fortieth anniversary of his execution would pass largely unnoticed, commemorated mainly by cultural events. Lino Del Fra, a self-described Communist and well-known film-maker, began work on a four-hour documentary about Bukharin's last years for Italian television. In London, Andy McSmith's play "The Trial of Bukharin" was scheduled for August at the Royal Court Theatre.

A letter from Moscow suddenly turned the anniversary into an international political event. On March 3, 1978, Bukharin's son wrote to the head of the Italian Communist party, Enrico Berlinguer, asking him "to participate in the cause of justice for my father." Yuri Larin's letter, which related the "intolerable" situation of his sixty-four-year-old mother, was published in many Western newspapers and confronted the Italian Communist party with an important decision.[30] On June 16, a leading representative, Paolo Spriano, publicly endorsed Larin's appeal as "a moral and political necessity," making it clear that he spoke for the party leadership.[31] A copy of Larin's letter also reached the Bertrand Russell Peace Foundation in London, which decided to organize a supporting petition, addressed to the Soviet authorities, among Western Communists and socialists. The response, according to British reports, was dramatic; signatures "were flooding in." The list soon included representatives of Communist and socialist parties across Europe and as far away as Australia, as well as cultural figures such as Tom Stoppard and Simone de Beauvoir.[32]

Larin's letter and the Russell Foundation's campaign made Bukharin's status a topical and highly publicized issue. It bore particularly on the Eurocommunist parties and their relationship both to the Soviet Union and the European left. Larin chose wisely, of course, in appealing to the Italian Communist party. Long the most anti-Stalinist of Western Communist parties, its historians had been writing sympathetically about Bukharin for several years.[33] Italian Communist sympathy toward Bukharin derived partly from his anti-Fascism in the 1930s, in contrast to Stalin's pact with Hitler, and his close relationship with the late Italian party leader Palmiro Togliatti. But the main appeal was Bukharin's different road to socialism, which in some important ways anticipated the Italian party's espousal of a gradualist road to socialism, a two-sector economy, and peasant farming. For the Italian Communist party, as Spriano explained, Bukharin's rehabilitation therefore "has a general significance which is of historic importance, as well as having moral, theoretical, educational, and political coherence."[34]

Leading spokesmen of other parties loosely called Eurocommunist—the Spanish, Australian, Belgian, and British—also quickly endorsed the appeal.[35] The slowest response came from the French Communist party, the second largest in Europe, reflecting perhaps its own half-hearted anti-Stalinism and larger divisions within Eurocommunism. Though three of its most eminent intellectuals—Louis Althusser, Etienne Balibar, and Jean Elleinstein—signed the Russell Foundation petition, the French Communist leadership emulated Moscow's silence for several months. Finally, in an article in the party newspaper in November 1978, Jean Burles, a Central Committee member and director of the Maurice Thorez Institute, issued a strong call for Bukharin's rehabilitation.[36] Eurocommunist unanimity on this issue was complete.

At the same time, prominent Western social democrats joined Eurocommunists in the Bukharin campaign, rallying around a Soviet Communist symbol. This was yet another sign that the historic division in the European left, perpetuated by the Soviet experience, could be overcome. Some socialists in power refused to sign the petition to the Soviet leadership on the grounds that it "would be tantamount to interfering with the internal affairs of a party—a party identical with a state."[37] But many socialists did sign, including the international secretary of the French Socialist party, the chairman of the British Labour party, and eleven other members of Parliament, three of

whom personally raised the Bukharin question with the Soviet embassy in London.[38] If nothing else, these socialists and Communists
agreed, as a petition circulated in Italy put it, that Bukharin's rehabilitation could help in "erasing from the image of socialism the obscure,
inhuman aspects which Stalinism gave it."[39]

Opponents of socialism, on the other hand, worried aloud about the
popularity of the Bukharin campaign and Eurocommunism's ability to
attract broader support on this and other issues. In an editorial on
July 28, 1978, pointedly entitled "A Victim, Not a Hero," the *Times*
of London attacked the whole idea of a Communist alternative to
Stalinism in Soviet history or in Europe today. While lamely endorsing the call for Bukharin's rehabilitation by Soviet authorities, the
Times warned: "But he cannot be used as a means to rehabilitate
communism itself."

IV.

Though it may slow the drift toward the restoration of overtly
Stalinist symbols, no international campaign can bring about Bukharin's official rehabilitation in the Soviet Union. That would require a
major victory by Soviet party reformers, who have been routed almost everywhere in Soviet politics since the late 1960s. For now
Bukharin's standing in the Communist world is in the hands of party
reformers outside the USSR. It will certainly continue to grow. The
Times's complaint that he is being falsely portrayed as a "legendary
lost leader" misses the point.[40] Bukharin was an inept politician and
as such exercises no appeal. His real significance is as the historical
representative of lost anti-Stalinist ideas, which may be taking root
today even in China. Bukharin's writings did not generate the contemporary revival of these ideas, but their rehabilitation and his are
inextricable.

Even so, there should be no cult of Bukharin, even in the most
anti-Stalinist of Eurocommunist parties. Several of his most relevant
ideas, such as the role of consumption and the market in planned
economies, were only embryonic and have been surpassed by
present-day reformers in Eastern and Western Europe. Still more,
though Bukharin's opposition to the Leviathan state and his cultural
liberalism remain pertinent, he was not a democrat. He, like other
original Bolsheviks, bears some responsibility for the Stalinist regime
that emerged after 1929. He never challenged, among other things, the
principle of one-party dictatorship, or even the banning of factions
within the party. Insofar as Eurocommunism involves a uniting of
Communist social ideals and political democracy, Bukharin is not rel-

evant. As the de-Russification of European Communist movements continues and as these parties return to their own native traditions, they will find less and less that is relevant in the Russian experience—less that they have to justify and thus less need for any symbol from the Soviet past.

Bukharinism was a more liberal and humane variant of Russian Communism, with its native authoritarian traditions. The real potential of Bukharinism as a source of change today—anti-Stalinist if not Eurocommunist in spirit—is, therefore, in the Soviet Union itself, from within the party itself. Bukharin's relevance is understood not only by antagonists inside the Soviet party but by those dissidents who believe that the whole Communist idea and the entire Soviet system are corrupt beyond salvation. For them, because "Bukharin is probably the only Bolshevik whom anyone in Russia remembers with a good word," his name has become central to the topical question: "What should be preserved from the revolution?"[41] For some anti-Communist Russians, he is, if not a hero, at least "the Don Quixote of Bolshevism"; others, such as Alexander Solzhenitsyn, the avatar of Soviet anti-Communism, are content with nothing less than a complete demolition of Bukharin's reputation.[42]

Neo-Stalinist conservatives in the Soviet party are no less determined to guard against Bukharin's rehabilitation. They understand that to rehabilitate this founding father would legitimize reformist ideas inside the party itself. And that would open the way to a reconsideration of the pillars of the existing system, from the unproductive collective farms and the malfunctioning planning structure to the oppressive censorship of literature. Clinging to the past, Stalin's heirs must continue the ban on Bukharin. And yet the ghost and his heretical "right deviation" are loose, from Moscow to Western Europe. It is as though Bukharin had hurled Danton's curse: "You have laid hands on my whole life. May it rise and challenge you."

NOTES

This essay is a considerably revised and expanded version of an article that appeared in the *New York Times Magazine,* December 10, 1978. It grows out of a larger project supported at different times by the John Simon Guggenheim Memorial Foundation and the Center of International Studies at Princeton University. I wish to acknowledge my gratitude to these institutions.

1. V. I. Lenin, *Polnoe sobranie sochinenii,* (55 vols., Moscow, 1958–   ), XLV, p. 345.

2. For Nikolai Bukharin's career, see Stephen F. Cohen, *Bukharin and the Bolshevik Revolution: A Political Biography, 1888–1938* (New York, 1973).

3. See, for example, N. I. Bukharin, *Doklad na XXIII chrezvychainoi leningradskoi gubersnskoi konferentsii VKP(b)* (Moscow, 1926), pp. 16–17; *International Press Correspondence*, VII (1927), p. 1423; and N.I. Bukharin, *Tekushchii moment i osnovy nashei politiki* (Moscow, 1925), pp. 5–6.

4. Cohen, *Bukharin and the Bolshevik Revolution*, pp. 237–238. Boris Pasternak's poem "Volny" is reprinted in Boris Pasternak, *Vtoroe rozhdenie* (Moscow, 1934).

5. It is worth noting that the first use of "spring" as a metaphor for liberalization in Stalinist policy seems to have been in a document inspired by conversations with Bukharin in 1936. See *Letter of an Old Bolshevik* (New York, 1937), p. 54.

6. For examples of Soviet reformers, see G.S. Lisichkin, *Plan i rynok* (Moscow, 1966) and A. Birman, "Mysli posle plenuma," *Novyi mir* (No. 12, 1965), p. 194; and for an East European, see Laszlo Szamuely, *First Models of the Socialist Economic Systems* (Budapest, 1974). The best discussion of the New Economic Party in this context is Moshe Lewin, *Political Undercurrents in Soviet Economic Debates: From Bukharin to the Modern Reformers* (Princeton, 1974), ch. 12, passim.

7. *Leningradskaia organizatsiia i chetyrnadtsatyi s'ezd: materialov i dokumentov* (Moscow, 1926), p. 110.

8. Jiri Valenta, "Eurocommunism and Eastern Europe," *Problems of Communism* (March-April 1978), p. 44.

9. F. Janacek and J. Sladek, eds., *V revoluci a po revoluci* (Prague, 1967), p. 281. The search for "lost" ideas is explained on page 9.

10. For a fuller discussion of these ideas and policies, see Cohen, *Bukharin and the Bolshevik Revolution*, especially chs. 5, 6, and 9.

11. "Bukharin-Kamenev Meeting, July 1928," *Dissent* (Winter 1979), pp. 82–88.

12. *The Case of the Anti-Soviet "Bloc of Rights and Trotskyites": Report of Court Proceedings* (Moscow, 1938), pp. 626–31.

13. Ibid., pp. 656–7.

14. Roy A. Medvedev and Zhores A. Medvedev, *Khrushchev: The Years in Power* (New York, 1978), p. 20.

15. Nikita Khrushchev, *Khrushchev Remembers*, Strobe Talbot, ed. (Boston, 1970), pp. 29–30, 352–353; and Roi Medvedev, "Diktator na pensii" (*samizdat* manuscript, 1978).

16. Nikita S. Khrushchev, *The Crimes of the Stalin Era* (New York: New Leader Pamphlet, n.d.), p. S-13.

17. Khrushchev himself mentioned the intervention of foreign Communists (*Khrushchev Remembers*, pp. 352–353), but Zhores Medvedev was the first to identify the role of Maurice Thorez and Harry Pollitt. See his letters in Ken Coates, *The Case of Nikolai Bukharin* (Nottingham, 1978), pp. 101–103, and in *Tribune* (London), September 15, 1978. In a private interview with the author, Jean Elleinstein, the French Communist, has confirmed Medvedev's account of Thorez's role.

18. For a discussion of some of these historical writings, see Nancy Whittier Heer, *Politics and History in the Soviet Union* (Cambridge, Mass., 1971), ch. 8.

19. Lewin, *Political Undercurrents in Soviet Economic Debates*, p. xiii.

20. The letter is quoted in full, in a somewhat different translation, in Roy A. Medvedev, *Let History Judge* (New York, 1971), pp. 183–184.

21. *Vsesoiuznoe soveshchanie o merakh uluchsheniia podgotovki nauchno-pedagogicheskikh kadrov po istoricheskim naukam: 18–21 dekabria 1962 g.* (Moscow, 1964), p. 298.

22. For a discussion of these events, see Stephen F. Cohen, "Reformism and Conservatism in the Soviet Union Since Stalin," *Slavic Review,* 38 (June 1979), pp. 187–202.

23. For a classic example of this literature, see F.M. Vaganov, *Pravyi uklon v VKP(b) i ego razgrom* (Moscow, 1977). The first edition appeared in 1970.

24. The *samizdat* document relating this event is published in *Khronika zashchity prav v SSSR* (New York), No. 27 (July-September 1977), pp. 16–17.

25. It is possible that this first official reply to the Bukharin family in sixteen years was promoted by a neo-Stalinist faction as an early move toward a full rehabilitation of Stalin during the centenary of his birth in 1979.

26. The first evaluation is quoted in Roi Medvedev, "N.I. Bukharin: Poslednie gody zhizni" (*samizdat* manuscript, 1978), p. 1. The second appears in an anonymous and untitled essay by a Soviet historian.

27. Medvedev "N.I. Bukharin," p. 116.

28. B. Shragin, "Nikolai Ivanovich Bukharin," Radio Liberty Seminar Broadcast, No. 38 012-R (1978).

29. On this question, see Stephen F. Cohen, "Bolshevism and Stalinism," in *Stalinism: Essays in Historical Interpretation,* ed. Robert C. Tucker (New York, 1977), pp. 3–29.

30. The letter appeared in this country in several publications, including the *New York Times,* July 7, 1978.

31. "Il caso Bucharin," *L'Unità* (Rome), June 16, 1978. Paolo Spriano's aritcle is translated in Coates, *The Case of Nikolai Bukharin,* pp. 91–94.

32. Coates, *Case of Nikolai Bukharin,* pp. 87, 99–100. Samples of the response by the international press are collected in a mimeographed publication, "Dossier on Bukharin," by the Bertrand Russell Peace Foundation.

33. See, for example, Giuseppe Boffa, *Storia Dell'Unione Sovietica,* (Milan, 1976), vol. I, part 3.

34. *L'Unità,* June 16, 1978; translated in Coates, *Case of Nikolai Bukharin,* p. 93.

35. Coates, *Case of Nikolai Bukharin,* pp. 87, 99–100.

36. "La question de la réhabilitation de Boukharine," *L'Humanité* (Paris), November 28, 1978. About the same time, the French party published a book—*L'URSS et nous* (Paris, 1978)—highly critical of the Soviet system and its Stalinist past and containing favorable references to Bukharin. The Soviet leadership replied with a sharp attack on the book. See E. Ambartsumov, F. Burlatskii, Iu. Krasin, and E. Pletnev, "Protiv iskazheniia opyta real'nogo sotsializma," *Kommunist,* no. 18 (December 1978), pp. 86–104.

37. This is how one European socialist leader explained the matter in a letter to the Bertrand Russell Foundation.

38. Coates, *Case of Nikolai Bukharin,* pp. 99–100; *Morning Star* (London), July 3, 1978.

39. The petition, organized by Lino Del Fra, is included in "Dossier on Bukharin."

40. "A Victim, Not a Hero," *Times* (London), July 28, 1978.

41. David Anin, "Aktualen li Bukharin?," *Kontinent,* (No. 2, 1975), pp. 313–314.

42. Ibid., p. 312; and Aleksandr I. Solzhenitsyn, *The Gulag Archipelago* (New York, 1974), pp. 412–18.

CHAPTER IV

Eurocommunism and the Decline of Proletarian Internationalism

Jan F. Triska

Communism in Europe is emerging in a new, historically unknown form. It challenges Soviet international authority and control, "proletarian internationalism," the Soviet model of socialism, the dictatorship of the proletariat, international coercion, ideological orthodoxy and dogma, and the status quo. Instead, it argues for equality, independence, sovereignty, nonintervention, national identity, peaceful change, and free consensus of and for all Communist parties. What kind of Communism is this? The USSR is deeply worried because, frankly, it understands neither the meaning nor the import of this change. Its own as well as its allies' interests seem to be profoundly threatened. What is to be done?

In this chapter I will examine this new Communist trend in Western Europe. First, I will discuss the two events that for the first time openly revealed the current breadth and depth of this development, namely the Twenty-fifth Congress of the Communist Party of the Soviet Union and the Conference of the European Communist Parties,[1] both of which took place in the first half of 1976. Then I will take a closer look at the Communist parties that, singly and jointly, have played the most prominent innovative roles. Next, I will focus on the major conflicting issues in the dispute, the Soviet international Communist strategy of "proletarian internationalism" and the Soviet model of building socialism. Finally, I will attempt to evaluate the impact of this development on the Soviet Union.

The Twenty-fifth Congress of the CPSU of February 1976 marked the first formal public display of the scope, intensity, and degree of differences and disagreements between Moscow and the West European Communist parties, principally the Italian and the French—currently the most influential nonruling parties—but also the Spanish, British, Swedish, Belgian, and other parties, as well as the Yugoslavian and Romanian. (The Japanese Communist party declined the Soviet invitation and did not send a delegation to the congress.)

The congress itself was an uninspired, routine, and predictable affair. True, Nicolae Ceausescu of Romania and Stane Dolanc of Yugoslavia (Josip Tito decided not to attend) repudiated Soviet superordination in the Communist movement and put emphasis on the equality of all parties. Ceausescu called for "the right of every party independently to elaborate its own political life and revolutionary strategy and tactics," while Dolanc stressed "the principles of equality, independence, and responsibility of each party toward its own working class and people." These appeals annoyed the Soviet host, but the themes were familiar, and only the place and time made them conspicuous.[2]

The congressional atmosphere changed, however, with the speeches of the West European Communist leaders. For the first time in history, a Soviet party congress became an open stage for the public revelation of the deep—and growing—dissension in the ranks. The 5,000 Soviet delegates had never heard anything like it before. The Western Communist leaders demanded not only "independence," "sovereignty," and "equality and respect for the autonomy of all parties," but also proclaimed their full support for individual and collective freedoms, religious freedoms, cultural freedom, pluralistic democracy, national (rather than Soviet or international) socialism, free trade unions, and freedom for research and artistic and scientific activities. Enrico Berlinguer, the leader of the Italian Communist party; Gaston Plissonier, the third-ranking member of the French Communist party (Georges Marchais, the secretary general, like Tito, decided not to come to the congress); Gordon McLennan, the General Secretary of the Communist party of Great Britain; Hans Werner, the leader of the Swedish Communist party; and even Franz Muhri of the Austrian Communist party—all went to the podium to profess, to subscribe to, to emphasize, and to demand principles, policies, and strategies never professed, subscribed to, emphasized, or demanded there before. It must have sounded like a conspiracy against the CPSU.

After the congress, Leonid Brezhnev and Berlinguer issued a joint statement pledging "respect for independence" of each other's party.[3] But two weeks later Mikhail Suslov, the Politburo member charged with the international Communist movement, in a major address to the Soviet Academy of Sciences branded those who interpret Communist ideology in their own fashion as "enemies of Marxism":

"They slander real socialism, try to wash out the revolutionary es-
sense of Marxist-Leninist teaching, and substitute bourgeois
liberalism for Marxism."[4]

The much-postponed Conference of the European Communist Parties (of the thirty-one European parties, only the "isolationist"
Icelandic and the "intransigent" Albanian ones abstained) took place
in June 1976 in East Berlin. It was more than just a ratification of the
Communist parties' dissent expressed at the congress. Both in form
and in content, the conference proved to be a learning experience for
both sides. At the congress, the West European Communist party
leaders announced publicly their individual differences but did not
discuss them. At the conference, on the other hand, the differences
were *discussed*—in fact, they were discussed and argued for almost
two years in the many meetings preparatory to the conference. In
addition, differences at the conference were broader and deeper than
at the congress; they became the focal point that ultimately caused
the conference to be postponed for more than a year. The party leaders talked to each other as well as to the Soviet and East European
Communists for an extended period of time and about previously un-
speakable matters.

The final document of the conference, for the first time in CPSU
history,[5] was arrived at by free consensus of all participants after an
extensive free exchange of views, was not critical of any party, and
was not binding on any of them (the delegates did not even sign the
document).[6] It was unlike any other document of its kind: "proletarian internationalism" and "single communist strategy" were
dropped and replaced by "voluntary cooperation and solidarity"
based on "principles of equality and sovereign independence of each
party, non-interference in internal affairs [as well as] respect for [the
parties'] free choice of different roads in the struggle for social change
of a progressive nature and for socialism." Peace, democracy, and
humanism were singled out as the major goals, and cooperation and
understanding among all peoples as the means. "A prerequisite and
indispensable condition for this is respect for the right of the people of
each country to choose and develop its political, economic, social and
legal system independently and without outside interference, and to
protect and multiply its historical and cultural heritage." Criticism of
Communist parties' activities and disagreement with their policies
should no longer be interpreted simply as "anti-Communism." Communist parties' "dialogue and collaboration with democratic forces"
should be encouraged. Nonaligned countries should be viewed as
"one of the most important factors in world politics." Common strategy was formally rejected when the Soviet proposal that the European

parties "function as vanguard forces, pursue identical objectives, and be guided by a common ideology" was dropped from the text.[7]

This, then, was the conference which, according to Tito, "must have no past and no future." Or, as Berlinguer put it, "An international communist body does not, and cannot, exist in any form."[8] The Communist parties of Italy, Spain, Britain, Sweden, the Netherlands, San Marino, Yugoslavia, and Romania became, in East Berlin, a successful pressure group and ultimately a winning coalition.

The differences revealed at the congress and discussed prior to and at the conference were important because they were stated and maintained in open confrontation. They were also important because they concerned fundamentals—Soviet moral and political leadership; the legitimacy of Soviet authority and the propriety of its international direction; and the adequacy of the Soviet model for building socialism. The group of dissident upstarts questioned and challenged proletarian internationalism as a strategy and direction of the Communist movement, as well as the utility of the Soviet socialist model for others.

Who Are the "Eurocommunists?"[9]

The "Eurocommunists" are an amorphous group in *statu nascendi*. While some Communist parties in the group appear committed (like the Italian, Spanish, French, and probably the British), others oscillate from issue to issue (like the Swedish and Belgian), and still others procrastinate (like the Dutch, Finnish, and Austrian). The Austrian party probably does not even belong in the last group. The Yugoslavs and the Romanians are highly supportive, but they are both ruling parties; neither is dedicated to the democratic parliamentary road to power as yet. The Japanese party would qualify if it were not in Asia.[10]

The Italian Communist party (PCI)—because of its history, its size, its electoral gains, its international concerns, and its leadership—is the leading and most influential nonruling Communist parliamentary party. In spite of the PCI's sustained opposition to policies of the CPSU—including its international strategy, its model of building socialism, its repressive domestic politics, its policy toward China, its invasion of Czechoslovakia, and its censorship—the PCI would like to be known best for its cooperative, conciliatory attitudes and activities, and its hopeful role of a broker and mediator in conflicts, not only at home, but vis-à-vis the USSR as well.

The French Communist party (PCF), the second largest nonruling party, had been traditionally loyal to Moscow. It came, therefore, as a

surprise when shortly before and during the PCF Twenty-second
Congress in February 1976 the party leaders not only sharply
criticized Soviet violations of human rights and Soviet "democracy"
in general, but formally rejected the dictatorship of the proletariat
doctrine as well. According to Jean Kanapa, member of the PCF
politbureau, "Reflections on Stalinism, and then the Soviet military
intervention in Czechoslovakia in 1968, led the French Communists to
develop further the specific *national* aspects of their policy and thus
to define an original perspective."[11] Georges Marchais, the leading
advocate of electoral alliance with the Socialist party, thereupon refused to attend the Twenty-fifth Congress of the CPSU because of the
"deep differences" between the two parties.

The Spanish Communist party (PCE) has been the most consistent
and vocal in its opposition to the CPSU. The PCE was the first illegal
party to defy Moscow. It criticized Nikita Khrushchev's dismissal in
1964, castigated the USSR for its invasion of Czechoslovakia, berated
the CPSU at the 1969 Moscow meeting, and refused Soviet material
assistance. It has collaborated closely with non-Communist forces.

The British Communist party condemned the Soviet invasion and
the subsequent "normalization" process in Czechoslovakia, proclaimed its support for civil liberties and political pluralism at the
Twenty-fifth Congress of the CPSU, and collaborated closely with
other opposition Communist parties at the European conference.

The Swedish Communist party (SKP) has often played its parliamentary representation into a pivotal vote. It stands for autonomy of
all parties and for parliamentary democracy. In fact, the SKP was the
first Communist party to assert, in 1965, that it could be voted out of
power just like any other political party.[12] At the European conference the SKP worked prominently with the opposition group. (Afterward, the pro-Soviet faction split from the SKP.)

Although traditionally a pro-Soviet party, the Austrian Communist
party opposed the occupation of Czechoslovakia and, on occasion,
has stood for development of "socialism within democracy."

The Finnish Communist party is Finland's second-largest political
party (now in government), and it is still viewed as pro-Soviet, though
progressively less so than in the past. Since 1965 the leaders of the
party's moderate wing (called the "progressive majority") have spo-
ken openly of their party's peaceful way to power, civil liberties, and
adherence to party plurality.

The Dutch Communist party (CPN) introduced its autonomous, independent line in the "new orientation" program in 1964. The CPN
proclaimed its primary concern with national electoral politics, rather
than with the international movement, and its wish for collaboration

with socialists, for pluralism, and for the electoral road to power. In 1975 the CPN sought to normalize its relations with the CPSU, but its priorities have not changed.

The Belgian Communist party (PCB) has repeatedly advocated alliances and collaboration with non-Communist political forces, especially the socialists. Although it generally supports Soviet views, the PCB has at times offered relatively strong criticism of the CPSU, especially for the invasion of Czechoslovakia. The PCB has tended to take a conciliatory attitude toward the Chinese.

Although not West European, the Japanese Communist party (JCP), should be at least mentioned. The JCP declined an invitation to attend the Twenty-fifth Congress of the CPSU in February 1976. (It was also the first party to denounce—in January 1974—the Soviet plan to hold a world Communist conference.) It dropped both the concept of the dictatorship of the proletariat and Marxism-Leninism from its platform, and introduced "scientific socialism" instead. The JCP claims to stand for pluralistic, constitutional democracy, civil liberties, and strict independence in the international Communist movement—especially from the CPSU but also from the Chinese Communist party. This strategy brought the JCP success, both in party membership (some 350,000 members) as well as in votes (almost seven million votes and fifty-eight seats in both houses of the Diet in 1974). (In the December 1976 elections votes for the JCP remained approximately the same, but several of its seats were lost.) The JCP condemned the Soviet invasion of Czechoslovakia as an outright aggression and criticized the Polish government's suppression of workers' demands in 1970. The Spanish, Italian, French, and other West European Communist party delegations visit the JCP often and sign joint communiques that emphasize the parties' independence as well as their dedication to civil liberties, human dignity, religious freedom, pluralism, and democracy.[13]

The Yugoslavs were the earliest dissenters from Soviet international strategy—a consequence of Stalin's clumsiness that forced the break upon them. They were alone. Not a single Communist party raised its voice in defense of Yugoslavia. There was no criticism and no protest against the Soviet treatment of Yugoslavia. In fact, many Communist parties denounced "the Yugoslav heresy" in the 1950s. The PCI was the first Communist party to approve the Yugoslav defection. The two parties have since become close friends. Because of their commonality of attitudes and interests, and because they have tended to agree on most political and ideological issues affecting them, they have kept in close touch for almost twenty years. The relationship has grown warmer over time. The Yugoslavs defend their independence and autonomy vigorously, of course; they have also on numerous occasions rejected the Soviet socialist model.[14]

Not so the Romanians. Although at times fiercely outspoken in their criticism of proletarian internationalism since 1964,[15] at other times their stand has been softer than that of the Yugoslavs. Domestic policies of the Ceausescu regime are practically Stalinist. The occasional Romanian flexibility, cautiousness, and even equivocation suggest a degree of strain, frustration, and pressure absent in the Yugoslav position.[16] While Romanian leaders maintain unstrained, warm relations with the Yugoslavs, the PCI and PCE representatives, and others in the Eurocommunist group, the Romanian press still occasionally uses the term "proletarian internationalism" as synonymous with international solidarity.

There are virtually no relations between the dissident Communist parties and the Chinese. This is no fault of the Eurocommunists; they would like to establish relations with the Chinese Communist party and have been seeking ways toward a *rapprochement* or at least a *modus vivendi*. The Italian, Spanish, and French parties have been in the forefront of these attempts, both singly and jointly, but to no avail. The Chinese have rejected all advances—even the messages of condolence on Mao's death—from the "revisionist" West European Communist parties. Of the group, only the Romanians and the Yugoslavs are in good graces with China. There have been no attempts to utilize the Romanian and the Yugoslav connection for Eurocommunist bridge-building with China.[17]

There is as yet no formal Eurocommunist alliance. There have been many sustained bilateral contacts, consultations, visits, and communiques among them, but, with the exception of the European conference, the individual Communist parties have acted by and large on their own. The European conference brought the parties together for the first time as a group but still on an ad hoc basis. It is true that there have been many West European regional meetings of Communist parties in the last twenty years: in Rome in 1959, Brussels 1965, Vienna 1966, Paris 1970 and 1971, London 1971, and several meetings in 1973 (Stockholm, Copenhagen, Paris, Rome, and Dusseldorf) to prepare a meeting in Brussels in 1974. All West European Communist parties attended most of these meetings, even the independent Dutch; only the Turks were absent often and the Icelanders usually stayed away. But because most Communist parties attended, including the pro-Soviet parties, these meetings did not advance Eurocommunism, at least not directly. Nevertheless, by 1974 international Communist unity had become "as meaningless as it was in the pre-1914 Second International."[18]

The Eurocommunists have thus kept in touch. In their opposition to the CPSU they have tended to share each other's views, emulate the more successful ones among them, especially the PCI, support each other, devote media coverage to each other's views, and consult on strategies.

The fortunes of the PCI, the original Eurocommunist trend-setter, were followed with intense interest by others critical of Soviet policies since the early 1960s. The crucial jolt, however, was provided by the Soviet invasion of Czechoslovakia: the Italian, French, Spanish, British, Austrian, Greek, Belgian, Dutch, Swedish, Yugoslav, Romanian, and other Communist parties (including the Japanese and Australian) openly criticized the invasion. This was the strongest censure of the CPSU up to that time. Afterwards, West European Communist parties began to seek mutual contacts and support in their efforts to gain more independence from the CPSU. Increasingly, they began to use exclusive national strategies to reach national goals. And since cooperation with socialists and other non-Communists required greater differentiation and distance from the CPSU, the new direction began to be set.

Soviet International Communist Strategy: Proletarian Internationalism

The Communists have no theory linking the Communist parties together. The closest they come to a theory is a mental construct called "proletarian internationalism," a concept of considerable historical significance dating back to the Communist Manifesto and the programmatic postulate of Marx, "Workers of the world, unite," now almost 130 years old. Defined variously as an intermediate international unity of Communist and progressive forces based on their common struggle against imperialism and for peace, proletarian internationalism has been historically juxtaposed as an antithesis to bourgeois, capitalist nationalism. It would eventually culminate in a synthesis of the stateless Communist world.[19]

In the process of its development and application, proletarian internationalism has acquired connotations and characteristics that are specifically Soviet. This is not surprising. The Soviet Union has been the original organizer of the Communist movement. Its problem was—and has remained—how to construct and maintain a rational international organization that would produce a minimum of undesirable side effects but bring a maximum satisfaction compatible with the aims of the organizer. In spite of the monumental Soviet effort that has gone into its organizational and strategic development, however, proletarian internationalism still remains little more than an assortment of conjectural, normative, and hortatory postulates.

With the remarkable growth of the Communist movement since the Bolshevik Revolution, with the elevation of over a dozen Communist parties to ruling parties, and with the impressive electoral successes of several other parties, it was no wonder that Soviet management, direction, and control of the Communist movement via proletarian internationalism could not keep pace. This simple strategic concept could not accommodate complex developmental relations among individuals—both party members and nonparty progressives; among parties—large and small, developing and developed, revolutionary and reformist, conformist and neutral, dependent, semi-dependent, and independent; and among states (here proletarian internationalism is called socialist internationalism, but the difference is purely symbolic)—some friendly, some neutral, and some hostile. Coercion may have been successfully applied in specific historical periods or against small or weak parties and neighbors, but as an overall organizing device it became inadequate, useless, and even dangerous. Proletarian internationalism, now perceived by many within the movement as a mechanistic continuation of an established habit of Soviet strategic control over other parties, has been increasingly under severe attack.[20]

Despite many Soviet invitations under Khrushchev and Brezhnev, Yugoslavia, expelled from the Communist camp in 1948, never came back to the fold. The final Sino-Soviet split, the Soviet invasion of Czechoslovakia, and the shabby Soviet treatment of its East European clients contributed to the sharp questioning of proletarian internationalism within the movement.

But there was more. The shock of de-Stalinization, a real blow to Soviet legitimacy in the eyes of many; the obvious and increasingly incongruous Soviet identification of proletarian internationalism with Soviet state interests, which the Yugoslavs criticized;[21] and the "forced exterior uniformity" that Palmiro Togliatti singled out in his political testament,[22] made, in the Chinese view, "a mess of the splendid Socialist camp." Soviet "great-power chauvinism and national egoism" eroded the relations among ruling parties and spread among the nonruling parties, adversely affected their allegiance and participation.[23]

Insistence on national roads to socialism may not mean much. It depends on the context. "Full and effective autonomy" may mean "full and effective solidarity with the USSR." When Maurice Thorez said in 1946 that the French Communists should follow a road other than that of the Russian Bolsheviks,[24] for example, he did not say much. Or when a document printed in Moscow in 1945 emphasized a

"German road to socialism," or when the Swedish Communist party began to discuss in 1946 a "Swedish road to socialism,"[25] no challenge to the CPSU was intended or implied. In fact, even the CPSU itself claims that it "invariably opposed the mechanical imposition of some parties' experience on others." True, "the Party believes that it would be a grave mistake to disregard and underestimate—citing national, particular features—the truly tremendous experience accumulated by the world revolutionary movement and the experience of real socialism." But "owing to specific historical conditions, the role of individual parties in the international communist movement and their responsibility for it are not identical." Still, it must be admitted that in the past "the leading detachment of the international working class has been the Soviet working class and its vanguard—the CPSU." After all, it was the CPSU that has made "the really significant contribution" to "the change of the correlation of forces in the world arena in favor of socialism"; it was the CPSU that has borne the principal burden of "curbing the aggressive imperialist forces"; and it is the CPSU that has the power "to assist the international working class in its struggle against imperialism."[26]

Similarly, in his opening speech at the Conference of the European Communist Parties, Brezhnev, while speaking of proletarian internationalism, was subdued:

> Sometimes one hears the question: Is proletarian internationalism as urgent as it once was or has it become obsolete? And some people are apprehensive: Do not calls for strengthening of the international bonds that unify Communists signify a desire to recreate some kind of organizational center? These are strange apprehensions. As far as is known no one, nowhere, is proposing the idea of creating such a center. As far as proletarian internationalism is concerned, i.e., the solidarity of the working class and the communists of all countries in the struggle for common goals, their solidarity in the peoples' struggle for national liberation and social progress, and the voluntary cooperation of the fraternal parties while strictly observing the equality and independence of each of them—we believe that this comradely solidarity, whose standard-bearer the Communists have been for more than 100 years, fully retains all its great importance in our time as well. It has been and remains a mighty and tested weapon of the Communist Parties and of the workers' movement in general.[27]

Proletarian internationalism was omitted from the final document of the Conference. This must have been a painful concession for the CPSU delegation, but it was a price they had to pay if they wanted to hold the conference at all. After the conference, the CPSU spokesman and writers returned to the theme. A number of articles and essays appeared in the Soviet press discussing the meaning of proletarian internationalism in the light of the Eurocommunist objections. One of the more interesting was a piece by Vadim Zagladin, deputy of Boris Ponomarev, Head of the International Department of the Central Committee. Zagdalin wrote of "a dialectical interdependence," stating that "The independence and self-dependence of the fraternal parties is a precondition for the development of equal cooperation among them." But he cited Ceausescu, who wrote that "one must not for a moment forget the natural laws and truths of universal significance by which every Party must be guided in order to fulfill successfully its historic mission." And, he reaffirmed, "one of these natural laws of universal significance" is proletarian internationalism.[28]

Zagdalin thus further softened the impact without retracing any steps. Judging from subsequent reactions, however, this interpretation was not acceptable either. In particular, the dissenters rejected the view that the independence of each Communist party can be best preserved by international solidarity. To them, common goals facing the movement cannot take precedence over their own independence, autonomy, and equality; and democratic socialism is neither a distorted form of the new society nor a camouflaged form of the old.[29]

Moscow may now interpret "monolithic unity" as "unity in diversity" and "discipline" as "coordination without subordination." It may profess "respect for the equality and independence" of Communist parties while denying any "desire to recreate some kind of organizational center." It may even approve of and actively support diversity as a necessary dialectic step to the future, more perfect union.[30] Its credibility, however, is at a very low ebb. Soviet proletarian internationalism, underdeveloped, abused, exploited, and on the defensive, has been steadily losing ground. In fact, the critics have complained, both the old, simple "internationalism" as well as the glorified "proletariat" lost their meaning a long time ago: "The hypothesis that *the nation* would begin to wither away when capitalism, the bourgeoisie, and the proletariat disappear" was tested and disproved by social reality. Moreover, in many African countries "the apparatus of the political and state bureaucracy has created *new nations*. This process of birth is going on before our very eyes; and even in highly developed societies one can observe the birth if not of nations, then at least of ethnic groups." Is this bourgeois nationalism? In fact, "every attack on national independence within the context of the international relation . . . is nothing but an opening of the road toward an extension of hegemony."[31]

Similarly, "the mystique" of the proletariat is a thing of the past: "Have not the workers in the United States been one of the major pillars of American policy? Was it not the German working class which fought in the uniform of the Wehrmacht? . . . To imagine that [the proletariat] had always been *a priori* progressive would mean closing one's eyes to plain facts. . . . It is evidence of error, ignorance or manipulation if one sticks firmly to the thesis that one social stratum is always and in all situations revolutionary while another social stratum is always reactionary."[32]

In addition, an ideology of one country cannot serve as the ideology of an international movement: "Ideology is a reflection of the socio-economic structure of a country, of its views and interests. [Therefore,] arbitrariness in such a situation cannot but turn into enforced monolithism, [and] the striving for monolithism leads necessarily toward a center which, arbitrarily, interprets such an ideology. [This is why] a united ideology no longer exists."[33] It cannot exist simply because "to attribute to certain nations the characteristic of being permanently revolutionary," or to claim that "there are nations that are invariably revolutionary . . . is only a step toward racism."[34]

As a consequence, there are today

> two completely different approaches from which emerge two different, even contradictory, strategic, political, international and other consequences. [The dissident CPs'] concept runs directly counter to the approach that imposes a common strategy and common tactics, and consequently a unique center that decides and controls them, a common "general staff" that sends the troops into battle. Whenever and wherever this [proletarian internationalism] concept has become standard in relations among the communist and workers' parties . . . and there are many historical examples . . . their policies were inevitably subordinated to a single policy, and this has never ensured success. On the contrary, on the basis of the so-called unity and compactness of monolithism, conflicts, sometimes very sharp, have arisen. *And not one of them has ever been resolved on such a basis.*[35]

Like all political parties, the parliamentary Communist parties are responsive to electoral outcomes. Victories do mean success, and defeat does mean failure—for the membership as well as the leadership. The responsiveness of Communist parties to elections has been growing simply because greater responsiveness has meant more votes. The lesson of the PCI has not been lost on its neighbors and friends. The electorate seems increasingly to have demanded—among other things—national independent Communist parties offering policies and strategies based on domestic needs. Moreover, electoral success has meant easier and greater access to resources—money, offices, respectability, and local influence—thereby untying the strings attached to Soviet aid. Thus, between their own policy needs and the incongruent strategic demands of the Soviet Union, the Eurocommunists had to choose. They opted no longer to give in to the CPSU without fight.

Since the early 1960s the West European Communist parties have begun to develop international strategies suitable to their own electoral profiles. The harsh Soviet insistence on proletarian internationalism had often created sharp tensions within the Communist parties in the past. These tensions were progressively relieved—by peaceful coexistence after 1956 and by détente from the mid-1970s. But peaceful coexistence and détente, while encouraging the cooperation of Communist parties with other political parties and forces and vice versa, created, in turn, progressively new tensions with the USSR. The Communist parties would no doubt have preferred to adopt electorally winning foreign policies that would not clash with Soviet interests. The zig-zag stands of Communist parties on the Common Market and especially on NATO illustrate this reluctance well. But while the electoral push was hard to resist, the fate of Chile was not lost on the Communist parties of Western Europe. This reinforced the disagreement between the Soviets and other Communist parties on China. Many non-Soviet parties could not go along with the Soviet excommunication of China and the possible further loss of their autonomy related to that break. The European conference showed this stance well.

Proletarian internationalism, the Soviet international Communist strategy, another dominion that "cloaked itself in a legitimacy derived from the will of its subjects,"[36] has lost another group of legitimizing supporters. After the schismatics (China and Albania), the independents (such as Yugoslavia and the Communist parties of Mexico, Iceland, the Netherlands, and Reunion), the neutrals (such as Romania, Vietnam, North Korea, Laos, and the Communist party of Malaysia), and the split parties (such as Canada, Brazil, Bolivia, Peru, and Paraguay), came the heretics, the so-called Eurocommunists. They are not willful, just circumstantial; they profit from objective conditions. They further weakened what was left of Soviet Communist stature, authority, standing, and legitimacy. When Berlinguer said in West Berlin after the European conference in June 1976 that "an international communist body does not exist, and cannot exist, in any form on a European or world level," he was stating a fact.[37] Proletarian internationalism has failed. Communist unity is dead. The leaders of the CPSU, to borrow their language, have failed to develop Marxist-Leninist teaching on internationalism in keeping with the conditions of the time, the relations among Communist parties, and the developments in the Communist movement.

The Soviet Model of Socialism

The Leninist Bolshevik party links political underdevelopment with revolution. In backward Russia, as in other backward societies, such as China, "where the peasant [was] the primary class of the masses, where the task of struggle pending solution [lay] in the fight against the remnants of medievalism, but not in the fight against capitalism," the Leninist party proved to be the right organization with the right strategy at the right time.[38] Communism, an urban theory, did well when implanted in a rural setting. In developed societies where capitalism and democracy have advanced in satisfying the masses, however, Leninist parties with revolutionary strategies have proved to be out of place. They ceased to be effective. As Kanapa put it, "There is ultimately another guarantee that the policy the French Communist Party follows will be a truly democratic one, relying in every case on the free choice of the people: this guarantee is that *there is no other possible way to effect the social changes necessary. France of 1977 is not Russia of 1917.*"[39]

Indeed, in backward developing states, with societies not yet integrated and often not politicized, Communist parties have tended to follow the Leninist Bolshevik model of dynamic revolutionary forces. Communists became the socializers toward modernity, mobilizing members for the rapid transformation of their societies. In developed states, where there was no legitimate function for a revolutionary party, Communist parties had three alternatives: follow the Leninist prescription and persist, and, if outlawed, go underground; protest, defend, and articulate the negative interests and dissatisfaction of isolated and alienated segments of the population not integrated into their social and political systems; or, finally, give in, adapt, conform to the national political model, and become electoral parties. In the first two instances of revolutionary or protest parties, the national environment-party relations tended to be hostile, while the party-Soviet relations tended to be friendly. In the third instance, the national environment-electoral party, relations tended to be friendly, while the party-Soviet relations tended to be less friendly — principally because of the lack of understanding caused by diametrically different political environments. In terms of influence, a party's deviation from the Bolshevik model and its replacement by a fitting local model tended to lead to success in national politics and, moreover, it tended to make the deviant party more influential in the Communist movement. The trade-off, therefore, became attractive to some parties.

Time, it seems, has been on the side of nonrevolutionary, non-

deviant, nonexclusive, national Communist parties. Overall, they
have either gained in membership or remained the same. Because
they ceased to challenge the national political process but, for all
practical purposes, accepted it, conformed to it, participated in it, and
played according to the rules of the political game, they ceased to be
viewed as national adversaries. Revolutionary or protest parties, on
the other hand, have been subject to powerful adversities. A few have
won and become ruling parties. The rest faced hostile governments
that circumscribed or even outlawed them. Some turned into amorphous movements and became victims of "objective conditions."
Others were pushed out on a limb by the new radical left. The growing dissension and conflict orientation of the ruling parties have produced strains, pulls, and pressures within the nonruling parties. Some
have even split into two or more factions. Deprivation, isolation, and
the struggle to remain alive have not proved conducive to the maintenance, let alone growth, of the revolutionary Communist parties.

Communist parties that aspire to function as electoral parties must
compete for votes with other political parties. To be successful they
have to alter their structure to accommodate their new function. The
Leninist model ceases to be applicable or useful. A small, elitist,
tightly-knit, well-disciplined, dictatorial party is not suited for vote-
getting. For this purpose, a broadly-based, open, conciliatory, pragmatic, nonheretic, flexible, cooperative national party is preferable to
a militant, centralist, closed, ideological, orthodox, exclusive, dogmatic, international party. The direction toward which the electoral
parties move seems to be established. They are not all in line as yet,
but the revolutionary-to-electoral trend persists.

In 1961 the members of the Central Committee of the PCI called for
an analysis of the causes of corruption of Soviet democracy, and in
1962 Togliatti was speculating about whether the classical class struggle made sense in advanced countries. In 1963 Thorez said that "the
theory of the single party in a socialist regime was an error of Stalin";
in 1966 adherence to a plurality of parties in a socialist state became a
part of the PCF platform; the Danish Communist party said the same
thing in 1968; and the Spanish Communist party announced that one-
party rule was a deformation of Marxism not suitable for advanced
countries.[40] The invasion of Czechoslovakia "helped to crystallize the
[dissenting] parties' determination that every party should have the
right to construct its own socialist system independently."[41] The
"dictatorship of the proletariat" phrase almost disappeared from the
vocabulary of electoral Communist parties—only to be explicitly
abandoned in the 1970s. When the PCF "very logically" decided to
go against the dictatorship of the proletariat formula, "this was not a

question of mere change in terminology but in an entire political approach."[42]

To view Lenin's theory on the dictatorship of the proletariat as completion of the theory set forth by Marx and Engels, or even worse, as a dogma and to regard Leninism as a law, was a mistake, argued Tetsuzo Fuwa, the Head of the Central Committee Secretariat of the Japanese Communist party. "In adopting the basic tenets of scientific socialism, the Japanese Communist Party is working to bring about the creative development of its own ideas and theories."[43] Marx and Engels envisaged a possibility of peaceful transition from capitalism to Communism. Lenin did not. Revolution was inevitable: "Soviet republics in more developed countries, where the proletariat has greater weight and influence, have every chance of surpassing Russia *once they take the path of the dictatorship of the proletariat*."[44] Lenin's revisionism of Marx and Engels made for this crucial distinction.

Communist parties, like other social organizations, contain the seeds of their own transformation. They are not exempt from the laws of history. They change with conditions of time. According to Neil McInnes, the "dynamic" structure of West European Communist parties (which he differentiates from the "formal" or "static" structure) consists of three complex, distinct forces in "stable equilibrium": (1) the party bureaucracy, the beneficiary of the electoral road to power; (2) the Leninist party structure and the utopian workers, a minority of the party membership who are the legitimizers of the Soviet rule fighting "a variety of social democracy"; and (3) the Soviet influence, the traditional Soviet direction and control of Communist parties. These three forces are at war, and "their shifting relations explain the evolution of the Western parties."[45]

This is the major theme of McInnes' penetrating study. The three forces can be seen in another way, however: they may be neither in "stable equilibrium" nor "shifting"; they have shifted, gradually and irrevocably, in favor of the party bureaucracy. This is the position toward which the center of gravity of electoral Communist parties has been moving. To accommodate a change in party function, the Communist parties had to change their structures. Otherwise, they could not adequately play the parliamentary game and compete with other parties for votes.

A Communist party that gives up revolution and the dictatorship of the proletariat for the electoral road must win votes. To get into office, it must win a majority of votes. Since it cannot do it alone, it needs electoral allies. To secure such alliances, it must reassure its allies—by playing down its major liabilities, namely its militance and its loyalty to the USSR. Once in the alliance, the Communist party, to be credible, must prove its support of the alliance through thick and thin, however harsh such a posture may be—as many Communist parties have found out the hard way (such as the Finnish, the French, or now the Italian Communist parties)—by keeping the contract.

To justify the change in the function and structure of the Communist parties, the alliance must be a winning, or at least a successful, coalition. The more successful it is the more jobs there are to be filled by the party. The more jobs there are, the more influential is the party bureaucracy that fills those jobs, and the less influential are the utopians who stay out in the cold. Since the party bureaucrats, in order to stay in office, must vest their interest in national strategies, the Soviet connection gets less attention. The militance and the Soviet influence do not necessarily become the dead weight in the party— they just become gradually displaced to reduce the risks.

The Impact of Eurocommunism on the USSR

The Eurocommunists have learned that their opposition to the USSR on fundamentals may bring votes at election times at home, but they have also learned that up to now their opposition abroad, vis-à-vis the USSR itself, is only marginally effective. Their most notable success was the European Party Conference. Their other criticisms and protests, whether in public or in private, sharp or diplomatic, single or sustained, at low or high levels, in concert or alone, brought only limited results—as, for example, the altered Soviet view on the Common Market. They have been constantly and sharply rebuked by the USSR when criticizing either Soviet and East European domestic policies—political repression, human rights violations, oppressive measures against dissidents, the content of Soviet-type "socialist democracy," censorship, subjugation of trade unions, and so forth—or Soviet oppressive policies in Eastern Europe—such as the invasion of Czechoslovakia. It is precisely here that the dissenting Communist parties have become threatening to the USSR. Calling for their independence and autonomy from the USSR is one thing: it is irritating, to be sure, because it decreases their utility to the USSR in the Sino-Soviet dispute, in Eastern Europe, and for Soviet foreign policy generally. But by attacking Soviet domestic politics and Soviet policies in Eastern Europe, they touch the nerve: Soviet power and prestige is at stake and so is the legitimacy of the CPSU.

Eurocommunism offers an alternative model to Soviet Communism. For obvious reasons it is less of a menace to the USSR proper. But because of its emphasis on national independence and individual roads to socialism, and in view of its historical ties with East European parties, geographical proximity, close association with Yugoslavia and Romania, and growing influence, it is a model fraught with danger in Eastern Europe. This is where it poses the most serious threat to the USSR.

For this reason, the emerging Czechoslovak "socialism with a human face," a Eurocommunist variant, was suppressed so brutally: it was indeed perceived as contagious. For the same reason it was supported by Eurocommunists. They have not accepted the Soviet occupation. They disagreed with the wisdom of Soviet armed intervention and have kept bringing up the issue in public. The Soviet invasion has aroused and solidified the Eurocommunist stand and its opposition to the USSR more than any other issue. The PCE has been the most outspoken and eloquent in its denunciation of the Soviet action; in fact, the two parties broke relations over the incident. The PCI repeatedly and publicly condemned the invasion, and it deplored the subsequent purges and trials. Morally, financially, and politically it supported Czechoslovak Communist exiles and published letters from preinvasion Czechoslovak leaders and other dissidents in Czechoslovakia. It has urged withdrawal of Soviet troops from Czechoslovakia ever since.[46] The PCF was at first less vociferous than the French socialists in expressing support for antioccupation sentiments and forces. Since then, however, the PCF position has hardened because, the party claims, the Soviet intervention has contributed to the democratization of the PCF itself.[47] The British and Australian parties, highly critical of the occupation, published letters and messages from Czechoslovak dissidents. The Yugoslavs and Romanians sympathized with the deposed Czechoslovak regime. The Austrian, Belgian, Dutch, Swedish, Japanese, and a faction of the Greek Communists censured the invasion.

Similarly, when Wladyslaw Gomulka and his associates took severe punitive measures against workers who were striking and rioting over prices and wages in Polish cities in 1970, several Communist parties, including the Italian and Japanese, protested the Polish government's stern measures. In 1976, responding to Polish historian Jacek Kuron's open letter to Berlinguer, the Central Committee of the PCI voiced its concern for the Polish workers tried in connection with the disturbances of June 25, 1976, and expressed its "hope that measures showing moderation and clemency may be adopted and publicized."[48]

Examples of a dialogue between East and West Europe include an article in the *World Marxist Review* by Deszo Nemes, member of the Hungarian party Politburo, and an article in *France Nouvelle* by Jean Kanapa on the dictatorship of the proletariat. Can socialism be attained without the dictatorship of the proletariat? No, argued Nemes, because "events [in socialist states] refuted the idea." Yes, replied Kanapa, because it would mean "banning opposition parties, establishing censorship, forbidding freedom of expression, association, demonstration, etc. . . . This is not necessary for the construction of socialism in France during our era. We do not want it."[49]

The Yugoslav international conference on Socialism in the Contemporary World included participants from the West, Africa, Asia, Latin America, as well as from the USSR, Bulgaria, Romania, and Czechoslovakia. In "a spirit of free discussion," apparently a "confrontation of ideas" took place. Different roads to socialism, dictatorship of the proletariat, Eurocommunism (sometimes called "Eurosectarianism"), state ownership, strategy of social forces, and similar disputed topics were openly discussed.[50]

When Czechoslovak authorities arrested leading dissidents in a continuing crackdown on signatories of a manifesto for civil rights guaranteed by the Helsinki agreement, the "Charter 77," published in West European newspapers, *L'Unità* wrote that "the virulence . . . leaves no doubt as to the spirit and methods with which the Czechoslovak authorities intend to confront the problems posed by Charter '77," and condemned the Czechoslovak government.[51] Similarly, *Rinascità* said that "the question of the realization of democratic socialism in Czechoslovakia remains unanswered."[52] A PCE spokesman in Madrid was reported to have called "particularly scandalous . . . the lack of freedom of expression in socialist states."[53]

The relationship between Eurocommunists and dissidents in socialist states is mutually reinforcing. Eurocommunists monitor events in Eastern Europe and in the USSR, and new trends and developments in West European Communist parties are not lost on the East Europeans and the Russians. The dissidents appeal to Eurocommunists for moral support, and the Eurocommunists criticize the socialist states for their excesses. True, censorship is still a potent barrier, but enough filters through to suggest that, at least in Eastern Europe, "critical socialists" not only know what is going on but feel less isolated and deserted. For example, in an open "Letter to the PCI from the supporters of the Czechoslovak 'New Course,'" the dissident writers in Czechoslovakia praised the PCI's "authentic democracy": "Your position constitutes an important component of the effort to give the cause of socialism in the advanced countries of Europe a new impulse and ensure its progress. It also provides support for the efforts of all those within the socialist countries who are convinced that the further progress of socialist society is the condition for overcoming the deformations that still exist."[54]

Similarly, when the East German popular poet, singer, and political critic Wolf Bierman, while on tour in West Germany, was stripped of his citizenship and forbidden to return, he claimed that Eurocommunists, particularly the French, Italian, and Spanish parties, had encouraged dissidents in East Germany to become "more daring, less embarrassed, more courageous, and more clear-sighted."[55] In turn, the French, Italian, Spanish, Belgian, and Swedish parties defended Bierman's right to travel and his cultural freedom, while the Austrian Communist party denounced the singer for serving anti-Communist interests.[56]

The Eurocommunists like to win votes, but they also want to be right. One of the few rewards available to a minority is the feeling of righteousness associated with supporting an untainted cause. Such a minority has no reason to compromise as there is little justice—or benefit—in compromise. Moreover, given the fairly rapid growth of Eurocommunism and the sustained fragmentation of the Communist movement, the dissident parties think that time is on their side, not on the side of the CPSU. They know from their own experience that if the CPSU fails to meet the rising expectations of its associates and supporters, then its legitimacy will be further undermined and its intrinsic value to all further depreciated. The Eurocommunists' verbal interventions and meddling in the USSR and East Europe, however ineffective in the short run, appear to be potentially significant, especially in East Europe.

Conclusion

Have the Eurocommunists "really changed"? I think they have. Their new, historically unknown form of Communism may go against the grain of Communism as we have known it since its split with social democracy, but it is here to stay. The major West European parties have sought in a variety of ways to produce a setting in which they could carry out more adequately their electoral, parliamentary function. They adapted their party structures, their political direction, their alliances, their daily political activities, and their party mentality to this function. They cannot go back even if they should want to. Their political organization would tear at the seams. They are captives of their own progressive democratization and political integration. "A party that puts its finger in the parliamentary machine to the extent that the major Western parties have is unlikely ever to overturn society."[57]

Relations between the Communist parties and the Soviet Union used to be a two-way street: "The Soviet rulers needed the ideological endorsement of Marxists in capitalist lands as much as Western communists needed the prestige of the proletarian state that 'expropriated the expropriators.'"[58] The non-Soviet Communists historically shared the feeling that by themselves, through their own power, they could not attain their goals. They therefore willingly bestowed the legitimacy of leadership and authority on the CPSU and obeyed its commands. The CPSU, in turn, interested in the contribution of the foreign parties to the maintenance and growth of the Communist movement that the CPSU organized and led, tried to motivate them to remain committed to the Soviet "common strategy" and "common model of socialism."

Since then the street has become narrow; it is no longer two-way. The trade-off is no longer what it used to be. The "rally 'round the flag" mentality of earlier years is gone. It is not only that the non-Soviet parties have changed and that they can do better, given their political arrangements and values, and so long as they are more independent and autonomous. Neither is it simply that domestication brings votes and votes bring power. It is also the cumulative effect of Soviet behavior over the years, perceived as oppressive and exploitative deprivation of others, which brings into question the legitimacy of Soviet authority. Has not the CPSU, the socializer of norms, so internalized the relational ties with Communist parties that historical changes could no longer cope with the prevailing rigidities? Last but not least, men do seek more than satisfactory and profitable relationships; they seek just ones. There seems to be a scarcity of those in the relations of other Communist parties with the CPSU.

Exchange theory posits that the more an activity is valued, the more it will be rewarded. Since the CPSU needs the other Communist parties more than they need the CPSU, one would expect concessions and benefits to flow to the other parties on the theory that the degree of renewed solidarity is a function of the value and frequency of benefits bestowed. I doubt that this would work. It may retard the alienation, but it will not stop it. The CPSU may negotiate itself out of the deadlock but not back into a movement. Neither does it seem probable that the Eurocommunists would attempt to gain influence by forming a coalition to change the CPSU to the degree the coalition can agree on. The odds against the latter, I think, are fairly high.

If the Eurocommunists do well, others will emulate them, thus further increasing the pressure on the Soviet Union. That may influence Soviet policy in Eastern Europe and, in the longer run, at home as well. Heretics have traditionally contaminated the orthodox more than the schismatics, the independents, or the neutrals.

Given the changes in West European Communism and in view of

the discussion above, it is not surprising that Soviet pronouncements have changed as well. It is now Moscow that advocates diversity, equality, and individual initiative:

> Monolithic unity is understood not as the unity of identical elements but as unity in diversity; and discipline is understood as the definitely coordinated activity of all socialist countries without any kind of subordination of some to others, but with broad individual initiative on the part of each country in the interests of carrying out its own and the common tasks. . . . One cannot be a good Communist by giving commands in international relations or blindly obeying even the best orders and slavishly copying what others are doing.[59]

Change in verbal behavior is comparatively easy. But can the CPSU "really change"? Can it come up with alternative lines of policy that would bring satisfaction compatible with the Soviet aims to Eurocommunists while producing a minimum of undesirable side effects to the CPSU? I do not think so. The Eurocommunists have learned that they can live—and prosper—without Soviet legitimation. Their aims and Soviet aims are only marginally compatible, and the marginality expands and contracts from issue to issue. The impact of their dissent may produce results in Eastern Europe only to Soviet detriment. The collision course is not yet set, but compatibility has been decreasing. To arrest this trend, cosmetic changes, such as the Soviet statement cited above, virtually an instant reflex defensive mechanism, are no longer relevant.

At the time of writing, over three years have passed since the Twenty-fifth Congress of the CPSU in Moscow and the Conference of the European Communist Parties in East Berlin. These three years have not proved to be years of unilateral progress, development, or growth for Eurocommunism. In fact, some of the intensity, zeal, and vitality seem to have gone from the Eurocommunist game. It is not just that the Eurocommunist parties have remained too many things to too many people, and neither is it that with time the Eurocommunist momentum has simply declined, as was expected. Instead, it is that the initial Eurocommunist success raised expectations that remain largely unfulfilled today. This has eroded the initial credibility of the West European Communist parties as parties of strength, discipline, and progress. As time passes, the parties' appearance of equivocation grows, and friends and foes alike find it increasingly difficult to take these parties seriously.

Yet, on closer examination, it appears that the many constraints that have acted on these Communist parties have been more of form and style than of substance. Sitting on the fence and talking to many different audiences at the same time, while coping with unrest in the ranks and hostility abroad, the Communist parties have overstayed their welcome at the threshold of power. Since the Berlin Conference they have not been the parties of efficiency and change they had purported to be and had been perceived to be by their respective electorates. After three years of euphoria, they face the real dangers of *stagnation* (either doing nothing, or, what is worse, taking half-measures), *isolation* (being out of the political mainstream and no longer politically relevant at home and abroad), and *loss of identity* (if they are really not social democrats, what are they?).

With respect to the first danger, that of stagnation, Berlinguer announced at a January 1979 meeting of the five Italian parties that made up the parliamentary majority backing Prime Minister Giulio Andreotti's minority government that the PCI was withdrawing its parliamentary support from the Christian Democratic government. Berlinguer accused the Christian Democrats of using the Communists, of not taking their views into account, of waging a campaign against the PCI, of making the PCI responsible for terrorism, and in general of excluding the party from decisions while demanding its support. The Andreotti-Berlinguer 1978 agreement, according to which the PCI became a member of the parliamentary majority backing the government in exchange for the promise of being consulted on all major decisions, came to a final halt. The PCI opted for an end to its "neither fish nor fowl" casting in Italian politics. The strain became untenable.

The second danger, that of isolation, prompted Berlinguer to take a trip to Paris, Moscow, and Belgrade in October 1978. In Paris, he and Marchais reaffirmed the 1977 Carrillo-Berlinguer-Marchais agreement on Eurocommunism. In Moscow, Berlinguer was said to have reached a compromise on Eurocommunism with Brezhnev, according to which West European parties were free to dissent from Moscow. (But in *Pravda* on November 6, 1978, less than a month after Berlinguer's visit, Zagladin again condemned Eurocommunism as "a dangerous delusion.") In Belgrade, Berlinguer was reported to have discussed with Tito Chairman Hua Kuo-feng's visit in Romania and Yugoslavia. (Peking is still opposed to resumption of relations with the major West European Communist parties.)

The third danger, that of the loss of identity, is probably the gravest. Here the Eurocommunist parties are vulnerable in the extreme. Given the many contradictory demands, pressures, and expectations at home and abroad, and the parties' professed concern for balance, equilibrium, and symmetry between issues such as autonomy and solidarity; the reformist perspective of the historic compromise and "revolutionary Marxism"; democratic centralism and "socialist pluralism"; democracy and Communism; and so forth, the new identity of the Eurocommunists is confusing to all, friends and foes alike. In the short run, such conceptual schizophrenia is not harmful and if properly manipulated may bring advantages, as when different audiences identify with their preferred party images. Over time, however, such equivocation to please all becomes detrimental. The electorate becomes confused. This is what the PCI found out in the 1978 electoral contests when it attempted to attract new voters.

All three major dangers can be averted by performance. There is still time. Confidence can be regained and disillusion replaced by support when political goods are actually delivered. Seriousness of purpose is seldom wasted on concerned observers. Successful electoral parties do eventually discover a middle course, at home as well as abroad.

The impact of so-called Eurocommunism on "proletarian internationalism" and the Soviet model of socialism is significant. The ongoing search of West European parties for autonomy is having a profound adverse impact on their solidarity with the USSR and with Eastern Europe, the area of contest. Not that the Eurocommunists want it: Carrillo, in spite of his open, sharp polemics with the Soviet leadership, does not want it; Marchais, ill at ease in his new role, does not want it; and Berlinguer is too reasonable to want it. The Soviet spokesmen always come back, as Zagladin did after Berlinguer's Moscow visit, defending both the universal ties of "proletarian internationalism" and the international validity of the Soviet model of socialism. And yet, there is no question in my mind that if the Eurocommunist leaders indeed become ministers—and they may not, of course—their parties will sooner or later present a clear and present danger to Soviet Communism—in the world, possibly in the Soviet Union proper, and certainly in Eastern Europe.

NOTES

This is an updated version of a paper originally prepared for the Conference on Soviet-American Relations in the 1970s, Kennan Institute for Advanced Russian Studies, the Smithsonian Institution, Washington, 1977.

1. Kevin Devlin, "The International Communist Movement. The Pan-European Conference," Radio Free Europe (RFE) Research, *RAD Background Report*, No. 171, August 5, 1976, p. 13. Useful materials not cited in this paper include the following: William Ascher and Sidney Tarrow, "The Stability of Communist Electorates," *American Journal of Political Science*, XIX (August 1976), pp. 475–499; Donald M. Blackmer and Annie Kriegl, *The International Role of the Communist Parties of Italy and France* (Cambridge:

Harvard University Press, 1975); Donald M. Blackmer and Sidney Tarrow, *Communism in Italy and France* (Princeton: Princeton University Press, 1975); Guido Carli, "Italy's Malaise," *Foreign Affairs,* 54 (July 1976), pp. 708–718; "Concerning a United Ideological Front of the World's Communists," *World Marxist Review,* 19 (February 1976), pp. 47–60; Gastone Gensini, "Component of Unity: Communists in the Struggle for Unity of All Anti-Imperialist Forces," ibid., 17 (May 1974), pp. 85–87; W. Lacquer, "Eurocommunism and Its Friends," *Commentary,* 62 (August 1976), pp. 25–30; Peter Lange, "What Is to be Done—About Italian Communism?" *Foreign Policy,* no. 21 (Winter 1975), pp. 224–240; Luigi Longo, "A Powerful Force for Change," *World Marxist Review,* 19 (April 1976), pp. 12–20; Neil McInnes, "World Communism in Fragments," *Problems of Communism,* 24 (November 1976), pp. 43–46; Peter Nichols, "On the Italian Crisis," *Foreign Affairs,* 54 (April 1976), pp. 511–526; Richard Pipes, "Liberal Communism in Western Europe?" *Orbis,* 20 (Fall 1976), pp. 595–601; Alceste Santini, "From Dialogue to Joint Action," *World Marxist Review,* 19 (April 1976), pp. 116–123; Simon Serfaty, "An International Anomaly: The U.S. and the Communist Parties in France and Italy," *Studies in Comparative Communism,* 8 (Spring/Summer 1975), pp. 123–149; John Barth Urban, "Contemporary Soviet Perspectives on Revolution in the West," *Orbis,* 19 (Winter 1976), pp. 1359–1402; Dale Vree, "Coalition Politics on the Left in France and Italy," *Review of Politics,* 37 (July 1975), pp. 340–356.

2. This account of the Twenty-Fifth Congress of the CPSU is based on Jan F. Triska, "The 25th Congress of the CPSU: Communist States and Parties," in Alexander Dallin, ed., *The 25th Congress of the CPSU: Assessment and Context* (Stanford: Hoover Institution Press, 1977), pp. 95–99.

3. *Pravda,* March 1, 1976.

4. Ibid., March 18, 1976.

5. Compared with the previous meetings and conferences of Communist parties, the European Conference stands out as a watershed; the influence began to flow unmistakably in the opposite direction. On closer examination, the growing conflictual trend may be traced over time even here. In the 1960 Communist Parties Conference, all the Communist parties toed the Moscow line, at least on the surface. The 1967 Karlovy Vary Conference was still an organizationally streamlined meeting, which only the Yugoslav and Romanian leaders failed to attend. At the 1969 Moscow Conference, on the other hand, not only speeches critical of the Soviet position were delivered (and published in *Pravda*) but fourteen of the seventy-five parties made reservations to or stated disapproval of the final document, which already contained mild Soviet concessions.

6. Stane Dolanc, "Confirmation of Democratic Cooperation and Solidarity," *Socialist Thought and Practice* (Belgrade), 14 (July-August 1976), p. 22.

7. "Conference of European Communist Parties," Foreign Broadcast Information Service (FBIS), *Daily Report, USSR,* Nos. 126–133, 1976. See also *Neues Deutschland,* June 30, July 1, 1976; *Pravda,* June 30, July 1, 1976; and Devlin, "International Communist Movement."

8. Devlin, "International Communist Movement," pp. 13–14.

9. Like Jean Kanapa, member of the Politburo of the French Communist party, I do not much care for the term "Eurocommunism." It is imprecise, fluid, exclusive, and at times too suggestive. But like Kanapa, I use it because it is a convenient shorthand for "several communist parties in industrialized capitalist countries [which], though in quite different situations, have had the feeling of being confronted with fundamentally common problems, so that

they have come up with similar answers, thereby outlining a socialist perspective which is strongly marked by a common concern for democracy." Jean Kanapa, "A 'New Policy' of the French Communists?" *Foreign Affairs,* 55 (No. 2, 1977), p. 284.

10. For more information on and background of the Communist parties discussed in this section, consult Richard F. Staar, ed., *Yearbook on International Communist Affairs* (Stanford University: Hoover Institution Press, 1966–1979).

11. Kanapa, "International Communist Movement," p. 283. Italics added.

12. Neil McInnes, *The Communist Parties of Western Europe* (London: Oxford University Press, 1975), p. 178.

13. Hong M. Kim, "Deradicalization of the Japanese Communist Party under Kenji Miyamoto," *World Politics,* 28 (No. 2, 1976, pp. 273–299; *Asahi Evening News,* May 12, 1976; *Bulletin* (Tokyo). *Information for Abroad. Central Committee of the Communist Party,* no. 356 (July 1976).

14. Yugoslavia is the only East European country that accepts "without qualification two significant political principles: the legitimacy of special interests and the autonomy of social organizations." Andrew C. Janos, "The One-Party State and Social Mobilization: East Europe between the Wars," in Samuel P. Huntington and Clement H. Moore, *Authoritarian Politics in Modern Societies* (New York: Basic Books, 1970), pp. 444.

15. Jan F. Triska, "The Socialist World System in Search of a Theory," in Dan N. Jacobs, ed., *The New Communisms* (New York: Harper and Row, 1969), pp. 29ff.

16. Thus, for example, in a speech to a congress of socialist culture in Bucharest, Nicolae Ceausescu, while praising the dissolution of the Comintern in 1943 because "a leading center was no longer necessary" and while defining internationalism as mutual support and not an excuse to meddle into internal affairs of others ("internationalism cannot be synonymous with sacrificing the interests of any people for the so-called general interests"), he reaffirmed, with reservations, Romania's adherence to the Warsaw Pact and Comecon. *Scinteia* (Bucharest), June 2, 1976. Similarly, Stefan Nastasescu, former secretary in the foreign ministry, in answer to the Soviet articles on proletarian internationalism that appeared after the European party conference, took the soft stand. He attacked both "limited" and "absolute" sovereignty, the former because it disregards rights of others and the latter because it "justifies unleashing of aggression against independent states." Still, Nastasescu emphasized international reciprocity and "the replacement of unilateral dependencies by multilateral interdependence among all states as equal and self-supporting entities in international society." Only "a sovereign entity can renounce some of its sovereignty." Stefan Nastasescu, "Sovereignty, Security, and International Cooperation," *Era Socialista,* no. 17 (September 1976), p. 3. See also *Die Welt,* September 18, 1976, p. 6.

17. *L'Humanité,* September 10, 1976; *L'Unità,* August 11, 1976; *Volkstimme,* August 11, 1976. See also Silvio F. Senigalia, "The PCI and China," *New Leader,* October 25, 1976, pp. 3–4.

18. McInnes, *Communist Parties of Western Europe,* p. 156.

19. Triska, "The Socialist World System," pp. 18ff.

20. Yugoslavia was condemned and expelled from the Cominform because the Comintern practices "of censuring and even disowning communist parties" were extended to state relations "rendering their consequences the more serious." For almost seven years Josip Tito protested such treatment in vain. Then the Chinese leaders accused the CPSU of having "arbitrarily in-

fringed upon the sovereignty of fraternal countries, interfered in their internal affairs, carried on subversive activities and tried in every way to control fraternal countries." In fact, "the leaders of the CPSU have themselves undermined the basis of the unity of the international Communist movement and created the present grave danger of a split by betraying Marxism-Leninism and proletarian internationalism." The Romanians, for their part, pointed out that there should be no "parent" and "son" parties—parties that are superior or inferior—but only equal parties. They should not interfere in each other's business and should respect each other. Ibid., pp. 35–41.

21. Jovan Raicevic, "From Dogmatism to Ideological Monopoly," *Socializam* (Belgrade), May 1976; *Politika* (Belgrade), October 24, 1976; Aleksander Grlickov in *Borba* (Belgrade), November 28–30, 1976.

22. *New York Times,* September 5, 1964, p. 2.

23. Triska, "Socialist World System," p. 41.

24. Kanapa, "International Communist Movement," p. 282.

25. McInnes, *Communist Parties of Western Europe,* p. 145.

26. *Krasnaia Zvezda* (Moscow), August 5, 1976, p. 6; see also *Mezhdunarodnaia Zhizn* (Moscow), no. 9 (August 1976), p. 2.

27. *Pravda,* June 30, 1976; *Izvestiia,* June 30, 1976.

28. "Important Contribution to Peace and Progress," *Mirovaia Economika i Mezhdunarodnye Otnosheniia* (August 1976), pp. 4–27. See also G. Shakhnazarov, "The Socialist Future of Mankind," *Pravda,* July 23, 1976; *Izvestiia,* June 30, 1976; Boris Ponomarev, "International Meaning of Berlin Conference," *Kommunist* (July 1976), pp. 11–25; Yu. Ogazis'jan quoted in *Rabochii Klas I Sovremennyi Mir* (July-August 1976).

29. See Editorial in *Politika,* October 24, 1976. See also *Era Socialista,* no. 16 (August 1976) and *L'Unità,* December 4, 1976.

30. *The World Socialist System and Anti-Communism* (Moscow: Progress Publishers, 1972), pp. 110–122.

31. Dusan Bilandzic, "The International Policy and Practice of the LCY in Light of the Development of Marxism and Socialism," *Borba,* August 21–September 13, 1976 cited in Slobodan Stankovic, "Party Theoreticians Reject Soviet Supremacy," RFE Research, *RAD Background Report,* no. 199 (September 22, 1976). Italics added.

32. Ibid.

33. Drago Buvac, "Reaching the Center Through a Detour," *Nedelne Informativne Novine,* May 2, 1976. "The trouble is that," in spite of this fragmentation, tendencies exist whose supporters would like to achieve 'unity' by forbidding all differences and by imposing a single view of one center." *Ekonomska Politika,* May 31, 1976.

34. Dusan Bilandzic quoted in Stankovic, "Party Theoreticians," p. 6.

35. Editorial in *Politika,* October 24, 1976. Italics added.

36. Werner Jaeger, *Paideia: The Ideals of Greek Culture* (New York, 1945), vol. I, p. 326.

37. Devlin, "International Communist Movement," p. 13.

38. Lenin, quoted in Lucian Pye, *Guerilla Communism in Malaya* (Princeton: Princeton University Press, 1956), p. 26.

39. Kanapa, "International Communist Movement," p. 284. Italics added.

40. McInnis, *Communist Parties of Western Europe,* p. 175.

41. Z. Priklmajer-Tomanosic, "The Internationalist Policy and Practice of the LCY in Light of the Development of Marxism and Socialism," *Borba,* August 21–September 13, 1976, cited in Stankovic, "Party Theoreticians," p. 8.

42. Kanapa, "International Communist Movement," p. 282.

43. "Scientific Socialism and the Problem of Dictatorship," *Era Socialista*, no. 16 (August 1976). See also *Central Committee of the Communist Party of Japan Bulletin* (Tokyo), no. 356 (July 1976), "Draft Resolution of the 13th Extraordinary Party Congress," cited in RFE Research, *Romania*, no. 29 (August 26, 1976), p. 8.

44. Lenin, cited in *World Socialist System and Anti-Communism*, p. 120. Italics added.

45. McInnes, *Communist Parties of Western Europe*, pp. 140–156, 204.

46. As Enrico Berlinguer reminded the European Communist Parties' Conference in East Berlin on June 30, "we have more than once expressed critical judgments on certain events and situations, for example, with regard to Czechoslovakia." "Final Document," FBIS, *Daily Report, USSR*, nos. 126–133 (1976). Jan F. Triska, "Messages from Czechoslovakia," *Problems of Communism*, 24 (December 1975), pp. 26–42.

47. Kanapa, "International Communist Movement," p. 283. See also Georges Marchais, *La Politique Du Parti Communiste Française* (Paris: Editions Sociales, 1974). Compare with Jacques Fauvet, *Histoire du PCF 1939 —1965* (Paris: Fayard, 1965).

48. *L'Unità*, July 20, 1976. The Italian Metalworkers' Union also protested against the severe sentences passed on Polish workers after the Radom-Ursus riots. *L'Unità*, November 17, 1976.

49. Deszo Nemes, "Lessons of the Class Struggle for Power in Hungary," *World Marxist Review* (September 1976), pp. 11–14; and Jean Kanapa, "Socialism: The Past Has Not the Answer for Everything," *France Nouvelle*, October 2, 1976; quoted in Kevin Devlin, "Hungarian—PCF Polemic: Kanapa Counterattacks," RFE Research, *RAD Background Report*, no. 209 (October 6, 1976).

50. Slobodan Stankovic, "Yugoslav Symposium Affairs Validity of Ideological Differences," RFE Research, *RAD Background Report*, no. 212 (October 7, 1976).

51. *L'Unità*, January 12, 1977.

52. *Rinascità*, January 14, 1977.

53. "Communists in Western Europe Criticize Prague Authorities," *Frankfurter Allgemeine Zeitung*, January 15, 1977.

54. *L'Unità*, June 18, 1976.

55. *Le Monde*, November 21–22, 1976.

56. *L'Unità*, November 20, 1976; *L'Humanité*, November 17, 19, 1976; *Le Drapeau Rouge*, November 23, 1976; *Ny Dag*, November 22, 1976; *Volkstimme*, November 20, 1976.

57. McInnes, *Communist Parties of Western Europe*, p. 181. Could a Communist government be voted out of power? We do not really know. Since World War II, Communists in Europe participated in governments in France, Italy, Czechoslovakia, Belgium, Luxembourg, Austria, Greece, Denmark, Norway, Finland, and Iceland, but never by themselves. Only in Czechoslovakia did the Communist party take over the government by *coup d'etat*. The sample of one is too small for any generalization.

58. Ibid., p. 15.

59. *World Socialist System and Anti-Communism*, p. 121.

Part Two •

EUROCOMMUNISM AND EASTERN EUROPE

CHAPTER V

Eurocommunism and the USSR

Jiri Valenta

Eurocommunism is not a movement in opposition to the USSR
or the United States. It is a movement which stems from the
need to pursue and follow in the individual countries an original road to socialism which is certainly different from the one
followed in the Soviet Union and in other socialist countries.
ENRICO BERLINGUER

Eurocommunism exists and is a reality, no matter what the
Americans and the Soviets may think about it.
SANTIAGO CARRILLO

Communism, with or without "Euro"? The phenomenon of
Eurocommunism has become a subject of debate among analysts in
both the East and the West during the last three years. As chairman of
the Austrian Socialist party Bruno Kreisky put it, "The phenomenon
of Eurocommunism is wandering through Europe and everywhere
people are seeking to explain it."[1] Although lacking both geographic
and political precision, and therefore ambiguous and perhaps even
improperly used, the term Eurocommunism has become a working
part of the political vocabulary. As such it is frequently used by the
leaders of at least two influential West European Communist
parties—the Spanish (PCE) and the Italian (PCI)—and also, less frequently, by some officials of the French Communist party (PCF).

At the Madrid summit of March 1977, officials of these parties, notably Santiago Carrillo and Enrico Berlinguer, evidently recognizing
the appealing quality of the term, began, with some initial hesitation
and with varying degrees of ambivalence, to employ it. In their understanding, Eurocommunism does not define an exact concept or a
coherent doctrine. Rather it denotes a trend or process leading to an
independent, pluralistic concept of socialism, embracing respect for
individual liberties and developed primarily within the unified
framework of the democratic countries of Western Europe. Although
it is artificial and provisional, the term used in this manner will, it is
hoped, suffice for the purpose of inquiry into Soviet attitudes and
policies toward those West European Communist parties that profess
adherence to this different form of socialism.

Eurocommunism: A Soviet Dilemma

The rise of Eurocommunism has caused increasing apprehension in both the Soviet Union and the United States. Public Soviet attacks on those Eurocommunists least favored by Moscow, such as Spanish Communist leader Carrillo, and American diplomatic efforts to deny entrance of the PCI and the PCF into Italian and French coalition governments, demonstrate the extent to which Eurocommunism has become a subject of keen interest to both superpowers.

These shared (and often over-rated) apprehensions over the rise of Eurocommunism have led to a paradoxical situation. Whereas in the West policymakers and observers, such as former Secretary of State Henry Kissinger, continue to question the very existence of Eurocommunism (at times referring to it as only a temporary tactic of the parties involved), some of their counterparts in the Soviet Union and in Eastern Europe claim that Eurocommunism is part of a grand design devised by the West to undermine political stability not only in Eastern Europe but also in the Soviet Union. Many Western observers hold that the entry of West European Communist parties—such as the PCI—into full government status would present a serious challenge to NATO and to American influence in Europe. Although this is undoubtedly true, the evidence available suggests that the rise of Eurocommunism also presents a serious dilemma to the USSR, to its self-proclaimed role as leader of the world Communist movement, to its hegemony in Eastern Europe, and to its role as a great power.

The challenge to leadership in the world Communist movement poses an especially acute problem for the Soviet Union. The Soviet Union and the Eurocommunist-oriented parties of Spain and Italy have in common their support of Marxist and revolutionary regimes in Cuba, North Vietnam, Angola, Ethiopia (with criticism by the PCI over the Soviets' sudden shift from Somalia to Ethiopia and Soviet military intervention in Afghanistan), and of the radical national liberation movements of the Third World, including the Palestine Liberation Organization and Polisario. Yet, at the same time, the Eurocommunist-oriented parties directly challenge the Soviet interpretation of Marxism and thereby the authority of the CPSU and its influence in the world Communist movement. Despite strong Soviet objections, the Eurocommunist parties are gradually repudiating a number of fundamental Leninist tenets, including the dictatorship of the proletariat. In April 1978, the PCE's Ninth Congress—the first to be held in Spain since 1932—confirmed the Eurocommunist line as its political course. In addition, a majority of the delegates (968 to 248) approved the suggestion by Carrillo that thesis XV of the PCE's statutes be altered—a move that set a precedent by dropping the Leninist label and changing the party's designation from "Marxist-Leninist" to "Marxist revolutionary and democratic." The creation of a "genuine Eurocommunist party," as Carrillo calls the PCE, may serve as a stimulus for similar developments in some other Communist parties. The emergence of a new kind of socialism with genuine political democracy in several West European Communist parties could provide a respectable and attractive variant to the rigid Soviet and East European model of socialism. It is impossible to know whether the Eurocommunist-oriented parties' alleged commitment to democratic values and their pledge to leave office if they achieve power and are subsequently voted out will be honored. What is certain, however, is that their profession of belief in Western democratic values, though still untested, greatly undermines Soviet ideology and the image of the CPSU as the universal model of a Marxist party. Furthermore, from the Soviet viewpoint, the new brand of socialism may set a dangerous precedent for other Communist parties, both in Western and Eastern Europe and in other developed countries, such as Japan and Australia.

Eurocommunism could have destabilizing spillover effects on Eastern Europe and on the Soviet Union itself, becoming a reference point for advocates of democratic socialism, reformers, and dissidents. Herein lies perhaps the most dangerous aspect of Eurocommunism for the Soviet Union and some East European regimes. After all, it was the similar "taking stock" of another model of democratic socialism based on the expansion of civil liberties that led finally to the Warsaw Pact invasion of Czechoslovakia in 1968. In their program of pluralistic socialism and in their intervention on behalf of reformists and dissidents in the Warsaw Pact countries, however, the Eurocommunists go much farther than Alexander Dubcek and his reformists. They advocate, within the framework of European unity, a form of socialism even surpassing that envisioned by the architects of the Prague Spring. The success of such an experiment in Western Europe would legitimize the Prague Spring and provide further impetus for similar efforts in other East European countries. Moreover, some leading Eurocommunists, such as Carrillo, declare that it is not only the right but also the duty of the West European parties to criticize repression in the USSR and Eastern Europe. In fact, the Eurocommunist parties of both Spain and Italy provided selective political support in 1977–1979 to Eastern Europe's most prominent dissident groups, Charter 77 in Czechoslovakia and the Workers' Defense Committee in Poland.

Furthermore, the Communist-dominated trade union organizations in Italy and in France have begun to criticize and even to boycott the Soviet-dominated World Federation of Trade Unions, supporting instead the dissident trade unions and "free trade union" groups of both Eastern Europe and the USSR.

More important is the possibility that at least one of the West European Communist parties—the PCI—may soon become a governing party. During the period 1976–1978 it participated informally in government through regular consultations with the Christian Democrats before decisions were taken in return for abstaining on votes of confidence. Even after Prime Minister Aldo Moro's tragic death in 1978 and an election setback for the PCI in 1979, there is still a remote possibility that a new government may be formed in Italy with Communist participation, despite objections by the critics of Eurocommunist orientation in the PCI. The PCI also remains a politically unpredictable force despite the self-inflicted setback of the March 1978 elections and the debate within the party among advocates and opponents of a Eurocommunist orientation. The possibility that a successful West European Communist party-in-power might become a very attractive model of pluralistic socialism for Eastern Europe poses a threat to Soviet hegemony and ultimately to political stability in the Soviet Union itself.

The third aspect of the Eurocommunist dilemma is its challenge to the Soviet Union's interests as a great power. Again, the possibility that the PCI may participate (perhaps against its better judgement) in a new Italian government poses a significant problem for the Soviet Union. On the one hand, PCI participation in the Italian government may raise expectations in the Soviet leadership that the political and psychological repercussions of such a development would disturb the stability of the Mediterranean flank of NATO, thus enhancing Soviet political influence in Western Europe. With varying degrees of ambivalence, the PCI and PCE give qualified support to the European Economic Community and to NATO. Although the PCE views Spain's entry into NATO as undesirable, it accepts the presence of American bases in Spain as long as Soviet troops remain in Czechoslovakia and declares that it will accept Spain's entry into NATO should the Spanish parliament approve. Berlinguer even stated in 1976 and again in 1979 that socialism in Italy is safer under NATO's umbrella than in the Warsaw Pact.[2] The PCF also accepts NATO as part of the existing military equilibrium in Europe and has endorsed (since 1977) the *force de frappe* (the national-nuclear "strike force"). The Eurocommunist-oriented parties have also proposed some fundamental changes in the Atlantic alliance and advocate the simultaneous dissolution of both the Warsaw Pact and NATO. At the least these changes would weaken the influence of the two principal powers in the NATO alliance, the United States and West Germany. Actually, the Soviets may hope to exploit to their advantage this new brand of "communist Gaullism," perhaps through some of the violently anti-American elements of the PCF. The PCF's current stance vis-à-vis NATO (particularly its interest in weakening the American role) and European unity, its endorsement of a Gaullist *tous azimuts* defense policy (the concept of defense against all points of the compass), and its refusal to integrate the nation's defense into NATO's unified command coincide with important elements of Soviet strategy in Western Europe.

On the other hand, the entry of the Communists into West European governments may complicate Soviet relations with the West, even to the extent of destabilizing the overall European political equilibrium and the informal system of spheres of influence that the Soviets have maintained with the United States in Europe since 1945. Indeed, Soviet détente with the United States may be jeopardized, and a return to the Cold War may follow. This is not to say that the Eurocommunists challenge the overall direction of the Soviet foreign policy of détente; on the contrary, the Eurocommunist successes of the 1970s are partly a function of the détente process in Europe. Some of the European Communist parties, however, resented the Soviets' good relations in the past decade with governments in power and their failure to exploit the "crisis of capitalism." This was particularly true of the PCF, which felt embarrassed by the Soviets' good relations with Charles de Gaulle, Georges Pompidou, and Valéry Giscard d'Estaing, and of the PCE, which felt embarrassed by the Soviets' good relations with the Franco regime.

In the long run the foreign policy strategy of the Eurocommunists may pose an even greater dilemma for the Soviet Union. The vision of some Eurocommunists, such as Carrillo and Berlinguer, of a "united Europe" of "progressive forces" equidistant between East and West and their firm commitment to European unification and integration certainly hold no more appeal for Moscow than de Gaulle's earlier dream of a Europe "from the Urals to the Pyrenees." Obviously, the strengthening of "the new European forces" under the banner of Atlantism, Eurosocialism, or Eurocommunism would not automatically strengthen Soviet influence in Europe. On the contrary, it could be carried out at the expense of both superpowers and gradually lead to the creation of a Europe acting independently of the United States and the Soviet Union. The USSR has traditionally feared and opposed any policy of European political, economic, or military integration, preferring, on the contrary, any form of nationalism.

Despite some convergent foreign policy interests, such as the weakening of American and West German influence in NATO and support for the revolutionary regimes and national liberation movements in the Third World, there can be no doubt that some serious differences have arisen between some West European Eurocommunist parties and the Soviet Union. Eurocommunism offers some opportunities for the Soviet leadership, but it has also created a serious dilemma for both the Soviets and their East European colleagues. To assess further the significance of this dilemma it is necessary to try to decipher the perceptions that the Soviet and East European elites have of Eurocommunism.

Soviet Perceptions: Internal Debate in the USSR?

It is probably accurate to say that all Soviet leaders are somehow apprehensive about the already visible effects of Eurocommunism on Eastern Europe, although they probably differ in their assessments of whether Eurocommunism is likely in the long run to prove more beneficial, more costly, or outright dangerous to Soviet interests. They also take different views of how to deal with its impact in Eastern Europe.

Some of these differences about how to treat the dissenting West European parties have apparently persisted for some time. They seem to date from at least 1967 when, according to an eyewitness account, Secretary General Leonid Brezhnev implied that the Soviet leadership was divided over the issue of how to deal with the dissident West European Communist parties.[3] It became fairly obvious in the period 1974–1976, when preparations were under way for the Berlin Conference of European Communist Parties, that the gradual rise of Eurocommunism after the 1968 invasion of Czechoslovakia further exacerbated differences among Soviet leaders.[4] In December 1975 Berlinguer expressly called attention to certain "varying positions or at least varying nuances" in the Soviet press's commentaries on the issue of independent and pluralistic Communism in Western Europe. Berlinguer interpreted this as evidence that "there is a debate in progress even within the USSR."[5] This debate may have also been partially responsible for the noticeable but unexplained changes in Soviet policy in 1975 during the preparation of a collective document for the East Berlin Conference.

Needless to say, little is known about where individual Soviet officials stand on the issue of Eurocommunism. The very scattered evidence in open Soviet sources suggests that the most outspoken critics of the Eurocommunists include the First Secretary of the Belorussian Communist Party, P. M. Masherov, the First Secretary of the

Ukrainian Communist Party, V. V. Shcherbitskiy, and the Secretary of the Central Committee of the CPSU responsible for ideological problems, M. V. Zimyanin.[6] These officials are charged with internal, ideological responsibilities, which perhaps explains why they are especially dismayed by one facet of the Eurocommunist issue—its spillover into Eastern Europe and the Soviet Union itself. Indeed, Eurocommunism may embody a certain hope for nationalist elements in some of the non-Russian republics of the Soviet west and for reformist-minded intellectuals in the Soviet Union, such as R. Medvedev.[7]

Other Soviet officials, however, seem to have taken a somewhat more conciliatory approach toward the complicated phenomenon of Eurocommunism. Two examples are B. N. Ponomarev, the secretary of the Central Committee of the CPSU and candidate Politburo member, who supervises the International Department (whose main function is to conduct relations with nonruling Communist parties), and his deputy V. V. Zagladin, who is directly responsible for the West European section of the department. They have been somewhat more moderate in their approach toward West European Communist parties.[8] This is particularly true of Zagladin, who in the past three years has played an increasingly prominent role in Soviet relations with West European Communist parties. While advocating a cautious policy, Zagladin has implicitly questioned the wisdom of public criticism directed at the Eurocommunists by Bulgarian leader Todor Zhivkov and has suggested that the term Eurocommunism (which he claims was invented by Zbigniew Brzezinski) could be understood in different ways. As Zagladin further explained, "While the term is not exact, one cannot deny that the European Communist parties have shared characteristics, work under similar conditions and have to face and resolve similar problems."[9] The attitude of the International Department's high officials can be explained, at least partially, in terms of bureaucratic politics: they probably see Eurocommunism in the context of their functional responsibilities with nonruling Communist parties, and a break with the Eurocommunists—who are actually the International Department's main constituents—is to be avoided. These officials are, of course, also concerned about Eurocommunism's potentially dangerous effects upon Eastern Europe and the Soviet Union. But thus far these concerns apparently have been outweighed by the perceived long-term benefits of Eurocommunist advances in Italy and France.

As stated earlier, some of the foreign policy interests of the Eurocommunists coincide with those of the Soviets, such as their support for the revolutionary regimes and national liberation move-

ments of the Third World and their determination to limit the influence
of the United States and West Germany in Europe. There is probably
considerable hope in the International Department that a Eurocommunist ascension to power in Italy or France would, despite the long-
term dangers involved, be more detrimental to the United States than
to the Soviet Union because of its potentially destabilizing effects on
both the NATO alliance in the Mediterranean and the American presence in the rest of Europe. Thus, by skillful management, Eurocommunist victories could be turned to Soviet advantage.

Nevertheless, the trend toward independent, pluralistic socialism in
some West European Communist parties since the late 1960s has
greatly irritated Soviet leaders. Of course, in public they take a calm
and conciliatory view of the issue. Although this seems particularly
true in the case of CPSU Secretary General Brezhnev, it is obvious
from the scattered evidence that the private Brezhnev is no great
admirer of the West European Communist parties. As early as 1967,
an excited Brezhnev is reported by an eyewitness to have said in a
private conversation, "*K'chortu* [to the devil] with those parties that
set themselves up as our mentors!" According to the same source,
Brezhnev also stated that although the Soviet leadership can find "a
common language to discuss various questions of international politics with social democratic and even bourgeois regimes in Western
countries . . . communist parties and party leaders are always finding
different pretexts to swim against the tide."[10] At the historical Cierna
meeting in 1968, when Dubcek warned Brezhnev that a hard-line policy against Czechoslovakia would be condemned by West European
Communist parties, Brezhnev replied: "Whoever dares to do that, we
have the means of reducing to grouplets."[11]

In public, however, Brezhnev prefers to maintain a calm position
and to keep a relatively low profile on the issue, ever aware of his role
as broker or "balancer" among the various factions in the Politburo.
This may explain some of the visible shifts and inconsistencies in his
stand. These have ranged from the spectacular gesture of receiving
Konstantin Zaradov, the editor-in-chief of *Problemy mira i sotsializma* and author of several anti-Eurocommunist essays, in September 1975 when Eurocommunist protests against his articles were
at their peak, to his support for the conciliatory line the following
month. In November, he reversed his stance again and apparently
supported the hard line, but appeared to return to a conciliatory position after the Twenty-fifth Congress of the CPSU in February 1976.
Undoubtedly, some of these shifts, which occurred during preparations for the East Berlin Conference of European Communist Parties,
were also related to Brezhnev's bureaucratic and domestic interests in

connection with the forthcoming party congress. Perhaps the proposed compromises with the Eurocommunists were too bold to be
accepted shortly before it. At the congress itself, Brezhnev warned
the Eurocommunists not to ignore "proletarian internationalism," but
shortly afterward he went along with advocates of compromise with
the Eurocommunists.[12] Brezhnev's vacillation suggests that his stand
on the issue of Eurocommunism is much affected by the requirements
of his office and may change dramatically in the future, as may that of
the entire Politburo.

The East European Debate

Whereas signs regarding the internal debate in the Soviet Politburo
are still not completely clear, there is enough evidence available to
suggest that Eurocommunism has generated a serious debate among
and within the ruling elites in Eastern Europe. Two schools of thought
appear to have emerged. One is represented by the Romanian, and to
some degree, the Hungarian party leaders, who favor a more conciliatory policy toward the Eurocommunists. On the other hand, elements in the Czechoslovak, the Bulgarian, and, to some extent, the
East German leadership are very hostile and are unwilling to reconcile
themselves to this new kind of "revisionism."

Romania's leader, Nicolae Ceausescu, is not very happy about the
idea of democratic socialism, but he supports all parties striving for
more autonomy and independence from the Soviet Union. In Yugoslavia, Josip Tito views the Eurocommunists' opposition to Soviet
hegemony and their advocacy of a radical break with the "Stalinist
and dogmatic past" as positions that should be encouraged. Whereas
such leaders as V. Bilak in Czechoslovakia, Zhivkov in Bulgaria, and
to some degree, Erich Honecker in East Germany see Eurocommunism as a threat to their unpopular regimes, more liberal leaders,
such as Hungary's Janos Kadar, perceive Eurocommunism as holding
promise for the future. Zhivkov's stand on Eurocommunism is probably motivated by his fear that Eurocommunism may "infect" his
regime as Czechoslovak reformism did in 1968. Czechoslovak
hardliners, such as Bilak (the "famous Marxist theoretician," as the
Italian newspaper *L'Unità* ironically calls him), see Eurocommunism
not in terms of the sloppy, journalistic label perceived by some, but
rather as a sinister concept of "anti-communism and anti-Sovietism,"
in essence another form of Dubcekism. They fear that the "traitorous
and unprincipled" policies of the Eurocommunists, who support the
exiled Prague reformist leaders Jiri Pelikan and Zdenek Mlynar, might

help revive the 1968 Prague Spring, and thus they advocate a sharp course against the Eurocommunists, particularly the PCE.[13]

As one might expect, the East German regime is no less critical, but it often simply agrees with Soviet views without offering any comments of its own. At the same time there are signs that intraparty debates over Eurocommunism have been taking place among the East German and Czechoslovak ruling elites. Reportedly, the security factions (ideologists and security officials) in both leaderships have pushed for a harsh counteroffensive against the Eurocommunists.[14] In private, Polish leaders are probably more sympathetic than it appears because of the complex political and economic situation in Poland after June 1976 and possibly because of the ongoing factional struggle.

Like Czechoslovak reformism, Eurocommunism represents to Kadar and his reform-minded colleagues in the Hungarian leadership a boon to Budapest's policy of domestic flexibility and limited autonomy in foreign affairs. Despite severe public criticism by Soviet and East German ideologists, the quiet Hungarian economic reform, initiated in 1968, has managed to survive. Kadar has never conceded that Eurocommunism with democratic socialism and reforms appealed to him. When he was asked to comment on Bulgarian leader Zhivkov's public attack on Eurocommunism as "a new concept" involved with "anti-Sovietism" aimed at disuniting the Communist parties,[15] Kadar simply said, "I do not share this view. The parties in the West act within specific conditions and this should be taken into consideration."[16]

Whither the USSR and Eurocommunism:
Future Scenarios

As of fall 1979, Soviet and East European leaders have not reached any consensus on how to deal with the phenomenon of Eurocommunism. Indeed, a process of sharp differentiation on this issue was reported to have taken place during several meetings of Soviet and East European officials between 1976 and 1978.[17]

The unexpected attack on Carrillo, one of the most outspoken Eurocommunists, in *New Times* on June 16, 1977, marked a moment of acute crisis between the CPSU and the PCE, the most radical Eurocommunist party.[18] There is no doubt that the attack on Carrillo and his book *Eurocommunism and the State* almost two months after its appearance was the result of a calculated decision—a matter of "positive calculation," as the *New Times* editor-in-chief, M. Fedorov, called it. As Fedorov put it, "We did not want our stance to influence the elections in Spain."[19] In terms of timing, it does seem to have made more sense to attack Carrillo after the Spanish elections. (After all, Carrillo might have picked up a number of extra votes if *New Times* had attacked him earlier.) *New Times'* target, however, was not only Carrillo, but, through him, the Eurocommunist-oriented parties in general. Possibly the attack on Carrillo came as a result of pressures from Soviet and East European advocates of a hard-line policy toward Eurocommunism. Publication of Carrillo's book provided an excellent opportunity for this. Indeed, in many quarters the attack was seen as a move away from the "live and let live" compromise reached at East Berlin in June 1976 and toward a new offensive against the Eurocommunists.

Yet the wisdom of a public offensive against Eurocommunism seems to be questioned by advocates of a more conciliatory approach toward Eurocommunism in Eastern Europe and perhaps even in the USSR. For one thing, the Romanian and Yugoslav leaders sharply disagreed with the attacks on Eurocommunism. Kadar tacitly implied that he disagreed with those who advocated a total break with Eurocommunists.[20] In fact, Kadar went to Italy in June 1977, ostensibly as a guest of the Italian government. During his trip he met with Italian Communist leaders in what seems to have been a cautious gesture of support for the PCI. Polish leader Edward Gierek also met with Italian Communist officials during his visit to Italy in November 1977.

Significantly, other conciliatory voices were heard, even in Moscow. The Italian leader Gian Pajetta, who met in Moscow with Mikhail Suslov and International Department officials Ponomarev and CPSU secretary and Politburo member Zagladin, was assured that the attack on Carrillo did not reflect the "Soviet leadership's official position," and that "Soviet policy is not directed against the Spanish Communist Party and even less against other Communist parties in the West." Suslov, Ponomarev, and Zagladin made it clear to Pajetta that "they do want to rule out its being looked upon as the start of a campaign."[21]

In subsequent articles on Eurocommunism, *New Times* tried to mitigate the negative international effects produced by the attack on Carrillo. Although the first article was an open attack on the Eurocommunists, the second one did not even mention them. On the contrary, the journal, by now perhaps reflecting the conciliatory line, denied that it had ever meant to criticize the Eurocommunists. The third article, which was reprinted as a reply to an American reader who suggested that "Communist electoral victories in West European countries would in the long run create more problems for the Soviet bloc than for NATO," declared that the CPSU "has complete confidence in its class brother communists . . . of the developed countries," and that "the gossip about 'Moscow's annoyance' with West European communist parties is a pure figment of the imagination."[22]

These conciliatory voices from Moscow were accompanied in the political realm by equally conciliatory policies aimed at defusing the tension with the Eurocommunists. V. Pertsov, an official of the International Department, and V. Afanasyev, the editor-in-chief of *Pravda,* were sent to Madrid in October 1977 in an obvious attempt to smooth over relations with the PCE, which had been completely frayed after the attack on Carrillo. Presumably a kind of rapprochement between the PCE and CPSU was worked out during the visit. Carrillo was invited to Moscow for the October Revolution ceremony, where—it is said—Soviet officials had promised him the opportunity to deliver a short speech. When the time came for him to speak, however, he was not allowed to do so.[23]

In April 1978, in turn, Soviet officials Zagladin and Afanasyev led the Soviet delegation to the PCE congress and gave several public blessings to the PCE experimentation with its model of democratic socialism.[24] Thus far the treatment accorded the PCE and Carrillo himself seems to reflect uncertainties and perhaps even differing viewpoints among Soviet leaders. As Carrillo observed about his aborted appearance in Moscow, "There must be some kind of debate. . . . Otherwise, they simply would have told me right from the beginning they were not going to allow me to speak."[25]

Overall Soviet politics and the debate in the USSR and East European countries have only resulted in some selective attacks on the most outspoken of the Eurocommunist leaders, such as Carrillo. The question of whether Soviet attitudes and policies toward Eurocommunist-oriented parties will change in the future and if so how is still rather vague and uncertain at the end of 1979. For the moment, three different scenarios can be proposed with regard to this question: (1) reconciliation; (2) total break; and (3) continuation of the present cautious and selectively critical policy.

The scenario of reconciliation is based on the assumption that either the Eurocommunist-oriented parties or the CPSU would drastically alter its policies. This is very improbable, at least in the near future, particularly because there are some Soviet and East European officials who remain totally unreconciled to the issue of Eurocommunism. By the same token, the Eurocommunists, because of a variety of factors, the most important being domestic imperatives, can hardly denounce their Eurocommunist orientation or refrain from criticizing oppressive Soviet and East European domestic policies.

The indignation and violent criticism of the USSR by PCE, PCI, and some PCF officials after the trials of A. Shcharansky and A. Ginzburg in 1978 and the political trials in Czechoslovakia in October 1979 are cases in point. Some Soviet officials may be aware of the Soviet Union's increasing ideological, spiritual, and political isolation from the international Communist movement. Eurocommunism exacerbates this kind of isolation. Nevertheless, powerful elements in the Soviet Union and their counterparts in Eastern Europe—the so-called "security factions" (mainly in Czechoslovakia and East Germany) have probably been doing their utmost to prevent reaching any kind of meaningful *modus vivendi* with the Eurocommunists. Unless profound democratic reforms even greater than those witnessed during Nikita Khrushchev's de-Stalinization in the mid-1950s take place soon in the Soviet Union, a genuine rapprochement between the USSR and the Eurocommunist parties of the West seems highly unlikely.

Furthermore, it must be increasingly difficult for the Soviet leadership to swallow the growing criticism of its regime by radical Eurocommunists, such as PCE official Manuel Azcárate, who have referred to the Soviet Union as being "not really a socialist state" and have suggested that it should be transformed.[26] It would be rather naive to expect the Soviet leaders, even the most conciliatory ones, to approve these attacks or to accept quietly what they consider to be "excesses"—for instance, the absence of "class positions" on the part of PCE, PCI, and PCF representatives at symposiums devoted to Eurocommunism.[27] Overall, given the peculiar development of Eurocommunism and the Soviet and East European response to it, a genuine Soviet-Eurocommunist rapprochement is fairly unlikely.

The Eurocommunist parties of the West would view an unselective Soviet polemic against them as a hostile counteroffensive. Such a discussion could also lead to the deepening of the Eurocommunist alliance in Western Europe and thereby have many detrimental consequences for the Soviet Union. Inevitably it would lead to a rupture with some of the West European Communist parties. One factor to be considered is whether the Soviets would be willing to become deeply involved in a hostile offensive against the Eurocommunists when their relations with another ideological contestant—China—are worse than ever, and relations with a United States administration that actively pursues a human rights policy are very unclear. The prospect of involvement in an ideological and political struggle on two fronts is probably seen in the Kremlin as nothing short of a nightmare. There are fears in the Kremlin that the polemic with the Eurocommunists might indeed lead to an inevitable split, which in turn would be exploited by anti-Soviet forces in the West as well as by China. Discussion with the Eurocommunists, Politburo member Suslov has warned, "should not lead to the opening of 'loopholes'" and the class enemy "should not be given the opportunity to use such discussion to promote his own interests."[28]

In the Soviet bureaucracies, it appears that the advocates of a conciliatory approach try to discourage their colleagues from making the kind of frontal assaults on the Eurocommunists that could lead to a total break. To this end they have even shown, as Zagladin sometimes has, "some kind of respect" for Eurocommunist positions.[29] By the same token, it appears that even the most radical elements among the Eurocommunists are not interested, at least for the moment, in a total break with the Soviet and East European regimes. Extreme criticism of these regimes and outright support of the dissidents and reformists there would inevitably precipitate such a break. This could in turn lead to the imposition of more rigid controls by hard-line elements in Eastern Europe, spoil Soviet relations with the West, and even bring about a return to the Cold War. Détente made Eurocommunism possible, and thus the Cold War is undesirable. The Eurocommunist parties (in varying degrees) and the Soviet Union share some important foreign policy interests. Moreover, there are probably elements in the Soviet leadership who view Eurocommunism as creating *secondary risks* and *primary opportunities* for the USSR. For them, at least over the short term, the benefits exceed the costs. In spite of the risks involved—primarily the possibility of destabilization in some of the East European regimes—these conciliatory elements have thus far been able to prevent the adoption of hard-line policies that would completely alienate the Eurocommunists. A clash with the Eurocommunists may be inevitable, as Soviet leader Ponomarev was reported to say, but at the present moment nothing must be done to hasten its onset.[30] Thus, a break with the Eurocommunists in the near future appears to be rather unlikely.

Following a period of extreme concern, which climaxed in a brief although acute crisis in summer 1977, Soviet leaders realized that Eurocommunism is not a general trend affecting all West European Communist parties at the same time or in the same way. Consequently, it does not require a general response. Since this time Soviet policy toward the Eurocommunist-oriented parties has been a very cautious one, clearly designed to avoid the extremes of either reconciliation or total break in relations. Soviet leaders have chosen to deal with the Eurocommunist parties individually and to restrict their public attacks to only the most radical leaders in the most vulnerable Eurocommunist party, such as the PCE's Carrillo and Azcárate.[31] Soviet leaders have carefully refrained from publicly criticizing the somewhat less radical and much less vulnerable Communist parties of Italy and France and their respective leaders. In fact, Soviet relations with the PCI and the PCF suggest that they do not want to push matters to the point of rupture. In contrast to the treatment accorded Carrillo, Berlinguer and the PCF's Paul Laurent were allowed to give speeches at the October Revolution ceremony in Moscow in 1977. Moreover, although Berlinguer's and Laurent's views certainly could not have pleased the Soviet leadership, they were nevertheless reprinted in the Soviet press.[32] In the same vein, the PCI's domestic politics have so far had a rather positive reception in the Soviet press.[33]

This does not mean, of course, that actual Soviet policies toward the PCI and the PCF have been as supportive as their public pronouncements seem to indicate. After all, not permitting Berlinguer and Laurent to speak might have been interpreted not only as a frontal assault upon Eurocommunism, but also as a tacit admission that the two most powerful Communist parties in Western Europe were pursuing heretical policies. Thus the treatment of Carrillo might have been intended as a kind of indirect warning to PCI and PCF leaders. Carrillo was obviously the easier target because his party, with the support of only 9 percent of the voters in the 1977 election, was not close to becoming a "government party" as the PCI has been since the 1976 elections, or as the PCF may be in the future. Furthermore, Carrillo was much more audacious in his criticism of the USSR and in his encouragement of dissidents in Eastern Europe than were other Communist leaders. (PCI criticism is much more cautious, and the PCF leadership is generally silent.)

Though the Soviets probably do not view most of the PCF leaders as being genuinely "Eurocommunist" in their orientation, their behavior toward this party has also been quite ambiguous during the last several years. In 1974 François Mitterrand had high hopes of winning the French presidential elections as the candidate of the Union of the Left, which included both the Socialist and the Communist parties. During the campaign, however, the Soviet ambassador to Paris, S. Chervonenko, paid a well-publicized last-minute pre-election visit to the Center-Right candidate, Giscard d'Estaing, a gesture widely regarded as Soviet endorsement of Giscard d'Estaing at the expense of the PCF's candidate. Alain Peyrefitte, French Minister of Cultural Affairs, explicitly confirms the hostility of the Soviet leadership to Mitterand and the socialist-Communist coalition and gives a plausible explanation for it. According to Peyrefitte, Chervonenko called on him as well, and told him, as a Gaullist official, that "I am instructed to tell you that *we* would welcome the victory of *your* candidate,"

Jacques Chaban-Delmas, and that if Chaban-Delmas were eliminated in the first round of voting, that they would welcome the victory of Giscard d'Estaing rather than Mitterand.[34] As the conversation went on, the reasons for this surprising hostility to Mitterand became clear. Chervonenko explained, in Peyrefitte's words, that "General de Gaulle established a political course characterized by independence and cooperation. . . . Were François Mitterand to come to power, who—beginning with Mitterand himself—could say what would happen? One prefers the certainty of a known line to the uncertainties of chance." Peyrefitte felt Chervonenko feared "things would skid out of control [le dérapage incontrôlé]" if Mitterand were elected.

> If he won, the candidate supported by the French Communist Party would find himself confronted by a situation which was very likely to escape him, his allies and everyone. An unforeseeable series of reactions could be produced, among them 'Reaction itself,' which could tip France toward an American protectorate. The balance of Europe and the world could be upset. The results could be just the opposite of what one would expect from a Socialist-Communist victory.

In comparison to such risks, the victory of a man who would assure the continuity of French policy would guarantee the Soviet Union against fearsome serendipity.[35]

Soviet behavior prior to France's general elections of March 1978 was similarly ambiguous. Whereas Brezhnev deliberately avoided meeting French Communist leader Marchais from the 1976 Berlin Conference of Communist Parties until January 1980, he gave a very friendly reception in September 1977 to French premier and chief economic advisor to President Giscard d'Estaing, Raymond Barre. Moreover, Soviet diplomats stationed in Paris were uneasy about the prospects of the PCF coming to power and were rumored to favor a leftist defeat in the March 1978 election. While remaining aloof from the election issue, the Soviet media also seemed to hint at some displeasure with the Eurocommunist wing of the PCF and after the election attacked one of its leading theoreticians, Jean Elleinstein, a deputy director of the Marxist Study and Research Center of the Central Committee.[36] This attack was synchronized with the ongoing post-election debate between the orthodox and Eurocommunist wings of the PCF.

In fact, contrary to public pronouncements, the Soviets have, in the last decade, provided political and economic support, albeit somewhat selective and cautious, for pro-Soviet and anti-Eurocommunist elements in several of the more vulnerable West European parties.

Since the Czechoslovak invasion of 1968, the Soviets have successfully supported, by economic and political means, the expulsion
of the Eurocommunist-oriented leaders of the Austrian Communist
party (Ernst Fischer and Franz Marek), have encouraged the latent
schism within the Finnish Communist party, and, by securing a pro-
Soviet majority, have deepened the split within the Greek Communist
party.

During 1969–1974, the Soviets provided financial assistance for
anti-Eurocommunist elements in a group operating around General
Enrique Líster of the PCE (Líster calls Eurocommunism "Euroopper-
tunism"),[37] and the newly formed Swedish Workers' party-
Communist, which broke away from the Eurocommunist-oriented
Swedish Left party-Communist in March 1977.[38] The Soviets may
have also encouraged a similar break in the Communist party of Great
Britain in the summer of 1976. There the new Communist party of
Great Britain was created by a minority group that refused to follow
the Eurocommunist-oriented program of the existing party.

To be sure, there have not been any reports of Soviet efforts to
undermine the present leaderships of the largest and least vulnerable
Eurocommunist party—the PCI. Nevertheless, Soviet success in
splintering the more vulnerable West European Communist
parties—Greek and Swedish—might well be meant as a veiled warning to Berlinguer. When two Soviet editors of *Pravda*'s West European department were asked in a private conversation by Italian
newspaperman A. Gambino about Berlinguer's statement that he felt
more at ease building Italian socialism in a Western country that belongs to NATO rather than to the Warsaw Pact, they reportedly responded in the following manner:

> The words of Berlinguer constitute a rather strong move on the part
> of a communist leader. We are convinced that the Italian com-
> munists do not agree with them. Everyone would do well to recall
> the fate of Hermansson, former leader of the Swedish Communist
> Party. He was the real inventor of Eurocommunism. He was the
> first to make capital himself out of anti-Sovietism: for instance, by
> leading the protest demonstration in front of the Soviet Embassy in
> Stockholm in the summer of 1968. By so doing he maybe succeeded
> in gaining the support and the votes of part of the petite
> bourgeoisie, but he lost the trust of the working class. The party
> under his leadership split in two and he no longer counts for
> anything.[39]

Needless to say, it remains to be seen if this cautious, calm, and
ambiguously selective support of the most radical opponents of the

Eurocommunists will satisfy (and if so, for how long) the more hard-line elements in the Soviet leadership and their transnational allies in Eastern Europe who may still believe that, even over the short term, Eurocommunism confronts the USSR and Eastern Europe with *primary dangers* and *secondary payoffs*.

Conclusions

While the fashionable use of the term "Eurocommunism" may soon pass, the trend towards independent, pluralistic socialism in several West European Communist parties will likely continue. Whether called Eurocommunism or not, the trend presents a serious dilemma, not only to the United States but also to the Soviet Union. On the eve of the 1980s, it is impossible to determine whether the short- and long-term effects of Eurocommunism will prove costly or more beneficial to either superpower.

The results of the French and Italian elections in 1978–1979 meant a temporary setback for Eurocommunism, but it did not entirely remove the serious dilemma facing the USSR. The continuous attacks on important Eurocommunist leaders and theoreticians, such as Azcárate and Elleinstein, and the support of anti-Eurocommunist-oriented groups in various parties attest to the dilemma's powerful and persistent influence. Indeed, some of the perceptions (many exaggerated) of the political spillover effects of Eurocommunism have already produced a debate among East European and perhaps Soviet leaders as to how to cope with this new dilemma.

It is still too soon to draw any definitive conclusions about the outcome of this debate or about the long-term Soviet policy toward Eurocommunist-oriented parties. Thus far the existing cleavages regarding the issue of Eurocommunism in the Soviet Union and in Eastern Europe have produced a curious mixture of restraint, tolerance, and a relaxed attitude on the one hand and a policy of selective attacks on the other. Of the three scenarios presented here, it seems that the third, which sees Soviet policy toward the Eurocommunist parties of Western Europe continuing along its current course, is the most likely to materialize. Should the Soviet leadership decide to repress an unforeseen liberalization of an East European regime, however, or to exercise inadmissable pressure on Yugoslavia after Tito's death, this would certainly cement the unity of the Eurocommunist-oriented parties on an anti-Soviet basis and almost certainly facilitate a total break with the CPSU. Also, should one of the Eurocommunist parties, say for example the PCI, become unexpectedly a member of a government coalition, this could lead to the development of an entirely new situation and the increasing likelihood of open conflict with the CPSU. The future uncertainties notwithstanding, Eurocommunism, despite its ambiguities, is no myth. It may continue to be a serious dilemma, not only for the United States but also for the USSR. Carrillo was perhaps right when he asserted after his June 1978 meeting with Berlinguer in Barcelona that "Eurocommunism exists and is a reality, no matter what the Americans and the Soviets may think about it."[40]

NOTES

A shorter version of this article appeared in *Political Quarterly* (London) in April 1980. The author wishes to express his gratitude to his wife Virginia and to Vernon Aspaturian and David Burke for their useful suggestions, and to Diana Noble and Irene Dixon for their assistance in preparation of this manuscript.

1. Speech of Bruno Kreisky at the Twenty-fourth Congress in Vienna, *Arbeiter Zeitung* (Vienna), May 20, 1978. For a study on the origins of Eurocommunism and its effects in Eastern Europe, see Jiri Valenta, "Eurocommunism and Eastern Europe," *Problems of Communism* (March-April 1978), pp. 41–54.

2. *Corriere della Sera*, June 15, 1976 and *La Stampa* (Turin), July 14, 1979.

3. Erwin Weit, *At the Red Summit: Interpreter Behind the Iron Curtain* (New York: Macmillan, 1973), p. 139. Erwin Weit served as interpreter to Polish leader Wladyslaw Gomulka and now lives in the West.

4. For example, whereas the Soviet periodical *Partiinaia zhizn* (Moscow) sharply criticized Spanish Communist leader Manuel Azcárate in February 1974, *Pravda* several months later published a favorable commentary on the meeting with the Spanish leadership. See *Partiinaia zhizn* (February 1974), pp. 54–63, and *Pravda*, October 16, 1974.

5. *L'Unità* (Rome), December 12, 1975.

6. See P. M. Masherov's speech at the Twenty-fourth Congress of the CPSU, *Pravda*, April 1, 1971, and a rebuff of the Italian Communist official Giuseppe Boffa in *Rinascità* (Rome), April 9, 1971. See also even more explicit attacks by P. M. Masherov at the CPSU Twenty-fifth Congress, *Pravda*, February 26, 1976, and after the Berlin Conference, *Pravda*, October 2, 1976. For V. V. Shcherbitskiy's direct attack on "Eurocommunism" as a concept through which the "class enemy" seeks to disrupt the unity of the Communist movement, see *Pravda Ukrainy* (Kiev), July 28, 1978. For M. V. Zimyanin's view, see *Pravda*, April 23, 1977.

7. See an interview with R. Medvedev, *Cambio 16* (Madrid), July 11–17, 1977.

8. For B. N. Ponomarev's views, see *Pravda*, April 28, 1977, and B. N. Ponomarev, "The Cohesion of Communism Is the Right Way to Success for the Cause of Peace and Socialism," *World Marxist Review*, no. 7 (June 1977). For Zagladin's views, see *Pravda*, April 20, June 20, 1976. Vadim Zagladin, "Creator of a New Civilization," *New Times*, no. 18 (April 1976), pp. 4–6; *Pravda*, June 2, 1977; and Radio Moscow, April 22, 1978, reported in Foreign Broadcast Information Service, *Daily Report, USSR*, April 23, 1978.

9. See an interview with V. Zagladin, *L'Espresso* (Rome), December 26, 1976.

10. Erwin Weit, *At the Red Summit*, pp. 138, 140.

11. Roger Garaudy, *Die ganze Wahrheit oder für einen Kommunism ohne Dogma* (Reinbeck beim Hamburg: Rowolt Taschenbuch Verlag, 1970), p. 123. Roger Garaudy was a PCF Politburo member in 1968 who was expelled from the party because of his opposition to the invasion of Czechoslovakia.

12. For a contrast to Leonid Brezhnev's hard-line speech at the CPSU Twenty-fifth Congress (*Pravda*, February 25, 1976), see his conciliatory speech at the East Berlin Conference (*Neues Deutschland*, July 1, 1976).

13. For V. Bilak's view on Eurocommunism, see *Le Monde*, April 1, 1977; *Rude Pravo* (Prague), June 18, 1977; and *CTK* (Prague), April 27, 1977.

14. In the East German leadership, the so-called "security faction," composed of chief ideologist Kurt Hager and the Central Committee secretary responsible for foreign relations, Herman Axen, reportedly favored a much harder policy toward Eurocommunism than party chief Erick Honecker. Similarly, in Czechoslovakia, Bilak and his supporters in the political leadership and some top officials of the secret service favored a much harsher policy toward Eurocommunists and dissidents than party chief Husak. See reports in *Der Spiegel*, August 1, 1977, p. 19; Jiri Pelikan in *L'Espresso*, March 27, 1977; and H. Hager's speech, *Neues Deutschland* (Berlin), April 29–30, 1978.

15. T. Zhivkov, "Year of Peace and Year of Struggle," *World Marxist Review* (December 1977). For his views see also *Neues Deutschland*, June 30, 1976, and *Rabotnicheskoe Delo* (Sofia), December 1, 1977. T. Zhivkov's views received a sharp response by the PCI. See *L'Unità*, December 3, 1976.

16. Reported by all Western news agencies, December 7, 1976.

17. See reports in *Nin* (Belgrade), December 26, 1976; *Frankfurter Algemeine Zeitung*, March 21, 1977; *Le Monde*, April 1, 1977; and Radio Prague, December 28, 1978, as reported in FBIS, *Daily Report, Eastern Europe*, December 29, 1978.

18. "Contrary to the Interests of Peace and Socialism in Europe," *New Times*, no. 21 (June 1977), pp. 9–13.

19. *ANSNA* (Rome), July 13, 1977, as reported in FBIS, *Daily Report, Western Europe*, July 17, 1978.

20. See an interview with Kadar, *Frankfurter Rundshau*, June 30, 1977.

21. Gian Pajetta, "Talks in the Kremlin," *Corriere della Sera*, July 5, 1977; and *L'Unità*, July 4, 1977, (Pajetta is a PCI secretariat member.)

22. "Putting the Record Straight," *New Times*, no. 28 (July 7, 1977), and ibid., no. 29 (July 14, 1977). *Pravda*'s authoritative editorial of September 10, 1977, went even further in its commentary, denying that the CPSU is fearful of Eurocommunism. "This statement," as *Pravda* put it, "is designed for political idiots." The CPSU supports the "possibility and inevitability of various ways of advancing towards socialism, as was shown by the Berlin Conference."

23. Interview with V. Pertsov, *La Vanguardia* (Barcelona), September 13, 1977; and an interview with Santiago Carrillo, *Le Nouvel Observateur* (Paris), October 24–30, 1977, pp. 63–64. *TASS* explained that Carrillo did not speak at the ceremony because he arrived too late. Then, according to *TASS*, he was offered the opportunity to speak at a separate ceremony elsewhere, with the assurance that his speech would be published. However, he declined. *TASS*'s version does not seem credible, because Carrillo in fact attended the Kremlin ceremony.

24. See Zagladin's remarks, Moscow television, April 22, 1977, as reported in FBIS, *Daily Report, USSR*, April 22, 1977, and a series of interviews with V. Afanasyev in *Mundo Obrero* (Madrid), April 27–May 3, 1978.

25. *New York Times*, November 4, 1977.

26. For elucidation of this point, see the attack on the official of the PCE, Manual Azcárate, in B. Andreyev, "Playing up to Imperialist Anti-Soviet Propaganda," *New Times*, no. 3 (January 1978), pp. 12–14. Also see Azcárate's response toward Soviet attacks on Eurocommunism, "The USSR against dissidents and Eurocommunists," *Wiener Tagebuch* (Vienna), no. 11 (January 1979), pp. 26–29.

27. See a criticism of O. Nikiforov, "'Eurocommunism' through the Eyes of Anticommunists," *Sotsialisticheskaia Industria* (Moscow) (December 13, 1977), p. 5.

28. M. Suslov. "Marxism-Leninism and the Revolutionary Renovation of the World," *Kommunist* (Moscow), no. 14 (September 1977), pp. 13–18.

29. For an appreciation of Zagladin's position, see an interview with Pajetta, *Corriere della Sera*, November 8, 1977. Zagladin, however, also shows some criticism. See criticism of one of Zagladin's articles on Eurocommunism in *L'Unità*, November 7, 1978.

30. Reported by *Le Monde*, April 1, 1977.

31. Again, as in the case of Carrillo, *New Times*, in the subsequent issue, temporarily narrowed the focus of its attack on Eurocommunism to anti-Soviet charges by Azcárate. A. B., "Why This Distortion of the Truth," *New Times*, no. 6 (February 1978), pp. 10–11.

32. Enrico Berlinguer, among others, stated that the PCI was seeking to establish "a new socialist society which will guarantee all personal and collective, civic and religious freedoms, the non-ideological nature of the state and the possibility of different parties and pluralism in public, cultural and ideological life." *Pravda*, November 4, 1977.

33. See, for example, V. Yermakov, "The Face of Crisis," *New Times*, no. 41 (October 1977), pp. 20–22, and G. Smirnov, "Antonio Gramsci: Toward the Common Goal in the Joint Struggle," *New Times*, no. 40 (October 1, 1977), pp. 18–19.

34. See Alain Peyrefitte, *Le Mal Français* (Paris: Plon, 1976) p. 433.

35. Ibid.

36. See hints in "Crisis and Elections," *New Times* (February 3, 1978), and a critical response in *L'Humanité*, February 4, 1978. For an attack on Jean Elleinstein, see "Back to Eduard Berstein?: Elleinstein Discards the Mask," *New Times*, no. 22 (May 1978), pp. 14–15.

37. Z. R., "Carrillo Slandering Hero of Civil War," *Rudé Právo*, November 11, 1977.

38. For a discussion of limited Soviet contacts with the Swedish Left party-Communist, see a statement by Soviet official V. Shaposhnikov, *Svenska Dagbladet* (Stockholm), November 4, 1977, also reported in FBIS, *Daily Report, Western Europe*, November 18, 1977. For a veiled Soviet criticism of the Left party-Communist, see *TASS*, April 7, 1977.

39. See Antonio Gambino, "Visit to the USSR. Careful! Ice Moving," *L'Espresso*, January 22, 1978.

40. Radio Rome, June 13, 1978, reported in FBIS, *Daily Report, Western Europe*, June 13, 1978.

CHAPTER VI

Eurocommunism and Poland

Andrzej Korbonski

This chapter examines the relationship between Eurocommunism and Poland's foreign and domestic politics. At first glance the task appears fairly simple and straightforward. A closer look, however, reveals several caveats that ought to be mentioned before analyzing this relationship in greater detail.

The first caveat concerns the meaning of the concept of Eurocommunism. Seldom in the recent past has there been so much confusion about a single idea or term, and even today unambiguous definitions are hard to find. This is a rather unsatisfactory state of affairs, especially when dealing with a phenomenon that has been described as one that "may prove to be the most potent foreign stimulus to have affected Eastern Europe since the convulsion produced by de-Stalinization in the mid-1950s."[1]

The confusion centers not only on the intrinsic meaning of Eurocommunism—its program and objectives—but also on its place in, or relation to, the larger concept of the international Communist movement. In other words, there is still no agreement as to whether Eurocommunism represents a radical departure from the basic principles of Marxism-Leninism, which, until relatively recently, have elicited significant consensus among Communist parties throughout the world. Some observers insist that it does, while others believe that it does not. The latter see it either as a purely tactical maneuver by the local West European parties in search of legitimacy and electoral support, or as a clever move directed, aided, and abetted by Moscow for the purpose of further weakening the fabric of some Western societies that have been showing signs of wear and tear. This is not the place to discuss this particular problem, which deserves a separate treatment. It is mentioned here mainly as one of the underlying characteristics that condition the impact of Eurocommunism on Polish internal politics.

The second warning refers to the general question of the impact of exogenous variables on internal political processes. The growth of scholarly interest in the ideas of dependence, interdependence, and dependency with respect to the Third World was soon followed by attempts to apply these concepts to Eastern Europe and its relations with the outside. Efforts to conceptualize the transmission of influence ''across systems'' were accompanied by attempts to identify agents, channels, and targets of penetration, and to produce specific cases of foreign influences affecting the process of political and socio-economic change in the region.[2] While some progress has been made in this respect, we still know relatively little about the process of influence transmission and have to engage in speculation and informed guessing.

The same applies to the third area of concern—the actual process of political decision-making. As is well known, decision-making in Communist systems still tends to be shrouded in secrecy, and the only information available is derived from the study of decisions or policy outputs. Knowledge of policy inputs in Communist societies is highly limited, and here again we are forced to rely on impressions and intuition.

Despite these caveats, it is possible to discuss the interaction between Eurocommunism and Polish politics in a meaningful fashion. I shall start by looking at the relationship historically, bringing the story up to the mid-1970s. This will be followed by a discussion of the impact, if any, of Eurocommunism on contemporary Polish politics, with emphasis on internal systematic change. I shall then focus on Polish foreign policy, including the country's relations with the Soviet Union and the other countries in the region. Finally, I will summarize the conclusions and attempt to answer the question of whether or not Eurocommunism—however defined—has had a major impact on the conduct of Poland's internal and external policies.

I

A good case can be made that Polish Communism has been, over the years, highly sensitive to outside influences. In part this has undoubtedly been because throughout its history Poland, if only due to its geographical location, has been on the receiving end of foreign pressures. The country has traditionally been an object rather than a subject in international politics. During most of the nineteenth century it was not even on the map—at a time when many countries in

Europe were going through a process of rapid and radical change. Although Poland may have periodically influenced its immediate neighbors, it has, by and large, been strongly influenced by either the West or the East.

The above phenomenon greatly affected the entire Polish political system, including the political parties of various hues, all of which tended to reflect outside influences with regard to their programs and institutional structures. While this was particularly true with respect to the parties on the extreme ends of the political spectrum, it also applied to the parties of the traditional center. At the same time, however, the different parties also embodied another distinctive feature of Polish political culture—a rather fierce nationalism, so characteristic of peoples striving for independence. Even after the proclamation of independence in November 1918 nationalist feelings remained strong. The country's frontiers and its location between Germany and the Soviet Union did not guarantee much security, and its future appeared uncertain.

Therefore, together with the rest of Polish polity, the various parties have been exposed and subjected both to foreign influences and internal, highly nationalistic pressures. The Polish Communist party has been no exception in this case, and its entire sixty-year history has mirrored the conflict between these two tendencies.

The Polish Communist party (KPP) offers a good example of this conflict. Right from the start it tended to swing from one extreme to the other and, partly because of this, it never succeeded in developing a large following or a profile of its own.[3] Throughout the interwar period it was probably more rent with dissension than any other member of the Comintern; it may be speculated that this was one of the factors that contributed to the party's calamitous dissolution on Stalin's orders in 1938.[4]

There is no doubt that the destruction of the KPP—unique in the annals of international Communism—left an indelible mark on Polish Communists, not only on the leadership, but also on the rank and file. It most likely strengthened nationalist tendencies among the survivors of the destroyed party. Deep down they refused to accept the official explanation for the dissolution, even though on the surface they had to obey and conform to Stalin's edict. To put it differently, the veterans of the prewar party, without admitting it openly, saw themselves as victims of an international conspiracy, and this belief left a residue of bitterness that influenced the character of the party recreated in January 1942.[5]

While knowledge of the early history of the Polish Workers party (PPR) still has some gaps, the basic trends in its development have been discussed in the literature, and there is no need to recapitulate the main arguments.[6] Suffice it to say that the new party, formed as it was under the German occupation, tried from the very beginning to present a patriotic image and to maintain a low profile vis-à-vis Moscow in order to become a part of national resistance and to attract genuine popular support. The fact that the PPR failed on all counts testified to the inherent weakness of the new party, a lesson not lost on the so-called "native" wing, and its leader, Wladyslaw Gomulka.

The period 1944–1947, between the formation of the Polish Committee of National Liberation (the "Lublin Committee") in July 1944 and the establishment of the Cominform in September 1947, may be viewed as crucial in PPR history. It coincided, of course, with the process of the seizure of power by the Communists, who in the course of the takeover were forced, for the first time, to articulate openly their ideology and program.

Anyone comparing the statements made by various Eurocommunist leaders in the middle and late 1970s with those uttered by the Polish Communists thirty years earlier is bound to be struck by their similarity: both emphasize democracy and pluralism, deny the validity of such basic tenets of Marxism-Leninism as the dictatorship of the proletariat and the class struggle, question the necessity of emulating the Soviet model, and stress the unique aspects of their own national blueprint for building socialism.[7]

Then, as now, the question was raised whether such statements represented purely a tactical move aimed at allaying popular fears and suspicions and at portraying the Polish party as largely independent of Moscow, or whether they truly reflected the views and attitudes of the PPR leaders. From a perspective of three decades it may be hypothesized that the ideological and programmatic declarations were a mixture of both, traditional pro-Soviet sympathies and deeply rooted nationalist tendencies, with the latter probably in ascendance. Therefore, it is not surprising that the same individuals responsible for making these statements were soon thereafter branded as Titoists and national deviationists and summarily removed from high party offices after June 1948.

During the heyday of Stalinism (1948–1953) the Polish party, together with the other parties in the region, ostensibly emulated the Soviet model. But even in this period it managed to steer its own course, which was both less oppressive and more relaxed than elsewhere in Eastern Europe. This was as true in the political as in the economic arena: Poland had hardly any political trials and also made very slow progress on the road to agricultural collectivization, considered a touchstone of conformity to the Stalinist model. One

possible reason for this deviation from the norm may have been the
December 1948 merger of the PPR and the Polish Socialist party. Despite far-reaching purges, the new union was bound to strengthen
nationalist elements in the new Polish United Workers party (PZPR).
Ultimately all this meant that, on the eve of the radical changes in the
international Communist movement following Stalin's death, Poland
not only had an alternative leadership waiting in the wings to take
over but also had not succeeded in bringing an important segment of
society under party control.

Not much needs to be said about 1956, the *annus mirabilis* in the
history of international Communism. In the context of this discussion
its importance lay primarily in the exposure of various East European
countries for the first time in many years to influences emanating from
external environments and sources other than the Soviet Union, specifically China and Yugoslavia, and to some extent Western Europe.
Soon thereafter the Communist movement embraced the concept of
"polycentrism," which meant that Moscow lost its monopoly of doctrinal wisdom. It also meant the unofficial yet unmistakable recognition by the Kremlin of the doctrine of "many roads to socialism."
This, in turn, allowed the various Communist countries in Eastern
Europe to seek support, advice, and solutions in other countries and
parties. In the case of Poland it was primarily China, rather than
Yugoslavia or Western Europe, that provided key support during the
crucial period of late 1956 and early 1957 when Gomulka, freshly returned to power, found himself largely isolated within the Communist
bloc and under attack from various parties, including the French.[8]

This was a difficult period for the Polish party, and it may be speculated that one of its consequences was to strengthen certain latent
tendencies that came to the surface some twenty years later. One of
them was nationalism, now combined with a strong dose of
xenophobia and suspiciousness directed at other members of the international Communist camp. Even though Gomulka eventually
developed close personal ties with Nikita Khrushchev and later with
Leonid Brezhnev, there is evidence that throughout the 1960s and
1970s the PZPR has remained largely alienated from other parties in
the region, except for the Hungarian. Although by November 1957 the
Poles lost the support of the Chinese and were forced to acknowledge
once again the primacy of Moscow in the world Communist camp,
they continued to resist strongly the idea of a formal international
Communist organization. The memories of the Comintern were still
too painful to be forgotten.[9]

The other by-product of the Polish road to socialism that com-
plemented and reinforced the nationalistic tendencies was the growing
domestic unrest, especially among party intellectuals and the youth.

Here again the story is well known. The intellectual ferment had already existed prior to 1956 and reached its peak in 1957, when it had
to be suppressed by a party concerned with the rapid growth of revisionist thinking.[10] Dissent surfaced again a few years later in the
well-known Kuron-Modzelewski letter, which can be seen as the pre-
cursor of similar declarations produced by the Polish dissidents of the
1970s.[11] By 1966 the protests became more widespread and led to the
dismissal of several Warsaw University professors. The protests
reached their apogee in March 1968, which witnessed not only an
outburst of student riots but also the beginning of an anti-Semitic and
anti-intellectual witch hunt conducted by the ultra-nationalistic wing
in the party. The behavior of the Polish oligarchy reached its nadir
during the Czechoslovak crisis in the summer of 1968.[12]

Without going into much detail, it may be shown that the basic
ideological foundations of Polish revisionist and dissident thinking
were laid in the mid-1950s. Already in July 1956, some two decades
before the emergence of Eurocommunism, the Central Committee of
the Polish party approved a resolution that stated, among other
things, the following:

> The problem of the consolidation of socialist legality constitutes
> an integral part of the entire process of democratization of the coun-
> try. . . . The problem of full observance and strengthening of
> legality should be the subject of the constant concern of the entire
> Party and of all organs of people's power. Party organizations
> should show an uncompromising attitude with regard to any man-
> ifestation of abuse of power, with regard to injustice and wrongs
> suffered by citizens; they should combat with all determination in-
> fringements of law and stand guard over the equality of citizens
> before the law.[13]

and that

> The development of free, bold, and matter-of-fact criticism . . . at
> meetings and in the columns of the press is an indispensable pre-
> requisite of the democratization of the country's life, the most ef-
> fective means of combating deficiencies, errors and bureaucratic
> distortions. An indispensable condition of democratization is the
> openness of political life.[14]

It may be presumed that these statements would be perfectly acceptable to most Eurocommunists today.

In October 1956 the same Central Committee declared that

> The relations among Parties and states . . . should be based on
> mutual trust and equality of rights, on mutual assistance, on mutual

friendly criticism whenever necessary, on reasonable settling of all
controversial matters in the spirit of friendship and socialism.
Within the framework of such relations each country should pos-
sess full independence and sovereignty, and the right of each nation
to sovereign government in an independent country should be fully
and mutually respected.[15]

Again, this view is not likely to be faulted today by most leaders of
West European Communist parties.

In the economic sphere, Polish scholars and theoreticians were also
the first to raise the banner of revisionism, questioning the basic
tenets and assumptions of Stalinist economic theory and practice.[16]
Long before the Czechoslovak and Hungarian reforms of the 1960s,
Oskar Lange, Michal Kalecki, and Wlodzimierz Brus suggested new
models and blueprints of socialist economy. Even though their efforts
failed in Poland, their ideas were at least partly embraced by reformers elsewhere in the region.[17]

Apart from the Kuron-Modzelewski letter, which represented a
comprehensive attack on the post-1956 Polish political system, Marxist philosophers such as Leszek Kolakowski and Adam Schaff challenged some fundamental assumptions of Marxist ideology and paid
for it by being removed from their official and party positions. It is
probably no exaggeration to say that most of the intellectual ferment
of the 1960s, which culminated in the paroxysm of spring 1968, was
fueled by Marxists increasingly alienated from the political reality of
people's Poland. By the early 1970s many of the most vocal revisionists had left the country and settled in Western Europe, finding a
sympathetic reception among the local Communist parties.[18]

II

The PZPR entered the 1970s in a state of considerable disarray. The
December 1970 workers' riots on the Baltic coast, which brought
about the ouster of Gomulka and the accession of Edward Gierek,
could not help but create powerful shock and confusion. The impact
was strongest among the party elites, but it was also felt within the
rank and file. Both echelons could see for themselves the widespread
bankruptcy and corruption of the system. Moreover, the scars caused
by the March 1968 purges were far from healed, which meant that
many of the intellectuals remained alienated from the regime and
looked with considerable suspicion upon the new leadership. The
economic situation showed no signs of improvement, which in turn
did little to reduce the antagonism of both the workers and the peas-

ants. It was clear that only drastic policy changes could break the vicious cycle of inertia and immobilism.

In the international arena the situation looked more promising. Poland was not deeply involved emotionally in the Czechoslovak crisis. Therefore, the Soviet intervention had relatively little impact on either the party or the society at large. The big event was the Bonn-Warsaw treaty, signed by Chancellor Willy Brandt and Gomulka shortly before the latter's demise. This treaty, together with a similar agreement between Moscow and Bonn, was perceived by the Poles as auguring a new phase in East-West relations. As such it was welcomed by the new leadership, which was eager to utilize détente for its own purposes.

The new ruling oligarchy decided that in order to regain the confidence of the masses it had to mend its fences with various classes and groups who had become antagonized and alienated from the system during the latter part of Gomulka's rule. Thus, the workers were mollified by the price rollback and freeze; the peasants benefited from the elimination of compulsory deliveries and higher prices paid for farm products; the intelligentsia was pleased with the relaxation of censorship and of foreign travel restrictions; and the Catholic chuch was promised a better relationship with the state. A major regime drive to acquire some legitimacy was to be based on a quantum jump in the living standard of the population, propelled by a spectacular expansion in the volume of Poland's trade with the West.

The new economic policy proved quite successful in the early years of Gierek's rule when the country achieved one of the highest rates of growth in the world. The euphoria did not last long, however, and the boom, having leveled off in the mid-1970s, gave rise to a series of economic problems that soon tarnished the image of the new regime. Balance of payments difficulties, poor agricultural performance, growing shortages of foodstuffs and consumer goods, and increasing inflationary pressure forced the government to undertake a number of policies that in at least one case—the June 1976 food price reform—almost caused its own downfall. In a sense, by 1978 the Gierek regime and the party found themselves in the same precarious position as Gomulka a decade earlier. To some extent their situation at home was more difficult because of the emergence of a dynamic dissident movement. This, of course, also complicated the country's relationship with the Soviet Union and the rest of the international Communist camp. The mass domestic dissatisfaction with the system's performance coincided with the growing importance and visibility that Eurocommunism was acquiring in Eastern Europe.

If little has been said until now about the interaction between the

Polish party and the Communist parties of Western and Southern
Europe it is because, at least until the late 1960s, relations tended to
be rather formal and distant. The reasons for this are not difficult to
grasp. As suggested earlier, after October 1956 the Polish party felt
somewhat alienated from the parties in both East and West. It saw
itself betrayed by the Chinese in 1957, which may well be the reason
it did not imitate Romania's policy of maintaining good relations with
Peking, even at the height of the Great Cultural Revolution. The
PZPR's relations with Moscow throughout the 1960s were correct but
not particularly close. The same was largely true for the other East
European parties with the perennial exception of Hungary, with
which Poland has traditionally maintained a "special relationship."

Poland's attitude toward Yugoslavia deserves a brief comment.
Yugoslavia and Josip Tito have always been popular in Poland, mostly
because of their anti-German resistance record and their courageous
stand against Stalin. Nonetheless, this popularity has never had a
major impact on Poland's political, economic, and social systems. By
the late 1970s, Titoism as a systematic or societal model had lost a
good deal of its earlier luster. It had little to offer Polish society and
was found unacceptable by large segments of it.

For example, some of the Polish Communists felt that, because
Yugoslavia allowed mass migration and permitted a high level of unemployment, it no longer qualified as a socialist country. Others dis-
liked the continued cult of personality surrounding Tito, while the
party liberals were less than impressed with the Yugoslav treatment of
political, literary, and national dissenters. Thus, while it is likely that
Tito's independent stand was still widely admired, there was considerable agreement within and outside the party that even if it could be
transplanted without great difficulty, the Yugoslav model had little
applicability to Poland.

What about the interaction with the West European parties? Here
again, at least until the mid-1960s, the relations tended to be rather
formal. The period witnessed a growing rapprochement between
Eastern and Western Europe. France tried to reassert its traditional
influence in the East, while countries such as Poland and Romania
attempted to take advantage of this and to enlarge their freedom to
maneuver. It was obvious that sooner or later this was going to lead
to an estrangement between the Polish and French Communist parties. The Poles clearly welcomed Charles De Gaulle's initiative, especially after the general officially recognized the Oder-Neisse Line.
The French Communists' attitude toward Gaullist policies, however,
tended to be at best ambiguous, despite a clearcut improvement in the
relations between Paris and Moscow. Moreover, in contrast to the

PZPR, the French party at that time was still considered to be largely orthodox and strongly pro-Soviet. This perception was not drastically changed by its behavior before and after the intervention in Czechoslovakia. Consequently, the French party was not overwhelmingly popular among the Polish Communist leaders, who were eager to cultivate good bilateral relations first with De Gaulle and later with Georges Pompidou. In order to achieve this particular objective the Polish leaders did not mind antagonizing the French party.

The Italian Communist party had many admirers in Poland, especially after the publication of the Togliatti memorandum in 1964, which received strong support among the liberal elements in the PZPR. For the next few years mutual relations remained essentially cordial, and it was not until 1968 that the first major difference between the two parties came to the surface. There is evidence that the Italian party, together with other West European parties, was rather deeply embarrassed by the widely publicized anti-Semitic campaign conducted by Gomulka after March 1968. Soon thereafter the two parties found themselves on opposite sides in the Czechoslovak crisis. Still, the estrangement did not last long: the Polish oligarchy saw in the Italian party an important and valuable ally that had to be cultivated at all costs. The Italians apparently wanted to reestablish their influence in Eastern Europe. It had been considerably weakened by their anti-Soviet stance following the invasion of Czechoslovakia. The Polish-Italian rapprochement progressed rapidly, and by the early 1970s the status quo was largely reestablished.

To sum up, on the eve of the emergence of Eurocommunism, the Polish party maintained good, even friendly, relations with its Italian counterpart, while its attitude toward the French party could probably be described as lukewarm despite Gierek's personal ties to the French Communists. Insofar as the East was concerned, the Poles were close to the Hungarians and to some extent to the Yugoslavs. The interaction with the remaining ruling parties was correct, but probably no more than that, at least on the surface. At home, the rapidly deteriorating economic situation reduced Gierek's popularity and gave rise to opposition movements within and outside the party.

III

Through 1979, at least, Eurocommunism has had little impact on Polish domestic and foreign policy.[19] The question is, why? Is Poland unique in this respect or is it representative of other countries in Eastern Europe? Are the conditions and political climate in Poland less receptive to Eurocommunist influences than elsewhere, or is the

Polish resistance largely accidental and short-run? Keeping in mind
the caveats cited at the outset of the paper, Poland's attitude toward
Eurocommunism, it can be argued, represents a synthesis of uniquely
Polish and broader regional characteristics.

What does Eurocommunism have to offer Poland and the rest of
Eastern Europe? Not very much, at least in the Polish case. Without
going into the details of Eurocommunist programmatic declarations,
there appear to be very few objectives and ideas among them that
would greatly appeal to the Poles. Probably the most attractive one
would be the Eurocommunist insistence on equality and noninterference in the internal affairs of individual parties as spelled out, for
example, at the June 1976 conference of twenty-nine European Communist parties in East Berlin.[20] This demand did not represent anything radically new to the Poles, however, nor was it nearly as relevant in the second half of the 1970s as it would have been ten or
twenty years earlier. As noted, the belief in a far-reaching autonomy
of national parties had had a long tradition in Poland, and it may be
assumed that today only a small minority of party leaders still believes in absolute obedience to Moscow's *diktats*.

It can also be argued that for the past few years there has been
remarkably little interference by the Kremlin in the internal affairs of
its junior allies. There has been no evidence of overt Soviet pressure
on Poland or other East European countries to suppress their respective dissident movements and no visible Soviet insistence on greater
conformity to the Kremlin line. Thus Hungary has continued to
adhere to the economic reforms, Polish agriculture has remained
largely in private hands, and both countries have been trading furi-
ously with the West—without Soviet intervention. In fact, the USSR
has been taking great pains not to intervene or even show signs of
displeasure with some of the policies of its junior partners. On the
contrary, its concern for the maintenance of political stability in the
region has prompted Moscow to provide emergency aid to countries
such as Poland, faced with economic difficulties in 1976, and to
charge relatively low prices for its raw materials and energy exports
to Eastern Europe. In fact, there is now considerable evidence that
Eastern Europe, including Poland, has ceased to be an economic
asset to the Soviet Union and has in fact become an economic burden. This means that the Kremlin has most likely realized that the
leadership of a major politico-military and economic alliance carries
not only benefits but also duties and obligations.[21] If this is true, then
the Eurocommunist call for equality and noninterference may well
sound a bit hollow in Polish ears.

The second major postulate voiced by the Eurocommunists concerned democracy, human rights, and political pluralism. Here again it may be argued that this particular demand was not likely to generate much excitement in Poland of the late 1970s. All three of these ideas have had a venerable tradition in Polish political theory, and have been for years articulated by Marxists and non-Marxists alike, albeit without much success. The birth of the Workers Defense Committee in the fall of 1976, followed by the emergence of two other formal opposition groups (the Movement for the Defense of Human and Civil Rights and the Polish Independence Association) laid the foundations for a dissident movement that has not only exhibited a dynamic growth but also a remarkable capacity for survival. To put it differently, since 1976 the Polish political system has acquired a large dose of pluralism that has become unique in Eastern Europe. This also means that another Eurocommunist demand has been satisfied to a large extent.

Two questions should be asked in this respect. First, why has it been possible for the dissident movement to thrive in Poland but not elsewhere in Eastern Europe; and second, are the Communist parties of Western Europe—the purveyors of Eurocommunism—at all responsible for the survival of the opposition? The answer to the first question lies outside the scope of this chapter and will not be attempted here. The answer to the second question is a qualified yes. More than once high ranking members of the Italian Communist party urged the Gierek regime to be lenient with the opposition, and it is not inconceivable that these appeals played a part in the Gierek regime's policy of "benign neglect" with regard to the dissidents.[22] The latter policy may have been the outcome of many pressures, and while the Eurocommunist influence may not have been the most significant of these, it was not wholly without impact.

How do the Polish dissidents feel about Eurocommunism, and have they been grateful for the latter's support? It appears that their attitude is ambivalent. On the one hand, some of the dissidents thoroughly distrust Eurocommunism as a viable liberalizing movement and see it essentially as an appendage or even tool of Moscow. Others tend to view it more positively as a force that in the long run is bound to weaken Moscow's hold on international Communism.[23] In other words, the fact that the Kremlin and conservative East European party leaders have been harshly critical of many Eurocommunist statements and declarations is taken at face value as proof that the Soviet Union treats Eurocommunism seriously and is afraid of its influence. However, Soviet fear is seen as implying that the USSR would resist fiercely Eurocommunist inroads into Eastern Europe. Hence, this view holds that it might be better part of wisdom for

the Polish party and the dissidents alike not to identify themselves too closely with the Eurocommunists, as the cost might prove
prohibitive.[24]

Insofar as the official Polish party attitude toward Eurocommunism
is concerned, it appears to fall somewhere between the strongly negative and condemnatory stance taken by Bulgaria, Czechoslovakia,
and East Germany and the somewhat relaxed and benign view expressed by the Hungarian party. Thus, at the June 1976 East Berlin
conference Gierek supported the Soviet Union, yet he also made
some conciliatory statements addressed to the Eurocommunists.[25] It
must be kept in mind that the East Berlin meeting took place right
after the ignominious surrender of the Polish party to the workers
protesting the increase in meat prices, and the Polish leader was in a
poor position to assume an independent stand vis-à-vis Moscow.
It also ought to be noted that the Poles waited a rather long time before they formally (and mildly) condemned Santiago Carrillo's
"Eurocommunism" and the State, which was proclaimed as heretical
by most of the other East European parties immediately after its
publication.[26]

This ambivalent stance most likely reflected the sharp divisions
within the Polish leadership. These have become even more pronounced since the June 1976 workers riots. Because of these divisions, the leadership has found itself unable to move resolutely
against the dissidents. The lack of consensus at the top has also probably been responsible for the regime's failure to assume a more
decisive—positive or negative—posture toward Eurocommunism.

Altogether, it seems that the PZPR has been keeping all its options
open in dealing with Eurocommunism. Its official attitude might be
characterized as one of restrained silence. The party has clearly been
reluctant to roundly condemn all Eurocommunist ideas, yet at the
same time it has been equally reluctant to give aid and comfort to
fraternal parties too critical of Moscow's leadership. Thus far, at
least, this highly ambiguous stance appears not to have harmed Poland's relationship with both the Soviet Union and the Eurocommunist camp, which, by the way, has become much more restrained
in its anti-Soviet pronouncements as time has passed.

IV

What then has been the impact of Eurocommunism on Poland? In
light of the foregoing discussion it may be concluded that the
influence of Eurocommunism on Polish domestic and foreign policy
has been relatively slight. There are several reasons for the lack of a
stronger impact.

To begin with, the ruling Communist party has been strongly nationalistic and even xenophobic, mirroring to a large extent the traditional Polish political culture. This has meant that it has had little interest in learning from others, whether in the East or the West. It has had considerable faith in its own ability to solve its own problems even though history has shown that ability to be somewhat suspect.

Moreover, for the past twenty-five years or so, the Polish party has nearly always been divided into two or three different factions. The result has been a lack of consensus on some fundamental policies or frequent inertia and immobilism. Thus, even if one faction were strongly interested in getting closer to the West European parties, it would be prevented from doing so by the other factions.

Third, it appears that Eurocommunism as a garden variety of Marxism-Leninism has little if anything to offer the Polish Communists. Ideologically, the emphasis on democratic freedoms and a pluralistic political system has not represented a *novum* to the Polish party. Indeed, as early as the 1950s some of its brightest theoreticians, such as Kolakowski and Brus, who were subsequently branded as revisionists and anti-Marxists, attempted to combine Marxism with democracy and pluralism, albeit unsuccessfully. Similar attempts in the 1960s and 1970s also proved less than successful, yet all of them provide vivid testimony that in this particular area the Polish Communists have frequently been ahead of their West European brethren and have had little, if anything, to learn from them.

The one area where the interests of the Polish and West European Communists appear congruent concerns the questions of equality of all Communist parties throughout the world and of noninterference in the internal affairs of individual Communist states and parties. There is no doubt that the Polish party would be the first one to subscribe to both principles, yet the country's membership in the Warsaw Pact and its economic dependence on the Soviet Union have made this impossible, at least for the time being. Instead, Poland has managed to allow much greater internal freedom. Its domestic policies in this respect stand in sharp contrast to Romania, which traded off political liberalization at home for autonomy in its foreign policy.

What about the future? There are signs that in the most recent period Eurocommunism, for a variety of reasons, has lost a good deal of its initial appeal and attraction and has consequently become a much less tempting alternative to those among the East European Communists who only a short time ago looked to Rome rather than to Moscow for inspiration, leadership, and models to emulate. If this is the case, then the impact of Eurocommunism—potential or actual— is likely to become even weaker than before. Throughout most of its existence West European-style Communism has had little relevance to

Eastern Europe in general and to Poland in particular. It seems that as time goes on Eurocommunism is becoming even more irrelevant. Its future impact on the region as a whole, as well as on individual countries, appears questionable.

NOTES

1. Charles Gati, "The 'Europeanization' of Communism," *Foreign Affairs*, 55 (April 1977), p. 547.

2. Andrzej Korbonski, "External Influences on Eastern Europe," in Charles Gati, ed., *The International Politics of Eastern Europe* (New York: Praeger, 1976), pp. 253–274, and Sarah M. Terry, "External Influences on Political Change in Eastern Europe: A Framework for Analysis," in Jan F. Triska and Paul M. Cocks, eds., *Political Development in Eastern Europe* (New York: Praeger, 1977), pp. 277–314.

3. Adam Bromke, *Poland's Politics: Idealism vs. Realism* (Cambridge, Mass.: Harvard University Press, 1967), pp. 52–56.

4. For details, see M. K. Dziewanowski, *The Communist Party of Poland* (Cambridge, Mass.: Harvard University Press, 1976), chs. 5–8.

5. Andrzej Korbonski, "The Polish Communist Party 1938–1942," *Slavic Review*, XXVI (September 1967), pp. 442–444.

6. Dziewanowski, *Communist Party of Poland*, chs. 9–11.

7. One of the good examples was the Polish Workers party's attitude toward agriculture. See Andrzej Korbonski, *Politics of Socialist Agriculture in Poland 1945–1960* (New York: Columbia University Press, 1965), pp. 136–139.

8. For details, see Zbigniew Brzezinski, *The Soviet Bloc* (Cambridge, Mass.: Harvard University Press, 1967), pp. 271–279, and Bromke, *Poland's Politics*, pp. 57–62. According to Brzezinski, both Josip Tito and Palmiro Togliatti praised the Polish regime's initial firm response to workers riots in the city of Poznan in June 1956. Brzezinski, *Soviet Bloc*, p. 248.

9. It may be speculated that the open admission, published in February 1956, that the dissolution of the Polish Communist party in 1938 was wrong and unjustified, did little to change that attitude. The text of the resolution rehabilitating the prewar Polish party was first published in *Trybuna Ludu*, February 19, 1956.

10. Brzezinski, *Soviet Bloc*, pp. 243–245 and 352–356. See also, Hansjakob Stehle, "Polish Communism," in William E. Griffith, ed, *Communism in Europe* (Cambridge, Mass.: MIT Press, 1967), vol. I, pp. 100–176, and Zbigniew Jordan, "Rewizjonizm Polski," *Kultura* (Paris) (December 1961), pp. 15–29, and (January-February 1962), pp. 21–44.

11. Jacek Kuron and Karol Modzelewski, *List otwarty do Partii* (Paris: Instytut Literacki, 1966). It is, clearly, no accident that Kuron has been one of the top leaders of Polish dissidents after 1976.

12. For a detailed account of the political developments in Poland in the second half of the 1960s, see Peter Raina, *Political Opposition in Poland 1954–1977* (London: Poets and Painters Press, 1978), chs. 5–6.

13. Resolution adopted by the Central Committee of the Polish United Workers party at its Seventh Plenary Session, July 18–28, 1956, in Paul E. Zinner, ed., *National Communism and Popular Revolt in Eastern Europe* (New York: Columbia University Press, 1956), pp. 172–173.

14. Ibid., p. 174.

15. Resolution adopted by the Central Committee of the Polish United Workers party at its Eighth Plenary Session, October 19–21, 1956. Ibid., p. 256.

16. For an interesting discussion of this phenomenon, see Andrzej Brzeski, "Poland as a Catalyst of Change in the Communist Economic System," *Polish Review*, XVI (Spring 1971), pp. 3–24.

17. This emerged clearly from many conversations I had during my stay in Prague, September 1966 to July 1967.

18. According to Kevin Devlin, "the most radical indictment of the East European regimes produced by the PCI's publishing house was written by a dissident Polish Communist (in exile) [Wlodzimierz Brus]." Kevin Devlin, "The Challenge of Eurocommunism," *Problems of Communism*, XXVI (January-February 1977), p. 19.

19. Thus, I seem to be less optimistic than Jiri Valenta, who claims that "Eurocommunist influence appears to be strongest in Czechoslovakia, Poland and East Germany, all of which have political and cultural traditions similar to those of Western Europe." Jiri Valenta, "Eurocommunism and Eastern Europe," *Problems of Communism*, XXVII (March-April 1978), p. 50. Moreover, while one may agree that Czechoslovakia did indeed share political and cultural traditions with democratic Western Europe, this was less true for Poland and East Germany, whose experience with democracy has been of a rather short duration.

20. For a detailed account of the developments leading up to the conference, see Devlin, "Challenge of Eurocommunism," pp. 1–20. See also, Neil McInnes, "Eurocommunism," *Washington Papers*, IV (No. 37, 1976), and Manfred Steinkühler, "Eurocommunism: Myth and Reality," *Aussenpolitik*, 28 (No. 4, 1977), pp. 375–402.

21. For a good discussion of this particular question, see Paul Marer, "Has Eastern Europe Become a Liability to the Soviet Union? II. The Economic Aspect," in Gati, ed., *International Politics of Eastern Europe*, pp. 59–81.

22. See Radio Free Europe Research, *Situation Report Poland 25*, July 23, 1976, and Raina, *Political Opposition in Poland*, pp. 248–249.

23. For an interesting discussion of these issues, see Gustaw Herling-Grudzinski and Adam Michnik, "Dwuglos o eurokomunizmie," *Kultura* (Paris), no. 355 (April 1977), pp. 3–15. In the eyes of one Western observer, "The Communist parties of Italy and Spain epitomize the Eurocommunist movement . . . they thus represent not an asset to the Soviet Union but a problem that developments in the Soviet Union and Eastern Europe themselves will naturally exacerbate." Bogdan Denitch, "Eurocommunism: A Threat to Soviet Hegemony?" in Grayson Kirk and Nils H. Wessell, eds., *The Soviet Threat* (New York: Academy of Political Science, 1978), pp. 153–155.

24. "Eurokomunizm i Europa Wschodnia," *Kultura*, no. 367 (April 1976), pp. 70–73.

25. "Real socialism has existed for less than sixty years. It is a young formation . . . which is still in the process of development, constantly searching for better solutions of current and future problems." "Konferencja partii komunistycznych i robotniczych Europy, Berlin, 29–30 czerwca 1976," *Nowe Drogi*, no. 367 (August 1976), p. 25.

26. Bogumil Sujka, "W kwestii solidarnosci socjalistycznej," ibid. (August 1957), pp. 52–57. See also, *Trybuna Ludu*, August 3, 1977.

CHAPTER VII

Eurocommunism and East Germany

Melvin Croan

Introduction

If there is anything surprising about East Germany, it is that the German Democratic Republic (GDR) should have produced any genuine political surprises at all. Elemental geopolitical and strategic considerations all but sealed East Germany's fate at the outset of the post-World War II period. Barring a fundamental change in the balance of power on the European continent, the GDR's margin of international maneuverability and scope for domestic development seem destined to remain narrowly circumscribed. But is this really the case?

Looking back over the almost three decades of the GDR's existence as one of postwar Germany's two successor states, one is struck by the various ways in which it has confounded Western observers. The legatee of an authoritarian political culture, not exactly noted for its experience of popular revolution, East Germany was unexpectedly convulsed by the first mass uprising against Communist rule in June 1953. Thereafter, for a decade or more, it was commonplace in the West to dismiss the GDR as an utterly artificial political construct, bereft of a genuine social base. The regime of the Socialist Unity party (SED) was treated as a faithful mirror of the Soviet political system, incapable of self-generating domestic change. The GDR itself resembled a penitentiary, an image that was graphically projected by the monstrous Berlin wall, erected in August 1961. Yet East Germany's veteran Stalinist boss, Walter Ulbricht, somehow managed to survive the politics of de-Stalinization under Nikita Khrushchev. Moreover, inflexible dogmatist though he was supposed to be, Ulbricht somehow presided over the innovations in economic policy of the 1960s. In the wake of these innovations, economic growth replaced economic stagnation, and the GDR came to attain a real measure of relative prosperity. Once Western observers acknowledged this East German accomplishment, they generally concluded that the GDR was a durable political entity. A major consequence of this fresh Western view was Willy Brandt's *Ostpolitik* and, more particularly, its *Deutschlandpolitik* component, which recognized the existence of "two German states," albeit within "one nation." Many Western commentators—academic no less than journalistic—also began to argue that the SED regime had developed authentic social roots after all, and that its leadership had accomplished the extraordinary feat of "transforming dissenters into participants,"[1] to employ Samuel Huntington's phrase connoting a major facet of the general process of the institutionalization of one party's rule. As one knowledgeable English commentator expressed it, the GDR appeared to many to have succeeded in substituting "progress for politics."[2]

Given the foregoing interpretation, the political reawakening of the East German population comes as no small surprise. Thus, the 1975 Final Act at Helsinki, to which the SED leadership proudly affixed the GDR's signature, led to a widespread popular demand for permission to emigrate to the West. Similarly, critical departures from Soviet orthodoxy on the part of "Eurocommunists" in the West have nurtured dissidence within the SED itself. At issue now is only the question of the origin, extent, and significance of these developments.

In order to address properly such topical considerations, it is necessary to bear in mind one basic point: although the GDR has undergone many changes, it still remains in one crucial respect what it has always been—an anomaly by virtue of what its own leaders euphemistically refer to as the "national question." As a result of Germany's national division and West Germany's greater size, larger population, higher standard of living, and demonstrated attraction to the East German population, the GDR's ruling elite continues to suffer from a political inferiority complex, rooted in an acute sense of what Peter C. Ludz has termed "deficient legitimacy."[3]

Domestic developments within the GDR thus remain inextricably intertwined with inter-German relations in a context that, despite its many changing modalities, has always been determined by East Germany's dependent relationship with the Soviet Union. This relationship remains absolutely crucial. Without belaboring the obvious, the Soviet Union's predominance over the GDR in terms of geographic expanse, population, economic wealth, and military strength is enormous. Moreover, the East German leadership remains acutely aware of all these basic power disparities, as do the Soviet political elites.

Finally, the inferiority complex of East Germany's Communist rulers toward West Germany serves to heighten their psychological dependence on the Soviet Union, whose continued support they deem indispensable to the GDR's very survival.

These conditions and circumstances have contributed to the forging of a crucial constant in the East German–Soviet relationship: the GDR has always constituted, in the parlance of one American school of foreign policy analysis, a "penetrated system," that is, a political system whose bureaucratic decision-making processes have always been open to active Soviet influence and direct Soviet intervention.[4] It is small wonder that the official stance of East Germany's SED leadership toward the heterodoxy embodied in "Eurocommunism" should hew closely to the Kremlin's own position.

The complexities and anomalies of the GDR's domestic and international situations go beyond its relationship with the Soviet Union. East Germany must be considered a doubly penetrated system. While its political structures are penetrated to an extraordinary degree by the Soviet Union, its domestic society is deeply penetrated by the West and, quite specifically, by West Germany. If anything, Western social penetration of the GDR has increased in recent years due to East-West détente in Europe and Bonn's *Ostpolitik*, which led to the proliferation of personal contacts between the two halves of Germany. Inasmuch as the SED is a mass-based party, comprising slightly more than two million members or approximately 12 percent of the adult East German population, the challenge posed by ideologico-political deviations originating in the West is exceptionally acute. This, in turn, has prompted East German leadership reactions that at times have been even more intransigent than Moscow's. East Berlin has also shown signs of seeking to exploit Moscow's ideological and political tribulations with other Communist parties so as to elevate the GDR's status as a Soviet client-state and to enhance its bargaining position vis-à-vis the USSR.

The picture that emerges, then, far from being simple or straightforward, is full of contradictory and often quite subtle elements. These elements will be assessed after first seeking the domestic East German roots, if any, of "Eurocommunism." To this end, the SED's reactions to the Eurocommunist phenomenon and East Berlin's most pressing current domestic and international concerns need to be examined.

Early East German Heterodoxy as Eurocommunism?

Most students of Eurocommunism agree that the term, initially coined by a Yugoslav journalist, was given wide currency by Western non-Communist commentators as a convenient shorthand expression to cover various (and not always consistent) deviations from, and criticisms of, Soviet positions evidenced by the Spanish, Italian, and French parties in the 1970s. In other words, Eurocommunism ought to be regarded less as a single, integrated ideologico-political platform juxtaposed to Soviet Marxism-Leninism than as an updated expression of polycentrism and national Communism. From this perspective, one can argue, as Charles Gati and Jiri Valenta have, that Eurocommunism began in Eastern Europe many decades ago.[5]

The search for the pristine origins of the Eurocommunist phenomenon in East Germany can be revealing precisely for its meager findings. To be sure, in the initial aftermath of the collapse of the Third Reich, some German Communists did nurture hopes of unfolding their own revolutionary blueprint, independent of Moscow's dictates.[6] It is also true that in early 1946 a ranking German Communist ideological functionary, Anton Ackermann, even formulated an explicit doctrine of "the special German road to Socialism."[7] At that time Ackermann's position coincided with that of entire German Communist party (KPD) leadership and, unquestionably, of the Soviet authorities as well. It was meant as a tactical appeal to the Social Democrats to facilitate the KPD-SPD organizational fusion, which took place with the foundation of the SED in April 1946. Moreover, the doctrine of a "special German road to Socialism" was soon renounced, and Ackermann himself was castigated for having propounded it. It is conceivable that Ackermann and others may have developed a personal commitment to the notion of a separate German road to socialism, for such has frequently been the experience of Communist politics and, indeed, many other varieties of politics. Whatever the case, Stalin's determination to tighten Soviet control over Moscow's zone of occupation in Germany effectively precluded any domestic political autonomy in East Germany. For political life as a whole, the basic note had been sounded at the outset by Ulbricht when he cynically remarked that "it's quite clear. It's got to look democratic but we've got to have everything in our control."[8]

In any event, Ulbricht managed to concentrate control of close to "everything" in his own hands. The challenge to his position as Stalin's viceroy posed by the KPD veteran Franz Dahlem, whose downfall Ulbricht engineered in 1952, was utterly devoid of ideological content. A much more serious affair involved the "Zaisser-Herrnstadt group," which Ulbricht purged in the aftermath of the June 1953 uprising. Its members had been preparing to take over the leadership of the SED, at the behest of Moscow, or at least with the backing of powerful figures in the Kremlin, including Lavrenti Beria, probably Georgi Malenkov, and quite possibly Nikita Khrushchev as well.[9] Little is known of the alleged platform of the 1953 anti-Ulbricht group of East Germany. Apart from its support for Soviet diplomatic initiatives regarding the German question as a whole (and these did seem to call for an end to the drive to "construct socialism" in the GDR) and for a relaxation of the SED's political controls, the anti-Ulbricht cabal probably did not have a platform as such. Furthermore, the industrial workers who brought about the June uprising received virtually no open support, official or intellectual, from the East German elite. The sole exception was the East German Minister of Justice and former Social Democrat, Max Fechner, who touchingly insisted that the workers had acted legally because they had a constitutional right to strike.[10]

Intellectual dissidence in the GDR first gained public expression in 1956, as a result of Khrushchev's initial assault on Stalin, which was echoed by Ulbricht as early as March 1956. The ensuing months of intellectual ferment and student unrest produced one genuinely sweeping program of reform, authored by the young SED philosopher, Wolfgang Harich. Although the aspirations he expressed were certainly widely shared, Harich himself was something of an eccentric who proved to be utterly naive as a would-be activist. His program to "enhance Marxism-Leninism" claimed inspiration from such disparate sources as Leon Trotsky, Nikolai Bukharin, Karl Kautsky, certain contemporary West German social democratic thinkers, and "aspects of Yugoslav experience and those new elements which mark theoretical discussion in Poland and China."[11] The hodgepodge of sources that sustained Harich's thought was not, however, the major point. Nor, for that matter, were the specifics of Harich's program to transform the GDR into a democratic collectivist rival to West Germany. Much more significant was Harich's stipulation that the attainment of his entire program of domestic East German reform would provide only a *transitional* stage on the road to Germany's national reunification. On these grounds alone it was virtually inconceivable that this program would appeal to any members of Ulbricht's entourage. Far less could they receive the endorsement of the Soviet authorities, although poor Harich seems actually to have believed that such would be the case.[12]

As it happened, 1956 saw the stirrings of intellectual heterodoxy in a wide variety of areas, including Marxist philosophy (Ernst Bloch and Robert Havemann), literary criticism (Hans Mayer), and economics (Fritz Behrens, Arno Benary, and Kurt Vieweg). Although they were subsequently denounced for harboring "certain Yugoslav theories,"[13] the reformist economists were loyal supporters of the East German regime; certainly they had nothing in common with the

Harich opposition. It is all the more striking that they enjoyed little, if any, contact with figures within the party hierarchy, like Fred Oelssner, who were seeking methods to render the East German economy more efficient.

For his efforts at practical reform, Oelssner found himself lumped together with Karl Schirdewan, Ulbricht's one time heir-apparent, and Ernst Wollweber, the secret police chief, both of whom had sought to oust Ulbricht during 1956. After some delay, the purge of the Schirdewan-Wollweber-Oelssner group was announced in February 1958. The affair deserves mention because it reflects the state of both East German domestic politics and GDR-Soviet relations in the 1950s. Domestic political considerations undoubtedly prompted the regime to charge a single anti-Ulbricht "faction" with attempted subversion. In reality it seems clear that two or more separate groupings were involved and that they never really coalesced. Furthermore, the activities of the various factionalists were conducted entirely *in camera*. As a result, the Ulbricht regime's intellectual critics of 1956 were denied access to leaders of the party opposition. In effect, they found themselves politically disarmed from the very outset. Like Wilhelm Zaisser and Rudolf Herrnstadt before them, Schirdewan, Wollweber, and Oelssner did not seek rank and file SED support in their drive to replace Ulbricht, and they sought to enlist popular disaffection outside the party even less. Rather, they jockeyed for backing from the Soviet leadership in Moscow. In particular, Schirdewan apparently counted on the favor of Khrushchev, basing his calculations on Ulbricht's seeming vulnerability due to his long record as a subaltern of Stalin. Schirdewan clearly miscalculated, as an Ulbricht spokesman was later to take satisfaction in pointing out.[14]

Thus the reasons for the weakness of the Eurocommunist phenomenon throughout the Ulbricht era, if not beyond, involved both situational and psychological considerations. In the first instance, Germany's national division and the fragile domestic foundations of SED rule in East Germany meant that the logic of revisionist thought pointed toward the eventual liquidation of the GDR. Harich called for precisely that. Even if he had not done so, that very outcome would still have constituted a specter for all contestants for power within the top echelons of the SED. Their ingrained sense of the vulnerability of Communist rule in turn opened up all crucial decision-making arenas to Soviet penetration and, in effect, rendered the Kremlin the immediate, rather than merely the ultimate, arbiter of East German domestic politics.

Moreover, exercise of this Soviet rule was greatly facilitated by the psychological impact of the GDR's missing national base. The SED had been thoroughly conditioned by German Communism's long and debilitating experience of Moscow-oriented internationalism. Major segments of its old "strategic elite," and many newer sub-elites as well, tended to subscribe, quite genuinely, to "proletarian (later socialist) internationalism" as a surrogate political community or *ersatz* patriotism.[15] This was the fundamental reason for the total absence of any Titoist deviation within the SED, notwithstanding Wolfgang Leonhard and his tiny coterie.

Finally, latent oppositionist currents that might have surfaced were constantly siphoned off through flight to the West. Disaffected Communists and ex-social democrats availed themselves of this outlet as readily as other East Germans. In 1961, however, the Berlin wall largely put a stop to this process and effectively sequestered the population. It also inaugurated a drive toward domestic consolidation that reached a high point a decade later when the GDR at last gained general international recognition as a separate sovereign state. Bearing this background in mind, the ways in which later developments affected political trends within East Germany must be considered.

Recent Domestic Developments

The decade of the 1960s may be said to have witnessed the substitution of "progress for politics" in East German domestic developments. With respect to economic affairs, Ulbricht practiced a kind of institutionalized revisionism to remarkably good effect. And as the fate of the GDR's chief economic planner, Eric Apel, illustrated, opposition to the primacy Ulbricht accorded Soviet interests was, quite literally, suicidal.[16] All this was true at least until Ulbricht's last few years in office when he abandoned himself to unrealistically ambitious growth goals and simultaneously moved to replace economic decentralization with computerized central planning. Even more importantly, however, the experience of substituting "progress for politics" was augmented and was ultimately overshadowed by the displacement of domestic politics onto the international arena. Ulbricht's efforts to shape Soviet policy toward West Germany in the context of Bonn's initiation of an active *Ostpolitik* amounted to studied self-assertion. In its own way it was an expression of national Communism. That Ulbricht's efforts came to grief and resulted in his retirement from office in May 1971 only served to demonstrate anew the practical limits on GDR maneuverability and autonomy.

The international strategy to which Ulbricht committed the GDR presupposed the appearance of steadfast ideological loyalty to Moscow and the maintenance of the strictest political discipline at home. It is hardly surprising that Ulbricht should have reacted so quickly and forcefully to the Prague Spring and cracked down so swiftly on the first intimations of support within East Germany for the Dubcek experiment. As a result, the GDR's domestic landscape at the end of the 1960s was one of ideologico-political sterility. Except for the idiosyncratic protestations of the *chansonnier* Wolf Biermann, and the humanistic critiques of the East German system persisted in by the courageous physicist-philosopher Robert Havemann, the rest was silence.

The Honecker era of the 1970s has differed from the decade that preceded it in a number of crucial respects. First, despite the Honecker regime's simultaneous efforts at *Abgrenzung* (delimitation) against the West and *Verflechtung* (integration) with the Soviet Union and Eastern Europe, the GDR has been compelled by the requirements of Brezhnev's *Westpolitik* to open its borders to a massive invasion of visitors from West Germany and West Berlin, numbering many millions of people annually. Secondly, East Germany has experienced a reversal of previously favorable economic trends, a development that has been increasingly aggravated by such extraneous factors as Western inflation and the global energy shortage. Given Erich Honecker's commitment to consumerism to secure popular allegiance, this reversal has had the unwelcome practical effect of heightening the GDR's economic dependence upon West Germany. Finally, the Honecker regime has been confronted both by growing social restiveness and renewed intellectual dissidence.

The problems posed by unruly, if largely apolitical, youth and by manifestations of a fresh sense of class consciousness among industrial workers are obviously unwelcome. Still, such restiveness can be controlled by tried and true police-state methods. The challenge posed by renewed intellectual ferment may prove less immediately tractable, especially when the critical spirit and major social forces are linked. It is one thing for the regime to mete out Solzhenitzyn-like treatment to Biermann by refusing the unconventional balladeer permission to reenter the GDR and stripping him of his citizenship, as happened in late 1976, and subsequently to expel other, lesser known artistic dissidents. It is quite another for it to know how best to cope with Rudolf Bahro, who has connections with the industrial labor force and personal ties with members, some possibly ranking, of the SED's own apparatus.[17] It was scarcely coincidental that Bahro's sentencing to eight years imprisonment on the charge of having worked for West German intelligence was announced the day after the eighty-fifth anniversary of Ulbricht's birth, an event which saw the extraordinary rehabilitation of the dead East German leader from nonperson to near patron saint of the GDR.[18]

As in the case of Havemann, Bahro's devastating critique of the bureaucratic deformation of "real existing socialism" (the East German system in practice) owes much to the aborted Czechoslovak reform and even more to the doctrinal departures of Eurocommunism in the West. The latter is true, even though Bahro himself was careful not to embrace openly the pluralistic currents of Eurocommunism, probably in the interest of presenting his work as genuinely theoretical rather than merely programmatic. Nonetheless, Bahro does take heart from the emergence of the Eurocommunist phenomenon in the West. Indeed, he seems to assume that its growth will serve not only to nurture the movement for genuine reform in the Eastern bloc, but also to stay the hand of the dogmatic, reactionary defenders of the Communist bureaucratic dictatorship in Moscow and elsewhere and thus, in effect, prevent a repetition of the knockout blow struck against the Czechoslovak experiment in August 1968.

No brief summary can do justice to the complexities and contradictions of Bahro's thought, but several salient points deserve mention. Shorn of its abstruse Marxist formulations, Bahro's critique of "real existing socialism" is directed primarily at the economic malfeasance, social malaise, and individual human repressiveness of socialist systems of the Soviet type. As he sees it, these systems suffer from latent but quite basic conflicts, and they are everywhere in a state of crisis. For Bahro, the center of the fundamental systemic crisis is located in the Soviet Union. Its origins are traced to the "noncapitalist road to industrialization," which he regards as having grievously distorted Marxist socialism. The process began under Lenin, whose policies, however, Bahro considers to have been historically necessary and well intentioned. Not surprisingly, Bahro's real culprit turns out to be Stalin, whom he holds responsible for erecting an all-powerful state based upon a pervasive bureaucracy, amounting to a particularly reprehensible version of Asiatic despotism. This Stalinist system embodied all the repressive features of historical Russian political experience. Furthermore it has perpetuated a division of labor. For Bahro, this directly violates genuine Marxist conceptions of state and society. In attributing the Stalinist deformation of Marxism to Russia's historic backwardness, Bahro's analysis exudes resentment at the political, cultural, and human costs exacted by the imposition of Soviet power over more advanced societies, such as Czechoslovakia and East Germany itself. According to Bahro, these societies, which belong to "Western civilization," now need both a "permanent cultural revolution" corresponding to the level of development of their forces of production and a simultaneous "national restoration" to reestablish continuity with the best of their national traditions and social forms.

Although Bahro sought to present a "theoretical base" rather than to develop a detailed action program, the practical implications of his thought subsequently gained unequivocal expression. This occurred in the form of an extraordinary "Manifesto of the Opposition" of an ostensible "League of Democratic Communists" within the SED, which was published in the West in January 1978.[19] The manifesto's close kinship to the doctrines propounded by Santiago Carrillo is unmistakable. Even more to the point, the document links its platform for internal reform in the GDR to a call—at this late date—for a reunified, democratic, and neutral Germany. As the version of the manifesto that was published in West Germany formulated it: "We are for an offensive national policy, for a concept that aims at the reunification of Germany in which Social Democrats, Socialists and Democratic Communists will enjoy preponderance over conservative forces. . . . This Germany can and must become a bridge between East and West, a factor stabilizing peace."[20]

The SED and Eurocommunism

The link between domestic reform and national reunification was first explicitly broached by Harich in 1956. Its reappearance twenty-two years later in a major document of political dissidence aptly suggests the enormously high stakes with which the SED still has to contend. This, in turn, helps to explain the East German party's reaction to the phenomenon of Eurocommunism, even though it does not by itself fully exhaust the subtleties that have gone into the SED's relationship to the major West European Communist parties.

In the first instance, SED spokesmen have consistently denounced pluralistic, democratic pretensions and conceptions whenever and wherever they have arisen within what used to be called "the Communist world movement." Conversely, they have explicitly championed anew the "dictatorship of the proletariat" as well as the Soviet version of "socialist internationalism."[21] They have lumped Eurocommunist deviations from these positions together with "social democratism." Thus, for example, Kurt Hager, the SED's ranking ideologue, recently issued a stern warning that there can be "only the alternative between the genuine revolutionary Marxist-Leninist course and the Eurocommunist, Social Democratic course of Biermann and Havemann."[22] In other words, the SED has sought to impose much the same kind of ideological *Abgrenzung* (delimitation)

against Eurocommunism as it has decreed against the West German
Social Democratic party. Furthermore, as the 1976 Conference of
European Communist Parties, held in East Berlin, demonstrated only
too amply, the SED has been eager to champion all Soviet positions,
doubtless in order to enhance its status with the CPSU and that of the
GDR with the USSR.

Similar considerations of East Germany's "national" interest have
also dictated considerable flexibility in relations with the individual
West European parties as well as with Yugoslavia and, for that matter,
Romania. Under Honecker, relations with Yugoslavia, previously
much troubled, have substantially improved, in part because Josip
Tito's ideological challenge is no longer taken very seriously. East
Berlin's interest in improved relations with Belgrade also reflects an
appreciation of the unique role that Yugoslavia has fashioned for itself
in East-West relations and in international Communist affairs, as well
as the East German desire to cultivate openings to the West and to the
Third World that Yugoslavia may be able to offer. Much the same set
of considerations operates with respect to Romania, which had previously borne the brunt of scathing East German attacks for its assertion of "narrow-minded nationalism" and is still unofficially treated
by SED leaders with a mixture of contempt and envy.

Broadly speaking, the SED's relations with the Italian, French, and
(to a lesser extent) Spanish Communist parties have evolved through
three distinct phases.[23] The first of these, dating back to the mid- to
late-sixties, precedes the emergence of the Eurocommunist phenomenon, the Italian Communist party's venerable commitment to
polycentrism notwithstanding. In this first phase, the SED enjoyed
more or less uncritical support from the West European parties which,
in turn, were regarded as valuable political assets against West Germany and its allies in the GDR's drive to obtain international diplomatic recognition.

A second phase, coinciding with the unveiling of distinctive
Eurocommunist doctrinal conceptions, ran to the mid-1970s. It was
characterized by general ideological hostility and sharp rebuffs to
specific criticisms of the East German system emanating from the
West European Communists. Perhaps the lowest ebb in SED-
Eurocommunist relations in this phase occurred in late 1976, in the
immediate aftermath of Biermann's expulsion from the GDR. That
action was roundly criticized by the Spanish, Italian, and French parties in terms that stressed not only the injustice of the individual case,
but also the damage it inflicted upon the cause of socialism
everywhere and on the Communist image in the West.[24]

A third phase, in evidence in the late 1970s, combines doctrinal
disdain and ideological distance with the attempt, awkward by its

very nature, to maintain and further develop close party relations. The inspiration behind the SED's current strategy toward the West European Communist parties is much the same as that which has animated the GDR's increasingly sophisticated attitude toward Yugoslavia and Romania. It consists of two basic sets of concerns. The first is to arrest any further pluralistic decay of international Communism, in the service of the interests of the Soviet Union, to be sure, but also in the SED's own interests with respect to the internationalist bases of its claim to domestic legitimacy within the GDR. The second, paradoxically enough, is to support the degree of autonomy already enjoyed by the West European parties with a view to balancing, at least partially, the GDR's own integration into the Eastern bloc with contacts to the West. Stated in other terms, the SED now seeks to couple ideological *Abgrenzung* with political rapprochement. In a sense, it has an interest in sustaining the Eurocommunist ideological challenge to the Soviet Union, if only to increase the GDR's value to the Kremlin as a trustworthy protagonist of Soviet orthodoxy.

East German-Soviet Relations and the GDR's Future Prospects

Despite the novel subtleties that have come to attend the GDR's relationship to the phenomenon of Eurocommunism, it would be wrong to assume that the SED has the ability, or even the desire, to play the Eurocommunist card against the Soviet Union, any more than it ever really had a chance to play the Chinese card against Moscow. Elemental geopolitical considerations rule out the one as they did the other.

In the first instance, the Eurocommunist ideological challenge is potentially far too explosive to be too closely embraced, given the GDR's "deficient legitimacy" due to the absence of a national base. To be sure, Eurocommunism's appeal to dissident East German intellectuals can be contained with relative ease. In this, as in all other manifestations of intellectual dissidence, the traditional German cleavage between *Macht* (power) and *Geist* (the critical spirit) still plays a major role. But for East German society and for the SED, a mass party that mirrors the economic and national frustrations of East German society as a whole, the Eurocommunist option may be too attractive for comfort. In this connection it is important to note a development that has enormous potential significance. In addition to the traditional German Communist Soviet-oriented internationalism, manifestations of a renewed sense of German cultural superiority toward the Russians have become legion.[25] While anti-Russian sentiment has always permeated the East German population as a whole, it may now have come to infect the GDR's new elites, including those whose careers have been made within various Soviet-East German and multilateral East European bureaucracies.

The latter development reflects the larger paradox of the GDR's international position, which has come to feature greater scope for activity abroad and the simultaneous imposition of tighter restraints on the actual conduct of East German foreign policy. This has been the case because Brezhnev's *Westpolitik,* forced upon a reluctant East German leadership, has created new threats to domestic stability in the 1970s. The SED has sought to counter these pressures by means of closer and ever more comprehensive integration into the Soviet-led Socialist community, with particular emphasis upon bilateral ties to the Soviet Union.[26] For its part, Moscow has shown an unflagging determination to keep the development of inter-German contacts within precisely circumscribed bounds and to monitor the development of these contacts with the greatest care. As a result, the bonds of the Soviet-East German patron-client relationship have proliferated rather than decreased and have grown stronger rather than weaker. That, in turn, has enhanced the Soviet Union's prerogatives as a patron and correspondingly diminished the GDR's status as a client. Concomitant East German aspirations to a second order patronage within the Socialist community (with respect to tutoring Czechoslovakia in the Husak regime's quest for ''normalization'' or in the division of labor attendant upon the USSR's recent heavy involvement in Africa) seem unlikely either to loosen Soviet restraints upon GDR policy toward the West or to fashion any new room for East German autonomy vis-à-vis the Soviet Union. In the final analysis, the twenty Soviet divisions still stationed on East German soil—now typically augmented, at the first signs of domestic restiveness, by special KGB detachments—militate against this.

Of course, differences of emphasis and accentuation persist between East Berlin and Moscow. They reflect the different priorities of policy between the Soviet Union as a global superpower and the GDR as a client state with a narrow range of intensely felt concerns focused on West Germany and the Berlin issue. As long as the Soviet Union continues to regard the division of Germany to be essential to its own national security, it is bound to heed the concerns of the East German leaders. To that extent, GDR interests have become an integral part of the decision-making process in the Kremlin. The East German leadership is in turn anxious that the Soviet Union properly appreciate the challenge that inter-German relations pose to the GDR's domestic stability. To a certain extent it remains in the Soviet interest that such

East German anxieties not subside entirely. Nevertheless, recent developments within the GDR have also served to highlight anew the precariousness of Communist rule and the prevalence of national feeling and latent popular anti-Soviet sentiment. As far as these issues are concerned, the interests of the leaderships in Moscow and East Berlin are virtually identical. Their common position is pretty much in keeping with the dictum recently expressed by the East German secret police chief: "Clarity in the question of power was, is, and will remain the basic requirement of the Marxist world view and politics."[27]

As long as considerations of domestic security predominate, the GDR seems destined to remain suspended between "the desire to stand on its own feet and the need for continued dependence,"[28] with pronounced emphasis on the latter in its relationship with the Soviet Union. A major, protracted crisis of the Soviet system at home could endanger much of the bilateral integration achieved during the Brezhnev-Honecker era. Barring such a crisis, it is highly improbable that the East German elite will acquire the leverage it needs to pursue policies at variance with those of the Soviet Union. On grand strategic issues it has little reason to do so, unless East Berlin perceives a direct threat to its vital interests. Even in this case, its chances of success are minimal, as the fate of Ulbricht's defiance of Moscow between 1969 and 1971 demonstrated. Since he succeeded Ulbricht, Honecker has consistently responded with alacrity to Brezhnev's quest for comprehensive, multi-faceted integration so as to strengthen the bonds of East German clientage in "an association which the GDR by itself will not be in a position to sever, at least for the foreseeable future."[29]

As long as that is the case, Eurocommunism is likely to remain of marginal significance to the GDR. At least this will be true as concerns those who actually wield power over its system of "real existing socialism." To be sure, they may continue their recent soft-pedaling of doctrinal differences between the SED and the Western Eurocommunist parties.[30] Moreover, the inspiration behind such a course may continue to involve the quest for a measure of self-assertion on the part of East Berlin against Moscow. Yet the limits of self-assertion are sharply circumscribed, and the margin that has become available to the SED is itself the result of the Soviet leaders' own recent, more relaxed attitudes toward Eurocommunist deviations.[31]

All of this could change, of course, with any major alteration of present circumstances. If, for example, any one of the Western Communist parties were to come to power or even substantially to enhance its present domestic role, that might prompt Moscow to pay renewed attention to the Eurocommunist challenge and impel the

Kremlin to take tough measures to counter it. If that were to occur, East Berlin would be expected to fall into line behind the Soviet lead and could be counted upon to do so, given the Soviet Union's imposing leverage on the GDR.

On the other hand, if the Soviet Union were to prove delinquent in using its channels of penetration into the GDR's decision-making processes and consequently relaxing its hold over the East German domestic scene, quite different perspectives might emerge. Vernon Aspaturian persuasively argues for a view of Eurocommunism as a cultural phenomenon distinctively tailored to Western conditions.[32] As such, its potential appeal could prove quite substantial to East Germany, a society now thoroughly penetrated by the West, though only problematically "Western" in terms of its historical experience. Indeed, given a measure of Soviet disengagement from Germany and a corresponding reassociation (not even necessarily reunification) between the two present-day German states, Eurocommunist currents could become a genuinely potent political force. They could easily forge practical political bonds between dissident Communists in the GDR and left wing Social Democrats and other radical elements in the Federal Republic of Germany, with truly far-reaching consequences, not least of all for the present international balance of power in Europe.

For the time being, however, an observation of Karl Marx with respect to the relationship between philosophy and politics in the German lands of his time, well over a century ago, seems particularly pertinent. "The German nation is obliged," Marx wrote, "to connect its dream history with its present conditions, and to subject to criticism not only these existing conditions but also their abstract continuation. Its future cannot be restricted either to the negation of its real juridical and political circumstances or to the direct realization of its ideal juridical and political circumstances."[33] In other words, one need not expect, but dare not rule out, an alteration of circumstances that might render Eurocommunism of considerable significance to the future of Germany as a whole.

NOTES

1. Samuel P. Huntington, "Social and Institutional Dynamics of One-Party Systems," in S. P. Huntington and C. H. Moore, eds., *Authoritarian Politics in Modern Society* (New York: Basic Books, 1970), p. 44.

2. Neal Ascherson, "Progress, Not Politics," *New York Review of Books* (March 9, 1967).

3. Peter C. Ludz, "Two Germanies in One World," *The Atlantic Papers*, No. 3 (Paris, 1973); and Peter C. Ludz, *Die DDR zwischen Ost und West von 1961 bis 1976* (Munich: C. H. Beck, 1977).

4. See, for example, James N. Rosenau, ed., *Linkage Politics* (New York: Free Press, 1969) and James N. Rosenau, *The Scientific Study of Foreign Policy* (New York: Free Press, 1971). Compare the earlier, considerably less rigorous and less "scientific" study, Andrew M. Scott, *The Revolution in Statecraft: Informal Penetration* (New York: Random House, 1965).

5. Charles Gati, "The 'Europeanization' of Communism," *Foreign Affairs* (April 1977) and Jiri Valenta, "Eurocommunism and Eastern Europe," *Problems of Communism* (March-April 1978).

6. Thus, in the early postwar days, rank and file Communists expressed views to the effect that "we must build Socialism in Germany without the Red Army and, if it should become necessary, against the Red Army." Wolfgang Leonhard, *Die Revolution entlässt Ihre Kinder* (Cologne: Kiepenheuer and Witsch, 1955), p. 395.

7. Anton Ackermann, "Gibt es einen besonderen deutschen Weg zum Sozialismus?" *Einheit* (Berlin) (February 1946).

8. Leonhard, *Die Revolution*, p. 358.

9. There was circumstantial evidence in mid-1953 to support this hypothesis. Ten years later, Nikita Khrushchev revived speculation about what may have transpired by charging that Berlin, in association with Georgi Malenkov, had in fact advocated "the provocative proposal that the German Democratic Republic be liquidated as a socialist state." *Pravda*, March 10, 1963.

10. See the discussion, with citations of the original sources, in Martin Jänicke, *Der dritte Weg* (Cologne: Neuer Deutscher Verlag, 1964), p. 38.

11. "Die politische Plattform Harichs," *SBZ-Archiv* (Cologne) (Sondernummer 1957), p. 8. Harich's platform was first published by the SPD *Ostbüro* (Eastern Bureau) as "Das Wort hat Dr. Wolfgang Harich," Sonderausgabe, *Einheit* (an illicit SPD series intended for East Germany). The text subsequently appeared in a special issue of *SBZ-Archiv* as well as elsewhere in West Germany and abroad.

12. See the account of one of Harich's confidants, Manfred Hartwig, "Wie es zu meiner Verhaftung kam," *Die Welt* (Hamburg), September 22, 29, 1959.

13. See the discussion in Melvin Croan, "East German Revisionism: The Specter and the Reality," in Leopold Labedz, ed., *Revisionism: Essays on the History of Marxist Ideas* (New York: Frederick A. Praeger, 1962), pp. 239–256.

14. See the excerpts from the Thirty-fifth SED Central Committee Plenum, in *Neues Deutschland*, February 25, 1958.

15. See Eberhard Schulz, *Braucht der Osten die DDR?* (Opladen: Leske, 1968).

16. The 1965 suicide of Eric Apel, head of the GDR Planning Commission, was widely regarded as a protest against Soviet economic exploitation of East Germany. This seems highly probable although it has yet to be fully proven. See the discussion in Joachim Nawrocki, *Das geplante Wunder* (Hamburg: Wegnet, 1967), pp. 172–84.

17. See the coverage in *Der Spiegel* (Hamburg), January 2, 9, 16, 1978. For Rudolf Bahro's text, see Rudolf Bahro, *Die Alternative, Zur Kritick des real existierenden Sozialismus* (Cologne: Europäische Verlagsanstalt, 1977) and Rudolf Bahro, "Die Revolution steht erst bevor. Sechs Vorträge über das Buch 'Die Alternative'" *L76 Demokratie und Sozialismus*, no. 5 (1977), pp. 93–137.

18. See *Neues Deutschland,* June 30, 1978.

19. The text of the "Manifesto" appeared in two parts in *Der Spiegel,* January 2, 1978, pp. 21–24 and January 9, 1978, pp. 26–30. Although the language of the version appearing in *Der Spiegel* seems suspect, specialists do not doubt the authentic existence of the manifesto.

20. *Der Spiegel,* January 2, 1978, p. 24.

21. Allegiance to the Soviet version of "socialist internationalism" was elevated to a basic principle of GDR constitutional law through the 1974 Amendment of the GDR's Constitution of 1968.

22. See *Der Spiegel,* December 13, 1976. This statement, attributed to Hager, was never published in East Germany but its tone rings entirely true.

23. See Heinz Timmermann, "Die Beziehungen Ost-Berlins zu den jugoslawischen und zu den 'Eurokommunisten,'" *Berichte des Bundesinstitut für ostwissenschaftliche und internationale Studien* (Cologne), no. 41 (1977).

24. See the commentaries of the Western Communist parties as reproduced in *Deutschland-Archiv* (Cologne) (No. 1, 1977), pp. 102–103.

25. See *Der Spiegel,* January 16, 1978, *Die Zeit* (North American Edition), April 28, 1978, and *New York Times,* August 8, 1978.

26. See Melvin Croan, *East Germany: The Soviet Connection* (Beverly Hills: Sage Publications, 1976).

27. Erich Mielke in *Neues Deutschland,* September 10–11, 1977.

28. Ernst Richert, "Zwischen Eigenstandigkeit und Dependenz," *Deutschland-Archiv* (No. 9, 1974), pp. 955–982.

29. Ludz, "Two Germanies in One World," p. 14.

30. Examples of the recent, more relaxed and nuanced SED attitude include Erich Honecker's matter-of-fact acknowledgment of differences with the Eurocommunist parties in the context of wishing them success "in the realization of their goals" (*Neues Deutschland,* February 22, 1977) and the absence of any SED polemics against the Spanish party in the context of the attack by *New Times* (Moscow) against Santiago Carrillo, which was, of course, dutifully reproduced in East Germany. See Timmermann, "Die Beziehungen Ost-Berlin," pp. 36–37.

31. See the discussion in Richard Lowenthal, "Moscow and the 'Eurocommunists,'" *Problems of Communism* (July-August 1978), pp. 38–48.

32. Vernon V. Aspaturian, "Conceptualizing Eurocommunism," in this volume.

33. Karl Marx, "Critique of Hegel's *Philosophy of Right,*" in Robert C. Tucker, ed., *The Marx-Engels Reader* (New York: Norton, 1972), p. 16.

CHAPTER VIII

Eurocommunism and Czechoslovakia

Jiri Valenta

Eurocommunism of the 1970s and the pluralistic Communism of Czechoslovakia in the 1960s shared some important similarities. Thus an exploration of the origins and development of Czechoslovak Communism during this period may help to reveal the roots and the evolution of Eurocommunist ideas and tenets. In addition to the historical aspects of this phase of Czechoslovak Communism, I will discuss the mutual influence exerted by Eurocommunism and Czechoslovak Communism upon one another in the 1960s and 1970s and the consequences of this interaction.

A disquisition on Eurocommunism is not necessary at this point, as Vernon Aspaturian and I have discussed the subject elsewhere.[1] I shall use the term not to designate a concept or condition but, in a somewhat more imprecise and ambiguous fashion, to describe a current trend in the international Communist movement. This trend can be loosely identified as a movement toward an independent form of Communism that, unlike the Soviet, is pluralistic in nature. Despite the ambiguous confines of this tendency, Eurocommunism emerges as something more than a myth or "pseudophenomenon," as some have labelled it.[2] Indeed, such West European Communist officials as Spanish Communist party (PCE) leader Santiago Carrillo and Italian Communist party (PCI) leader Enrico Berlinguer have embraced the term as a convenient, though somewhat sloppy, shorthand for their parties' searches for a pluralistic, independent form of Communism. Carrillo traced the evolution of the Eurocommunist trend in his *"Eurocommunismo" y Estado,* the publication of which brought him into collision with conservative ideologists in the USSR and Eastern Europe.

The concept of Eurocommunism also exists in the minds of many conservative leaders in Eastern Europe. While there are those who

continue to doubt its existence, some (such as the Czechoslovak leaders Vasil Bilak and Jan Fojtik) see Eurocommunism as a viable threat.
For these men, Eurocommunism is an instrument of anticommunism
designed to undermine the foundations of "real socialism" in
Czechoslovakia and to return to power such "right-wing oppor-
tunists" and "traitors" as Alexander Dubcek.[3]

Unlike most East European countries, Czechoslovakia shares many
cultural values and political traditions with Western Europe. The prevailing democratic tradition there has been a main force in the development of a Communism that is unique in Eastern Europe.[4] My initial
hypothesis asserts that Czechoslovak Communism is characterized by
two main tendencies: the first authoritarian (Leninist and Stalinist);
the second more democratic and pluralistic. H. Gordon Skilling has
persuasively argued that this dualism helps to explain some of the
dramatic shifts and crises in Czechoslovak Communism since 1921.[5]
The prevailing traditions and political culture in Czechoslovakia as
they have affected the dualism in Czechoslovak Communism must
first be explored in order to assess the origins and development of the
opposite trend toward pluralistic, reform Communism, leading to the
Eurocommunist-type renaissance of 1968.

Democratic Traditions in Czechoslovakia

The dominant tradition in Czechoslovakia has been pro-Western
and democratic. There is a deeply rooted heritage of Protestant religious reform—Hussitism—that came to life in the Czech lands one
hundred years before it surfaced elsewhere in Europe. The Czech
Protestant ethic stressed the ideas of equality, tolerance, reason, and
individualism.[6] Despite the forced conversions to Catholicism in the
seventeenth century, the oppression of the Protestants during the
early stages of Austrian rule, and the numerical majority of Catholics,
the Protestant ethic survived and was an important factor shaping the
character of Czechoslovak political culture. The spirit of the
Enlightenment, the French Revolution, and Austrian liberalism provided an encouraging environment for the flourishing of these democratic traditions. At the same time the politico-economic framework
of the Austrian Empire, as well as the proximity of Germany,
facilitated extensive modernization, industrial maturity, and westernization in Czech lands, particularly in the second half of the nineteenth
century. By the end of the nineteenth century, the process of modernization had produced a respectable level of socioeconomic development and a strong proletarian working class and socialist movement.

Even so, it can be argued that three hundred years of foreign domination and long association with the Austrian Empire introduced into the Czech political culture a behavioral tendency often associated with the hero of the famous World War I novel by Jaroslav Hasek, *The Good Soldier Svejk:* an unwillingness to resist foreign rule by violent means; a passive, compromising behavior; and the sly opportunism of the *maly Cesky clovek* (petty little Czech), serving foreigners and submitting to foreign rule for the sake of survival.[7] Other East European nations, notably Poland and Hungary (where democratic traditions were not so engrained), struggled for political freedom in a fiercely nationalistic, but perhaps unrealistic, fashion. During the nineteenth-century national awakening, the Czechs, lacking a comparable revolutionary passion, negotiated for national and political rights in the Austrian parliament. Armed conflict and revolutionary zeal were generally avoided, since positive political results could not thereby be ensured and lives could be lost.[8]

The historical experience and traditions of the Slovaks were separate from those of the Czechs until 1918. Although the Czechs and Slovaks had similar languages and cultural values and strong ethnic ties, their different historical experience produced different socioeconomic structures and political cultures. In contrast to the Czech lands, Slovakia, as a result of a thousand years of association with Hungary, was a backward, agrarian society with neither political rights for its citizens nor a significant socialist movement.

These differences notwithstanding, the tradition in the Czech lands and, to a much lesser degree, in Slovakia was more pro-Western and democratic than anywhere else in Eastern Europe. It is true, however, that both Czechs and Slovaks (unlike the Poles and Hungarians) shared a sentimental admiration for the Russians, since their history had not been marked by armed clashes with Russia. Unlike the Slavic nations in the Balkans, however, neither the Czechs nor the Slovaks were strongly influenced by pro-Russian pan-Slavism. Western culture had a greater impact on them, and most pro-Western Czechs and many Slovaks felt little or no need to learn from the political experience of the authoritarian and oppressive Tsarist regime. This view was particularly well articulated by the leading Czechoslovak thinker, philosopher, and founding father of the 1918 Czechoslovak republic, Tomas G. Masaryk. As a social and humanist thinker, Masaryk rejected Russian pan-Slavism as reactionary.

The nonviolent establishment of the Czechoslovak republic and political system (modeled after the democracies of the West) was very much affected by a rich legacy of democratic traditions and by the influence of Masaryk and his values: nationalism, but also democracy, pluralism, equality, and human rights. Despite the economic shocks and subsequent social pressures, Czechoslovakia—in contrast to the rest of Eastern Europe and to Germany, Italy, and Spain as well—did not seek a solution in totalitarianism. From this time, when Fascism was on the offensive throughout Europe, until the German occupation of 1939, Czechoslovakia preserved its democratic character.

The Roots of Pluralistic Communism

The democratic traditions of Czechoslovakia and the prevailing Czechoslovak political culture produced an unusual style of Communism. Its historical predecessor was a strong socialist movement organized around the Social Democratic party. Founded in 1878, this party was a curious product of Austro-Marxism and parliamentarianism—a unique political phenomenon in Eastern Europe. The influence of Masarykism as a philosophy and a political orientation was also strong. Whereas Masaryk rejected the revolutionary views of Marx and later, after World War I, even more vehemently those of Lenin, he was interested in the social questions they raised. Some of his views on social justice, equality, and alienation are remarkably similar to those expressed by the young Marx in his *Economic and Philosophical Manuscripts* and later by the Marxist thinkers of the Prague Spring and Eurocommunism. Masaryk felt that there were basically two Marxs, and that Lenin incorrectly cited the Marx that both Marx and Engels themselves later repudiated. While Marx stated that Communism is "a fully developed humanism,"[9] Masaryk declared that "socialism will be either humanistic or it will not be at all."[10]

The serious cleavage in Czechoslovak social democracy, also evident in many other European socialist parties, led to the foundation of the Communist party of Czechoslovakia (CPCz) in 1921. The origins of Leninism can be traced to that year when the Czechoslovak left-wing social democrats opted openly for the Comintern's Twenty-One Points, formed a united, centralized, multinational party, and adopted revolutionary aims. Yet the CPCz came into being only after two years of serious ideological and political disagreements with an impatient and demanding Comintern. Party leader Bohumir Smeral hesitated for some time even to adopt the Communist label, instead calling the party the "Marxist Left" of social democracy.[11]

Smeral may be considered one of the first advocates of pluralistic Communism in the international Communist movement. Like many other left-social democrats, he was sympathetic to Soviet Russia and the Bolshevik Revolution. He also believed, however, as do some Eurocommunists today, that, although the Soviets can serve as an inspiration, their form of socialism should not serve as a universal model for other Communist parties. For Smeral, blind imitation of the Soviet model, disregarding local conditions, could only lead to political disaster, with the party soon losing its mass character and declining to an insignificant sect. Thus Smeral, himself a left-social democrat rather than a Bolshevik, favored parliamentarianism, gradualism, and legalism. It is interesting to note that for some time in 1918 Smeral did not favor a purely Czechoslovak national solution for the Czechoslovak workers' movement, calling instead for transformation of the Austro-Hungarian Empire into a socialist central European federation and for a future "united socialist Europe."[12]

The Executive Committee of the Communist International was impatient, to say the least, with Smeral's views and policies. It criticized him for his hesitation, which was described as "counterrevolutionary" in the Comintern's letters.[13] Finally in 1921, after the Comintern exercised considerable pressure, the Unified Congress of the Left-Social Democrats voted to found the CPCz.

Unlike other Central and East European parties, the CPCz was a mass party, able to boast of important popular strength. This did not escape the attention of Lenin, who told the Czechoslovak Communist leader Karel Kreibich in 1921 that "the location of Czechoslovakia in Central Europe and the mass character of your Party are very important to the future development of events." Lenin is said to have promised that he would learn the Czech language so that he could follow developments in Czechoslovakia directly.[14]

The interest of Lenin and other Soviet leaders in the Czechoslovak party in the 1920s was by no means only theoretical. The Czechoslovaks were called to Moscow and criticized by the Soviet leaders and by Comintern officials at numerous sessions of the Comintern in the 1920s. The Czechoslovak Communist leaders were faulted for their neglect of indoctrination and their lack of revolutionary fervor.[15] In 1923 the CPCz was singled out as being "burdened more heavily than other parties with the remnants of social-democratic ideology."[16] In the 1925 parliamentary election the party received 13 percent of the vote in what amounted to a six-party system, thereby becoming the second strongest party in Czechoslovakia. In the same year, Soviet representative to the Comintern Dimitrii Z. Manuilski said that the Czechoslovak question was to assume "great international significance." The Czechoslovaks were criticized for their "good-natured sentimental attitude" and their conciliatory approach to hostile ideologies, and they were asked to combat the "rightist" danger.[17]

According to an authoritative Soviet source, only at its Fifth Congress in 1929 did the CPCz score a "decisive victory over opportunism and establish itself solidly as a Marxist-Leninist party."[18] At this congress the young, radical leaders—the so-called *Karlinsti kluci* (rascals of Karlin)—took over the party with the help of the Soviets. Many less radical leaders were purged or demoted. Subsequently, and throughout the early 1930s during the process of "Bolshevization," Czechoslovak Communism took on Stalinist tendencies. The effect was twofold: in internal policy, a predominantly Leninist and even more so Stalinist culture (democratic centralism) was established; in foreign affairs, proletarian internationalism (dependence on and obedience to the CPSU) was followed.

The introduction of Leninism and Stalinism—essentially a Byzantine amalgam—into the political environment of a country with predominantly democratic traditions, however, was costly to the CPCz. In the early 1930s it lost its mass character as membership declined through purges and massive defections from 100,000 to about 20,000. On the whole, Stalinization caused the authoritarian character of Czechoslovak Communism to prevail during this period.

Nevertheless, Bolshevization did not totally suppress the democratic traditions of Czechoslovak socialism. Even in the 1930s the CPCz had to struggle, according to Soviet sources, with social-democratism and Masarykism, which were looked upon as "two mutually complementary forms of reactionary ideology prevailing in bourgeois Czechoslovakia."[19] In any case, following a decision of the Comintern in 1935, the Czechoslovak party's revolutionary policies were modified by the popular front as they had been in France and Spain. In foreign affairs, the popular front emphasized the defense of Czechoslovakia against the threat of Fascism and sought to generate popular support for President Edvard Benes's foreign policy of alliance with the USSR, which was initiated in the same year.

The popular fronts of Europe in the 1930s are often cited by Eurocommunist spokesmen, such as Carrillo, as historically important antecedents of Eurocommunism. The CPCz, it should be stressed, was at that time one of the few European parties that remained legal. Consequently, despite its Bolshevization, the CPCz lacked a significant underground Bolshevik tradition. While German and Italian comrades were being deported to concentration camps and most other East European Communists were working in the underground, the Czechoslovak Communists continued to function through the parliamentary system. In the general elections of 1935 the CPCz was the fourth strongest party, earning 10 percent of the popular vote.

As in the case of the French Communist party (PCF), the popular front strategy of the CPCz was destroyed by the events at Munich and by the Nazi-Soviet pact of August 23, 1939. Czechoslovak Communists, like their comrades in France and elsewhere in Europe, were asked to sacrifice their interests for the *Realpolitik* benefit to the USSR. Support for the new Comintern line, however, came only after a few months of confusion—perhaps even opposition—and the possible purge of several members of the Central Committee in Prague.[20]

Czechoslovakia's "Specific Road toward Socialism": 1945–1947

Elements of Smeralism or democratic Communism were revived briefly during the period 1945–1947. By 1945 the CPCz, like the Communist parties of France and Italy, had become a massive movement on the threshold of power. Like its West European counterparts, the PCI and the PCF, the CPCz was able to attain, with the general European "swing to the left" shortly after World War II, the image of a progressive movement fighting against Fascism and for national liberation. Like the Italian and French parties, the CPCz did not attempt to seize power in 1945. Instead, Klement Gottwald, like Palmiro Togliatti and Maurice Thorez, advocated a strategy of broad alliances and parliamentarianism. In 1945 the CPCz began to experiment with a mixture of Smeralism and popular front strategy on a large scale but under a different name—"a specific road toward socialism." This strategy, which was elaborated in the top echelons of the party in their Moscow exile, was in many ways similar to the strategy of the Eurocommunists. In 1968 Dubcek and his supporters would turn to them for inspiration.

Although Czechoslovakia's "specific road toward socialism" lacked a precise theoretical elaboration, it evolved into a coherent, pragmatic program. In domestic affairs it was characterized by a thrust toward an essentially pluralistic form of government: a coalition of four ruling parties in a parliamentary system under the concept of a "National Front." In 1945 Gottwald actually had to defend his policy favoring a coalition government against some radical party officials, saying that the party's "immediate goal" was not a "Soviet Republic, a socialist state" and that it would be a "great strategic mistake if the Party had such an immediate perspective."[21] True, all rightist and conservative parties were forbidden and the National Front was a "closed" coalition. The democratic process, even more than during the interwar period, was limited to a search for multiparty consensus, often bypassing Parliament behind closed doors. One essential ingredient of a pluralistic system was missing—an opposition party. Yet the Communist party made a commitment to tolerate human and civil rights, including religious rights. In economics, the party favored an essentially mixed economy of nationalized and private industries and the synthesis of the planned and market systems. While favoring land reform, nationalization, and state control of large enterprises, it tolerated large sectors of private industry and private agriculture. In foreign affairs the CPCz, like all other Czechoslovak political parties, favored a close alliance with the USSR. However, as Klement Gottwald declared, this policy was not supposed to prevent the reestablishment of good relations with friendly Western powers.[22]

For some leaders, perhaps including Gottwald, the commitment to "a specific road toward socialism" had greater tactical than strategic significance. Nevertheless, from 1945 to 1947 there appears to have been widespread belief among many Communist officials and rank-and-file members that Czechoslovakia, because of its different traditions, political culture, and national conditions, might take a different path toward socialism from the one taken by the USSR in 1917. This belief was probably encouraged by the Soviets and by Stalin himself, who saw Czechoslovakia as an example for potential Communist victories through the parliamentary system in Italy and France. At that time the Czechoslovak Communists associated their program with the traditions of Hussitism, the Reformation, and Masarykism.[23]

Not surprisingly, the CPCz's policies enjoyed widespread popular support, particularly in the industrialized Czech lands. In agrarian Slovakia, however, the party received less support. This was well demonstrated by the free elections of May 1946, in which the CPCz (numbering over a million members) secured 38 percent of the total vote—by far the largest proportion ever won in free balloting by any Communist party. While the Communists received an overwhelming 43 percent in the Czech lands, in Slovakia they received only 30 percent. As a result, the dominant political force in Slovakia became the Democratic party, which received 62 percent of the vote, again confirming the weakness of the Communist movement in that part of Czechoslovakia.

The experiment with "a specific road toward socialism" lasted only until 1947. There are several reasons for this. First, it took place following World War II and within a climate of moral erosion, weakened national self-confidence, and loss of identity resulting from the six-year German occupation, during which many Czechs and Slovaks collaborated with the Germans.

Second, Czechoslovak internal policies and coalition politics were affected, even conditioned, by the great-power interplay in Europe following World War II. In 1947 Czechoslovakia, like Italy and France, became a cold war battleground for the ideological and political maneuverings of the USSR and the Western powers. The Soviet leadership's negative response to the Marshall Plan placed obstacles on the Czechoslovak path toward socialism.[24] In July 1947 Stalin vetoed the CPCz decision that, along with that of at least one other Communist party (the Polish), approved the acceptance of an invitation by Western powers to discuss the Marshall Plan.[25] The founding of the Cominform in 1947 as the institutional device of the Soviets' European control system and the acceptance of Andrei Zhdanov's thesis of "two camps" undoubtedly affected the CPCz strategy of seeking "a specific road toward socialism."

These developments similarly affected the parliamentary path to socialism of the PCI and PCF, both of which were severely attacked by the Soviet and Yugoslav leaders at the Cominform session of September 1947.[26] It became clear that the Soviet leadership had decided to abandon the idea of separate paths toward socialism in the advanced countries of Europe in favor of the theory of the universality of the dictatorship of the proletariat. The fate of the representatives of the Communist parties of France and Italy, who were forced from their governments in the spring of 1947, was used as a warning to the CPCz. In September 1947 Czechoslovakia was the only country in Eastern Europe where a coalition government still existed and where the power struggle between Communist and non-Communist forces had not yet been settled. At the first session of the Cominform the USSR made it clear that it wished to alter this situation.

Third, internal developments in France and Italy in 1947 had an impact on the perceptions of Czechoslovak officials. Many were particularly shaken by the expulsion of the PCF and PCI from their respective governments. The *ultras* (radical forces in the CPCz) viewed "a specific road toward socialism" as only a temporary tactic and never gave up the Leninist dictum of the dictatorship of the proletariat. They began to warn both the Czechoslovak leadership and Moscow of an impulse in the non-Communist parties to isolate the Communists, adding that this would result in the expulsion of Communists from the government, as had happened earlier in France and Italy. The *ultras* doubted that in the forthcoming elections of May 1948 the party would be able to maintain its leading position in the National Front coalition by constitutional means. Consequently, they called for a confrontation within the front.[27]

Fourth, some of the blunders of American diplomacy vis-à-vis Eastern Europe and the inept actions of non-Communist politicians in Czechoslovakia in 1946 and 1947 had actually strengthened the hand of the Communists in their power play, which led to the unresisted, bloodless, and even elegant Communist takeover of February 1948.

All these factors bore heavily on the CPCz shift from its emphasis on "a specific road toward socialism" to "dictatorship of the proletariat." International factors, both global and regional, were perhaps the most important variables in this process. The cold war between the United States and the USSR and the pressures of radical elements in the international Communist movement forced the CPCz (and also some West European Communist parties, particularly the PCI and PCF) into a Stalinist mold.

Even before the establishment of the Cominform in 1947, Czechoslovakia was criticized by Yugoslav and Polish leaders for its "politics of opportunism." Soviet and some East European leaders viewed the political situation in Czechoslovakia, unlike that in other East European countries, as unresolved, and the country itself as being "the weakest link" in the socialist camp. In 1948 the Hungarian leader Matyas Rakosi and the Polish leader Boleslaw Bierut began to press the Czechoslovak party leadership into a search for internal Titoist "enemies" in the CPCz.[28] The Soviet leadership felt that the Czechoslovak party was more susceptible to Western "deviations" than any other party in Eastern Europe. This may at least partly explain the intensity and scope of the massive wave of purges and political trials in Czechoslovakia during 1949–1954. These involved many Communist officials, a number of whom had advocated, with Soviet blessings, "a specific road toward socialism." Some found their end on the gallows.

In this period Stalinism became the prevailing trend in European Communism. The mode of "a specific road toward socialism" was replaced again by the Bolshevik political culture and the Soviet model of socialism. Gottwald, who at times probably hesitated to accept all of Stalin's orders (particularly regarding the political trials), eventually yielded to Stalin, whom he feared and whose authority he had learned to respect in the old days during the Bolshevization of the CPCz and the Comintern. In January 1953, at the very peak of Stalinism in Czechoslovakia, Gottwald revised his own dictum of the specific road, declaring that there is "only one road, the Soviet road, toward socialism in Czechoslovakia."[29]

Prague Spring 1968: Czechoslovakia's Experiment with Eurocommunism

The story of Stalinism in Czechoslovakia and of Antonin Novotny's rule in the 1950s need not be readdressed here. It suffices to say that Stalinism as a system was more intense and devastating in Czechoslovakia (despite its democratic tradition and pluralist culture) than in most other countries of Eastern Europe. It survived at least until the early 1960s. De-Stalinization was a gradual process interrupted by temporary lapses into counterreformism during 1957–1960 and 1963–1965.

It is often overlooked that the first criticisms of Stalinism within the CPCz were heard as early as the mid-1950s. Indeed, the "national Communism" in Yugoslavia and the wave of reforms and "national Communism" in Poland and in Hungary in 1956, following the Twentieth Congress of the CPSU and Togliatti's advocacy of "polycentric" Communism, produced reverberations not only among intellectuals and students in Czechoslovakia but also among a number of party members. During the revolutionary spring of 1956 some CPCz members called for an extraordinary party congress and for far-reaching de-Stalinization. By October, during the crisis in Poland and Hungary, the Presidium of the CPCz probably feared not only for the future of the Communist regime in Hungary but also for the regime in Czechoslovakia.[30] Only after the revolution in Hungary and the subsequent Soviet intervention were Stalinist forces in the CPCz leadership able to start coping effectively with those party members who advocated rapid de-Stalinization in Czechoslovakia. Under Novotny's leadership, the party then unleashed its propaganda campaign against "national Communism" in Yugoslavia and Poland and against revisionism and Masarykism in Czechoslovakia, thereby slowing the process of de-Stalinization.

Yet gradually, in the late 1950s and 1960s, reformers in the CPCz, as in some West European Communist parties (particularly the PCI and in the 1960s the PCE), began to move away from the Stalinist model. Their respective evolutions were influenced by many of the same circumstances, as well as by comparable political necessities. The common feature was the recognition that Stalinism was out of harmony with the prevailing traditions and political cultures in their countries. The reformers also saw the need to win popular support. "Stalinism" in Czechoslovakia, as H. Gordon Skilling aptly put it, was a "grotesque manifestation of Byzantinism in a profoundly Western country."[31]

Undoubtedly, Czechoslovakia in 1956 lagged behind the revolutionary élan characteristic of Poland and Hungary. De-Stalinization came about more slowly and gradually there than in neighboring countries because of a combination of factors: a traditional unwillingness to resist oppression and terror by violent means, a weakening of the national morale as a consequence of the shocks of 1938 and 1948, and the terror of the early 1950s, which killed or temporarily silenced the potential Nagys, Gomulkas, and Kadars who would have embarked upon a sharp program of de-Stalinization. The gradual de-Stalinization and subsequent slow process of democratization that led to the Prague Spring were possible because of the legalistic and pluralistic traditions of Czechoslovak political culture. Also countering the Bolshevization of 1929–1935 and the Stalinization of 1948–1954 were legacies of the pluralistic Communism of Smeral in the early 1920s, the popular front policies of the latter 1930s, and the "specific road toward socialism" of the latter 1940s, which paved the way for the Eurocommunist experiment of spring 1968.

Czechoslovak Communism of 1968 exhibited some similarities with Eurocommunism and shared with it certain mutual influences. Like Eurocommunism, the Prague Spring was not just a product of de-Stalinization; it was also a by-product of various reformist trends in European Communism (both East and West) present since the mid-1950s—"national Communism" as practiced in Yugoslavia since 1951 and for a short time in Poland and Hungary in 1956 and the evolution toward democratic socialism in the PCI. From the early 1960s, reform-minded intellectuals of West European parties—Roger Garaudy, Lombardo Radice, Ernst Fischer, and Franz Marek—began conducting a transnational dialogue with leading Marxist intellectuals in Eastern Europe—the Hungarian Gyorgy Lukacs, Leszek Kolakowski in Poland, and Czechoslovakia's Karel Kosik, Ivan Svitak, Edvard Goldstucker, and others. This promising dialogue was based on a genuine and critical revival of the philosophy of the "authentic" Marx and of Marxist humanism. In a philosophical-intellectual sense it laid the theoretical foundations for both the Prague Spring and Eurocommunism.

In Czechoslovakia, the renaissance of the philosophy of the young Marx was supplemented in the 1960s by the revival of a critical interest in the socialist humanism of the "old" Masaryk and the great Prague writer Franz Kafka.[32] Kafka's work became a symbol of the breaking away from the grotesque Byzantinism imposed by Stalinism. Not surprisingly, some of the most orthodox East European leaders, such as East Germany's Walter Ulbricht and his ideologists, dated the origins of "revisionism in Prague" from the famous 1963 conference in Liblice, Czechoslovakia, where Marxist theoreticians from the East and West "rehabilitated" Kafka. A leading post-Dubcek-era ideologist and veteran fighter against revisionism in Czechoslovakia, Fojtik, goes even farther, dating the origins of Czechoslovak revisionism back to the late 1950s, when Kosik and Svitak and "their idols, the various Fischers and Garaudys," began their attack on Marxism-Leninism.[33] In the 1960s Garaudy and Fischer, as the Soviet writer M. Silin has pointed out, "had devoted special works and speeches, including some right in Prague, to prepare for the 'Prague Spring' and the 'Czechoslovak experiment'!"[34] This is a remarkable tribute to the ability of West European Communist theoreticians to influence political developments in Czechoslovakia.

In Prague during the 1960s, Marxist intellectuals displayed considerable interest, not only in the West as a whole, but specifically in liberalizing trends current in West European Communism and particularly in the PCI.[35] While some West European Communist intellectuals and officials viewed the process of de-Stalinization and the gradual democratization in Czechoslovakia as significant developments of real relevance to them, Marxist intellectuals in Czechoslovakia and at least one high Czechoslovak official, Secretary of the Central Committee Vaclav Koucky, looked with hope to the reformist tendencies of the Italian party.[36]

Both the Prague Spring and Eurocommunism were the product of a trend that began and developed within formerly Stalinist parties, often by erstwhile radicals. Some of the leading figures of the Prague Spring, like Josef Smrkovsky, Frantisek Kriegel, and Josef Pavel, were men who had played an important role in the coup of 1948. As Carrillo has observed, "In Prague, as here in the PCE, the initiators of the movement came from the Czechoslovak Party itself and had been formerly Stalinistic."[37] In the political arena the Czechoslovak reforms (spearheaded by some Slovak politicians in 1962–1963) were prepared and carried out by a coalition in the CPCz; old party veterans joining forces with younger moderate officials, both Czechs and Slovaks, in their struggle against more conservative elements. This struggle, which intensified in 1967–1968, led to Novotny's fall and his replacement by Dubcek.

The program of Dubcek's leadership came about as a result of several years of theoretical work by several brain-trusts or interdisciplinary teams within the party. One of them, dealing with political reform, was headed by Zdenek Mlynar;[38] another dealing with economic reform, by Ota Sik. Overall, the peaceful revolution of early 1968 was the outcome of a "revolution from above" rather than from below—a struggle from within and not from without the party. It was the result of the theoretical and practical work of reformers who tried to link economic with political reform of the system.

The reform-minded leaders of the CPCz had incorporated their more pluralistic concept of socialism into the Action Program accepted by the leadership in April 1968 as the Magna Carta of Dubcek's new leadership. In it the Prague Spring reformers turned for inspiration to some of the concepts of the "specific Czechoslovak road to socialism" espoused during 1945–1947. Its main features in domestic politics were the legalization of democratic procedures within the CPCz; the granting of more autonomy to state bureaucracies, the other political parties, and the Parliament; the restoration of civil rights and freedom of expression and association; the more vigorous continuation of political rehabilitation; the restoration of the national rights of ethnic minorities within a federally organized state; the consistent implementation of economic reform; and the decentralization of the economy. Free discussion of Dubcek's reformist program of socialism "with a human face" was given increasing play in Czechoslovak politics. During the Prague Spring the ethics of Marxian democratic socialism were linked to and synthesized with a critical but nevertheless objective reassessment of Masaryk's humanism.

In terms of pluralism and human rights, Dubcek's reforms were much broader in scope and more comprehensive than those of Imre Nagy or Wladyslaw Gomulka in 1956—more, even, than any Yugoslav reforms. Reflecting essentially Western, democratic traditions, the Prague Spring was more gradual, protracted, legalistic, and tolerant than any previous reform movement in Eastern Europe. Unlike the reform movements in Poland and Hungary in 1956, the reform movement in Czechoslovakia was a very broad, very thorough program, initiated from above and carried out without excesses or violence.

Thus, it is not surprising that the Prague Spring was viewed in the reform-oriented circles of West European parties, particularly the PCE and the PCI, as well as by reformers in the PCF and in neighboring countries (Poland, East Germany, and even the USSR) as an example of democratic socialism relevant to the European Communist movement as a whole. Many West European Communist parties saw the Prague Spring experiment as transcending Czechoslovak borders and having significance for the West European Communist movement. Thus, shortly after publication of the Action Program, a high official of the PCE, Santiago Alvarez, expressed his approval of Dubcek's Czechoslovakia as a "type of socialist society which, given our concrete conditions and experiences, we think we must have in Spain."[39] After a visit to Czechoslovakia in May 1968, Luigi Longo, secretary general of the PCI, declared that the Czechoslovak experiment not only "helps the parties of certain socialist countries" but also assists "the Communist parties of the capitalist countries in their struggle to create a new socialist society—young, open and modern."[40] In April of the same year, PCF Secretary Waldeck Rochet also praised Dubcek and pledged support for his program, which the French leader claimed contributed to the "expansion of Socialism."[41]

Seen from the point of view of conservative elements in the Soviet and East European establishments (including those in Czechoslovakia), however, the reforms implemented by Dubcek's leadership created a dangerous political situation and threatened to spill over into neighboring countries, primarily Poland, East Germany, and the USSR. As the Prague Spring advanced into summer, evolving gradually from a "revolution from above" into a "revolution from below," but always nonviolent and controlled by the party leadership, apprehensions increased. So did pressures against the Czechoslovak reformists by the leaders of the three neighboring countries. Again, as in 1947–1948, the Stalinist elements in the Czechoslovak leadership warned Moscow and asked for "fraternal assistance."

Simultaneously, support for Dubcek's regime grew more vociferous among reformist elements in the European Communist parties, particularly in Western Europe. Fearing that conservative bureaucracies in the USSR and in Eastern Europe would attempt to crush the Prague Spring, the PCI, PCE, and PCF mobilized seventeen West European Communist parties in behalf of the embattled country. During the crisis, this coalition brought considerable pressure to discourage intervention. Among other tactics, the member parties threatened to convene a separate conference to condemn the USSR. Longo and Carrillo figured prominently in efforts to prevent the invasion, and Rochet served as mediator between Czechoslovak and Soviet leaders. Although Eurocommunist pressure did not deter the invasion, it caused much confusion and procrastination before the decision was taken, and it probably moderated Soviet behavior both during and after the intervention.[42]

Thus, the Prague Spring and Eurocommunism, especially as practiced by the PCE and PCI, bear some important similarities. These are particularly evident in their independence in applying the principles of Marxism; their renunciation of violent revolution; and their commitment to Western values of humanism and pluralism, and freedom of opinion, association, and the press.

Simply put, the Prague Spring can be considered the forerunner of Eurocommunism, and the Czechoslovak reformers can be considered its precursors in their attempt to create a model of socialism that, rooted in the Western tradition, differs from that of the USSR. So similar is the process of democratization that took place in the CPCz in 1968 to the trend manifested in the Eurocommunist parties of Italy and Spain in the late 1970s that Carrillo ventured this striking analogy: "If the term 'Eurocommunism' had been invented in 1968, Dubcek would have been a Eurocommunist!"[43]

There are, to be sure, some important differences between Prague reformism and Eurocommunism. In domestic affairs, the reformers in the ruling Czechoslovak party sought to modify the existing authoritarian structure of state, whereas the PCI and, to a lesser degree, the PCE, both nonruling Communist parties, operate within a state structure of pluralism. Also, unlike some West European parties, the CPCz under Dubcek did not embrace a genuinely parliamentary system with free elections nor even approximate the parliamentary system of 1945–1947. On the contrary, the Czechoslovak reformers made it clear that they would not allow fully free and universal suffrage but only a "limited pluralism," with the party maintaining its leading role.

There are also important differences in the approach to foreign affairs by the CPCz and the Eurocommunist parties of Western Europe. Unlike the latter, whose foreign policies diverge in some areas from those of the USSR, the Czechoslovak reformers never questioned their foreign policy dependence on the USSR. Berlinguer has said that the development of socialism in Western Europe is safer under NATO's umbrella, and Carrillo stated that the PCE would physically oppose the USSR in any military offensive against Spain, but Dubcek never questioned Czechoslovakia's membership in the Warsaw Pact and the socialist camp, and he did not resist the Soviet military intervention. Thus, the importance of the Prague Spring lies in its being not so much a model for the West European Communist parties as an inspiration to their political development—and, significantly, a warning.

After events in Czechoslovakia, the Leninist version of socialism in the USSR and in Eastern Europe became an even greater liability and embarrassment to the Communist parties in Western Europe. The invasion marked a crucial turning point, since most of the West European Communist parties had never before openly opposed the USSR on a major policy issue. Furthermore, support for Dubcek was the first joint anti-Soviet venture of the Italian and Spanish Communist parties and their first shared action as Eurocommunists.

On the whole, the invasion encouraged a broad trend toward greater autonomy for Communist parties in developed states, particularly in Western Europe. As Manuel Azcárate, head of the PCE's Foreign Policy Department, pointed out, "It posed for Communist parties the need to assert their independence with renewed vigor." More significantly, the invasion spawned a new trend toward "socialism with a human face" that embodies even greater departures from the Soviet model than the architects of the Prague Spring had contemplated. Although the idea that each party should enjoy autonomy was not new, the notion that democratic socialism constitutes a relevant model for the West was new for most of the West European

Communist parties. Czechoslovakia's "socialism with a human face" may not have served as a model, but perhaps, in Azcárate's words, it did serve as "the most specific point of reference" for the rejection of the Soviet model of socialism and "for pointing out the rise of the new trend in the Communist movement which later took the name Eurocommunism."[44] Or, as Milovan Djilas simply put it, Eurocommunism "was born in Czechoslovakia in 1968."[45]

Eurocommunism and Czechoslovakia

Like West European Communism, Communism in Czechoslovakia has been characterized by two conflicting tendencies. The more democratic tendency first became apparent under the leadership of Smeral in the early 1920s. It reemerged under a different form in the popular front strategy of 1935–1938 and even more strongly in the 1945–1947 thrust toward "a specific road to socialism." Finally, it was the strong force behind the Prague Spring of 1968. The authoritarian tendency manifested itself particularly during the so-called Bolshevization in the late 1920s and early 1930s, the Stalinism of 1948–1954, and the period following the Soviet invasion of 1968. Stalinism, the extreme version of this tendency, was able to develop and survive in Czechoslovakia mainly because of external pressures and coercion from the USSR and some neighboring East European countries. The CPCz was a mass party with strong popular support only when the democratic trend, in tune with the democratic traditions of the country, prevailed. Whenever the party fostered Stalinist policies, which were imported from and imposed by the USSR and were at variance with native tradition, the party became, before taking power, an insignificant, dogmatic sect and after taking power, a numerically strong but purged organization that could not rule without Soviet support and the use of coercion or terror.

This is the situation in which the CPCz finds itself at the end of the 1970s. After the Soviet intervention and Dubcek's dismissal in April 1969, the Prague Spring experiment was gradually reversed. This happened, as in the past, through the efforts of *ultra* elements in the party, and again with substantial aid from the CPSU and other East European parties. Although the so-called normalization in the 1970s did not reach the proportions of 1949–1954, it brought about the revival of a moderate version of Stalinism in Czechoslovakia.[46]

Czechoslovakia in the early 1980s is a country with one of the most oppressive regimes in Eastern Europe. Those from the "party of the expelled," among them many former supporters of Dubcek's Eurocommunism and Marxists in general, suffer the worst persecution.

The Czechoslovak secret police, ironically called the "anticommunist squad," specialize in the persecution of dissidents, among them many leftists and former Communists.[47] Former Czechoslovak officials who became dissidents, such as Jaroslav Sabata, are described as "common criminals," while others both at home and abroad are labeled "Zionists" and "counterrevolutionaries." In the postinvasion purge of 1970 approximately 500,000 of a total membership of 1,500,000 were removed from the CPCz. Ninety percent of the casualties, many of them prewar party veterans—individuals with a high degree of education and party seniority, many of whom supported Dubcek— were in the Czech lands. Although most have become politically apathetic, some may still be viewed as potential supporters of the "party of the future"—the potential cadres for Czechoslovak Eurocommunism.

The future of Eurocommunism in Czechoslovakia, despite the Stalinist relapse, may still be relevant. A form of Eurocommunism existed in Czechoslovakia during the Prague Spring and links between this Czechoslovak Communism and West European Communism are significant, developed through interaction and strong mutual influence. The Eurocommunist-oriented parties in Western Europe have not lost their interest in the ideas of the Prague Spring. Thus in July 1978, the PCI's *L'Unità* organized a seminar on the topic of "the Czechoslovak Experience of the Spring of 1968" at the Gramsci Institute's Center for Studies of Socialist Countries. There, Central Committee member Radice pointed out that the Prague Spring showed the development of reform Communism in the East and the West to be "parallel," and "two interconnected processes."[48]

The experience of the Prague Spring, brief though it was, was important to the Eurocommunists. As PCI Foreign Section Deputy Chief A. Rubbi stated, it motivated and accelerated PCI theoretical study and political development for the West European independent and original road to "socialism in democracy and freedom."[49] Similarly, the PCE's *Mundo Obrero* asserted in 1978 that "there is a fundamental connection between the road followed during that Spring and the plan for 'socialism in freedom' called 'Eurocommunism.'"[50]

The interest in Czechoslovakia among Eurocommunists of the PCE and PCI is not merely of a theoretical or academic nature. Since 1968, together with the Communist-led trade unions in Italy and France, they have provided a degree of moral and political support for exiled Marxists from Czechoslovakia and occasional political and, it seems, financial support for Czechoslovak dissidents. The PCI and PCE periodicals—*L'Unità, Rinascità,* and *Mundo Obrero*—have often provided an opportunity for exiled Dubcek-era politicians from

Czechoslovakia (Jiri Pelikan and Mlynar, for example) and for others still living in Czechoslovakia (such as Dubcek, the late Smrkovsky, and the late Kriegel) to present their views. These periodicals, as well as the PCF's *L'Humanité,* on occasion, have reported on and criticized the oppressive policies against the dissidents in Czechoslovakia. Special publicity was given in 1977–1979 to the affair surrounding Charter 77, a document that proved that democratic traditions and some ideas of the Prague Spring had not disappeared in Czechoslovakia. The several hundred signatories of this charter—a broad coalition of Eurocommunist-minded and non-Communist intellectuals (including several former members of Dubcek's government), politicians, and workers—called for a strong defense of the civil liberties and political rights of citizens. There is inconclusive evidence that the chartists received some political support from Eurocommunist parties and trade unions, and East European dissident groups such as the Polish Worker's Defense Committee.[51]

Although Eurocommunist support for the Czechoslovak dissidents is very limited, Czechoslovak officials nevertheless fear Eurocommunist influence. The "healthy forces" in the CPCz, who in 1968 opposed Dubcek's version of Eurocommunism and asked for "fraternal assistance" from the USSR, are those who criticize Eurocommunism most harshly in the East. They include Presidium member Bilak and old "fighters against revisionism," such as Secretary of the Central Committee Fojtik. In their view, Eurocommunism exists as a well-defined movement created by Western ideologists such as Zbigniew Brzezinski, who is said to be a "spiritual father of Eurocommunism."[52] According to Czechoslovak sources, Eurocommunism is a hostile strategy "being foisted as a 'cuckoo's egg' on Western European Communist parties. Their leaders, such as Carrillo, have completely taken over and are cultivating with unconcealed pleasure that cuckoo's egg of 'Eurocommunism.'"[53] Eurocommunism, Fojtik observes, is an expression of the "geopolitical prejudice of Eurocentrism." It is "subversive" and is advocated by those who want to turn Czechoslovakia "back to Western civilization."[54]

As Czechoslovak officials see it, important similarities exist between the men of the Prague Spring and leading Eurocommunists. Prague Spring reformists like Mlynar, Sik, Smrkovsky, Dubcek, Hejzlar, Pelikan, and others fought in the late 1960s, just as the Eurocommunists do in the late 1970s, for ideological independence and a breakaway from Moscow.[55] In the view of hard-liners in Prague, Eurocommunism is subversive and plays the role of a fifth column. According to Fojtik, that "anticommunism obviously wants to incite the opposition elements in the socialist countries with the aid of

Eurocommunists' and our dissidents, with has-beens of the 'Prague Spring,' with oppositionists and renegades heckling our country from the anti-communist centers and bourgeois communications media, is a sufficient warning sign."[56] Eurocommunists, such as the PCE's Azcárate (Carrillo's right-hand man who holds the record as the Eurocommunist most frequently attacked by the Czechoslovak press), are "spreading the contagion of liberated Eurocommunism from Western to Eastern Europe" and preparing the "takeovers of Eurocommunists in socialist countries."[57]

The foregoing discussion does not mean to imply that Eurocommunism's limited influence in Czechoslovakia could produce the new Prague Spring in Czechoslovakia that is feared by paranoid elements in the leadership of that country. Such apocalyptic judgments, perhaps purposely exaggerated, clearly run counter to the facts. Several factors limit the influence of Eurocommunism in Czechoslovakia. The Eurocommunists have only selectively criticized violations of human rights and only very selectively supported the dissidents in Czechoslovakia. The Eurocommunist parties do not want to aggravate their disagreement with the Soviet leaders or to risk excommunication by Moscow. Likewise, Soviet leaders do not wish, at least for the moment, a total break with the dissident Eurocommunist parties.[58]

Eurocommunist support also varies from party to party. The general rule is that the more commitment there is to Eurocommunism, the more commitment there will be to support of the dissidents in Eastern Europe. Whereas the PCE leadership maintains ties with the men of the Prague Spring outside and inside Czechoslovakia and supports the dissidents openly, the PCI leadership does so more cautiously. In contrast, the PCF leadership maintains a hands-off policy and is silent. In the Eurocommunist wings of both the PCI and the PCF, many intellectuals and militants would like to see their parties follow the PCE's policies.[59] Another constraint on Eurocommunist influence in Eastern Europe is the USSR and its hegemonic interest in that region. It is doubtful that the Soviets will permit a Eurocommunist-type government in any East European country in the near future.

Despite the paranoia of segments of the ruling elite, Eurocommunist influence on the dissident movement in Czechoslovakia is limited. First, the movement is confined to several hundred members. Second, the dissidents express varying political orientations—some of them Eurocommunist, even Trotskyist, others Christian, and still others clearly anti-Communist with ultraconservative leanings.[60] Many dissidents in Czechoslovakia do not believe in Eurocommunism, but they do hope the Eurocommunists will play a role in aiding the dissident movement and perhaps in moderating the behavior of local officials.[61] Moreover, so long as the Eurocommunists are not excommunicated from the common fold, the hard-liners in Eastern Europe and in the USSR will find it difficult to monitor the two-way flow of Eurocommunist ideas between Eastern and Western Europe and to prevent their flourishing in the East.

The dissident movement in Eastern Europe poses a very serious dilemma for the West European Communist parties that profess a Eurocommunist orientation. It is a fundamental issue touching on the essential problem of Leninism and on Communist party attitudes and policies toward the USSR and the East European regimes. Only the PCE leadership has consistently attempted to assert Eurocommunist options, including initial steps toward de-Leninization of the party. There is an ongoing struggle in the PCI and PCF between both tendencies, Leninist and Eurocommunist, with the latter strongly opposed by the parties' pro-Soviet wings. Many leaders of these two parties (particularly the PCF) have not yet undertaken a thorough and comprehensive analysis of the failings of the Prague Spring as Carrillo, Azcárate, and Jean Elleinstein have done. If they had done so, they would have concluded that some elements of their domestic programs (for instance, the PCF insistence on immediate nationalization of most industrial firms) and their foreign policy (PCI acceptance, perhaps against its will, of certain rules of international solidarity and PCF support for various Soviet foreign policy actions such as the invasion of Afghanistan) are unrealistic and self-defeating.

The future of Eurocommunism in Czechoslovakia depends on the fate of Eurocommunism in Western Europe. If Eurocommunism is defeated in the West, it will be remembered as a broken trend in the history of European Communism that succumbed to the Leninist and Stalinist legacy. If Eurocommunism succeeds in becoming a genuine political force in Western Europe, a new, indeed still to be imagined, version of "socialism with a human face" may emerge in the West, and perhaps also in Czechoslovakia, and with it a credible alternative to Leninism.

NOTES

In writing this chapter I used my previous research on the history of Czechoslovak Communism undertaken with the late Professor Josef Korbel in preparation for his book *Twentieth-Century Czechoslovakia: The Meanings of Its History* (1977). I have also benefited from interviews that I conducted with many Czechoslovak officials—former members of Alexander Dubcek's government—and many of Dubcek's advisers, including scholars and dissidents now living in Western countries. This chapter also appears as an article in *East Central Europe (L'Europe du Centre-Est)*, VII (1980).

1. See Jiri Valenta, "Eurocommunism and Eastern Europe: Promise or Threat?" presented at the National Convention of the American Association for the Advancement of Slavic Studies, October 14, 1977; Jiri Valenta, "Eurocommunism and Eastern Europe," *Problems of Communism*, XVII (March-April 1978), pp. 41–54; and Jiri Valenta, "Eurocommunism and Eastern Europe," in Teresa Rakowska-Harmstone and Andrew Gyorgy, eds., *Communism in Eastern Europe* (Bloomington: Indiana University Press, 1979), pp. 290–307. See also Vernon V. Aspaturian, "Conceptualizing Eurocommunism: Some Preliminary Observations" in this volume.

2. Angelo M. Codevilla, "Eurocommunism, Pseudophenomenon," *Strategic Review* (Fall 1978), pp. 62–70.

3. See, for example, Jan Fojtik, *Tribuna* (Prague), April 19, 1978.

4. Aspaturian, "Conceptualizing Eurocommunism."

5. See H. Gordon Skilling, *Czechoslovakia's Interrupted Revolution* (Princeton: Princeton University Press, 1976), pp. 21–42. Skilling has also scrutinized the Stalinist trend in an excellent essay. See H. Gordon Skilling, "Stalinism and Czechoslovak Political Culture," in Robert C. Tucker, ed., *Stalinism: Essays in Historical Interpretation* (New York: Norton, 1979), pp. 257–282.

6. For studies treating Communism and Czechoslovak tradition, see H. Gordon Skilling, "Communism and Czechoslovak Traditions," *Journal of International Affairs*, XX (No. 1, 1966), pp. 118–136; Paul E. Zinner, *Communist Strategy and Tactics in Czechoslovakia, 1918–48* (New York: Praeger, 1963), pp. 5–24; and Galia Golan, "The Democratic-liberal Traditions in the Czech Lands," an unpublished paper.

7. See the discussion of Czechoslovak sociologist Emanuel Chalupny, *Narodni filosofie ceskoslovenska* (Prague, 1932) and of David W. Paul, "The Repluralization of Czechoslovak Politics in the 1960s," *Slavic Review*, 33 (December 1974), pp. 721–740; David W. Paul, "Nationalism, Pluralism and Schweikism in Czechoslovakia's Political Culture" (Ph.D. dissertation, Princeton Unviersity, 1973); and Ivan Pfaff, "Kolaboranti mezi nami: tradice nebo complex?" *Svedectvi* (Paris), XI (1971), pp. 45–58. For a different interpretation, see Skilling, *Czechoslovakia's Interrupted Revolution*, pp. 16–19.

8. For an analysis, see Ferdinand Peroutka, *Jaci jsme* (Prague: Borovy, 1934) and Korbel, *Twentieth-Century Czechoslovakia*, pp. 4–24.

9. Karl Marx, *Economic and Philosophical Manuscripts* in Erich Fromm, *Marx's Concept of Man* (New York: Frederick Ungar, 1967), p. 127.

10. As quoted in Korbel, *Twentieth Century Czechoslovakia*, p. 17. See also T. G. Masaryk, *Svetova revoluce* (Prague: Cin, 1925), p. 211; Karel Capek, *Hovory S. T. G. Masarykem* (Prague: Ceskoslovensky spisovatel, 1969), p. 260.

11. For a discussion of Smeral's views, see Ferdinand Peroutka, "Jmeno, jez vyhaslo: Smeral," *Svedectvi*, XI (1971), pp. 59–68; and Zinner, *Communist Strategy and Tactics*, pp. 28–35.

12. Korbel, *Twentieth-Century Czechoslovakia*, pp. 72–73.

13. Zinner, *Communist Strategy and Tactics*, p. 34.

14. Karel Kreibich, *Tesny domov—siry svet* (Prague: Lupa, 1969), p. 296. Kreibich also mentioned that after Lenin's death an anecdote was told about Lenin reading a book under the table during a Politburo session. It was a textbook on the Czech language. See also Jindrich Vesely, *O vzniku a zalozeni* (Prague: Statni nakladatelstvi politicke literatury, 1953), pp. 164–165.

15. Korbel, *Twentieth-Century Czechoslovakia*, p. 73.

16. Zinner, *Communist Strategy and Tactics*, p. 39.

17. See D. Manuilsky, "The Czech Example—a Lesson for the Entire Comintern," *Communist International* (1925), pp. 19–20, as quoted in M. Silin, *A Critique of Masarykism* (Moscow: Progress Publishers, 1975), p. 164.

18. Silin, *A Critique of Masarykism*, p. 169.

19. Ibid., p. 171.

20. Vojtech Mastny, *The Czechs under Nazi Rule: The Failure of National Resistance, 1939–42* (New York: Columbia University Press, 1971), pp. 150–151.

21. Korbel, *Twentieth-Century Czechoslovakia*, p. 232.

22. Ibid., p. 233.

23. Zinner, *Communist Strategy and Tactics*, p. 179.

24. See the Central Committee's study, *Zprava Komise UV KSC o politickych procesech a rehabilitacich v Ceskoslovensku 1949–68* (Vienna: Europe-Verlag, 1970), p. 6.

25. E. Lobl, *Svedectvo o procese* (Bratislava: Vydavatelstvo politickej literatury, 1968), pp. 47–48.

26. *Zprava*, p. 7 and the minutes of the PCI's Eugenio Reale, who participated at the first Cominform session in Szklarska Poreba, in Milorad Drazhkovitch and Branko Lazitch, eds., *The Comintern: Historical Highlights* (New York: Frederick A. Praeger, 1966), pp. 259–268.

27. See the study by Pavel Tigrid, "Ve stinu lipy," *Svedectvi*, XI (1971), pp. 69–96, and its English version, "The Prague Coup of 1948: The Elegant Takeover," in Thomas T. Hammond, ed., *The Anatomy of Communist Takeovers* (New Haven: Yale University Press, 1975), pp. 379–432.

28. *Zprava*, pp. 12–13, and Karel Kaplan, "Zamysleni nad politickymi procesy," *Svedectvi*, X (1970), p. 447.

29. Korbel, *Twentieth-Century Czechoslovakia*, p. 232.

30. See hints in the Czechoslovak press at that time. For example, *Mlada fronta* (Prague), November 5, 1956, and an account of Z. Mlynar, former secretary of the Czechoslovak party under Dubcek: Z. Mlynar, *Mraz prichazi z Kremlu* (Cologne: Index Listy, 1970), pp. 50–65.

31. H. Gordon Skilling, *Communism, National and International: Eastern Europe after Stalin* (Toronto: Toronto University Press, 1964), p. 88.

32. See, for example, Milan Machovec, *Tomas G. Masaryk* (Prague: Melantrich, 1968), pp. 23–25, 53.

33. *Rude pravo*, July 1, 1971.

34. Silin, *A Critique of Masarykism*, p. 262.

35. This observation is based on the author's personal experiences.

36. Mlynar, *Mraz prichazi z Kremlu*, p. 76.

37. *Le Figaro*, April 26, 1978.

38. See Mlynar, *Mraz prichazi z Kremlu*, pp. 77–117.

39. *Mundo Obrero* (Madrid), May, 1, 1968.

40. *L'Unità*, (Rome), May 8, 1968.

41. *L'Humanité* (Paris), April 20, 1968.

42. For the discussion, see Jiri Valenta, *Soviet Intervention in Czechoslovakia, 1968: Anatomy of a Decision* (Baltimore: Johns Hopkins University Press, 1979).

43. *L'Unità*, July 14, 1977.

44. M. Azcárate, "Europe and Eurocommunism," and *El País* (Madrid), July 30, 1977.

45. *Corriere della Sera*, August 25, 1978.

46. See Valenta, "Eurocommunism and Eastern Europe," p. 47.

47. See an interview with exiled Dubcek supporter F. Janouch in *Mundo Obrero*, June 29–July 5, 1978.

48. *L'Unità*, July 10, 1978.

49. Ibid., August 21, 1978.

50. *Mundo Obrero*, August 17–23, 1978. See also a similar evaluation of the British party in *Morning Star*, August 18, 1978.

51. See Valenta, "Eurocommunism and Eastern Europe," and *Le Monde*, April 26, May 4, 1978.

52. *Rude pravo*, January 11, 1978.

53. "For Peace and Progress in Europe" [editorial], Ibid., June 29, 1977.

54. J. Fojtik in *Tribuna*, April 19, 1978, and J. Fojtik in *Pravda*, August 17, 1978.

55. Ladislav Hrzal in *Rude pravo*, December 15, 1978. Also see V. Bilak's speech in *Pravda*, December 16, 1978.

56. Fojtik in *Tribuna*, April 19, 1978.

57. *Tribuna*, February 28, 1979 and March 5, 1980.

58. See Jiri Valenta, "USSR and Eurocommunism" in this volume.

59. French Communist party leaders came under attack in the spring of 1979 by members who circulated a petition referring to democratic rights in Eastern Europe, particularly in Czechoslovakia, and demanding expulsion of the official representatives of the CPCz from the Congress of the PCF. A few PCF members travelled to Czechoslovakia in May 1979 to meet with Charter 77 spokesmen; they were arrested and later expelled. For details, see reports in *Le Monde*, May 11, 23, 1979, and *Le Matin*, March 22, 1979.

60. Private interviews conducted by the author with Czechoslovak refugees in 1978–1979.

61. See report of H. Camps in *Le Soir*, August 22, 1978.

CHAPTER IX

Eurocommunism and Romania

Trond Gilberg

Introduction

Considerable differences exist among many of the West European
parties purportedly advocating "Eurocommunism," and it may be
premature to attach real permanence to this concept. Even without
the precautionary use of quotation marks, Eurocommunism is best
understood as an approximation, rather than a definition, of a trend
that currently predominates in West European Communism.[1] In many
respects it is easier to explain Eurocommunism in terms of what it is
not: it is not dominated by the CPSU and its views on political and
socioeconomic pluralism, civil rights, and the road to socialism;[2] its
view of the party's relationship to the rest of society is not as rigid as
the Soviet and East European position;[3] and it does not call for the
party to exercise the degree of social and political control that characterizes Communist rule in the Soviet Union and Eastern Europe.[4]
However, the Eurocommunist parties' interpretations of these points
is by no means uniform either. Thus, any discussion of the influence
that Eurocommunism may exert in Eastern Europe should initially
specify which representatives of West European Communism it proposes to examine.

There is another important reason to be selective. Most of the West
European Communist parties have, at best, a minuscule prospect of
actually capturing power (and presumably of implementing the ideals
of Eurocommunism). Only two parties are in a position to reasonably
expect such a development in the near future. At present the Italian
Communist party (PCI) is on the threshold of sharing power at the
national level. The French Communist party (PCF) had such an opportunity in the spring of 1978, and even though its immediate pros-

pects for recovery of that momentum are dim, the future may resurrect the chances of Georges Marchais and his party. Similarly, over the long term, the Spanish Communist party (PCE) may also have chances to exert significant political influence at the national level. The relative prominence of these three parties, both in terms of ideological innovations and the prospects for power and influence makes them the logical choice as representatives of Eurocommunism. The primary question to be investigated, then, is this: What is the impact of Eurocommunism, as represented by the PCI, PCF, and the PCE, on the ideology and policies of the Romanian Communist party (PCR)?

I. Dominant Aspects of the PCR's Ideological Stance and the Resultant Policies

The PCR and its leader, Nicolae Ceausescu, are somewhat unlikely allies of the Eurocommunists. Most analysts agree that the Romanian regime is characterized by policies that violate most of the major characteristics of the Eurocommunist variant represented by the French, Italian, and Spanish parties. Ceausescu's system is characterized by the following policies:

1. Romania has one of the most centralized political systems in Eastern Europe, and Ceausescu holds all of the primary reins of power: he is president of the republic, general secretary of the Communist party, and an active ex officio member of a host of "mixed" commissions (which include representatives from the party, the governmental and administrative agencies, mass organizations, and research institutions) that play an increasingly important part in policy formulation and execution. Ceausescu has also strengthened his position in the PCR by means of frequent purges and "rotation of cadres." In addition, he has supervised a massive and sustained campaign of ideological mobilization, and his territorial reorganization of the country in the late 1960s considerably strengthened his hand in the provinces by means of the appointment process. The general secretary's political style allows for frequent "inspection visits" to economic units outside of the capital. These enable him to use the rank and file as a control on the performance of administrative and technical cadres. An unprecedented personality cult has developed around Ceausescu, and through judicious use of nepotism he has further tightened his grip on the "commanding heights" of the Romanian political system. This, then, is personalized political rule, which bears very little resemblance to the professed ideals of political pluralism,

currently advocated by the three parties chosen as representatives of Eurocommunism.[5]

2. Ceausescu is not merely an autocratic leader who has succeeded in acquiring an amazing amount of political power; he is also an original ideologue with a definite view of his historical mission and that of the PCR. Briefly, this mission is to "lay the material base of socialism and communism" by creating a highly developed political, socioeconomic, and cultural system—a "multilaterally developed society." This society is to be characterized by social cohesion, political awareness and activism, and high economic productivity by individuals fully and enthusiastically integrated into the societal efforts led by the PCR. Such a system will give Romania a respected place among the nations of the world and will allow it to achieve national liberation and fulfill its national mission, goals which were pursued by the great heroes of the Romanian past, Michael the Brave and Stephen the Great. The "multilaterally developed society" is therefore conceived of as the end product of Romanian national development. Ceausescuism is a unique synthesis of Marxism and traditional Romanian nationalism. It is a well-developed and constantly articulated vision of the *integrated, administered,* and *managed* society in which the only "leading" (and thus supreme) political, socioeconomic, and cultural force is the PCR and Ceausescu.[6] Such a view of society is particularly inimical to political pluralism, even of the most limited kind.

The Ceausescu vision also prohibits economic pluralism. Romania is one of the few countries in Eastern Europe where even most of the service industry has been nationalized. Collectivization of agriculture was completed in 1962, and economic planning and management remain quite centralized by comparative standards; in fact, cautious decentralization during the latter half of the 1960s was soon followed by recentralization. Romania has one of the most hierarchically organized economic systems in all of Eastern Europe. Any resemblance between its system and the limited economic pluralism advocated by the French, Italian, and Spanish Eurocommunists is visible only in the black market activities and other illegal phenomena in an economy beset by significant and perennial scarcities.[7]

3. The integrated society also rejects individual autonomy and the civil rights called for by critics of the existing regime, as well as the possibility for the individual to "opt out" of the nation-building effort now under way in Romania. A lengthy debate over this issue between intellectuals, and the general secretary and the administrative-coercive apparatus of state and party, led to the "little cultural revolution" in Romania in the early 1970s. The ideological offensive initiated by Ceausescu in the summer of 1971 is still under way, and it

has enforced the principle that the arts are to be used as weapons in the struggle for the "multilaterally developed" (read "fully integrated and directed") society. Ceausescu has enforced his particular vision of socialist realism in Romania: the individual is free to be the best carpenter, mathematician, or collective peasant that the regime needs but not at liberty to decide to drop out of socialist society. An individual can only reach his or her potential consistent with this vision. The "new socialist man and woman," therefore, enthusiastically accept the guidance of the collectivity, as expressed by the leading force of society, the PCR and its leader, and work diligently for the fulfillment of prescribed societal goals. Ceausescu appears to be one of the few East European leaders who still believes that human nature can be perfected according to prescribed notions of the "new" individual. This vision certainly stands in sharp contrast to the ideas of individual rights expressed by the three selected Eurocommunist parties.[8]

Thus it is clear that the one major area in which there is considerable agreement between the PCI, PCF, and the PCE, on the one hand, and the PCR, on the other, is the quest for national roads to socialism and Communism and the political autonomy that this implies. The four parties, in short, agree that there can be no one center of world Communism and that there is no all-encompassing, specific doctrine, as interpreted by a set of high priests in a specific party. Furthermore, it follows logically from this premise that no international forum (let alone any national party) can authoritatively excommunicate a party or movement from the international fraternal order of Communists. The notion that diversity is essential to the well-being of international Communism is qualified only by the conviction (expressed or genuine) that ultimately all systems will reach socialism and Communism, and that there can be no regression to "capitalism" in societies where political power has already been obtained by Communist parties. Beyond their consensus on rather general principles, the four parties agree that each of them has the right to conduct its own affairs as local conditions might require. Their affinity, therefore, derives much of its strength from the existence of a common "enemy," namely the efforts by the CPSU to reintroduce hegemonic control (or some fraction thereof) in the international movement and its constituent parts.[9]

Cynics may argue that the ties between selected Eurocommunists and the PCR are merely a marriage of convenience based on the mutual desire for autonomy from the CPSU and the Soviet state. Such considerations are undoubtedly very important, but they may not be exclusive. It can be argued that the four party leaderships may be convinced that an autonomist policy is the only feasible way to achieve socialism and Communism everywhere and anywhere. I would like to consider both of these propositions as reasons for the expanded relations between the Eurocommunists and the Romanians.

II. The Impact of Eurocommunism on the PCR in the Fields of Foreign Policy and Autonomism

Within the parameters established above, the impact of the Eurocommunism practiced by the selected parties has been considerable. First of all, the views of the PCI, PCF, and PCE have served to reinforce views and policies already advocated and practiced by the Romanians. The Italians have advocated party autonomy ever since the 1950s, but the French did not adopt this position until the 1970s. The PCE became a particularly forceful exponent of autonomy after the party was legalized in Spain in the post-Franco era. The PCE did, of course, advocate these views even while the party was illegal in Spain, but its underground status gave it less weight at that time. Scholars differ as to when the PCR began articulating nationalistic and autonomist views and instituting comparable policies. Some put the inception in the early 1950s, while others suggest it began with the publication of the famous "Romanian Declaration of Independence" in 1963. Whatever the point of departure, it is clear that the PCR leadership was advocating (and practicing) autonomist policies in its relations with the CPSU and the other ruling parties of Eastern Europe well before the advent of Eurocommunism per se in the 1970s. It should also be pointed out, however, that the concept of "polycentrism" was originally proposed by the then head of the PCI, Palmiro Togliatti, in the mid-1950s—a time when most analysts would consider the Romanian leadership very much within the parameters of Soviet-defined foreign policy. It is therefore difficult to determine who influenced whom in the early stages of autonomism in Eastern Europe.

By the early 1960s it was clear that a special relationship had developed between the PCR and the PCI. During that decade, this relationship was further strengthened by common reactions in Bucharest and Rome to the many crises in the international Communist movement. The most important crisis points with respect to the issue of autonomism were the following: (1) the 1960 Bucharest conference of Communist parties, when the Sino-Soviet rift came into the open, and Albania launched its crusade of political orthodoxy and anti-Sovietism; (2) the continuation, indeed exacerbation, of the Sino-Soviet rift throughout the decade (even after the ouster of Nikita

Khrushchev); (3) the 1963 "Declaration of Independence" of the PCR; (4) the Cultural Revolution in China and the full-fledged equality of Moscow and Peking in the international movement; (5) the 1968 crisis over the Prague Spring and the subsequent invasion of Czechoslovakia; (6) the negotiations of the Mutual and Balanced Force Reduction, the Strategic Arms Limitation Treaty, and the European Security Conference during the first half of the 1970s; (7) the Portuguese revolution and subsequent policies of the Portuguese Communist party; (8) repeated Soviet attempts to convene an international Communist conference and the resulting meetings in various East European capitals; (9) the 1975 Helsinki Agreements; (10) the 1976 conference of Communist parties in East Berlin; (11) events in France, Italy, and Spain during 1976, 1977, and 1978, which significantly increased the political chances and enhanced the influence of the PCI, PCF, and PCE; (12) various national party congresses during this period, which gave the parties under discussion the opportunity to state their views on interparty relations and the international Communist movement.[10]

During this period, the PCR and the PCI enjoyed the good fortune of having their positions accepted by other European parties. There was a significant increase in support for the autonomist position throughout the two decades or so in which this tendency evolved in European Communism. Thus, the original autonomists, the Yugoslav Communists, supported the PCR's position at the earliest sign of Bucharest's intransigence toward the CPSU. Similarly, the British, Norwegian, and Swedish parties increasingly accepted the Romanian position during the 1960s. Although the Icelandic party is strictly isolationistic in terms of participation in international Communist forums, it severely criticized the CPSU and the pro-Soviet parties of Eastern Europe on numerous occasions during the 1960s, especially after the invasion of Czechoslovakia, and can certainly be counted in the autonomist column. The PCE also joined the ranks of the autonomists at a relatively early stage. The PCF did not make the full transition to this position until the mid-1970s.[11]

During the period of growing autonomism, the four parties repeatedly reinforced each other's position and often acted in unison in their quest for increased autonomy from the CPSU and its close associates in the international movement. Thus, the Romanians and Italians (in addition to the Yugoslavs, the Swedes, Norwegians, and others) refused to become involved on the Soviet side in the dispute between Moscow and Peking. Instead, both Bucharest and Rome argued forcefully that there could be no one center, and that in fact only national centers were feasible. Indeed, Ceausescu managed to capitalize on both Romania's good relations with the autonomists and its membership in the Warsaw Pact. The PCR assumed the role of well-intentioned go-between, attempting to mediate among the squabbling giants in the interests of international solidarity and the common front against the threat of "imperialism." Furthermore, the PCI and the PCR were in the forefront of those emphasizing the familiar principles of noninterference in internal affairs, mutual respect and advantage, and full recognition of autonomy as the primary principles of interparty relations. The two parties also directly criticized Soviet attempts to formalize CPSU primacy in the movement. The Italian party was particularly active in this regard, but the Romanians were not far behind. As a result of the Sino-Soviet rift and the debate that followed, the two parties succeeded in establishing themselves as major representatives of the autonomist position and have maintained this role ever since.[12]

When the PCR decided to expand its quest for autonomy by rejecting Soviet-sponsored proposals for increased economic integration in the Comecon, the PCI applauded the decision in the name of polycentrism and the principle of national roads to socialism and Communism. Similarly, the two parties supported each other in their refusal to use vitriolic Soviet rhetoric to condemn the many excesses of the Cultural Revolution in China. But the most striking example of close cooperation between the Romanian and Italian party leaderships came during the Prague Spring and in the aftermath of the Czechoslovak invasion. The PCI strongly supported the Dubcek regime's policy of internal liberation and its presumed semiautonomous position in the movement. For Ceausescu the main element to be supported in Prague's policies was the principle that each system has the right to develop its own road and policies. Thus, both the Italian and Romanian Communist leaders had strong words of support for Alexander Dubcek, and Ceausescu even paid an official visit to Prague in August, prior to the invasion.[13] When the Czech invasion aroused Romanian fears that the Soviet leadership might decide to deal similarly with the other autonomist thorn in their side, frantic consultations ensued between Bucharest and Rome, and between the PCR leadership and other Communist parties in Western Europe. During this grave crisis, the PCR clearly used its good relations with like-minded elites in West European Communist parties to marshal support for its position and thus help fend off a possible invasion by the forces of the Warsaw Pact.[14]

The activism in interparty relations exhibited by the PCR during the Czechoslovak crisis and its aftermath continued into the 1970s. The Romanian party continued its close contacts with the PCI and expanded its relations with the French and Spanish parties as well.

Frequent bilateral contacts during these years often took the form of visits by Eurocommunist party delegations to Bucharest, or PCR delegation visits to Paris, Rome or some other city where the autonomist parties could deliberate on issues of mutual interest. Particularly close relations developed between Ceausescu and Santiago Carrillo of the PCE.[15]

Bucharest was even more active during the negotiations over the European Security Conference and Mutual and Balanced Force Reduction (MBFR) during the first half of the 1970s. The Romanians participated primarily as a ruling party and advocated certain policies pertaining mainly to the relations among states rather than among Communist parties. Even in this capacity the PCR line reflected the debate inside the international Communist movement, and its arguments were strongly supported by the autonomist parties in Western Europe. The Romanian arguments in the security and MBFR discussions were also designed to enhance the autonomy of individual states—a point which was clearly appreciated by the Italian and Spanish parties, and to some extent by the PCF as well. In addition, the PCR leadership argued forcefully for the dismantling of power blocs and for the removal of foreign troops from European territory. Ceausescu and his spokesmen went so far as to advocate stronger cooperation against "big-power chauvinism" among small- and medium-sized states, regardless of the political and socioeconomic systems of the states involved. Such arguments again found ready support among the leaders and members of the West European autonomist parties, whose primary concern was the need to reduce the commitment of their national leaders to NATO and to other Western cooperative efforts and at the same time elude direct Soviet control. Once again, however, the PCF was considerably less enthusiastic about the Romanian position than were Italian and Spanish party leaders.[16]

Several major events during the remainder of the 1970s clearly demonstrated the close relationship among the PCR, PCI, and the PCE, and the emerging congruence of views between the Romanians and the French. In the early 1970s, and particularly after 1973, the CPSU sponsored efforts to convene an international conference of Communist parties that would debate major problems of ideology, strategy, and tactics of the movement, and possibly establish guidelines for policy. In 1973, the tiny (and strongly pro-Moscow) West German Communist party called for such a conference, and this initiative was endorsed by the Bulgarian party after some hesitation. Subsequently, other loyalist parties also responded favorably, while the CPSU remained discreetly in the background. During 1973 and

1974, the West German proposal was firmly endorsed by enough parties so that arrangements for the conference could be formalized. Representatives from most of the West European Communist parties, together with their East European ruling counterparts, participated in a series of preparatory meetings in various East European capitals. The story of the tortuous progress of these meetings is well documented and need not be repeated here.[17] Late in 1975 the PCF finally supported the autonomist bloc of the PCR, the Yugoslav League of Communists, the PCI, PCE, and assorted smaller West European parties in their efforts to block any Soviet and loyalist attempt to enforce adherence to a rigid program or a set of theses that would in any way reestablish an international center and firm policy guidelines. The autonomists' campaign was successful, and the CPSU and its close collaborators were obliged to accept the principle that the planned conference could only issue general statements and could not castigate or otherwise bring sanctions against any party for its policy. The French party's accession to the autonomist group and the emerging alliance among the PCI, PCE, and PCF as a Eurocommunist bloc also profoundly upset Soviet strategists, who were now confronted by a formidable coalition of autonomist ruling and nonruling parties.

The PCF's acceptance of the autonomist position was a major development. During the first half of the 1970s the French party had refused to accept fully the "revisionist" approach to internal politics advocated by the PCI and the "autonomist" view of the PCR, PCI, and PCE. The major issues on which the parties differed were the Portuguese revolution, the policies of the Portuguese Communist party (PCP), and the Romanian stance at the Helsinki conference in 1975. The PCF had supported the hard-line position of the PCP in questions pertaining to the relationship between Communist parties and other political forces in a revolutionary situation. Marchais and Alvaro Cunhal were also united in advocating a much more loyalist attitude towards the CPSU than their Italian and Spanish counterparts.[18] This significant split, which had weakened the forces of Eurocommunism in international councils, was at least partially remedied by the French adherence to the autonomist line—formally established as a PCF policy at the party's congress in February 1976. The PCP, on the other hand, continued its orthodox policies in this field—a policy that undoubtedly contributed to the increasing isolation of the Portuguese party in its own society and thus the abatement of revolutionary possibilities in Portugal.

The alliance of the three major West European parties and the PCR on the issue of international Communism continued to prosper during the final preparations for the June 1976 East Berlin Conference of

European Communist Parties. During the conference the autonomist group of parties forcefully reiterated their positions, and the conference itself contributed little, if anything, to the CPSU's hopes of increased influence. In fact, the PCF, that most recent convert to Eurocommunist views in the international field, went out of its way to demonstrate its independence and its willingness to criticize the Soviet Union and the CPSU, while the PCI, PCE, and PCR, long-standing advocates of autonomism, could afford to be less abrasive on this point, although they firmly reiterated their traditional views and positions.[19] The PCF was engaged in complicated maneuvers to establish a solid left-wing coalition in France, and its desire to show its "reformist" colors to the French electorate accounted for the strong words of independence. The PCR, however, was not concerned with the source of the French conversion as long as it resulted in PCF support for Bucharest's position. This kind of support continued through the late 1970s.

The cohesion of "the bloc" was further strengthened by a series of developments in France, Italy, and Spain. In the 1976 Italian elections, the PCI came very close to achieving a plurality, and the continuing weakening of the Christian Democrats propelled the Communists into a pivotal political role. In France, the Communist-socialist electoral alliance was defeated in the 1978 elections. Nevertheless, it was subsequently recognized as a legitimate political "player" by President Valery Giscard d'Estaing, who invited Marchais to come to the Elysee Palace for a discussion of major French political problems and ways to solve them. Marchais's willingness to appear at the presidential palace was a significant gesture of "reformism." During Spain's transition from the Franco dictatorship to a working multiparty democracy, the formerly outlawed PCE was recognized as a legitimate participant in the reconstituted Spanish system and subsequently scored some significant, if modest, successes in the national elections. These positive results were further enhanced by the party's strong showing in the 1978 senatorial by-elections.[20]

The successes of the three Eurocommunist parties have helped to strengthen their leaderships' conviction that their policies are the correct strategy for obtaining political power in their respective societies. This has enhanced their willingness (indeed eagerness) to defy Moscow and the CPSU on many issues. Carrillo has been the most outspoken critic of Moscow, but PCI leader Enrico Berlinguer has not been far behind, and the French leaders have made considerable progress in "catching up" with their Eurocommunist partners in criticism. The most important French spokesmen in this regard are Jean Kanapa and Jean Elleinstein.[21]

The "alliance" of the three major West European parties and their increasingly outspoken support of autonomy and national roads to socialism and Communism have been extremely important to Ceausescu and the PCR. This development has provided outside support for Romania's foreign policies—a mainstay of the PCR and the Communist regime. Ceausescu and his party head one of the most directed and restrictive systems in all of Eastern Europe, and the PCR sorely needs an autonomous and nationalistic foreign policy to maintain at least a modicum of popular support. The West European Communists' support of the Romanian position enhances Ceausescu's reputation at home and provides a welcome source of strength for Ceausescu in his dangerous balancing act with Moscow and the CPSU.

III. The Challenge of Eurocommunism for Ceausescu's Directed Society

Since Ceausescu's vision of the "multilaterally developed society" and its political institutions and processes differs fundamentally from the views expressed by the leaders of the PCI, PCF, and PCE, Ceausescu and the PCR face a dilemma. On the one hand, the Eurocommunist emphasis on national roads to socialism, Communism, and autonomy is crucial to the PCR's own attempts to increase its autonomy vis-à-vis the Soviet Union and the CPSU. On the other hand, most of the Eurocommunist views on political revolution, the road to power, relationships with other political forces in society, economic development, and individual autonomy and freedom do not conform to either the ideology or practices of the PCR and its general secretary. Implemented in Romania, such ideas would signal the end of Ceausescu's personal power and lead to the destruction of the PCR's political, socioeconomic, and cultural hegemony. The problem for Ceausescu, therefore, is how to take advantage of the autonomist ideas of Eurocommunism in the international movement while preventing its revisionist aspects from gaining a foothold in Romania.

This problem is not uniquely Romanian in all of its manifestations. The other ruling parties of Eastern Europe also confront the dangers that increased post-Helsinki contacts with the West pose to the monopolistic political and socioeconomic controls they exert in their respective societies. It is clear, however, that no other ruling party in Eastern Europe (with the exception of Yugoslavia, which is not strictly comparable in the first place) relies so heavily on West European Communist support for crucial elements of foreign policy and domestic legitimacy as does the PCR. It is therefore important to look closely at the Ceausescu approach to the possible influx of "nefarious" and dangerous ideas from the Eurocommunist support community.

Ceausescu and the PCR have approached the problem of dealing with pluralistic political, socioeconomic, and cultural ideas emanating from the West (and increasingly from the Eurocommunists) in a variety of ways. The most important are the following:

1. During the 1970s the PCR has launched an unprecedented political and ideological campaign designed to raise the level of consciousness among both the party cadres and the general population. Specific manifestations of this campaign include such policies as expanding the teaching of Marxism-Leninism, the history of the international working class movement, and the history of the PCR; frequent purges of unreliable party cadres; expanded propaganda and agitation activity in the schools, associations, and in places of employment; frequent appearances by the general secretary in political, cultural, and socioeconomic institutions, where his views and, presumably, those of the PCR, are forcefully expressed; an unprecedented expansion of publication of political treatises, discussions, seminars, and other regime views; mass mobilization and enforced participation of cadres and the public in rallies, meetings, and other regime-sponsored activities; and, finally, the expansion of "volunteer work" that consists primarily of discussions of political matters and ideological exhortations by the relevant agitprop section.[22]

2. During the same period, the regime has perceptibly tightened its control over the arts and literature, theatre and cinema, as well as academic research and publication. The artist's function in Romanian society has been severely restricted. Ceausescu has repeatedly emphasized that artists, writers, and other members of the intelligentsia may criticize certain concrete aspects of regime performance but must refrain from drawing general conclusions about the viability of the system or PCR hegemony in Romania. Furthermore, the regime perceives the artistic intelligentsia mainly as an instrument of state policy, which should extol the regime, use its art to inspire greater enthusiasm among the masses, and generally act as a catalyst for political and cultural mobilization. Attempts by the artistic intelligentsia to do otherwise are severely criticized and condemned, as is any tendency towards "elitism." Indeed, Ceausescu has repeatedly stated that artists and writers must not stand above the people, but must consider themselves one with them, to the extent of recognizing that the real artistic impulses within Romanian society originate with the masses. (The 1976 song-festival "Hymn to Romania" was an at-

tempt to implement this principle. It emphasized mass participation rather than the production of the artistic elite.)[23]

3. There has been a perceptible tendency towards limited economic nationalism during the 1970s in the following sense: Ceausescu has emphasized the need for domestically generated technological innovation, rather than the indiscriminate import of technology and know-how from the West. Furthermore, he has severely castigated the tendency among the Romanian intelligentsia to defer to the West in the technical field; Romanians, says the general secretary, should be capable of generating their own innovations. This campaign is an integral aspect of Romanian economic policy towards the West, which aims at enhancing the export of machinery and reducing the image of Romania as primarily a supplier of agricultural goods and raw materials.[24]

4. Concomitantly with the efforts at economic nationalism, the PCR has moved during the 1970s to expand its already considerable control over the growing technical, educational, and managerial intelligentsia, an action that underscores the party's rejection of any notion of "convergence" based upon common needs of modernized societies. This further underlines Ceausescu's conception of Romanian modernization as a unique phenomenon that aspires to the simultaneous development of the political, social, economic, and cultural sector, the attainment of "socialist culture," and the making of "socialist men and women"—an achievement that is supposed to usher in a form of society that surpasses any currently in vogue in the West. Presumably, it would also be higher than the type of society advocated by the Eurocommunists, who now profess to accept pluralism and limited societal conflict. The methods used to control societal elites emerging from the modernization process range from increased political indoctrination to frequent purges and "rotation of cadres," even when such practices result in reduced economic performance.[25]

5. During the 1970s the PCR and its leader have also striven to reduce Western influence in the cultural field and in interpersonal relations, despite the regime's attempt to expand tourism as an indispensable source of hard currency. Ceausescu has repeatedly derided the tendency of Romania's younger generation to ape all aspects of Western culture, especially its pop music, long hair, blue jeans, and attempts at hippie behavior, now occasionally found in Romanian cities. The general secretary has tried to counter such nefarious leanings by emphasizing the value of indigenous Romanian culture and its behavior patterns. Unfortunately he has made little impact on the teenage population, which seems to continue its worship of all things

Western. Another aspect of the movement towards cultural self-sufficiency and fear of undue Western influence has been the increasingly restrictive approach that Romanian authorities have taken towards academic exchanges with the West in recent years.[26]

Ceausescu's emphasis on a Romanian road to socialism and Communism and his admonition that each country must develop its own policies without interference from any quarter has occasionally resulted in an indirect attack on the Eurocommunists. A representative sample of such views is the following, taken from a recent speech by the general secretary:

> On various occasions I have referred to Eurocommunism. Certainly, this notion as such does not say a great deal. It will not lead to a new orientation in the process of revolutionary struggle and building the socialist society which is taking place under very diverse social, economic, historical and geographical circumstances. The communist and workers parties, their practice and revolutionary strategy cannot be labelled by the areas or regions in which they carry out their activity, but rather on the basis of how they resolve the basic problems of changing society, of social and national justice and equity in each country. . . .

> Questions also have been raised in connection with criticism by certain parties in the West of a number of specific problems in the life of some socialist countries and of the policy promoted by them in one case or another.

> We have discussed these problems with several parties, including the parties that have voiced such criticism, openly expressing our own views. Certainly, as I have already mentioned, not everything is ideal in the socialist countries. Unfortunately, certain problems have not been completely resolved in these countries, including Romania. . . . To question the entire work accomplished in the socialist countries will not contribute to the just and objective understanding by the people's masses of the realities of socialism and will not help the struggle waged by the workers' class and the democratic forces in the capitalist countries. We understand that a number of aspects of realities in the socialist countries can be criticized. However, it is difficult to understand the involvement of certain communist parties in official statements against certain acts and events taking place in these countries. We believe that such positions do not serve the respective parties, the socialist countries, or the policy of détente and international cooperation.

> In criticizing certain negative states of affairs, one also must depict what is positive in the socioeconomic development of the socialist

countries. One must objectively depict how socialism has resolved a number of vital problems of the great majority of people in a completely different manner, and infinitely more rationally, than the capitalist system has done and can do. In defining certain mistakes and abuses in the socialist countries, the communist parties in capitalist countries also must objectively depict the essential state of affairs in these countries, the great efforts to develop them and to raise the peoples' level of civilization—the great prospects that have been opened and are being opened by socialism for material and cultural prosperity and for well-being and freedom of the whole of mankind. . . . [applause]

As for the discussions on democracy and on human rights, socialism always has held that genuine democracy and true humanitarianism are incompatible with the perpetuation of man's exploitation by man, with the grave economic, social and political inequalities preserved under capitalism, with national, social and racial discrimination.[27]

This speech represents the most clear-cut statement to date of the PCR's official views on the possible effects of "Eurocommunism" on internal politics in Romania.

6. The obvious corollary to official rejection of "alien" and "foreign" influences is increased emphasis on nationalism. To this end the Ceausescu regime has launched an unprecedented campaign to glorify the historical tradition of the Romanians, thus rejecting any other tradition. Romanian historical research has not only extolled the reign of Stephen the Great, Michael the Brave, and Vlad the Impaler, but Romanian historians are also enthusiastically propounding the existence of a link between the ancient Romans and the contemporary Romanians. There is also a growing tendency to link the Romanians of the 1970s with the Geto-Dacians, who inhabited the territory of contemporary Romania before the advent of the legions. Even more interesting is the emergence of a line of reasoning that argues that the Geto-Dacians were culturally superior to the Romans and in fact influenced them. Some recent publications have argued that certain aspects of this culture were superior to all other cultures in Europe at the time; thus, ancient Dacia was in fact a catalyst for the transmission and diffusion of a higher culture.[28]

This campaign reached its highest point so far in Romania's centennial independence celebration in 1976–1977. The Ceausescu regime used the occasion to legitimize the system among the Romanian portion of the population. The policies of 1976–1977 have continued since, almost constantly, and the fervor of the message has not abated.[29]

A predictable and perhaps inevitable result of the intensely nationalistic, occasionally chauvinistic, campaign of the Ceausescu regime has been the alienation of Romania's ethnic minorities. Even though the general secretary has always emphasized that Romanian socialist culture is not limited to its Romanian aspects, the fact remains that the symbols used to implement the concept and the leaders who do the implementing are Romanian. Thus the general secretary would respond to any manifestation of minority unhappiness with this state of affairs by calling them tendencies towards "bourgeois-landowner mentality" and "old-fashioned nationalism," and by further intensifying the efforts of Romanian cultural diffusion. This is indeed a vicious cycle that is unlikely to be broken as long as nationalism remains an essential weapon in the regime's struggle to insulate itself from alien Western ideas.[30]

7. Finally, the holistic and nationalistic character of the present regime results in severe rejection of any form of opposition, dissent, or other manifestations of pluralism or societal antagonism. Thus, Ceausescu frequently decries those who would leave the fatherland for reasons of material gains or the false idea of "going home." He has, for example, repeatedly pointed out to the German minority that a group whose ancestors came to Romania eight hundred years ago cannot possibly consider another country (West Germany) its national or cultural home. In the same vein, Ceausescu has harshly criticized those who have engaged in political dissent, especially those who used the Helsinki agreements as a basis for demanding greater civil rights. (But it should be pointed out that his words have for the most part been followed up by milder policies that have allowed most of the dissenters to emigrate. This is a feasible solution, however, only as long as the number of dissidents remains small.)[31]

Ceausescu's reaction is understandable on at least two grounds. First of all, those who claim that the regime is deficient in human rights are in fact arguing that such rights have validity in and of themselves, regardless of regime. This notion has particularly obnoxious implications for a leader who is attempting to create the fully integrated society, in which individual rights can only be exercised in the context of the needs of the collectivity, the society. Secondly, the human rights campaign smacks of Western ideas and influences, including those of the Eurocommunists. From Ceausescu's point of view, staunch countermeasures against the dissemination of such inimical ideas are not only justifiable, but fundamentally necessary.

IV. Eurocommunism and the Multilaterally Developed Society: Conflict and Accommodation

Although the relationship between Eurocommunism, as represented by the PCI, PCE, and PCF, and the PCR exhibits a dual nature, the four parties have certain common interests, and these interests have been assiduously promoted by the respective leaderships during the 1960s and 1970s. Specifically, the major area of common interest is international Communism: all four parties strongly advocate autonomy for each individual party in terms of policy, and indeed even some autonomy in doctrine. A mutually reinforcing relationship has therefore developed in this field among three successful but nonruling parties, and one of the ruling parties of Eastern Europe. At the same time, the ruling status of the PCR, in contrast to the other parties, has created wide areas of policy and issues in which there is little if any congruence between positions held on a host of issues. These divergences in policy positions stem from the fundamental differences between the Ceausescu view of the party and its position in society, and the Italian, Spanish, and French views on this matter.

The Romanian position, which advocates political, socioeconomic, and cultural hegemony for the Communist party in society, is a mixture of ideological tenets applied in practice and shrewd *Realpolitik*. Ceausescu and his associates clearly believe in the hegemony of the PCR in Romanian society and are willing to go to great lengths to safeguard it. At the same time, it seems abundantly clear that, even if its leaders wanted to, the PCR could not implement the pluralistic policies advocated by the Eurocommunist parties. The "Italian approach" would fundamentally alter political conditions in Romania and would most likely result in a drastic drop in PCR power, perhaps even its demise as a ruling power. Such a development would be watched very carefully in Moscow, and armed intervention would be well-nigh inevitable. It seems that Ceausescu has little choice but to attempt to limit the impact of Eurocommunism on his own society while using it to strengthen his quest for foreign policy autonomy (and thereby increased domestic legitimacy as well).

The leaders of the PCI, PCE, and PCF are well aware of this dilemma. For this reason they have abstained from sharply criticizing the performance of the PCR in fields such as nationality policy and human rights, even though they harshly criticize other East European ruling parties on these issues. The Eurocommunist leaders clearly have little inclination to begin a campaign against the PCR and

Ceausescu as long as the four parties remain in fundamental agreement on issues pertaining to the international Communist movement. This process of accommodation, then, is one of the most important aspects of the relationship between Eurocommunism and the PCR.

Despite the restraint of the PCI, PCE, and PCF toward the PCR on matters concerning domestic policy, there is nevertheless a challenge in the relationship. This challenge is indirect but important all the same. Specifically, Ceausescu is confronted by the following problem: How can close relations be maintained with advocates of limited political, socioeconomic, and cultural pluralism without engendering a "spillover" effect in Romanian society? This danger is exacerbated by the very successes of the Romanian modernization process, which have created social stratification, a literate citizenry, an expanding technical intelligentsia, and a working class whose political quietism is beginning to wear thin in the face of continued economic hardship and the practices of "transmission-belt" policies. There is a dissident movement in Romania that utilizes Western documents, some of them written by Eurocommunists, as bases for their demands for human rights. Ethnic minority groups are bound to be attracted to the ideals of limited societal pluralism now advocated in the PCI, PCE, and the PCF. Elements of the Romanian working class, notably the miners of the Jui Valley, have shown that they are capable of challenging the regime and even winning some concessions from it. The restlessness among other elements of the industrial working class, especially younger workers, is spreading. Elements within the emerging societal elites, especially the technical and managerial intelligentsia, are increasingly vocal in their demands for political influence. For the masses, widespread political apathy represents another kind of pluralism: the choice of nonparticipation in the mobilization society. All of these problems are likely to persist, indeed to intensify and to spread. Will the regime perceive this development as at least partly a result of "alien ideas" emanating from the Eurocommunists? If so, will Ceausescu or his successor withdraw from active contacts with his Western allies, or will the leadership allow limited pluralism to develop in Romania? If the latter occurs, how is it to be controlled?

On the basis of the problems discussed above, Romania and the PCR stand before a period of potential fundamental crisis whose resolution will entail making choices that may ultimately determine the fate of the entire system. Ceausescu faces the unenviable dilemma of meeting the challenges that his foreign policy success poses to the equilibrium of his own society. Under these circumstances, Eurocommunism is of fundamental importance, for good and evil, in Romania. Even though Romania may represent an extreme case, similar problems will increasingly face the other ruling parties of Eastern Europe as well.

The Romanian balancing act among Eurocommunism, the Soviet quest for hegemony, and the attempts by the Chinese to reduce the influence of the CPSU in Eastern Europe was poignantly illustrated in late 1978 by the visit of Chairman Hua of the Chinese Communist party to Bucharest and Belgrade. The Romanian press gave prominent coverage to the visit, and Ceausescu's statements once again made it clear that the Romanians intend to continue their attempts to relate to all of these disparate strands of the so-called international movement, while maintaining a clear national profile. This, then, is the *Romanian* solution to the triple challenges from Western Europe, the Soviet Union, and China. In the past Ceausescu and his colleagues have handled these challenges with considerable skill. It appears likely that their policies will be successful in the future as well, until the dynamics of Eurocommunist ideas begin to wear away the crucial elements of centralized leadership in the Romanian domestic system. When that happens, the crisis of leadership may indeed come to pass.

NOTES

1. An example of some of the best writing on Eurocommunism is Kevin Devlin, "The Challenge of Eurocommunism," *Problems of Communism* (January-February 1977), pp. 1–20.

2. Santiago Carrillo of the Spanish Communist party has been the most vociferous critic of the CPSU; this debate continued at the recent PCE congress. See Kevin Devlin, "Spanish CP holds historic 'Eurocommunist congress,'" *RAD Background Report*, no. 80, (April 25, 1978).

3. See, for example, the statement by the French Communist Jean Kanapa, one of the leading spokesmen for contemporary Eurocommunism, in *France Nouvelle*, October 5, 1976.

4. The policies of the Italian Communist party are illustrative here. For an excellent article on the PCI, see Giacomo Sani, "The PCI on the Threshold," *Problems of Communism* (November-December 1976), pp. 27–51. The Italian position on most of these issues was forcefully stated at the Berlin Conference of European Communist Parties in June, 1976 and discussed by Sergio Segre in *Rinascità* (Rome), July 9, 1976.

5. I have summarized a great deal of material in this exposition. For two major documents in which the Ceausescu "vision" has been stated, see Nicolae Ceausescu, *Report to the 11th Congress of the Romanian Communist Party* (Bucharest: Meridiane Publishing House, 1974), and Nicolae Ceausescu, *Romania on the Way of Completing Socialist Construction: Reports, Speeches, Articles* (6 vols., Bucharest: Meridiane Publishing House, 1969–).

6. See, for example, Nicolae Ceausescu's major speech to the PCR Central Committee in November 1971. Nicolae Ceausescu, *Exposition on the Programme of the Romanian Communist Party for the Improvement of Ideological Activity, for Raising the General Level of Knowledge and the Socialist Education of the Masses, for Grounding the Relations in Our Society on the Principles of Socialist and Communist Ethics and Morality: Decision of the Plenum of the Central Committee of the Romanian Communist Party* (Bucharest: Agerpres, n.d.).

7. The performance of the Romanian economy is discussed in Trond Gilberg, *Modernization in Romania since World War II* (New York: Praeger, 1975).

8. See Ceausescu, *Exposition on the Programme*, especially pp. 18–21, 58–64.

9. The PCR and the Eurocommunists took very similar positions on this issue. See for example, the report on the Berlin conference in *Scinteia* (Bucharest), July 1–3, 1976.

10. This summary is based on a multitude of sources. For capsule commentary, see appropriate national profiles in the *Yearbook on International Communist Affairs* (Stanford: Hoover Institution Press, 1966–).

11. Ibid.

12. See, for example, Ceausescu's report to the Eleventh PCR Congress, in *Congresul al XI-Lea al Partidului Comunist Roman* (Bucharest: Editura Politica, 1975), especially pp. 21–44.

13. Further contacts between the two parties took place in Yugoslavia in July; here, the three parties (PCR, PCI, and the Yugoslav League of Communists), debated the tense situation in the bloc; see Richard F. Staar, ed., *Yearbook on International Communist Affairs 1969* (Stanford: Hoover Institution Press, 1970) p. 727.

14. I have a detailed discussion of these events in "The PCR and West European Communist Parties During the Last Decade: Autonomy and 'National Roads' in Practice" (paper prepared for the 1978 Annual Conference of the International Studies Association, Washington, D.C., February 22–25, 1978, published by Pergamon Press in 1979).

15. Ibid., especially pp. 4–16.

16. See, for example, Trond Gilberg, "Ceausescu's Romania," *Problems of Communism* (July-August 1974), pp. 29–44.

17. Kevin Devlin, "Challenge of Eurocommunism."

18. Ibid.

19. For example, *L'Humanité*, July 1, 1976.

20. The Eurocommunist position on the PCE has been challenged internally, however. See "Die Spanischen Leninisten Erheben Sich Gegen den Parteichef Carrillo," *Frankfurter Allgemeine Zeitung*, March 29, 1978.

21. Devlin, "Challenge of Eurocommunism."

22. See, for example, Gilberg, "Ceausescu's Romania," pp. 21–44, and Trond Gilberg, "The Internal Political Order" in Stephen Fischer-Galati, ed., *Eastern Europe in the 1970's* (New York: Columbia University Press, 1980).

23. The "Hymn to Romania" was part of the "National Epic," which was further the official celebration of the centennial of Romanian independence. For the motivations behind the "National Epic" and the cultural congress in 1976, see *Contemporanul* (Bucharest), January 9, 1976.

24. An interesting example of how the trade unions now concern themselves not only with the fulfillment of plans and "catching up with the West,"

but also with problems of workers' relations to work and other socio-psychological matters can be found in *Munca* (Bucharest), January 30, 1976. While this approach does not stand in direct contrast to Ceausescu's emphasis on productivity and hard work, it is an interesting "deviation," especially in light of recent labor unrest.

25. Gilberg, *Modernization in Romania*, especially chs. 2 and 3.

26. See, for example, Ceausescu's speech to the PCR Central Committee plenum, April 14, 1976, on the need to emphasize the national traditions of the Romanian heritage. *Scinteia*, April 15, 1976.

27. Ceausescu speech to the party and state *aktiv*, August 3, 1978, broadcast by Bucharest Domestic Service in Romanian, August 3, 1978 (also printed in *Scinteia*, August 4, 1978).

28. Ceausescu commented on this during the Congress on Political Education and Socialist Culture, held in Bucharest June 2–4, 1976. His speech is reported in *Scinteia*, June 3, 1976.

29. See, for example, Ceausescu's statement on his perception of his role in Romanian life and history, in ibid., January 28, 1978.

30. Gilberg, *Modernization in Romania*, especially ch. 8.

31. For example, Ceausescu's speech on the centenary of Romania's independence in *Scinteia*, May 10, 1977.

CHAPTER X

Eurocommunism and Yugoslavia

Robin Alison Remington

Believing that practice is the final judge of the correctness of
theoretical propositions and interpreter of ideological movements, the Yugoslav Communists will continue to learn from
our own experience and from that of other socialist movements, not hesitating to correct whatever either practice should
designate as obsolete or untenable.
YUGOSLAVIA'S WAY (1958)

Comparative political analysis requires agreement on concepts. In this
respect "Eurocommunism" is a sloppy, journalistic shorthand, an inappropriate label for a political dynamic within the world Communist
movement by no means limited to Europe. To fit Yugoslavia into this
dynamic, one must understand that we are dealing with multiple political arenas and potentially conflicting political priorities.

International Communism is a 130-year-old transnational movement
composed of ruling and nonruling parties dedicated to changing the
present international system. Relations among these states and parties
are governed by rules that the participants agree do not apply to out-
siders. Communists in and out of power cling to the belief that for any
given time or circumstance a "right" course can and must be found.
No comparable consensus exists, however, with respect to methods
of decision making or, for that matter, the rules of the political game.

Prior to 1917 the international organizational efforts involved nonruling parties. These endeavors were essentially egalitarian and
wracked by personality conflicts; they never reconciled the clash between national and class interests. In other words, there was no
clearly established priority between proletarian internationalism and
socialist partriotism. The success of the Russian Revolution radically
altered the power configuration within the international Communist
movement. The Soviet Union took on the status of a giant surrounded
by dwarfs. Proletarian internationalism was subsequently equated
with Soviet national interest, a double standard reflected in the Comintern's Twenty-one Conditions of 1920.

After World War II the situation changed again. A significant
number of European states dedicated to the construction of Com-

munism emerged. At first, the dominant-subordinate relationship between Moscow and the East European Communist leaders seemed
unshaken. In most cases the East European leaderships consisted of
prewar Communists who were dependent on the Soviets for funds,
organizational support, ideology, and a legitimizing myth. Then,
gradually, challenges appeared, and with them an increasing number
of interpreters of Communist norms and values who faced the need to
relate them to domestic needs.

On the international level, Eurocommunism strives to return to the
egalitarianism that existed prior to 1917. At the same time, each party
engaged in this endeavor operates in a unique domestic political
arena. There are not one but many political contexts to be considered.
Thus, a primary tenet of Eurocommunism is that specific national circumstances should determine political tactics and allies on the road to
socialism.[1] It assumes that Communist goals can be best achieved by
national methods of socialist construction. Socialist patriotism, rather
than dedication to Soviet policy objectives, becomes the measure of
fulfilling international obligations. Conceptually, then, Eurocommunism may be seen as ideological acceptance of the pervasive demands of political culture on policy formation by an increasing
number of key political actors in the international Communist
movement.

Eurocommunism is by no means a recent tendency of West European Communist party influence to move from west to east.[2] Rather,
Eurocommunism is the process of adjusting to a changing balance of
power within the political arena of the international Communist
movement. It is a demand for democratization of decision making and
reordering of common priorities. Eurocommunism's bottom line is the
collective challenge it poses to the Russian national Communism that
Stalin imposed on the world Communist movement. This challenge
did not originate in Western Europe. The phenomena we now call
Eurocommunism began in the late 1940s in Eastern Europe, or more
precisely, in Yugoslavia. Its components—nationalism, pluralism,
and regionalism—are all central elements of documentable Yugoslav
experience.

Much of the substance of the Eurocommunist approach with respect to socialist humanism and expansion of the legitimate channels
for political participation appeared in the arena of Yugoslav domestic
politics as early as 1958. Perhaps even more importantly, defense of
Eurocommunism as a Yugoslav foreign policy priority has had
significant impact on ideological and organizational struggles over the
role of the party in contemporary society within the League of Communists of Yugoslavia (LCY). Although it is impossible to definitively
predict the shape and direction of policy in post-Tito Yugoslavia, this

analysis tentatively suggests the following hypotheses with respect
to the relationship between Eurocommunism and Yugoslavia's
experience:

1. The 1976–78 Soviet-Yugoslav Eurocommunist polemics have
operated as a functional equivalent to the historic 1948 schism in
terms of domestic repercussions.

2. At least temporarily this has led to a reversal of the LCY recentralization of the early 1970s.

3. Therefore, the fate of Eurocommunism will be less important to
Yugoslav intraparty politics in the post-Tito period than might otherwise have been the case.

In order to substantiate this view, the rise of a Yugoslav alternative
to the Soviet model must be kept in historical perspective.

The Lessons of History

The Yugoslav drive for autonomy in interparty relations, the lowest
common denominator of Eurocommunist demands, is rooted in party
history. Founded in 1920 during the wave of revolutionary euphoria
that swept Eastern Europe after the Russian Bolsheviks came to
power, the Communist party of Yugoslavia (CPY) was soon forced
underground, riddled with nationalism, and whiplashed by Comintern
intrigues. The party barely escaped the fate of the disbanded Polish
Communist party and almost shattered under the iron fist of Stalin's
great purge.[3] Josip Tito, however, survived his stay in Moscow at the
height of the purges to become head of the party in 1937. The new
secretary-general learned to deal with Comintern pressures and to operate effectively in a political subculture where political and ideological deviations could cut short far more than one's political career.

Two organizational developments became cornerstones of the subsequent Yugoslav demand for ideological self-determination. First, in
rebuilding the party from a scant 1,500 members, Tito created a loyal
indigenous cadre that worked as a team providing leadership during
and after World War II. Secondly, he forced the party to support itself. The Comintern no longer paid the bills.[4] Nevertheless, until the
war made communication virtually impossible, Moscow undoubtedly
continued to call the tune.

It is likely that party history also reinforces Yugoslav sympathies
for Western Eurocommunist commitment to parliamentary strategies.
The CPY itself had a successful, if brief, exposure to electoral politics. In the November 1920 general election for the first Yugoslav parliament, the party won fifty-nine seats, taking the third position at the
polls. This strong popular showing left many party members with the

opinion that, had the party not been declared illegal, Communists could have more than held their own in the parliamentary game.

By the end of the war the pattern of revolutionary take-over in Eastern Europe was creating an ever-expanding gap between the Yugoslav leaders and their comrades who rode to power on the coat-tails of the Red Army. The Yugoslav party had led an indigenous battle of national liberation in which the Communists succeeded in establishing the only effective, multi-ethnic, nationwide political organization in Yugoslavia. The myth of partisan solidarity functioned as the founding instrument of Communist Yugoslavia—a "revitalized belief system" that legitimized Communist leadership of the Yugoslav revolution.[5] In short, the Yugoslav party emerged from the devastation of World War II with both power and authority.

Ironically, Yugoslavia also emerged from World War II to all appearances the most ideologically dogmatic state in Eastern Europe, almost embarrassing in its dedication to the Soviet model of political and economic planning. Yet the Soviet-Yugoslav split was a logical consequence of the CPY's wartime experience. While it continued to profess loyalty to the first socialist state and expressed devotion for Comrade Stalin, the CPY subtly but steadily took issue with Moscow's order of priorities. In the Yugoslav view, it was not the Soviet Union but the Yugoslav people, aided by the Western allies, who were responsible for the success of the partisan struggle. As the ideologue Mosa Pijade expressed it: "The people are water, a partisan is a fish; a fish cannot live without water."[6]

The state of the CPY as it evolved from 1945 to 1948 can be summarized as follows: (1) The party's relationship to the indigenous population was one of mutual dependence. (2) The CPY possessed an experienced close-knit core of seasoned revolutionaries. For the most part, the local leadership also consisted of former partisans whose loyalty to the CPY was founded on Yugoslavia's wartime experience. Thus, the CPY leadership was united, had acquired considerable independent governing experience during the war, and had virtually no first-hand contacts with Soviet officials below the highest level. (3) The Yugoslav Communists were politically independent and accustomed to making their own domestic policy. In addition, Tito had a foreign policy agenda incompatible with Moscow's priorities. By 1948, therefore, the Yugoslav party was clearly pursuing a paradoxical course. It imitated the Soviet political-economic model while it resisted Moscow's advice on domestic policy and advocated foreign policies that actually undermined Soviet interests toward both the West and the international Communist movement.

The conflicts that culminated in the Yugoslav expulsion from the Cominform have been well documented elsewhere.[7] It is enough to note that the salient issues were autonomist: the Yugoslavs wanted to run the show in Yugoslavia. They insisted that proletarian internationalism become reciprocal and be demonstrated in the form of Soviet support for a Yugoslav Trieste and in the Greek civil war. Finally, Tito's revolutionary ambitions for a Balkan federation, despite Stalin's evident lack of enthusiasm for it, posed a regional challenge to Soviet hegemony.

The 1948 split, then, predated the Eurocommunists' autonomist and regionalist positions. It was not, as it has often been portrayed, simply a demand for national Communism. Yugoslavia's belief in the need for national roads to socialism did not precipitate the 1948 break, but rather resulted from it. Indeed, the younger generation of Western Eurocommunists might well have difficulty imagining the extent of the blow to the CPY's ideological self-image, and the organizational and personal identity crisis that wrecked the Yugoslav party at all levels.[8] Yugoslav attempts to term the split a monstrous "mistake" and to reassure Moscow with public statements of loyalty to the Soviet Union and Stalin collapsed under the weight of Soviet invective. Economic blockade, military pressure, and East European show trials of Titoist heretics ended hopes of reconciliation.

As the Stalinist model became patently inappropriate, a search for alternatives began. Its results can be seen as forerunners of contemporary Eurocommunist strategies. At the historic 1952 Sixth Party Congress, the name of the party was changed to the League of Communists of Yugoslavia to symbolize an increasingly decentralized organizational structure. The newly christened league's "leading role" was then restricted to political and ideological education. By this act, the Yugoslav Communist party renounced its official monopoly on political life, thereby legitimizing the creation of that complex political infra-structure known as self-managing institutions.

The "self-managing organs" were not intended to manage much in the beginning. They were perceived as mobilizing devices, not as competition. Nevertheless, the official commitment to mass political participation, the acceptance of legitimate social conflict, and the expression of interests outside the Communist party were an embryonic form of Eurocommunist "socialist pluralism." Moreover, these changes led to a major unintended consequence. The Leninist organizational principle of democratic centralism became virtually unworkable because the dilemma of how to make decisions simultaneously at all levels of the party seriously inhibited many of its organizations. One might go so far as to say that Yugoslav practice rendered Leninism obsolete long before Santiago Carrillo, head of the Spanish Communist party, renounced it as an overly Russianized brand of

Marxism inappropriate to Spanish experience.[9] But that is moving ahead of the story.

By the mid-1950s the relationship of the Yugoslav experiment to East and West European Communist parties was largely determined by the imperatives of Soviet factional politics. These ultimately led Nikita Khrushchev to attempt to woo Tito back into the Soviet bloc.

Repercussions of the Soviet-Yugoslav Rapprochement

Khrushchev's desire for a foreign policy coup that would normalize Soviet-Yugoslav relations prompted him to admit Soviet responsibility for the quarrel with Yugoslavia. He blamed it on certain "unmasked enemies of the people."[10] However, the Soviet leader's willingness to accept the earlier Yugoslav explanation and dismiss past differences as a mistake came too late. By 1955 the Yugoslav practice of self-managing socialism rested on the assumption that Stalinism went beyond Stalin's personality cult to a perversion of socialism that had seriously flawed the Soviet system. The Belgrade Declaration signed after eight days of negotiations was a state, not a party, document. In it the Soviets, using the Yugoslavic language of nonalignment, publicly endorsed the Yugoslav position on separate roads to socialism. They pledged "mutual respect and non-interference in internal affairs for any reason—whether of an economic, political or ideological nature—since questions of the internal structure, differences of social systems and differences of concrete forms of developing socialism are exclusively a matter for the peoples of the different countries."[11]

The essence of this formula was repeated when Tito triumphantly went to Moscow in June 1956 to extend the scope of the Belgrade Declaration to the sphere of party relations. Soviet concessions in the Belgrade and Moscow Declarations provide the ideological legitimization for contemporary Eurocommunist rejection of proletarian internationalism, general laws of socialist development, and the dictatorship of the proletariat. There have been many milestones on the road from Belgrade in 1955 to the Berlin Conference of European Communist Parties in 1976. These meetings represent the twenty-year process of efforts to institutionalize the rules of the game in interparty politics. Despite Soviet efforts at backtracking, Communists are no longer bound by the "myth" that proclaims their primary loyalty must be to the "first land of socialism" and their tactics can only be determined by one doctrinal center.

In 1956 the ripples of Yugoslav influence spread beyond Eastern Europe to the Italian Communist party (PCI). In May Palmiro Tog-

liatti visited Yugoslavia. Shortly after reestablishing party ties with
the LCY, the Italian leader held his historic interview in which he
proposed that "polycentrism" become the norm within the international Communist movement and in which he spoke of a certain "degeneration" in Soviet society.[12] It is not clear whether or not Togliatti
was expressing his own previously unvoiced opinions. In any case,
his statement supported long-standing Yugoslav views and established
a pattern of LCY-PCI bilateral consultation on interparty matters that
typifies relations within the Eurocommunist alliance today. Likewise,
Soviet angry reaction to these moves anticipated the nature of Moscow's current polemicizing against Eurocommunist propositions.[13]

Soviet-Yugoslav harmony collapsed under the strain of the Hungarian uprising and changing Soviet priorities. Bluntly, once Khrushchev had outmaneuvered his rivals in June 1957, he no longer needed
Tito. From the Soviet perspective, welcoming Yugoslavia back to
Eastern Europe had been about as successful as putting a reformed
fox in charge of the hen house. To repair the damage, Khrushchev
turned to the Chinese, who joined in his effort to upstage the Yugoslavs and reconstruct a Communist center at the 1957 Moscow Conference.[14]

Once again isolated and furious, the Yugoslavs justified their position in the 1958 Program of the LCY, thereby setting off the second
major Soviet-Yugoslav dispute. Much of the domestic substance of
this program was temporarily abandoned during the frenzied party re-
organizations following the so-called Croatian crisis of 1971. Nevertheless, it continues to constitute the ideological ground rules of party
life and was pointedly reaffirmed as the basis of the Eleventh LCY
Congress in June 1978. Indeed, as a programmatic statement, the
Yugoslav party program underlines the similarity between Eurocommunist positions and the Yugoslav experience.[15] Therefore, let us
look briefly at its specifics.

The 1958 Program of the League of Communists
of Yugoslavia

The Yugoslavs rejected Marxism as a system of dogma. Instead
they insisted that it had value as a social theory only to the extent that
the theory could be creatively applied to concrete situations at any
given moment. The LCY program made three major assumptions: (1)
development necessitates different roads to socialism and as a result
no form of socialism is intrinsically superior to any other; (2) the
changing balance of forces between world socialism and capitalism
had eliminated the tactical need to elevate Soviet interest above na-

tional considerations; (3) inasmuch as "pure capitalism" and indeed "pure socialism" did not exist, the prospects for a peaceful transition to socialism were better than ever before. Along the way Communists might find an increasing number of appropriate allies among socialist parties, labor movements, and even capitalist forces that knowingly or unwittingly furthered socialist progress. In these circumstances the dictatorship of the proletariat should be limited to situations in which the working class is strong enough to determine social policy with no special "form of state or method of organization." In other words, under contemporary political conditions, parliamentary politics are as tactically legitimate as Leninism.

The program goes on to state that relations among Communist parties must be based on equality, respect, and voluntary cooperation, and must be without formal organizational structure. Socialism should not be exported, nor can outside forces "prescribe the socialist forms of any one country." Socialist democracy must encourage freedom of expression and a "struggle of opinion," while "socialist humanism" necessitates protecting the rights of individuals from unjustified state action. In the end, not only the state but the Communist party itself must wither away.

The 1958 party program expressed the ideal, not the reality, of the Yugoslav political experiment. Its provisions not only included, but in some cases went beyond, the platforms of Western Eurocommunists, although it undeniably differs in other respects—for example, in its view of the relationship of any future Communist Italy to NATO. Moreover, even as it predated current developments in the West European Communist parties, the program set the stage for subsequent Yugoslav economic decentralization. It thus provided the rationale for Belgrade's "market socialism" that has influenced Western Communist thinking about the advantages and disadvantages of a mixed economy. All of which leads to a turning point in Yugoslav autonomous development that demonstrated the impossibility of separating economic and political reform. This is a matter of unquestioned relevance for Eurocommunist politics, with implications unmistakably spelled out in Czechoslovakia in 1968.

The Economic Reform of 1965 and the Fate of the Prague Spring

A detailed discussion of the intricacies of Yugoslav economics is beyond the scope of this paper.[16] It will suffice to say that the Economic Reform of 1965 testified to the influence of one school of Yugoslav economists inside and outside the party. This group convinced the LCY leadership that Yugoslavia had reached a "take-off" stage in which artificially depressed standards of living were no longer necessary to finance the country's industrial infrastructure. Their solution to the problems of waste, unutilized industrial capacity, and lack of worker incentive was to accept the logical consequences of the principle of market socialism: prices must measure supply and demand, and enterprises that do not make a profit go out of business.

Despite Tito's personal approval, trade union support, and a forceful restatement of the program at the Sixth Central Committee Plenum, implementation of these proposals met unending obstacles. The opposition to reform stemmed from the perception that whatever the long-term benefits, the proposed economic changes could only come at high cost to significant sectors of Yugoslav society. Managerial elites in unprofitable enterprises and underdeveloped regions allied with middle- and lower-level party and government functionaries who stood to lose power with any depoliticizing of the economy. Central Committee resolutions notwithstanding, these bureaucrats tenaciously fought the reforms as antisocialist. The opposition was protected at the highest level by Tito's designated successor, Alexander Rankovic, head of the State Security Administration (UDBA). It crumbled only after his fall in 1966.

As anticipated, the short-run result of the economic reforms was a painful rise in unemployment that the party temporarily alleviated by allowing large numbers of Yugoslavs to work abroad. By 1968, however, student strikes and Albanian rioting in Kosovo testified to the potential seriousness of social and political disorder. It appears certain that the party would have been forced into a major reevaluation of its policies had not the Soviet-led invasion of Czechoslovakia distracted attention from domestic dysfunction and refocused it on national security.

Not since 1948 had the party appeared so united. Party recruitment among the young became more successful. The National Assembly passed a law making it treason for any citizen to fail to resist foreign occupation. Tito even euphorically pronounced the "national question" solved—a premature assessment, in retrospect.[17] Once the storm over Czechoslovakia subsided, however, it became clear that the fundamental economic and political conflicts exacerbated by the economic reform remained unresolved. The domestic dilemma was to return full force in the 1970s as economic demands became the catalyst for rising ethnic nationalism. The nationalist movement in turn fed into an ongoing bureaucratic power struggle between the federal center and the republic party and government elites.

In short, Yugoslavia has a less than enviable track record with respect to the ability of socialist pluralism to resolve conflicts of interest arising from political and economic reform. These problems remain an open wound in the Yugoslav body politic. Unlike the earlier period, the nature and concerns of the Eurocommunist alliance in the late 1970s have reinforced the search for pluralistic solutions within Yugoslavia rather than the possibility of a Yugoslav model appropriate for West European Communist development. In this instance Eurocommunist influence has indeed moved from West to East. Nor in all fairness can it be said that Dubcek's "socialism with a human face" did any better in this area. We do not know what would have happened had the Prague Spring collided with the cold reality of substantial resource reallocation. Whether or not the Communist party of Czechoslovakia could have resolved conflicting demands without polarizing contending groups is academic. Soviet troops ended the attempt.

The Czechoslovak crisis of 1968 played a catalytic role in the development of the Eurocommunist alliance structure.[18] It signaled the coming of age of the West European contingent, particularly the PCI and the Spanish Communist party (PCE) and, to perhaps a lesser degree, the French Communist party (PCF). The sharp PCI and PCE criticism of Moscow's resort to force to resolve the differences with the Dubcek regime broke a number of the remaining taboos against public attacks on Soviet policy and severed the psychological umbilical cord that tied these parties to the socialist motherland in 1917. Unlike its reaction to the 1956 Hungarian crisis, in 1968 the PCI acted on the implications of Togliatti's polycentrist analysis of the relationship of the world Communist movement to the Soviet system. After the invasion of Czechoslovakia, the West European parties arrived at the political position that the Yugoslav party had been forced into after 1948. The failure of these parties' efforts to prevent the "allied socialist" intervention to "save" Czechoslovak socialism, their subsequent objections to the fate of the Prague Spring, and their condemnation of the nature of "normalization" strengthened Eurocommunism's East and West European proponents' determination to change the rules of interparty politics. The skill and sophistication of the Yugoslav participants in this alliance were eloquently demonstrated during the organizational maneuvering focusing on preparations for a pan-European Communist conference.

The Road to Berlin: "Diversity in Unity"

The obsessive Soviet insistence on using world Communist conferences to legitimate Moscow's policies in interparty and East-West arenas has consistently backfired since Stalin's death in 1953. The

Moscow Conference of 1957, designed to isolate the Yugoslavs and contain the Poles, opened the door to Chinese influence in Eastern Europe. The November 1960 meeting of eighty-one Communist parties produced at best a compromise platform in a futile Soviet effort to diffuse the challenge from Peking. Subsequently, the importance of the Chinese alternative reordered the political dynamics of interparty relations. As the Soviet-Chinese polemics intensified, Moscow's search for willing and unwilling allies gave rise to neutrals who skillfully benefited from their ostensible attempts to reconcile Sino-Soviet differences. Moscow's ambivalent policy of alternately attacking and wooing such parties only increased their importance, thereby confirming the advantages of independent political maneuver and increasing the appeal of neutralism.

In an atavistic, Comintern-conditioned reflex, the Soviets attempted to recoup these losses by mobilizing an international conferences to expel the Chinese. United Italian and Yugoslav opposition to isolating Peking led to Togliatti's January 1964 visit to Belgrade, where both parties endorsed a "unity in diversity" formula. This public rejection of Khrushchev's conference plans soon received support from the Romanians, who joined the Italians and Yugoslavs in forming the backbone of an East and West European Eurocommunist alliance that became known as the "southern axis" in the 1970s.[19]

When the World Communist Conference was finally held in June 1969, it accomplished anything but the desired confirmation of Soviet policy. The concessions necessary to hold the conference at all turned the meeting into a pyrrhic victory. Independents and neutrals responded to pro-Soviet attacks on China with public denunciations of the invasion of Czechoslovakia. Since delegates could publish their own speeches immediately and even hold press conferences, their widely differing views on the nature of revolution, on proper interparty relations, on socialist democracy, and on seeking out non-Communist allies became media events in the Communist and Western presses alike. Even *Pravda* published selected summaries of all the speeches.

The conference's final declaration supported the principle of "noninterference in the affairs of others" in interparty relations, and it included the explicit statement that "there is no leading center in the international communist movement." Nevertheless, it did not receive unanimous support. The document amounted to a public reversal of the interparty political game as established at the 1957 Moscow Conference. Even though the final document was not signed by some parties, signed in part by some, and signed with reservations by others, the end result was the agreement to disagree and the legitimization of public disagreement—what Kevin Devlin has aptly called "institutionalization of diversity" in the world Communist movement.[20]

Nonetheless, in 1973 the Soviet Union returned to the conference road, this time advocating a European conference to be followed by a world meeting. The resulting pan-European conference put European Communist regionalism center-stage. The autonomous parties played this advantage to the hilt. The drawn-out preparations for the meeting gave them an invaluable forum in which Yugoslavia gained increasing visibility as an important Eurocommunist ally. Indeed, the negotiations surrounding the preliminary Warsaw meeting in October 1974 might be considered a procedural concession comparable to the agreement in principle expressed in the Belgrade Declaration of 1955.

On October 16 Radio Belgrade announced that the rules of procedure adopted by the Warsaw meeting included a provision for "decision making by consensus." This concession was undoubtedly made to ensure Yugoslav participation. A substantial procedural victory, this meant that all collective documents adopted either at the Warsaw meeting or in subsequent preparatory sessions would have to be acceptable to all parties without opposition. As a consequence, the Eurocommunist parties had gained virtual veto power.

The head of the Yugoslav delegation, Alexander Grlickov, bluntly put forward the Yugoslav conditions for continued commitment to the conference project. Grlickov's insistence on maintaining the principles of equality and noninterference was combined with a sharp reference to the danger of "tendencies toward hegemony" in the world Communist movement and a flat rejection of the idea that conditions for a world conference existed in the present period.[21] That the Romanians, along with such West European parties as the Spanish, Italian, and British, reiterated more tempered versions of the Yugoslav line on interparty relations was to be expected. Soviet moderation, however, indicated by Boris Ponomarev's response limited to a call for "joint action," despite more dogmatic statements by hard-line East European delegations, seemed out of character.

Indeed, the Soviets immediately attempted to forestall the consequences of their procedural concession. At the Budapest meeting in December, Ponomarev spoke explicitly about the Soviet desire for the conference to take a stand against "all those in Europe and beyond it who try under the flag of anti-communism and anti-Sovietism to weaken socialism's international positions."[22] Undoubtedly directed primarily at the Chinese in 1974, this Soviet position foreshadowed Moscow's current campaign to have Eurocommunism condemned as anti-Soviet and by definition harmful to the cause of socialism. These efforts proved futile. Prolonged preparatory meetings, combined with a plethora of bilateral consultations, simply worked to solidify the Eurocommunist alliance. To make matters worse, by 1975 the PCF as well had joined the "southern axis" in opposing Moscow's policy priorities.

Ultimately the Soviets decided to cut their losses and abandon the pan-European conference project before it proved even more of an embarrassment at the Twenty-fifth Congress of the CPSU in February 1976. Whether or not this decision reflected a policy struggle, those involved may have perceived distinct advantages in keeping Tito and Georges Marchais, the leader of the PCF, at home. The Italians, however, retaliated by turning the CPSU congress into a platform for announcing the PCI dedication to intellectual freedom in the context of a pluralistic and democratic socialist society. The Soviets could not have considered this move useful or appropriate.

Under these circumstances, the reasons for the Soviets' urgent and sudden return to the idea of the pan-European conference remain a mystery. It is by no means clear what brought then party secretary Konstantin F. Katushev to Belgrade in early June 1976, where he reportedly "agreed to everything." Katushev's downgrading in May 1977 would imply power struggle and policy disagreements in the Kremlin, but we have no evidence linking his demotion to the Soviet failure to contain the Eurocommunist coalition at the pan-European conference, finally held in Berlin in June 1976. While Leonid Brezhnev and his colleagues may have derived consolation from the fact that the Berlin meeting did endorse the main lines of Soviet foreign policy, on balance the gathering was another victory for the Eurocommunists. Issues pertaining to proletarian internationalism, the dictatorship of the proletariat, and the need to establish a general line for the development of socialism were simply ignored. The conference's emphasis was on equality, sovereignty, noninterference in internal affairs, and respect for different roads to socialism. All of Moscow's efforts had culminated in multiparty sanctioning of the essence of the 1955 Belgrade Declaration.

The Nonaligned Dimension

Even as the success of Eurocommunist organizational maneuvering benefited significantly from Yugoslav tactical skill, the process provided the Yugoslavs with substantial opportunities to further their own policy objectives. Preparatory meetings and interparty consultations prior to major conferences proved ideal vehicles for putting forward the Yugoslav view that nonalignment was a desirable policy alternative for small- and medium-sized European states both within and outside the Communist world.[23] At the Budapest meeting of December 1974, Grlickov made the Yugoslav preferences explicit with his demand that the European parties adopt the Algiers action program of the nonaligned countries as the basis for their relations with the Third World. In 1975 Yugoslavia's concern over this issue led it to convene a Belgrade seminar on the struggle for more just economic relations between Europe and the Third World. Communist, socialist, and social democratic parties participated, as well as the Algerian National Liberation Front and the Dutch and Icelandic parties. These two parties had boycotted the pan-European conference project.

On the one hand, these efforts amounted to an attempt to build links between the Eurocommunist forces and the increasingly fragmented nonaligned movement in Asia and Africa. Such links were thought to have strengthened Yugoslavia's position within the nonaligned policy arena, reinforcing, for example, Belgrade's condemnation of Cuban aid to the Ethiopian offensive against the Eritreans. On the other hand (and more important from our perspective), to the extent that the Yugoslavs blurred the lines between the Eurocommunist and nonaligned blocs, they subtly transferred Yugoslav historic authority within the nonaligned movement to the interparty forum.

Thus, Yugoslav maneuvering within the Eurocommunist coalition must be seen as going beyond the strategy, evident in preparations for the Helsinki Conference on European Security and Cooperation, of expanding nonalignment from the Third World to Europe.[24] Yugoslav spokesmen held openly that Eurocommunism amounts to nonaligned Communism,[25] meaning a victory for nonaligned principles in interparty relations. This identification of Eurocommunists with the nonaligned nations, the intensity of Yugoslav polemics in response to the Soviet campaign against Carrillo, and Moscow's drive to equate Eurocommunism with anti-Sovietism set off major reverberations on the Yugoslav domestic political scene.

The Internal Political Dynamic

Since 1948 Yugoslav domestic politics have followed a cyclical pattern. Periods of liberalization and decentralization are succeeded by periods characterized by centralization, authoritarian solutions, and attempts to depoliticize the political forces previously encouraged. This oscillation results from the intrinsic dilemma that the Soviet-Yugoslav split poses for Yugoslav Marxists. The demand for national emancipation from Soviet hegemony and socialist emancipation from CPSU ideological domination legitimized wide-scale political participation at all levels in the name of self-managing socialism. In practice,

self-management not only served to justify the LCY's continued rejection of the Soviet model, but also reordered organizational relationships within the Yugoslav party itself.

Self-management inevitably increased decision-making autonomy at
the republic and commune levels. The decrease in the political
strength of the republic party organizations, in turn, had major ethnic
ramifications. Because the key republics also represent national
(ethnic) groups, self-management inadvertantly amounted to sanctioning ethnic politics in the form of bureaucratic power struggles within
the party. The unintended consequence was to evade the distinction
between socialist and national self-determination. By 1971 this situation had generated demands that self-management be carried to its
logical conclusion, that is that the LCY be reorganized along national
lines.[26] It is fair to say that this was the last thing that the drafters of
the party program of 1958 had in mind.

In retrospect, the so-called Croatian crisis of 1971 may be seen as
the result of Tito's effort to halt *de facto* development of a multinational, multiparty system in which the federal League of Communists
effectively yielded its power to the republic party organizations representing ethnic constituencies. The aging godfather of Yugoslav Communism struck to protect a united, country-wide Communist party
that had the power to "interfere when necessary." Tito's move to
reorganize the LCY went beyond suppression of alleged Croatian
separatism to contain the "mass national movement" that had infected the Croatian League of Communists. Rather, the seemingly ir-
rational expansion of the purge to other republics was part of Tito's
master plan to streamline and recentralize the LCY so that the party
could survive his passing without being torn apart by ethnic conflict
or suffocated by the weight of competing self-managing institutions.
In this light, Tito's insistence that "the rot" had begun with the historic Sixth Party Congress in 1952, and his statement that he had
"never liked that congress" seem less of an anomaly. Events play
tricks on the most skillful politician. Perhaps, after all, the Yugoslav
leader deserved the Order of Lenin awarded to him during his trip to
Moscow in June 1972. Yet whatever Tito's personal preferences, the
Sixth Party Congress inaugurated a political process that could not be
reversed by fiat.

A "pluralism of self-managing interests" is not the idealized
socialist pluralism of the PCI, it is Yugoslav reality. For more than a
quarter of a century, the Yugoslav party itself has strenuously labored
to build what Bodgan Denitch describes as a "new political culture"
characterized by "increasing differentiation of institutions, creating a
type of institutionalized pluralism."[27] Despite difficulty in adjusting to

its ambiguous role in society, the LCY has succeeded in instilling participation as a value and aggregation of interests outside the party as a social norm. Moreover, the problem for those who favor return-ing to Leninist solutions goes beyond convincing large numbers of Yugoslavs to give up channels of participation that they are accus-tomed to consider legitimate expressions of their own interests. Tito's efforts notwithstanding, there is no single "Yugoslav Communist party." The LCY is deeply divided on the question of the party's role in society and its implementation of that role. Self-managing institu-tions initially emerged and now operate because some leading officials believed and continue to believe that such institutions are essential to Yugoslav socialist development, or, as Dennison Rusinow has put it, "in part because internal dissention has periodically paralyzed these apparatuses (party/state bodies) sufficiently, at either the federal or a regional level, to provide the functional equivalent of permission."[28]

Historically, foreign policy variables have largely dictated the tim-ing of Yugoslavia's domestic political cycles. The Soviet-Yugoslav split put Tito on the road to socialist self-management. In 1955 Khrushchev's desire for rapprochement, coupled with the dangerous implications of the Djilas affair, temporarily sidetracked that process and might have halted it permanently. By 1957, however, Khrushchev had abandoned the Yugoslavs in his effort to reconstruct a Communist center. The 1958 party program was formulated primarily in response to this international embarrassment. It led to a further decentraliza-tion that Tito felt free to stop only after Brezhnev had renounced the "Brezhnev Doctrine" as a Western "fabrication" on his visit to Bel-grade in September 1971.[29] After the June 1976 Berlin Congress, Soviet-Yugoslav relations again deteriorated, this time in conjunction with Moscow's campaign to revive proletarian internationalism and the dictatorship of the proletariat as general laws of socialist devel-opment and to dismiss Eurocommunism as anti-Sovietism. Yugoslav opposition intensified as the Bulgarians became the chief proponents of this view.

Taking into account the timing involved, it is unlikely that the Soviet attack on Carrillo in *New Times* for his book *Eurocommunism and the State* had any direct connection with Edvard Kardelj's June 13, 1977 speech to the LCY Central Committee Presidency, which stressed the need for a "pluralism of self-managing interests" to op-erate more freely and criticized party misuse of power.[30] The strong Yugoslav defense of Carrillo and escalating Eurocommunist polemics, however, strengthened the hand of those who supported Kardelj's criticisms. These circumstances also made more difficult public op-position to his insistence that inasmuch as the distortions of the early

1970s were now under control, the party must draw back and allow "all creative socialist forces" to operate autonomously in their self-managing institutions. There is no doubt that other powerful forces within the party resisted this interpretation. The delayed publication of Kardelj's book *The Roads of Development of the Socialist Self-Management Political System,* as well as the postponement of the rumored amnesty for political prisoners, imply internal party struggle.

Kardelj's book was published in the autumn of 1977. In November the Yugoslav government announced that 218 convicted political prisoners would receive amnesty and that another 356 would not be brought to trial. These moves indicate that the balance of forces was once again tilting towards a period of permissiveness, a direction at least potentially ratified by the party reorganization that took place at the Eleventh LCY Congress in June 1978.[31] Kardelj's book and the 1958 party program were explicitly considered key sources for the basic theses adopted in preparation of the congress. This development amounted to a symbolic rehabilitation of the pluralistic ideas that had been systematically downplayed since the party upheavals following the Croatian events in 1971.

The reorganization of the party Presidium, which cut that body back to twenty-four members and eliminated the Executive Committee, tied the highest level of the party ever more closely to its republic party roots. The new Presidium has three members from each republic, two elected at republic party congresses plus the president of the republic central committee. Two members come from each autonomous province, and one from the army party organization. Representation on the Central Committee at the federal level consists of a delegation of nineteen members from each republic party plus the president of the republic central committee, fifteen members from each provincial party, and fifteen members from the army party organization. The revived Secretariat also reflects republic, province, and army representation.

Thus, despite the virtual adulation of Tito, the Eleventh LCY Congress may be seen as reversing the direction of his centralizing reorganization ratified by the Tenth LCY Congress in May 1974. The resulting composition of the Presidium certainly bears little resemblance to the seven-member Politburo rumored to be in the works in 1977. At that time, party sources were talking "unofficially" to Western correspondents about a streamlined Executive Committee.[32]

This is not to say the process cannot be reversed or that its proponents would not agree to "administrative measures" if these become necessary to maintain order after Tito is no longer in power. Nonetheless, the Soviet-Yugoslav Eurocommunist polemics between June

1977 and June 1978 operated as a functional equivalent to the split in 1948 and the dispute in 1958 with respect to their impact on Yugoslav domestic development. Even if I would not go so far as to call the current period "the third great debate" over the nature of the Yugoslav experiment, its significance is undeniable.[33]

Conclusions

The policies and principles laid down by the Eleventh LCY Congress stabilized the situation inside Yugoslavia. This congress provided domestic legitimization for expanding socialist pluralism that should help safeguard Yugoslav self-managing socialism as well as the country's nonaligned status even if their Western Eurocommunist allies suffer setbacks in the future. Throughout 1976–1978 the fate of progressive forces in Yugoslavia became entangled with that of the Western Eurocommunists, most notably the Italians. The debate with Moscow over whether Eurocommunist positions represented nonaligned politics or anti-Sovietism strengthened the position of those within and outside the LCY to whom socialist self-management meant expanding local autonomy, implementation of market socialism, legitimate interest aggregation and conflicting views, and the right to criticize without fear. The party congress did not end the importance of Western Eurocommunism to this amorphous Yugoslav grouping. It did make the Yugoslavs' position less vulnerable, although we have yet to assess the impact of Kardelj's death in early 1979.

Moreover, it is well to remember that the PCI-LCY alliance is a symbiotic relationship in which the PCI commitment to democracy and socialist pluralism is reinforced in turn by the existence of a nonaligned Yugoslavia dedicated to a pluralism of self-managing interests. The nature of post-Tito Yugoslavia is crucial to the PCI, for Yugoslavia physically separates Italy from the more dogmatic East European countries.

There is much concern in the West over the extent and sincerity of the Italian Communists' professed commitment to domestic pluralism, civil liberties, and the need to resist Soviet hegemony. Those attempting to evaluate American interests with respect to Italian Communism should bear in mind that Yugoslavia provides a precedent that is frequently overlooked. As with Yugoslavia, PCI differences with Moscow developed over time. The Italian party is indigenous, domestically popular, and experienced in governing at the local level. (Like the Yugoslav partisans, the PCI must euphemistically live off the countryside.) In terms of leadership, the Italians' independent line has

survived the succession from Togliatti to Luigi Longo to Enrico
Berlinguer—a better record of generational adaptability than the
Yugoslav party can boast. In addition, the PCI rank and file accepts
and values the party's autonomous tradition, equating it with domestic parliamentary politics and political pluralism. Thus the PCI is
farther down the road to genuine socialist pluralism in the late 1970s
than was Yugoslavia in 1948. The assessments of the Yugoslav alternative were not initially positive in the West.

It may well be that a strong, visibly successful Italian Communist
party, capable of leading the Western Eurocommunists, is just as
much in American interest as was supporting what amounted to
Yugoslav national Communism in the 1950s. The cold fact is that President Jimmy Carter has little direct influence on human rights in the
Soviet Union and hard-line East European countries. American outrage at abuse of dissidents, typified by the response to the 1978 trials
of Anatoly Shcharansky and Alexander Ginzburg, may have led to
Ginzburg's release, but it cannot be counted upon systematically to
improve the fate of such individuals.

The Eurocommunist outcry is certainly no more welcome in Moscow. In the long run, however, it is potentially more effective than
American protests, not so much in specific instances, but in the
example it provides of Communists working productively within the
framework of pluralistic, democratic society. The ghost of the Prague
Spring lives on in Rome. As long as Italy remains in NATO, the
Soviets are helpless to eliminate the threat of ideological contagion
that it took 600,000 troops to end in Czechoslovakia.

Most importantly, to the extent that Washington values the ability
of a nonaligned Yugoslavia to offer a genuine alternative to the Soviet
model for other East European regimes, it must realize that this
ability is at least in part dependent on the well-being of Eurocommunism in Western Europe. This is not to suggest that the Carter
administration should embrace the Eurocommunists. Positive appreciation would only backfire. The need to develop a balanced approach
that indirectly encourages Eurocommunism as a movement without
going so far as to endorse a Eurocommunist takeover in Italy, or
elsewhere in the West, is a challenge to the sophistication of American foreign policy.

NOTES

This chapter was first presented as a paper at the conference on Eurocommunism, Eastern Europe and the USSR held at the Naval Postgraduate
School, Monterey, California, August 21–22, 1978. It benefited from the

comments of our panel discussant, Lt. Paul W. Dahlquist, USN.

1. As emphasized by William E. Griffith and Rudolf Tokes, eds., *Eurocommunism and Detente* (New York: New York University Press, 1978).

2. Contrast the interpretation of Charles Gati, "The 'Europeanization' of Communism," 55, *Foreign Affairs* (April 1977), pp. 539–553.

3. Ivan Avakumovic, *History of the Communist Party of Yugoslavia* (Aberdeen, Scotland: University Press of Aberdeen, 1964).

4. Phyllis Auty, *Tito* (New York: Ballantine Books, 1972), p. 46.

5. See the discussion by M. George Zaninovich, *The Development of Socialist Yugoslavia* (Baltimore: Johns Hopkins University Press, 1968), pp. 17–24 and Bogdan Denitch, *The Legitimation of a Revolution: The Yugoslav Case* (New Haven: Yale University Press, 1976).

6. Quoted by Vladimir Dedijer, *With Tito Through the War: Partisan Diary, 1941–1944* (London: A. Hamilton, 1951), p. 39.

7. For basic documents, see Robert Bass and Elizabeth Marbury, eds. *The Soviet Yugoslav Controversy, 1948–1968: A Documentary Record* (New York Prospect Books, 1954). The Yugoslav version may be found in *White Book on Aggressive Activities by the Governments of the USSR, Poland, Czechoslovakia, Hungary, Rumania, Bulgaria, and Albania towards Yugoslavia* (Belgrade: Ministry of Foreign Affairs, 1951).

8. For an insightful anecdote that reveals the extent to which younger PCI cadres have come to accept PCI commitment to democratic principles as the norm and that indicates how easily party history can be submerged in current practice, see Joan Barth Urban, "Moscow and the PCI: Kto Kovo?" Paper delivered at the American Political Science Association Annual Meeting, Washington, September 2, 1977, p. 43.

9. See, for example Edvard Kardelj's statement that "Leninism is simply a series of ideas and methods that grew out of the Russian experience. Our experience is different." Quoted by George W. Hoffman and Fred W. Neal, *Yugoslavia and the New Communism* (New York: Twentieth Century Fund, 1962), p. 171.

10. For contemporary analysis, see the account of Dennison Rusinow, *The Yugoslav Experiment: 1948–1974* (Berkeley: University of California Press, 1977), p. 88ff.

11. Stephen Clisshold, ed., *Yugoslavia and the Soviet Union 1939–1973* (London: Oxford University Press, 1975), Document 174.

12. *Nuovi Argomenti* (Rome), June 19, 1956. A detailed, excellent analysis of the evolution of the PCI position is provided in Urban, "Moscow and the PCI: Kto-Kovo?"

13. *Pravda*, July 2, 1956.

14. See Zbigniew K. Brzezinski, *The Soviet Bloc: Unity and Conflict* (Cambridge, Mass.: Harvard University Press, 1971), pp. 271–309.

15. English language version translated by Stoyan Pribechevich, *Yugoslavia's Way: Program of the League of Communists* (New York: All Nations Press, 1958).

16. Those who want to pursue this aspect further should consult Deborah D. Milenkovitch, *Plan and Market in Yugoslav Economic Thought* (New Haven: Yale University Press, 1971).

17. *Borba* (Belgrade), September 22, 1969.

18. Robin Remington, "The Phoenix of Eurocommunism: From the Ashes of 1968." Paper presented at the Midwest Slavic Conference, Bloomington, Indiana, April 14–16, 1978.

19. See Kevin Devlin, "The Interparty Drama," *Problems of Communism,* XXVI (July-August 1975), pp. 18–35.

20. Ibid, p. 22.

21. *Tanjug,* October 17, 1974.

22. *Tass,* December 20, 1974.

23. Radovan Vukadinovic, "Small States on the Policy Nonalignment," in August Schou and Arne Olv Brundtland, eds. *Small States in International Relations* (New York: John Wiley & Sons, 1971), pp. 99–114. Also Vlado Benko, "Denconcentration of Power in the International Community and the Position of Small and Medium Sized State," in Ljubivoje Acimovic, ed., *Nonalignment in the World Today* (Belgrade: Institute of International Politics and Economics, 1969), pp. 131–152.

24. Elaborated in Robin Alison Remington, "Yugoslavia and European Security." *Orbis XVII* (Spring 1973), pp. 197–226.

25. Vjesnik (Zagreb), December 17, 1977 and April 26, 1978.

26. Ibid., February 11, 1971.

27. Denitch, *Legitimation of a Revolution,* p. 12.

28. Dennison Rusinow. "Yugoslav Domestic Developments," Paper presented at the conference, "Yugoslavia: Accomplishments and Problems," Wilson Center, Washington, October 16, 1977.

29. *Borba,* September 22, 1971.

30. *New Times,* 26 (June 1977), pp. 9–13. Quoted from Rusinow, "Yugoslav Domestic Developments," p. 2. Nor is it an accident to my mind that Kardelj has praised Eurocommunism as an "anti-bloc movement," emphasizing its function as an opponent of the Communist center in Moscow. Quoted by Slobodan Stankovic, "Edward Kardelj and Eurocommunism," *Radio Free Europe Background Report,* no. 184 (September 19, 1977).

31. Note the revised party statutes adopted at the Eleventh LCY Congress in June 1978, providing the right of the minority within the party to "maintain their views," although it is still obligated to help carry out the majority decision. Draft statutes published in *Komunist* (Belgrade), March 27, 1978. For further elaboration see Milorad Muratovic, "The Relationship between the 'Majority' and 'Minority' in the Light of the LCY's Experience," *Socijalizam,* 5 (May 1978), pp. 34–43. For coverage of the party congress itself, see *Borba,* June 24, 1978.

32. *Times* (London), June 2, 1977.

33. A question raised by Rusinow, "Yugoslav Domestic Developments," p. 5.

CHAPTER XI

Eurocommunism and Hungary

Paul R. Milch

I. Communist Power Seizures in the Wake of World War I and World War II

The Hungarian Communist party (HCP) has had several "beginnings" during its short but turbulent sixty-year history. Foremost among these was its meteoric rise and fall in 1918–19 in conjunction with the Hungarian Soviet Republic. The leaders of the new party, especially the charismatic Bela Kun, set out proudly to duplicate the Soviet model as prescribed by Lenin. Yet, when the opportunity arose in March 1919 to seize power in Hungary, Kun and his inner circle, just four months after their arrival from Moscow, allied themselves with the "opportunistic" social democrats to establish the Hungarian Soviet Republic. Although in the compromise agreement with the socialists the Communist program was adopted, including the establishment of the dictatorship of the proletariat, several questions of Communist ideological purity arose immediately.[1] In the final analysis, once in power, the Communists, under Kun's leadership, were forced to operate without help or interference from Soviet Russia simply because the latter was too preoccupied with its own problems. Communist rule was achieved without a violent revolution, and the dictatorship of the proletariat, although declared, proved to be neither absolute nor irreversible. Power had to be shared with the social democrats, whose political skill and sheer numbers (with their labor union organizations) were far superior to those of the Communists, who were soon outmaneuvered as a result.[2]

After the fall of the Hungarian Soviet Republic in August 1919, the HCP virtually disappeared for a quarter of a century. Although an underground party existed in Hungary in the 1930s, the police power of the authoritarian Horthy regime proved more than a match for the faction-ridden domestic Communists, isolated as they were from the group that had emigrated to the Soviet Union.

It was this small, well-disciplined core of Moscow-trained Communists, led by Matyas Rakosi, who took over the leadership of the HCP in 1945. At first, the Communists in general, and Rakosi in particular, took pains to appear accommodating and democratically inclined. Rakosi sought to reassure the population that the Communists had no intentions of using the military might of the Soviet army to take political control of the country. His party's organ, *Szabad Nep*, protested:

> According to Bela Kovacs [leader of the Smallholders Party, the Communists' first target at that time] and his group, the Communists are preparing to seize power. We have always said and still say that this is nonsense. The very fact that the democratic element in the Smallholders Party takes this absurdity seriously shows how much they are under the influence of reactionary gossip.[3]

Within a few months of that statement many Smallholders were arrested on charges of fascist conspiracy, and Bela Kovacs was himself abducted by the Russians.

Later, at the height of his power in February 1952, Rakosi explained the events this way:

> At the beginning of 1945 when our country was liberated . . . the majority of our Communists did not understand the strategy and tactics of our Party. . . . The greater part of those comrades who were not acquainted with or did not understand our strategical plan *devised during the war*, were surprised at such a broad coalition composed of heterogeneous elements, and treated it often with antagonism. . . . And they [these comrades] told us what they wanted. . . . "Now that the Red Army has liberated us—let us profit by this opportunity to restore the proletarian dictatorship."[4]

In the same speech Rakosi also admitted that "Soviet 'interferences' in our internal affairs were quite frequent and of great help in the strengthening of our Party, but not in a sense imputed by the imperialists." The fact remains, of course, that Rakosi's famous "salami tactics" of eliminating opponents, inside and outside the party, one by one, succeeded with clockwork precision until he managed to transform Hungary into a Stalinist dictatorship.

Although Western skeptics of the alleged Eurocommunist espousal of democratic ideals often refer to the postwar history of Communist power seizure in Hungary (and elsewhere in Eastern Europe) as examples of Communist perfidy, there are enough historical and geopolitical differences between circumstances in Eastern Europe then and those of Western Europe today to make the comparison quite remote. But even Rakosi's boast may well have been an *a posteriori* explanation of Communist tactics that just happened to work out to his best advantage in historical circumstances that could have turned out to be less fortunate for the Communists in Eastern Europe if it had not been for Western passivity towards the area.[5]

II. Imre Nagy and the Revolution of 1956

The Hungarian Revolution of 1956 is now widely accepted as one that ultimately tried to rid the country not only of Soviet domination, but also of Communist rule as well.[6] While this viewpoint may be essentially correct, it is also true that the events that led to the revolution were both inspired and led by Communist intellectuals and politicians who had nothing further from their minds than to undermine the leading role of the Communist party in Hungarian society.

The man who is commonly regarded as the "leader" of this movement, Imre Nagy, was an old-line Communist who received his training in Moscow during the 1930s and early 1940s. Although his political fortunes fluctuated within the party leadership during the years 1945–1953, he appeared to be a public supporter of all the policies of Rakosi. On Stalin's death in March 1953, Nagy delivered a eulogy full of frequent praises of "the great leader of humanity." Yet in July 1953, when the Kremlin chose him to lead Hungary into the reform period and forced Rakosi to relinquish the premiership to him, Nagy apparently embraced the program of liberalization wholeheartedly. Later, when Rakosi managed to fight his way back to power, Nagy retired to write his views on the Hungarian political and economic scene.

In his treatise *On Communism* Nagy revealed that his ideas on the modernization of the Hungarian economy had been different from those of Rakosi even during the 1947–1948 period. Rather than Rakosi's forced industrialization and compulsory collectivisation, he had then been in favor of pursuing policies similar to Lenin's New Economic Policy (NEP). Nagy saw the NEP as the most appropriate program for the transition to socialism in any country, such as Hungary, in which there was a significantly large number of small peasants.[7]

Nagy's program was finally adopted as party policy with Kremlin approval when he became premier in July 1953. Although Rakosi and his *apparat* sabotaged the program practically from the beginning,

Nagy's "New Course" included such reforms as slowing down the pace of industrialization, increasing the production of consumer goods, making membership in collective farms voluntary, and abolishing police terror and political prison camps. Coming on the heels of Rakosi's terror, the new course program seemed as liberal as today's Eurocommunism appears when compared to Soviet-style Communism.

It may seem forced, however, to compare Nagy's policies with Eurocommunism, particularly at this juncture. Although Nagy refused to exercise the usually mandatory self-criticism when he was forced to resign in the spring of 1955, he was also reluctant to assume openly the position of leader of the opposition within the party or nationwide even after the outbreak of the 1956 revolt. It was only in the last seven days of the revolution that he finally allowed himself to be caught up in the revolutionary fervor. It was only then that Nagy, with apparently sincere enthusiasm, announced the abolition of the one-party system, the reorganization of democratic parties, and Hungary's withdrawal from the Warsaw Pact, coupled with appeals to the United Nations to defend the country's neutrality.

It would be wrong, however, to assume that Nagy suddenly succumbed to ideas that had been alien to him just a few days earlier. The fact is that none of the aims of the revolution were either alien or new to him. This becomes quite evident on reading *On Communism*. This document, written just before the Twentieth Congress of the CPSU, where Nikita Khrushchev dethroned Stalin, is a strongly worded denunciation of the policies and practices of the "clique headed by Rakosi, which . . . crushed the basis of Hungary's young democracy and liquidated our people's democratic forces and the democratic partnerships of socialism."[8]

Although the treatise was written in Communist party official jargon, replete with quotations from Marx, Lenin, and even Stalin and Rakosi, the author's conception of a more humane and democratic socialism that accommodates national characteristics and aspirations comes clearly into view. Right at the start Nagy established his belief that Marxism is not a rigid dogma:

> Marxism-Leninism cannot rigidly adhere to its present ideological tenets within the framework developed by the genius of its great masters, nor can it confine itself merely to renewing its old theories, as there are no eternal, never changing teachings which remain applicable regardless of time or space and independently of concrete situations. The masters of Marxism-Leninism did not bind the hands of future generations with their theories.[9]

This statement is similar in content to Santiago Carrillo's early stipulation in his *Eurocommunism and the State* that "proletarian revolutions revise themselves and revolutionaries do so too. Lenin revised certain theses of Marx and put forward the thesis of the *unequal development* of imperialism and the breaking of its weakest links to lay the foundation of the Great October Socialist Revolution."[10] Nagy placed the blame for the dogmatization of Marxism-Leninism squarely on the "Stalinist monopoly over the science of Marxism-Leninism" that had led to the belief that the only admissible way to build socialism was the one practiced in the Soviet Union.[11] This ignored the obvious diversity of conditions in such disparate countries as the Soviet Union, China, Yugoslavia, and Hungary itself.[12]

Nagy's view was that the development of the peoples' democracies should have reflected their special "diversity of difference in conditions" from those of the Soviet Union, and the dictatorship of the proletariat in these countries should have been exercised without the excessive use of force.[13] Nagy explained the relevance of this position to the Communist parties of Western Europe in the following way:

> The Soviet form and methods of building socialism, its mechanical application, disregarding the special characteristics of various individual countries, raise serious obstacles in the path of international revolutionary workers' movements, primarily and especially to the work of the Communist and Workers' Parties in the Western capitalist countries in *their* battle for socialism. For Central and Eastern European countries, and last but not least for us, it is necessary that we find and use such forms and methods in building socialism in all phases of social, political, economic, and cultural life, and we must realize such a rate of progress that it will make socialism acceptable and desirable to the widest possible masses in the capitalistic countries and to all strata of the working classes.
>
> Our social, economic, and cultural situation from which we proceeded to build socialism is in many ways very close to the situation that prevails in the capitalist countries of the West. Therefore the similarities in the situations of the Western capitalist countries and the present People's Democracies in Central and Eastern Europe make it possible that by the application of a creative Marxism-Leninism, taking into consideration the special character of the transition period and the situation in the various countries, as well as the new road to socialism, one can extend immeasurable aid to the Communist and Workers' Parties of Western Europe in gaining the support of the working masses in their struggle for socialism. Our conspicuously proper or improper standpoint on principles, our good or our bad work, our success or our failure, can promote or impede the cause of socialism in Western Europe.[14]

That this "European" road to socialism should be a humanistic one

Nagy made clear when he wrote that the party membership and the Hungarian people wanted

> a system that is actually ruled not by a degenerate Bonapartist authority and dictator but by the working people through legality and self-created law and order. They want a People's Democracy . . . where human beings are respected and where social and political life is conducted in the spirit of humanism.[15]

As for the best course for Hungary in the postwar conflict between the Communist and non-Communist blocs, Nagy insisted that his country "must avoid becoming an active participant in any of the clashes between power groups or becoming embroiled in war, to serve as a field of battle or an area of troop passage."[16] And ever so cautiously, wrapped in the language of party functionaries, he dared to use the word "neutrality":

> For this reason, taking a stand against such power groups, whether that of neutrality or active coexistence, will mean the realization of consistent representation of the basic principles of cooperation within the countries of the socialist camp.[17]

Nagy's acceptance of the multiparty system during the revolution does not seem to have direct antecedent in his writings. His reference to the "clique headed by Rakosi" having crushed "Hungary's young democracy," however, is an obvious denunciation of the way the party eliminated the multiparty system of 1945–1947.

In sum, then, Nagy's acceptance of the more radical demands of the 1956 revolution is quite understandable, as his own earlier views were by no means incompatible with them. Of course, these were exactly the accusations made against him at his trial. Charges that he was a traitor to the cause of socialism, however, were a blatant falsehood.

The Communist credentials of the "1956 events," however, do not depend on Nagy's personality. The whole period of political and intellectual ferment that preceded the revolt was initiated and continually instigated by both veteran and young Communist intellectuals who were concentrated mainly in two centers of activity: the Petofi Circle and the Writers' Association. Other hubs of opposition activity existed in the offices of the official party daily, *Szabad Nep,* and the small circle of Communists around Nagy himself.

On the eve of the 1956 revolution these opposition Communists could well be described in today's terminology as Eurocommunists in that they embraced the goal of building socialism in a pluralistic, democratic society along independent lines that fully accounted for specific Hungarian conditions. For example, the ten-point resolution of the Petofi Circle included demands for a new "constructive program [for the economy] in accordance with the special conditions existing in Hungary," the "consolidation of Hungarian-Soviet friendship . . . on the basis of the Leninist principles of complete equality" and the replacement of Stalinist leaders of the party and state with "Comrade Imre Nagy and other comrades who fought for socialist democracy and for Leninist principles." The Writers' Association adopted a similar set of demands that called for the establishment of trade unions that "must truly represent the interests of the Hungarian working class" and the creation of "political and economic conditions for free membership in cooperatives." This resolution, voted on the night before the October 23 uprising, was perhaps the first public demand that "the PPF [Patriotic People's Front] should assume the political representation of the working class of Hungarian society. Our electoral system must correspond to the demands of socialist democracy. The people must elect their representatives in parliament, in the [Workers'] Councils, and in all autonomous organs of administration by free, secret ballot."[18] The demand for a free pluralistic society had finally been made in public.

The Hungarian Revolution of 1956, however, was a very short-lived, spontaneous affair. Consequently, it did not leave behind an elaborately developed ideological-political justification or explanation of the events that transpired. The foremost Hungarian Communist ideologue-philosopher, Gyorgy Lukacs, was an apparent supporter of the revolution and could have ideally performed such a function.[19] He did not do so for reasons that have as much to do with his personality as with the unexpected way the revolution took place. But after the second military intrusion of the Soviet Army and before conditions began to "normalize," a group of young, mostly Communist individuals, acting in total isolation from the population and even the rest of the intelligentsia, organized an underground group that prepared two statements referred to as the *Hungaricus* pamphlets.[20]

The *Hungaricus* pamphlets undertook nothing less than a Marxist reexamination of the history of socialism since the days of Lenin in light of the 1956 uprising. In its critical review of the socialist system in the Soviet Union, *Hungaricus* went beyond both Khrushchev's criticism of Stalin and the critiques of the Yugoslav Communists. It pointed out that the dictatorial, bureaucratic system Stalin built had become by necessity a violent, brutal, inhuman system that could not be changed by new leadership or the abolition of the "personality cult." Contrary to Khrushchev's claim that Stalin's distortions of

Marxism-Leninism led to the inequities of Soviet socialism, *Hungaricus* maintained that Stalin first instituted his system of terror and despotism and that this "reality of Russian socialism imposed by violence shaped Marx's and Engel's theory to its own image." *Hungaricus* blamed mainly Stalin both for the distortion of the Soviet system and for the vulgarization of Marxism-Leninism by turning it into a rigid, ossified dogma. It charged Lenin with some responsibility as well. In fact, quoting the then Italian Communist party secretary Palmiro Togliatti, *Hungaricus* questioned whether the Soviet way of building socialism was the right road even for the Soviet Union.[21] While agreeing that Lenin and the Bolsheviks were correct in seizing power in 1917, *Hungaricus* went beyond Carrillo's later criticism and maintained that even in backward Russia of 1917 Lenin overestimated the speed with which the building of socialism could begin.[22] Finally, *Hungaricus* suggested that the objective conditions in the Soviet Union of the time (1956–1957) were ripe for the democratization of socialism and expressed the hope that proletarian internationalism would help create subjective forces that would begin the fight for the total abolition of Stalinism and for the establishment of socialist democracy in the Soviet Union.

Turning to an analysis of the Hungarian situation, *Hungaricus* denounced the Rakosi regime as a totally misguided effort to build socialism "with foreign force and an apparatus designed along foreign lines. This increasingly anti-socialist socialism, this ever more counterrevolutionary revolution, this people's democracy against the people, rested on the basis of the bureaucratically concentrated planned economy."

Yet *Hungaricus* strongly rejected all "bourgeois criticism" of Soviet-style socialism in general and the Hungarian regime in particular. It made clear that members of the ruling classes of the former capitalist regime of Hungary had no claim for power in contemporary Hungary. It still considered the achievements of the Rakosi regime a basically progressive development despite all of the pain and suffering they had caused. With respect to the future, *Hungaricus* maintained that, while "the Hungarian Revolution has revealed the utter degeneration of the lofty ideals of the Russian October that, forty years ago, inspired half the world," the events of the Hungarian October of 1956 had shown that "new roads, different from Stalinist terror-communism or the social democratic trends fawning upon capitalism, are opening before the international working-class movement."

By distinguishing its views from both Soviet-style Communism and "social democratic trends fawning upon capitalism," the *Hungaricus* pamphlet revealed itself for what it was: a document by premature

Eurocommunists who had the misfortune to be in the wrong place at the wrong time. While Spanish and Italian Eurocommunists of the 1970s can disagree with, criticize, and even defy Soviet Communism, these Hungarian precursors of Eurocommunism could only conclude that future struggles would be necessary to achieve "a truly democratic and independent socialism, corresponding to Hungarian circumstances" and vow that "the next time we shall be better prepared to act."

Yet another set of political statements were left by a member of Nagy's cabinet. Istvan Bibo, although a non-Communist, held leftist, socialist views. In his proposals entitled "Plan to Solve the Hungarian Question on a Compromise Basis," he put forward a detailed plan whereby Hungary would follow the "third road" of a multiparty system.[23] Only those parties that wholly subscribed to the maintenance of socialism in Hungary would be allowed to participate. In addition, in exchange for a phased withdrawal of Soviet troops, Hungary would provide the Soviet Union with guarantees that it would not become a base for any anti-Soviet military or political activity.

The words from the last report of a Polish journalist (before returning home from Budapest when the revolt seemed victorious) provide some non-Hungarian documentation establishing the connection between Eurocommunist concepts and the orientation of the Hungarian Revolution. Victor Woroszilski noted:

> Naturally I do not know in what type of regime the Hungarian Republic will finally clothe itself. But it seems that we will be able to observe here a curious synthesis: a basic realization of a popular democracy (land in the hands of the peasants, socialization of factories and banks) and of a pluralism of parties, freedom of the press, and all the other liberties inherent in a liberal democracy. Does not such a regime constitute one of the possible roads — perhaps a very slow one — towards Socialism? I am not sure.[24]

III. Eurocommunism and the Kadar Regime

When Janos Kadar made his mysterious switch from ardent supporter of the Nagy government to the leader of "loyal Communist" forces who crushed the "Horthyite-Fascist-Hungarian-capitalist-feudal-counterrevolution" in a matter of a few days, most people inside and outside Hungary assumed that a return to the darkest days of Stalinism and Rakosiism would be the natural sequel. For about a year and a half, until the announced execution of Nagy and three of his supporters in June 1958, this was not far from the truth.

At the start of that period Kadar still kept up the pretense of advocating free elections and a multiparty system. Speaking to a delegation of the Central Workers' Council in the parliament building, he said:

> Let us consider the monopolistic position of the Party. We want a multi-party system and free honest elections. We know that this will be no easy matter, because not only by bullets, but also by the ballot can the Workers' power be killed. We have to take into account that we may be thoroughly beaten at the elections, but if we take on the election fight, the Communist Party can have the necessary strength again to obtain the confidence of the working masses.[25]

Yet in the same breath he also explained what he had against "a multi-party system and free honest elections." His objections to them may sound like a remarkably ironic counterpart to the arguments Western opponents of Eurocommunists make against Communist participation in the governments of Italy or France today:

> We have no reason to doubt the statements made by honest middle-class politicians that they want socialism; only, after an election defeat of Communists, these politicians could be set aside by their own parties. There is no middle-class politician, however well-intentioned he may be, who could defend the factories and the land, without the help of the Party of the working class.[26]

Although Kadar continued to talk for a while about an alliance with some non-Communist politicians, it was still too soon for reconciliation. Instead, a head-on collision took place between Kadar's "Revolutionary Worker-Peasant Government" and the people, or more precisely, the workers themselves. The workers' councils, which had come into being during the revolution and then started to fade away as the multiparty system had suddenly sprung back to life, now became a powerful, defiant force. These were not "middle-class politicians" endangering the rule of the party. They were working men elected by direct democracy in the factories of the most heavily industrialized sectors of Budapest. Their's was a "socialist revolution" directed against the party. Kadar broke its back the only way he knew how: by brute force of terror reminiscent of the worst days of Rakosi.

In 1958, however, Kadar appeared to embark, ever so cautiously, on a new road of national reconciliation. It was apparently the right time to do so. All open opposition to the regime had been destroyed, and the announcement of Nagy's execution made it clear that no compromise with the forces of the revolution would be tolerated. Had Kadar waited much longer to begin his process of liberalization, the national mood of bitterness against him would have solidified completely, forcing the regime to a permanent return to Stalinist methods of oppression.

By the early 1960s Kadar's new slogan, "He who is not against us is with us" began to take hold.[27] Three thousand political prisoners who had participated in the 1956 uprising received amnesty. As a signal that the regime would not revert to the Stalinist past, many former Rakosi supporters were expelled from the party. It is not the objective of this paper, however, to trace the very interesting process of liberalization by the Kadar regime,[28] but rather to examine the Kadar regime as it has evolved in the 1960s and 1970s and the way it relates to the contemporary phenomenon of Eurocommunism. Essentially, the argument will be made that the Hungarian People's Republic occupies a unique position among the East European allies of the Soviet Union, a position that also represents a significant break with recent Hungarian history.

This unique position has evolved gradually and is composed of apparently carefully orchestrated domestic and foreign policy components. Although the foreign policy element is the less interesting part of the whole, it is an important complement to the domestic element. Basically, Hungary's foreign policy may be characterized as one that takes its cues on important international issues from the foreign policy position of the Soviet Union, with appropriate changes in tone and stance to compensate for the vast difference in the international statures of the two countries. Recent studies of East European conformity in foreign policy to the Soviet Union have shown Hungary occupying a middle ground among her socialist neighbors.[29]

Hungary's attitude toward Eurocommunism is a case in point. When the Bulgarian Communist leader, Todor Zhivkov, harshly denounced Eurocommunism as "anti-Sovietism," Kadar openly contradicted him by saying "I do not share this view. The parties in the West act within specific conditions and this should be taken into consideration."[30] At about the same time *Tarsadalmi Szemle,* the theoretical-political periodical of the Hungarian Socialist Workers' party (HSWP), also expressed the view that socialism could be reached under the conditions of a multiparty system, and therefore Eurocommunism did not have to be viewed as anti-Soviet in nature. Yet one month later the same periodical depicted Eurocommunism as a new ideological device of imperialism created to destroy the unity of the international revolutionary movement.[31] While the contradiction may be difficult to explain, Soviet leaders have also expressed views on both sides of the issue.[32] It seems clear that the Hungarian leaders feel ill at ease discussing the issue in public. According to *Tanjug*, the Yugoslav news agency, the Hungarian party considered its participation in the polemics over Eurocommunism "not indispensable."[33] Yet, not long before that, Dezso Nemes, a member of the Central Committee of the HSWP, did engage in polemics with his French counterpart, Jean Kanapa, about the relevance of the East European experience for Western Communist parties.[34] At any rate, the Hungarian leadership has taken a moderate stand on this issue that is not very different from Leonid Brezhnev's own ambiguous public pronouncements.[35] Moderation remains the policy of the HSWP. The final resolution of the April 1978 Central Committee session included the following statement:

> According to the Party's views it is the right and the duty of every sister party to act independently and creatively in applying the teachings of Marxism-Leninism and the general laws of the Socialist Revolution and of construction, with allowance for the given country's peculiarities and traditions. This requires from every Party to adjust the national with the international interest, to strive for unity, for mutual solidarity and for comradely cooperation.[36]

The May 12, 1978 issue of the party daily, *Nepszabadsag*, took up the matter of Eurocommunism in a lengthy article entitled "With 'Euro' or Without It." After describing Eurocommunism in factual, not unfavorable terms, the article produced a long list of "capitalist" reactions to the ideas and practices of Eurocommunists. Quoting statements by Henry Kissinger, Zbigniew Brzezinski, Valéry Giscard d'Estaing, the "Italian right-wing," "various parties of French monopoly capital," Alexander Haig, and *Informaciones*, "the newspaper of the Spanish bank capital," all of which show the distrust of the "bourgeoisie" toward Communism of any kind, the article concluded with the following warning aimed apparently at Eurocommunists and perhaps their Hungarian sympathizers:

> Thus when the class struggle sharpens and sheer class interests clash, it emerges that the bourgeoisie does not differentiate much between the Soviet or Italian, the Hungarian or the French Communists. . . . Its fundamental goal is merely to divide these [Eurocommunist] Parties and pit them against the fraternal Parties which struggle in the Socialist countries and to divert them from consistently representing the interests of the working masses, from attaining power and liquidating private ownership of the means of production. It follows from this, among other things, that the

stronger the collaboration and unity among the Communist and Workers' Parties, the sooner this will fail.[37]

In accordance with this recommendation, the party has maintained close relationships with the three major Eurocommunist parties.[38] Kadar himself endorsed this position in his interview with a *New York Times* reporter in June 1978. Discussing the Communist parties of Western Europe, he stated, "It's all the same to me whether they're dictatorships of the proletariat or not, so long as they try to break the strength of monopoly capitalism and make steps toward socialism in their own way."[39]

Domestically, under Kadar's leadership Hungarians are certainly making "steps toward socialism *in their own way.*" Once some basic moves were made to relax the harsh administrative measures of the immediate postrevolutionary years, the regime began experimenting with economic reforms. When it became apparent that stopgap measures would not suffice, the party leadership initiated a lengthy planning period for a thorough change in the country's economic system. The planning that began in 1964 culminated in the inauguration of the New Economic Mechanism (NEM) on January 1, 1968.

The basic objectives of NEM were to decentralize the old Stalinist command economy to enable it to break out from its stagnation and permit the country to begin modernizing its technologically backward industry. The main feature of NEM was the granting of large measures of autonomy to individual enterprises coupled with a new system of prices that allowed market conditions to operate within the carefully delineated confines of an essentially centrally controlled economy. Since its inception NEM has had its ups and downs.[40] Its chief architect, Rezso Nyers, was removed from his position of head economic planner and from the party Politburo in March 1974. At that time Hungary experienced serious economic problems as a result of the business slowdown in the West, on whose trade the country had come to depend more and more under the new economic system. Yet, NEM has not been abandoned, and its mere survival past the tenth anniversary of its inauguration is a measure of its success.[41] Another such indicator is the widely reported increase in the living standard of the population. This achievement partially predates NEM and is the result of the increased attention given the production and importation of consumer goods after the defeat of the 1956 revolution.[42]

Although "since 1968, Hungary has been the pace setter of economic reform movement in Eastern Europe,[43] the economy has not been the only area in which careful, systematic liberalization has been in progress for some years. With the removal of harsh police methods in the immediate aftermath of the revolution's defeat, Kadar began his liberalization drive early in the 1960s. At the Eighth Party Congress in November 1962, Kadar announced the abolition of university admission requirements based on class origin. The jamming of Western radio broadcasts beamed at Hungary was eliminated in 1964. Similarly, a liberal direction became apparent on the literary scene, where the party made its peace with the writers. As a result, it was acknowledged that "different social, national, and artistic conditions will not only result in individual differences but can also establish certain trends, groups and schools," and that "the present development of socialist realism . . . increasingly offers the possibility of many roads.[44]

It was apparent that Kadar and much of the Hungarian leadership recognized that improved living conditions alone would not be sufficient to win the hearts and minds of the people. In 1962 Kadar stated: "The elementary obligation of our party is to work as hard as if there were twenty parties in Hungary and we had to win votes by secret ballot every day, for this is the only way for us to secure the support of the people."[45] Many other declarations by party officials and the press sought to reassure the population that the present leadership had a genuine desire to make changes in Hungarian life toward a freer and more humane socialism. *Nepszabadsag* editorialized in 1968: "In the past few years many ideological debates have been held about it, and all debates centered on ways and means to develop socialist humanism and democracy."[46] It was clearly recognized and openly acknowledged by the leadership that socialism by itself does not have to bring with it democratization. The Patriotic People's Front (PPF) daily, *Magyar Nemzet,* referred to the Chinese model to indicate "that not even a socialist system in and of itself can provide a guarantee against uncorrectable errors on the part of the country's leadership. Guarantees like this can only be achieved by the complete democratization of political life, by eliminating the possibility of cabinet politics, by creating a democratic atmosphere, and by developing suitable institutions."[47]

Indeed, the HSWP proceeded to prove by deeds what it had been preaching in word. Beyond such changes as the appointment to leadership positions of non-party experts on a mass scale, the reform moves began to take on institutional forms. Some of the "changes" were almost imperceptible by strictly legal standards. For example, on March 3, 1970, *Magyar Kozlony,* the official gazette for laws and decrees, published the rules and regulations governing the granting of passports. While the "new" regulations were basically the legal establishment of the existing practice and were by Western standards very restrictive, the very fact of informing the public of its rights had the effect of liberalizing past procedure. That this was indeed the case is obvious from the recent report that "in the past seven years the number of Hungarian citizens travelling abroad grew four times and reached 4,685,000 last year [1977].[48] The same report states that the Presidential Council adopted a new law decree on foreign travel and on passports. "The new law decree states that every Hungarian citizen is within his rights to travel abroad,"[49] while the rules and regulations were further liberalized and simplified.

It has long been recognized, however, that the Presidential Council, as well as the Council of Ministers and, of course, the Politburo of the HSWP have been usurping the authority and taking over the responsibility of the National Assembly.[50] Beginning in 1967, various attempts have been made to breathe new life into the functioning of the House of Representatives. Efforts have been made to increase the involvement of the National Assembly in the actual drafting of legislation through its committees. This is a huge improvement over the past when the House essentially served the function of rubber stamping new legislation drawn up by the appropriate ministry or the party. Another area of increased power of the National Assembly is the proper overseeing of the work of the entire state apparatus, including the ministries. Ultimately the crucial issue is how representative a body can a parliament become in a socialist state. Gyula Kallai, then House speaker, stated in 1969 before the party Political Academy:

> The expansion of socialist democracy in state life should be achieved mainly through representation. Without the application of [this] principle, scientific, systematic, optimally effective and . . . democratic direction of the life and development of a socialist society is inconceivable. Our socialist democracy should grow stronger and develop further principally as a representative democracy.[51]

Again there have been some very cautious actions to back up such promising words. The new electoral law of 1966 that permitted multiple candidate races in national elections has been put to test repeatedly since then. While the results are not much of a step toward the establishment of representative democracy, they do show that genuine contests can develop especially on local issues.[52] Another aspect of this process has been the electoral reform of 1970, which abolished the monopoly of the PPF in the nomination of single or even multiple candidates. This has permitted the nomination of potential candidates by individual electors at the nomination meeting of the PPF. In practice, however, progress has been agonizingly slow.

In 1967 there were 9 contested races out of a total of 349. In the 1971 elections 49 seats were contested out of a total of 352.[53] This progress was reversed, however, in 1975 when only 34 seats among the 352 were sought by more than one candidate.[54] While the leadership may have decided that the economic problems facing the country in 1975 warranted caution in the liberalization process,[55] the fact remains that none of these elections has given the electorate anything resembling a true choice on important issues.

Another institution where similarly slow and cautious progress has been made is the trade union movement. The signal for change here was the new labor code enacted in 1967 that defined the role of labor unions as simply "representing and protecting the interests of the workers."[56] While this may sound natural enough, it is significant that no mention is made of the Marxist-Leninist function of unions as "transmission belts for the party." At the same time, the new labor code has specified the rights of the trade unions within the enterprise vis-à-vis the management, such as the right to veto management decisions that violate the law, the collective contract, or "socialist morality." There is no doubt that the new code, including the use of the veto, has been put to the test in several instances.[57] Even some state officials of the highest level have occasionally been rebuked in public by trade union officials. Taking everything into account, however, the progress made in this area is again not particularly impressive, except perhaps in comparison with the trade union movements in other East European countries except Yugoslavia. It is clear that the memory of the remarkable energy and vitality that the multiparty system and the workers' councils manifested in 1956 reminds Kadar of the need to proceed with extreme caution on both the issues of representative democracy and of workers' representation in trade unions.

The real power behind all these institutions is, of course, the party. Bela Biszku, a member of the Politburo at the time, stated in 1969:

> The question is often posed whether, under a one-party system, there are institutional guarantees of the continuous development of democracy in our social life and the prevention of abuses of power. Although we have done a great deal in this area in the past decade, our tasks will be even greater in the future. Nevertheless, I believe that the supreme guarantee has already been given—namely, the Party itself, which has never forgotten the lessons of 1956 and which, in its inner life incessantly fosters democracy. We are doing everything to prevent any group from ever again monopolizing the Party and the socialist system and abusing power.[58]

The first and foremost task for the HSWP is to ensure democracy within its own ranks. Even the theme of becoming an example that the "fraternal parties in capitalist countries" can emulate was renewed by *Tarsadalmi Szemle* in 1968 without mentioning, of course, that this had been one of Nagy's arguments as well.[59] Words, again, were followed by moves to decentralize the HSWP and give more voice to local organs and the membership in general. Whether such measures are adequate to change the basic organization and spirit of a party originally formed in the "Leninist-Stalinist mold," and whether they could withstand the attacks of another Rakosi when and if one emerged, are questions that can be answered only by the future.

Nevertheless, visitors to Hungary in the past ten to fifteen years have returned with the undeniable impression of an increasingly free atmosphere coupled with growing improvement in material well-being. Thanks to the new labor code workers are free to change jobs. The new passport regulations have made it possible for most people to enjoy vacations abroad, many of them in Western countries, often driving in their own cars. Since the state has made its agreement with the Catholic Church as well as with other religious groups,[60] the freedom to worship is enjoyed by practically all who care to do so. Literature, the theater, and the cinema produce works whose freedom and variety are often the envy of Eastern Europe. There is considerable freedom of speech and opinion on most subjects.[61]

There are obvious limits to this list of freedoms: political organization is permissible only within the confines of the PPF, which of course is under the "leadership" of the HSWP. This has been made clear to everyone who needed further reminders after the crushing of the "counterrevolution" of 1956 by such statements as the one quoted above from Biszku's address. As a result, a great majority of the people have sought outlets for their interests in things nonpolitical. Kadar has seemed to encourage this process by not requiring people to be political (his turning Rakosi's slogan around served precisely this purpose) and by removing the political content from as many aspects of everyday life as possible. Thus, while, according to Hungarian foreign policy, Israel is the vilest agent of imperialist warmongers, Jews are free to attend their synagogues, and a state-owned department store may very well play popular Israeli folk songs for background music. Under Rakosi such dissociation was never permitted.

A striking feature of this nonpolitical atmosphere is the almost total lack of dissidents. This is all the more surprising because it is so contrary to Hungarian history and the Hungarian character. While other East European countries, as dogmatic as postinvasion Czechoslovakia and as liberal as Yugoslavia, feel compelled to keep a certain fragment of the intelligentsia in prison at any given time, in Hungary the *New York Times* could quote its basically accurate Hungarian source in 1975: "I don't think any of us know of a single writer or artist or scholar in a Hungarian jail for political reasons at the moment, and that's something."[62]

That is quite an achievement for a country with a Communist government. But even in Hungary there were other "moments," not so long ago, when the jails were not completely empty of political victims. In November 1974 two sociologists, Ivan Szelenyi and Gyorgy Konrad, were arrested and briefly detained for writing a sociological study about the role of the intelligentsia in a socialist country.[63] A similar fate befell the poets Tamas Szentjoby and (a year earlier) Miklos Haraszti.[64] Interestingly, all these dissidents were deviationists of the leftist variety. They were also either researchers in sociology or writers on sociological themes. Another sociologist who has managed to get himself into trouble with the party repeatedly is the former Stalinist premier, Andras Hegedus, who was accused of rightist revisionism.[65]

Hegedus, however, committed another sin considered political even in Hungary's nonpolitical atmosphere: he protested the invasion of Czechoslovakia in a private letter to the HSWP Central Committee.[66] Just how far Kadar's "normalization" process had succeeded by 1968 was shown by the near total lack of any protest in Hungary over an emotional issue that must have seemed so painfully familiar to Hungarians.[67] Although the government joined the invaders while the people simply went about their business without any visible support to either side, the gap between them was not as deep as it seemed. Kadar was apparently in sympathy with Alexander Dubcek's reform program and supported him practically to the last minute. Kadar also attempted to mediate between the Czechoslovak and Soviet leaders.[68] But, as R. Selucky reports, even in the fall of 1967 when he visited Hungary and talked to many of the reformers, they

> all expressed fears that the Czechoslovak reformers (who were then trying to go beyond the limits of the 1965 reform) were going too far by giving the reform a political and ideological content. . . . They [the Hungarian reformers] were, of course, aware of the deep correlation between the marketization of economy and the political system; instead of emphasizing the correlation, they tended to minimize it or kept silent about it. While their Czechoslovak colleagues believed that the choice was between a consistent reform and an inconsistent one, the Hungarians knew that the choice was between an inconsistent reform or no reform at all.[69]

Apparently, by 1967 not only Kadar, but also a large segment of Hungarian society, certainly those in leadership positions, had become experts in realistically assessing just how far the Russians could be pushed.

It is this attitude that A. A. Kadarkay refers to as "Hungary's remarkable coming of economic and political age in the sixties."[70] Apparently gone are the times when Hungary fluctuated between abject servitude and romantic heroism, which produced either a ready supply of quislings or bands of romantic revolutionaries, but no truly responsible leaders willing to work quietly for the national interest within the limits of international and domestic realities. It is in this sense that the Hungarian people's acquiescence in Kadar's decision to join Brezhnev's troops and help crush Czechoslovak hopes and aspirations must be understood. August 1968 was not the time for another heroic act of almost certainly inconsequential value to the Czechs. It was, indeed, the time to consolidate the slow but painful progress achieved on the front of economic reforms.

Yet this "coming of age" of the Hungarian people and leadership does raise another question. Selucky calls this process the "Kadarization" of the people and states that "successful Kadarism corrupts the nation, breaks its political morale, and disrupts its character, regardless of the country in which it is applied."[71] This corruption of an entire nation by granting it relative material well-being and a limited amount of individual freedom is an issue that some leftist dissidents have raised since the late sixties.[72] The most prominent man to raise the issue was the doyen of Hungarian Marxists, Gyorgy Lukacs.

Lukacs criticized the encroachment of the profit motive on the field of culture. By the 1960s his gradual development toward humanism and democratization had reached the point where he was willing to accept NEM with its economic stipulations. He maintained, however, that the application of the profit motive to the cultural area was an anti-Marxist regression to capitalism.[73] This position is similar to the views of neo-Marxists in the West, such as Herbert Marcuse, who have theorized extensively about the "alienation" of man in modern Western society. This is no coincidence. In the view of some analysts, "Lukacs is certainly a spiritual forefather of Western 'socialist humanism.'"[74] Interestingly, this position is based not on Lukacs's recent works, in which he has become increasingly critical of Stalin's bureaucratic distortions of Marxism-Leninism, but mainly on his early masterpiece, *History and Class Consciousness*, which is so imbued with romantic left-wing sectarianism that some critics view it as an *a priori* justification of the brutal terror methods of Stalin and Rakosi.[75]

Indeed, it was left-wing sectarianism for which Lukacs was criticized early in his Communist career.[76] In a 1920 pamphlet in

German entitled "On the Question of Parliamentarianism" he argued against Communist participation in bourgeois parliaments.[77] In his main work, mentioned above, he maintained that the proletariat "must develop a dialectical contradiction between its immediate interest and its long-term objectives" and must wage a struggle "against itself." It is precisely such views that force R. N. Berki to conclude that "Lukacs always was and professed himself to be a follower of Stalin."[78] Even after spending the war years in Moscow, where Lukacs had occasion to observe, at close range, Stalin's "road to socialism," he was unable to foresee and forewarn against Rakosi's terror.[79] While he may have been disdainfully aloof in watching Rakosi's machinations, he was quite content to continue with his critique of bourgeois society.[80] Nor was he among the first or the loudest to protest the terrorist methods when Rakosi attempted to return to them in 1955.

It was only after the 1956 revolution, in which he participated with reluctance,[81] and his subsequent brief imprisonment that he finally seemed to recognize some of the basic flaws in the system to which he had devoted a lifetime. Subsequently under Kadar he was able to enjoy the luxury of relatively free criticism of his society. He not only criticized Stalinism, but questioned the effectiveness of de-Stalinization by essentially Stalinist methods, that is, from above and under the control of the party leadership.[82] Shortly before his death in 1971 he even expressed the view that "in the socialist lands Stalinist ideology has not lost much ground."[83] He went back to Lenin and began to emphasize Lenin's "political realism." Even then he seemed unable to make the connection between his philosophical denunciation of Stalinism and the renewed practice of it in Czechoslovakia and Poland.[84]

There have been other prominent intellectuals who, from time to time, have fallen into disfavor with the regime for publicly expressing unorthodox views, among them the historian-philosopher Erik Molnar, who had been minister of foreign affairs and minister of justice. In 1959 and again in 1961 the dogmatists who were still strong in the party mounted vigorous campaigns to denounce Molnar's "revisionist" views expressed in two books published in those years.[85] In the first volume Molnar argued that the orthodox Marxist critique of capitalism does not stand up when applied to contemporary capitalism. Party dogmatists were quick to point out that Molnar's ideas implied that capitalism was not a doomed system and as such were clearly heresy.[86] This denunciation in turn probably helped Molnar to realize that the final demolition of dogmatism is of "immense importance" for the "very survival of Marxist social science," when, shortly after a second denunciation of his books by dogmatists, the Twenty-second Congress of the CPSU vindicated his fight against Stalinism. Molnar came to the conclusion that "if we know nothing but these [Marxist] theories, we can go wrong at every single turning."[87]

The same conclusion emerged more than fifteen years later from two remarkable volumes of *samizdat* publications.[88] The practice of *samizdat* itself is exceptional in Hungary, where it has not been used since the immediate postrevolutionary period. But these writings also attest to the remarkably novel conditions in Hungary in the late 1970s, for they contain no letters of protest or lists of political prisoners, as their counterparts in the Soviet Union or Czechoslovakia do. Instead these works contain a collection of non-Marxist (or even anti-Marxist) writings that simply could not find a publisher in Hungary. In the first volume, called *Marx in the Fourth Decade,* the authors (who were members of the radical left in the late 1960s) attest to their abandonment of Marxism as the basis of their philosophy of life.[89] "It would be a crude misunderstanding to imagine that Marxist theory ever played a determining role in any kind of major political decision making," writes one of the authors.[90] This by implication negates not only Stalinism but Leninism as well and, of course, questions the utility of Marxism itself as a social science.

The second volume is a collection of articles that, because of their topic or the manner of treatment of their topic, cannot be published in Hungary. The editor, Janos Kenedi, explains in his introduction how publishers prevent the publication of such articles even though no formal censorship exists. Instead, in addition to a subtle process of self-censorship, publishers turn down manuscripts, often with the remark that "it did not fit our profile."[91] At other times controversial pieces are rejected with the ingratiating explanation that it would play into the hands of some dogmatist who just happens to be in the process of mounting an attack against some liberal literary figure.

It is these subtle forms of censorship that have a demoralizing effect on the cultural life of the nation. It is an integral part of the process of Kadarization that may be slowly eating away the moral fabric of the nation. While Rakosi's crude despotism united almost the entire country in intense hatred against him, Kadar's sophisticated system of loose and yet quite well-defined controls makes any potential opposition to the regime likely to crumble even before it takes shape. The recent *samizdat* were an effort to overcome this difficulty and to show in a united form how one aspect (censorship) of the Kadarized control mechanism works.

Within Eastern Europe, Hungary's domestic system appears to be

unique. Only Poland, among the Warsaw Pact countries, has a regime
that is similarly liberal. In fact, in the countryside Poland is freer,
because only a small fraction of the land is collectivized, whereas
Hungary is almost totally collectivized. Yet Poland has a very different regime today. Just as Wladyslaw Gomulka was unable to keep his
people's trust for long, so Edward Gierek struggles today with economic problems and internal dissension.[92] There are no such occur-
rences in Hungary. The economic problems of 1975 seem to have
abated. Price increases announced in November 1975 and again in
1977 and in 1979 on consumer goods and services caused hardly a
murmur, in contrast to the Polish food riots that have occurred twice
in the 1970s.[93] Instead of discontent, protests or riots, Hungarians
seem to be satisfied that the present regime is the best they can expect
under the circumstances, and they try their hardest to make small
improvements in their individual everyday lives.

In contrast to Gomulka and Gierek, Kadar seems to have excellent
rapport with his people. He knows that Hungarians may be willing to
accept some hardships if the need arises but will not suffer the type of
lies and dishonesty so prevalent under Rakosi. Speaking of the recent
price adjustments necessitated by the elimination of subsidies to in-
efficient enterprises, Kadar declared that "If there is . . . a problem it
befits the Party's honest and frank policy to discuss it publicly before
our people as well, without beating around the bush. . . ."[94]

Such straight talk would certainly not be sufficient to allay discontent in countries like Poland or Czechoslovakia. There the events of
1956 and 1968 were resolved in a quite different manner from the
bloody destruction of all opposition during and after the Hungarian
Revolution. The memory of those days has not been erased in the
Hungarian consciousness. Nearly everybody in Hungary knows what
the limitations on freedom are and why. Kadar misses few opportunities to insert in his speeches the reminder:

> In our foreign policy, our endeavor is . . . to make it clear and
> unmistakable to everyone where we belong and what objectives we
> pursue. Therefore, we openly tell all that we are an ally of the
> Soviet Union and a member of the Warsaw Pact and CEMA.[95]

People understand the domestic implications of these "foreign policy" precepts. This is partly why there are no food riots when prices
increase and no dissidents when some liberties are somewhat cur-
tailed. It is a Hungarian phenomenon, but one that is quite new in
twentieth-century Hungary. The only similar period occurred during
the latter part of the nineteenth century when, after the bloody sup-

pression of the 1848 revolution, Hungary made its Compromise of 1867 with Austria, and a period of tranquility, relative affluence, and semi-independence ensued. It lasted almost fifty years.

If Kadar's regime has no parallel among the Warsaw Pact countries, its similarities to Tito's Yugoslavia are readily apparent. It is through this Hungarian-Yugoslav comparison that the relationship of the Hungarian system to Eurocommunism may best be examined. Yugoslavia is regarded by some authors as the initial source of the Eurocommunist phenomenon.[96] Perhaps the clearest Eurocommunist features of Tito's regime are to be found in his sometimes fiercely independent foreign policy. In this respect Kadar's regime provides a sorry spectacle of total and openly flaunted subservience to Soviet dominance. Domestically, however, Hungary has gone a long way to emulate the Yugoslav model without acknowledgement and with proper modifications to account for "Hungarian conditions." Much of the institutionalization of Hungarian reforms had their Yugoslav predecessors some years earlier. The Hungarian reform economy, with its system of semi-autonomous enterprises and some market controlled prices, has the Yugoslav economy as its closest relative. It even appears that the granting of some measure of independence to the trade unions (by statute and in practice) was modeled after the Yugoslav workers' councils. (The Hungarian leaders did not dare to duplicate them fully in view of the strong independent stance of such organizations in Hungary during and after the revolution.) It also appears that the HSWP is following in the footsteps of the League of Communists of Yugoslavia in trying to restrict the leading role of the party to ideological and political education. Whether the Hungarian regime will be able to travel much further on this road is highly questionable; after all "Hungarian conditions" are much "different" from Yugoslav conditions. In the mid-1960s, however, it would have been (and was) questioned whether Kadar had the will and the ability to lead Hungary as far as he has. Of course, Hungarians almost never acknowledge the relevance of Yugoslavia to their experiment in socialism and probably never will, lest they expose their hard-won reforms to the vicissitudes of Soviet-Yugoslav friendship. But if there is a road to a more humane, democratic socialism within the Soviet orbit, Kadar seems to have found the path leading to it. In terms of humanism and freedom of the individual, the Hungarian experiment in democratic socialism may prove to be more successful than the Yugoslav one if for no other reason than the lack of the serious nationalities problem that threatens to tear Yugoslavia apart after Josip Tito's death.

All of this, of course, is highly conjectural, partially because of the rumored ill health of Kadar. Notwithstanding all the new legal and institutional reforms that Kadar has been able to effect, the best guarantor of a more humane socialism in Hungary today is still Kadar himself. The succession problem that has plagued all Communist governments has baffled him as well.[97] It is, however, difficult to imagine that any successor to Kadar, or the Kremlin leadership for that matter, would be willing to risk stirring up trouble in Hungary, a country that is currently safely in the Soviet camp and seemingly content to stay there as long as its internal freedoms are not overly threatened.

The real problem for the future is more complex: just as the Hungarian governments that followed the Compromise of 1867 had to struggle to survive between the pressures of the selfish interests of a great power to the west and the national aspirations of a domestic population, so the current Hungarian regime will find it increasingly difficult to balance the ambitious designs of a great power to the east with the eventually inevitable demands for "total freedom" and "total independence" expressed by a new generation of Hungarians with no personal memories of 1956.[98]

IV. Conclusions

It has been pointed out by several authors that Eurocommunism—a term of the 1970s—covers concepts that actually predate the Russian Revolution of 1917.[99] However, Eurocommunist features of the HSWP do not go back that far. Indeed, it was only in the period of liberalization preceding the 1956 revolt that small flames of a more humane and democratic socialism were ignited in Hungary. The spirit and philosophy of that liberalization drive makes the comparison between the leaders of the drive and the 1970s Eurocommunists a readily apparent one. Chief among the 1956 liberalizers was, of course, Nagy, whose democratic and independent brand of Communism, previously hidden in a then unpublished manuscript, suddenly burst into the open during the final days of the 1956 uprising. Both his theories written earlier and his overt actions as premier during the revolt make him an essential "Eurocommunist" of the 1950s.

Although Kadar undoubtedly had the option to impose and maintain a dogmatic application of Marxism-Leninism (just as Gustav Husak did in Czechoslovakia after 1968), he chose to begin and to continue a campaign of liberalization that by the late 1970s has turned Hungary into the most relaxed and free country in the Soviet bloc. It now appears that Hungary is following its own road to socialism, and many Hungarians would so claim in private. Whether this is done independently of the CPSU is certainly questionable. Kadar may be stretching the limits of Soviet tolerance here and there, but it is obvi-

ous that he has the basic approval of the Soviet leaders for his experiment in "goulash Communism."[100] Yet under Kadar's realistic leadership, Hungary has effectively achieved many of the basic goals of
Nagy and the 1956 revolution.

It is quite likely that Kadar will continue to proceed with his cautious salami-tactics-in-reverse by which he introduces small reforms
one by one, sometimes almost imperceptibly. Whether true political
pluralism of the type Eurocommunists in Italy, France, and Spain
claim they embrace can ever be achieved this way is open to question. Certainly Kadar would disclaim any intentions of aspiring to
such ends. But just as Enrico Berlinguer, Georges Marchais, and
Santiago Carrillo are doubted when they profess adherence to a multiparty system even after a Communist takeover, so can Kadar's sincerity be questioned in disavowing political pluralism. After all, it is
politically expedient for him to do so at this time. In other words, it
could be that Kadar is a crypto-Eurocommunist.

Just as the practice of Eurocommunism in Western Europe is sure
to undergo changes, so the forms of East European Communism are
also likely to evolve. In the long run, such development should mainly
be in the direction of more democracy and humanism. Hungarian society has obviously been slowly advancing in that direction. It appears that East and West European concepts of socialism may be
converging. If so, it may be possible that some countries on opposite
sides of the once infamous iron curtain, such as Italy and Hungary,
may be governed before the end of the century by essentially similar
Eurocommunist parties. What this would mean for Italy and Western
Europe is hard to predict, but for Hungary and Eastern Europe such a
development would definitely be beneficial, even if Western-style
abundance of freedom and material goods brings with it many problems of a new kind.

NOTES

I would like to thank the editors for their encouragement and help during
the writing of this chapter. I also wish to express my gratitude to Charles
Gati, who read an earlier version of this chapter, for his numerous insightful
comments.

1. Lenin himself questioned Bela Kun on "what actual guarantees you
have that the new Hungarian government will be really communist and not
simply a socialist government, that is, one of the traitors of Socialism?" and
also "What does it really mean that the socialists acknowledged the dictatorship of the proletariat?" V. I. Lenin, "Text of Radiotelegram to Bela Kun,
March 23, 1919," *Sochineniia*, 3rd ed. (Moscow: Marx-Engels-Lenin Insti-

tute, 1931), vol. 25, p. 203, quoted in R. L. Tokes, *Bela Kun and The Hungarian Soviet Republic* (New York: Praeger, 1967), p. 79.

2. See Tokes, *Bela Kun*, pp. 154–174.

3. Szabad Nep, November 21, 1946, quoted in P. Kecskemeti, *The Unexpected Revolution* (Stanford: Stanford University Press, 1961), p. 25.

4. M. Rakosi, *The Way of Our People's Democracy* (New York: National Committee for a Free Europe, Research and Publication Service, 1952), pp. 6ff., quoted in Kecskemeti, *Unexpected Revolution*, pp. 22–23. Emphasis supplied.

5. C. Gati, "Two Secret Meetings in Moscow in October 1944 and the Communist Quest for Power in Hungary," presented at the 1978 Annual Meeting of the American Association for the Advancement of Slavic Studies, Columbus, Ohio, October 1978.

6. See, for example, Kecskemeti, *Unexpected Revolution;* P. E. Zinner, *Revolution in Hungary* (New York: Columbia University Press, 1962), pp. 29–99; and Bill Lomax, *Hungary 1956* (New York: St Martin's Press, 1976). This conclusion is, of course, in agreement with the otherwise extremely tendentious accounts of the Revolution published in Hungary, such as J. Berecz, *Ellenforradalom: Tollal es Fegyverrel, 1956 [Counterrevolution: With Pen and Sword, 1956]*, (Budapest: Kossuth, 1969).

7. Originally entitled "Dissertations," this work was published in English as *Imre Nagy on Communism in Defense of the New Course* (New York: Praeger, 1957), p. 33. Also quoted in Kecskemeti, *Unexpected Revolution*, p. 33.

8. *Imre Nagy on Communism*, p. 50.

9. Ibid., p. 3.

10. S. Carrillo, *"Eurocommunism" and the State* (London: Lawrence and Wishart, 1977), pp. 17–18.

11. *Imre Nagy on Communism*, pp. 5–6. Note the allusion to Leninist teachings about the application of Marxism to Soviet conditions, similar to the remark made by Santiago Carrillo in the passage quoted above.

12. Ibid., pp. 7–8.

13. Ibid., pp. 8–9. As this was written prior to the Twentieth Congress of the CPSU, Nagy found it necessary to call his enemies' views "anti-Stalinist."

14. Ibid., pp. 9–10.

15. Ibid., p. 49.

16. Ibid., p. 32.

17. Ibid., p. 33.

18. M. J. Lasky, ed., *The Hungarian Revolution, A White Book* (New York: Praeger, 1957), pp. 47–49.

19. Gyorgy Lukacs was a member of Nagy's cabinet when the revolution was crushed by Soviet troops on November 4, 1956. He was subsequently imprisoned until April 1957 and later allowed to resume his scholarly activities as one of the outstanding Marxist philosophers of his time.

20. The pamphlets were published clandestinely in two parts at the end of December 1956 and in the middle of February 1957 in Budapest. The first part was republished in English as *Hungaricus: On a Few Lessons of the Hungarian National-Democratic Revolution* (Brussels: Imre Nagy Institute for Political Research, 1959). The second part was entitled "A New Socialist Direction" and is available in Hungarian only. However, both parts are described in detail in Lomax, *Hungary 1956*, pp. 182–192. All subsequent quotations are from there.

21. See his interview in *Nuovi Argumenti* (Milan), no. 20 (June 16, 1956). This was recently republished as a party pamphlet.

22. According to Carrillo, "the *formal* Marxism of Kautsky could not be applied to the revolutionary crisis of Russia in 1917." See Carrillo, *"Eurocommunism" and the State*, p. 18.

23. Istvan Bibo's views were later published in Hungarian as *Harmadik Ut* [*The Third Road*] (London, 1960). For a description of Bibo's ideas, in English, see Lomax, *Hungary 1956*, pp. 171–174.

24. Victor Woroszilski in *Nowa Kultura* (Warsaw), December 9, 1956, quoted in Lasky, *Hungary 1956*, p. 212.

25. *Nepszabadsag* (Budapest), November 15, 1956, quoted in Lasky, *Hungary, 1956*, p. 262.

26. Ibid.

27. This was a deliberate reversal of Matyas Rakosi's old slogan of the 1950s: "He who is not with us is against us." Janos Kadar made the statement in his speech at the National Council of the Patriotic People's Front, quoted in *Magyar Nemzet* (Budapest), December 10, 1961.

28. By far the best detailed study on this subject containing much excellent factual material as well as careful analysis of the current regime is W. F. Robinson, *The Pattern of Reform in Hungary: A Political, Economic and Cultural Analysis* (New York: Praeger, 1973). Some others are: R. Selucky, *Economic Reforms in Eastern Europe: Political Background and Economic Significance* (New York: Praeger, 1972), pp. 135–150; B. Kovrig, *The Hungarian Peoples Republic* (Baltimore: Johns Hopkins University Press, 1970), pp. 131–187; A. A. Kadarkay, "Hungary: An Experiment in Communism," *Western Political Quarterly*, 26 (June 2, 1973), pp. 280–301. Another detailed study of contemporary Hungarian life is P. A. Toma and I. Volgyes, *Politics in Hungary* (San Francisco: W. H. Freeman, 1976).

29. For example, W. R. Kintner and W. Klaiber, in ranking the Warsaw Treaty Organization (WTO) countries, as well as Yugoslavia and Albania, in terms of their adherence to Soviet policy over the 1956–68 period, assign Hungary a high conformity index that is still lower than those of East Germany and Bulgaria. W. R. Kintner and W. Klaiber, *Eastern Europe and European Security* (New York: Dunellen, 1971), pp. 219–267. R. H. Linden, *Bear and Foxes* (New York: Columbia University Press, 1979), scored the same countries in terms of their deviation from a WTO "norm" in their international interactions and separately in their international attitudes over the period 1965–1969. Hungary's score comes out either next to least or the least deviant from the WTO average among the eight countries. The general validity of these studies would be hard to challenge. Nor are these results, covering periods of the late 1960s, necessarily outdated. J. G. Kuchinski and P. R. Milch, "Quantitative Analysis of Defense Expenditures of Warsaw Treaty Organization Countries" presented at the XX Annual Convention of the International Studies Association, March 23, 1979, in Toronto, Canada, finds that in terms of military expenditures over the period 1960–1974, Hungary occupies a similarly unexciting, nondeviationist position among the Warsaw Pact allies of the Soviet Union.

30. For Todor Zhivkov's statement, see *Rabotnichesko Delo* (Sofia), December 1, 1976. For Kadar's interview in Vienna, see *Associated Press Report*, December 7, 1976.

31. Contrast *Tarsadalmi Szemle* (Budapest), January 1977 with February 1977.

32. Contrast, for instance, Zagladin's comments in *L'Espresso* (Rome), December 26, 1976 with articles authored by Konstantin Zaradov in *Problems of Peace and Socialism,* September 1975.

33. *Tanjug* (Belgrade), January 12, 1977.

34. See D. Nemes: "Lessons of the Class Struggle for Power in Hungary," *World Marxist Review (Problems of Peace and Socialism),* September 1976, pp. 11–14, quoted in K. Devlin, "Hungarian-PCF Polemic: Kanapa Counterattacks," Radio Free Europe Research Report, October 6, 1976. In his part of the debate, Dezso Nemes, one of the few remaining Moscovites in the Hungarian Socialist Workers Party, reels off his not unpredictable "lesson" from the three relevant periods of Hungarian history, the Hungarian Soviet Republic of 1919, the establishment of Communist rule in 1947–48, and the counterrevolution of 1956: the dictatorship of the proletariat is absolutely necessary for the building of socialism.

35. See, for example, Leonid Brezhnev's speech at the Twenty-fifth Congress of the CPSU, *Pravda,* February 25, 1976, and Brezhnev's speech at the Conference of European Communist Parties in Berlin, in *Neues Deutschland,* July 1, 1976.

36. Foreign Broadcast Information Service (FBIS), *Daily Report, Eastern Europe,* April 24, 1978, p. F 5.

37. Article by Ferenc Varnai, quoted in ibid., May 17, 1978, p. F 5.

38. Representatives of the HSWP held talks with representatives of the French, Italian, and Spanish Communist parties during 1978 in Paris (June 14) Rome, (June 12–17) and Madrid (October 22–28) respectively. See ibid., June 16, 1978, p. F 6, June 20, 1978, p. F 8, and November 2, 1978, p. F 1.

39. *New York Times*, June 10, 1978.

40. See B. Buky, "Hungary's NEM on a Treadmill," *Problems of Communism,* 21, (September–October 1972), pp. 31–39, and Robinson, *Pattern of Reform in Hungary.* Also more recently, *New York Times*, June 12, 1975, p. 1.

41. *New York Times*, April 3, 1974, p. 9, March 23, 1975, p. 15.

42. This has been widely reported by all media. See, for example, the articles quoted in note 41. For more scholarly accounts see P. Lendvai, "Hungary: Change vs. Immobilism," *Problems of Communism,* 16 (March–April 1967), pp. 11–17, and Kadarkay, "Hungary: An Experiment in Communism," As one, admittedly inadequate, measure of affluence, the number of cars per 1000 inhabitants increased twenty-three fold to 69 during the period 1960–1977, according to the *Hungarian Statistical Pocketbook, 1978.* During a similar period (1960–1976) the portion of expenditure for foodstuffs by the population dropped from 39.3 percent to 30.2 percent, using figures provided by the *Statistical Yearbooks* of 1960–1977. This is a significant drop that permits the population to concentrate on such other essentials as better housing but also on such luxuries as foreign travel. Hungary is the only COMECON state where the share of consumer goods in the economy has increased during the years 1960–1974, according to H. Trend and R. Nikolaev, "'Consumer Communism': Myth or Reality?" in R. R. King and J. F. Brown, eds., *Eastern Europe's Uncertain Future* (New York: Praeger, 1977), pp. 145–158.

43. M. Gamarnikow, "Balance Sheet on Economic Reforms," in Joint Economic Committee, Congress of the United States, *Reorientation and Commercial Relations of the Economies of Eastern Europe* (Washington, 1974), p. 182.

44. These are quotations used by Robinson, *Patterns of Reform in Hungary*, p. 278, from various works by Bela Kopeczi, who was then deputy rector of Lorand Eotvos University in Budapest and later became secretary general of the Academy of Sciences.

45. *Nepszabadsag*, March 4, 1962, quoted by G. Mueller and H. Singer in "Hungary: Can the New Course Survive," *Problems of Communism*, 14 (January–February 1965), p. 33. Also quoted by Kadarkay, "Hungary: An Experiment in Communism," p. 283.

46. *Nepszabadsag*, editorial, September 22, 1968, quoted by Robinson, *Pattern of Reform in Hungary*, p. 196.

47. *Magyar Nemzet*, May 4, 1969, quoted by Robinson, *Pattern of Reform in Hungary*, pp. 198–199.

48. FBIS, *Daily Report, Eastern Europe*, October 30, 1978, p. F 5.

49. Ibid.

50. Lendvai, "Hungary: Change vs. Immobilism," p. 15, cites the example of only five laws passed by Parliament in 1962, while twenty-eight law-decrees promulgated by the Presidential Council, many of them of great enough importance to have been presented to Parliament, according to O. Bihari in *Tarsadalmi Szemle* (August 1965).

51. *Magyar Tavirati Iroda (MTI)* [Hungarian Telegram Bureau], May 8, 1969, quoted in Robinson, *Pattern of Reform in Hungary*, p. 268.

52. See, for instance, the occasionally melodramatic account of W. Shawcross, *Crime and Compromise: Janos Kadar and the Politics of Hungary since the Revolution* (New York: E. P. Dutton, 1974), pp. 99–100.

53. Robinson, *Pattern of Reform in Hungary*, pp. 207, 209.

54. *New York Times*, June 17, 1975, p. 4.

55. At that time NEM was forced to reintroduce stronger central control due to economic problems caused by the recession in the West. See interview with J. Bognar, Chairman of the Parliament's Committee of Budget and Planning, ibid., June 12, 1975, p. 1.

56. Robinson, *Pattern of Reform in Hungary*, p. 238, quoting the new labor code as given in *Magyar Kozlony*, no. 67 (October 8, 1967).

57. Robinson, *Pattern of Reform in Hungary*, p. 241. See also interview with Trade Union leader Sandor Gaspar, *New York Times*, July 1, 1974, p. 2.

58. *MTI*, March 12, 1969, quoted by Robinson, *Pattern of Reform in Hungary*, pp. 263–264.

59. Quoted in Robinson, *Pattern of Reform in Hungary*, pp. 197–198.

60. See C. E. Kovats, "The Path of Church-State Reconciliation in Hungary" in King and Brown, *Eastern Europe's Uncertain Future*, p. 301. See also *New York Times*, September 28, 1977, III, p. 2.

61. See, for example, the articles on the visit by Billy Graham to Hungary, *New York Times*, August 16, 1977, p. 5 and September 18, 1977, p. 56. See also ibid., July 7, 1978, p. 21 for a recent account.

62. Ibid., March 16, 1975, p. 8.

63. Ibid., January 29, 1975, p. 3 and February 8, 1975, p. 8.

64. Miklos Haraszti's book "Piecerate" was refused publication in Hungary. It was published in the West as *A Worker in a Workers' State* (New York: Universe Books, 1978).

65. A. Hegedus was prime minister of Hungary from April 1955, when he replaced Nagy, until October 24, 1956, when he was replaced by Nagy and forced to flee to Moscow. He returned to Budapest in the 1960s and "retired"

to academic life. Hegedus was dismissed from his post of director of the Sociological Research Group of the Hungarian Academy of Science in 1968. See Robinson, *Pattern of Reform in Hungary*, p. 261.

66. See G. Gomori, "Hungarian and Polish Attitudes on Czechoslovakia, 1968" in E. J. Ozerwinski and J. Piekalkiewicz, eds., *The Soviet Invasion of Czechoslovakia: Its Effects on Eastern Europe* (New York: Praeger, 1972), pp. 110–111.

67. Besides Hegedus, the only other protesters were the five Hungarian Marxists (Agnes Heller, Maria and Gyorgy Markus, Vilmos Sos, and Zador Tordai) who happened to be attending an international symposium on "Marx and Revolution" in Korcula, Yugoslavia. They issued a public declaration condemning the invasion. See R. L. Tokes, "Hungarian Intellectuals' Reaction to the Invasion of Czechoslovakia," in Ozerwinski and Piekalkiewicz, *Soviet Invasion of Czechoslovakia*, p. 140. According to this source, Lukacs (some of whose students are in the above group), also sent a letter of protest to the party Central Committee. According to Gomori, "Hungarian and Polish Attitudes," p. 111, Lukacs expressed his thoughts in private only. This latter version is more in character with Lukac's usual behavior. In January 1977 some of the Korcula protesters and Haraszti were part of a group of thirty-four signatories who supported the Czechoslovak "Charter 77" proclamation. Although the party members among the Korcula protesters were expelled from the party, no action was taken against the signatories on this occasion. See R. Staar, ed., *Yearbook on International Communist Affairs, 1978* (Stanford, Calif.: Hoover Institution Press, 1978), pp. 48–49.

68. See Shawcross, *Crime and Compromise*, pp. 250–251 and Tokes, "Hungarian Intellectuals' Reaction," pp. 147–149.

69. Selucky, *Economic Reforms in Eastern Europe*, p. 138.

70. Kadarkay, "Hungary: An Experiment in Communism," p. 280.

71. Selucky, *Economic Reforms in Eastern Europe*, p. 138.

72. Supporters of Mao Tse-tung and Che Guevara have come to the fore in the late 1960s to the chagrin of the leadership. See Robinson, *Patterns of Reform in Hungary*, pp. 258, 260 and Kadarkay, "Hungary: An Experiment in Communism," p. 296.

73. See Gy. Lukacs, "The New Economic Guidance and Socialist Culture" [in Hungarian], *Kortars*, 13 (April 4, 1969), pp. 507–518. See also Robinson, *Patterns of Reform in Hungary*, pp. 284–285 and Shawcross, *Crime and Compromise*, pp. 157, 175, 191.

74. See R. N. Berki, "Evolution of a Marxist Thinker," *Problems of Communism*, 21 (November-December 1972), p. 59.

75. Gy. Lukacs, *History and Class Consciousness* (London: Merlin Press, 1971). See Berki, "Evolution of a Marxist Thinker," p. 56.

76. In 1924 Zinoviev denounced Lukacs in the Comintern. See Berki, "Evolution of a Marxist Thinker," p. 55.

77. Later incorporated in Lukacs, *History and Class Consciousness*.

78. Berki, "Evolution of a Marxist Thinker," p. 57. Similar conclusions are reached by G. Lichtheim, "The Transmutations of a Doctrine," *Problems of Communism*, 15 (July-August, 1966), pp. 23–24.

79. Lukacs was once arrested and briefly imprisoned in Moscow. See J. Hay, *Born 1900, Memoirs* (La Salle, Ill.: Library Press, 1975), p. 263.

80. A. Aczél and T. Méray, *The Revolt of the Mind* (New York: Praeger, 1959), pp. 57–80; L. S. Feuer, "University Marxism," *Problems of Communism*, 27 (July-August 1978), p. 70.

81. Lukacs said in an interview in 1965; "even if Nagy had won his struggle, I would have retired anyway in January or February 1957 and returned to my books." See E. Alexander, "Memories of a Brief Encounter," *Problems of Communism*, 21 (November-December 1972), p. 70.

82. See G. Kline, "Impressions of the Man and His Ideas," ibid., p. 64.

83. D. Shanor, "Searching for Socialist Democracy: A Talk with Gyorgy Lukacs," *New Leader* (New York), October 18, 1971, p. 14.

84. See Berki, "Evolution of a Marxist Thinker," p. 58; Kline, p. 64. See also note 67.

85. The first one was E. Molnar, *Some Economic Problems of Contemporary Capitalism* [in Hungarian] (Budapest: Kossuth, 1959). The second one was E. Molnar, *The Fundamental Philosophical Problems of Historical Materialism* (Budapest: Szikra, 1961). See Robinson, *Patterns of Reform in Hungary*, pp. 43–45, 50–52.

86. See L. Hay, "Erik Molnar: Some Economic Problems of Contemporary Capitalism" [in Hungarian], *Tarsadalmi Szemle*, XIV (October 1959), pp. 153–165, quoted in Robinson, *Patterns of Reform in Hungary*, pp. 43–44.

87. *Magyar Nemzet*, March 11, 1962, quoted in Robinson, *Patterns of Reform in Hungary*, p. 51.

88. See *Times* (London), February 3, 1978, p. 7.

89. The title alludes to the fact that both the authors and Communist rule in Hungary are entering their fourth decade. Miklos Haraszti, for example, is one of the authors. See note 64.

90. *Times* (London), February 3, 1978, p. 7.

91. This is why the title of this 859 page *samizdat* volume is "Profile."

92. For a description of the uneasy stalemate between the Communist government and the increasingly better organized opposition, see A. Bromke, "The Opposition in Poland," *Problems of Communism*, 27 (September-October, 1978), pp. 37–51.

93. See *New York Times*, December 1, 1975, p. 55, and the interview with Kadar, ibid., June 10, 1978.

94. FBIS, *Daily Report, Eastern Europe*, June 16, 1978, p. F 2.

95. Ibid., p. F 3.

96. For example, R. A. Remington, "Eurocommunism and Yugoslavia" in this volume.

97. Biszku, Kadar's heir apparent, was relieved from his post of Central Committee secretary on April 22, 1978. See FBIS, *Daily Report, Eastern Europe*, April 24, 1978, p. F 1 and *Times* (London), April 27, 1978, p. 7.

98. There are indications that the Kadar regime recognizes the problems posed by the growing up of this post-1956 generation and is taking steps to prevent the "romanticization" of the period. See *Times* (London), April 27, 1978, p. 10.

99. Some possible ideological forerunners, such as Karl Kautsky, Rosa Luxembourg, and others are suggested by V. V. Aspaturian, "Conceptualizing Eurocommunism: Some Preliminary Observations" in this volume.

100. Vladen Kuznetsov wrote in *Novoye Vremya:* "Does a 'Hungarian model' exist? It does. But not in the way western papers write about it. In Hungary the general laws of socialist construction are in every respect clearly and tangibly asserted. It is not forgotten in Hungary what the country owes the socialist community." Quoted in FBIS, *Daily Report, Eastern Europe*, April 24, 1978, p. F 9.

CHAPTER XII

Eurocommunist Perceptions of Eastern Europe: Ally or Adversary?

Eric Willenz

Shortly before the legalization of the Spanish Communist party in the spring of 1977, a much-touted meeting of the leaders of the three principal West European Communist parties, the Spanish (PCE), French (PCF), and Italian (PCI), took place in Madrid. The conference came in the wake of growing conflict between these parties and Moscow, and the timing and locale of this West European Communist party summit seemed sufficiently portentous to raise expectations that something momentous was about to occur. This tension had characterized their relations since the conclusion of the June 1976 Conference of European Communist Parties in East Berlin. Would the Western Communist party chiefs throw down the gauntlet to the Soviets and East Europeans by jointly criticizing the lack of civil and political rights in their regimes and point to other serious flaws in those systems that would make a break between them unavoidable?

One can only speculate about that possibility, since the final communique from Madrid refrained from any joint criticism of the Soviet or East European regimes. The circumstances surrounding the sudden convening of an obviously Soviet-inspired meeting of senior East European party officials in Sofia at the same time, however, prompts the thought that Moscow might have been prepared to respond vigorously had such an attack materialized. In the end, the three Western Communist parties avoided a joint frontal assault on the Soviets and East Europeans, which in turn produced an equally bland response from those assembled in Sofia.[1]

The events of March 1977 illustrate the precariousness of relationships among growingly disparate elements in the Communist movement. The movement's history, ideology, and particular circumstances have tended to weld its members together in an often artificial and syncretic union whose continued cohesion has become increasingly doubtful. Hence the conditions that have given rise to what is called Eurocommunism reflect the underlying and often tortuous changes that are beginning to erode traditional assumptions about the nature of certain Communist parties. Their future remains clouded as they grope for a new role in their own political landscape. It is noteworthy that some key aspects of Eurocommunism also have surfaced in the Japanese and Australian Communist parties. The problem, as Sidney Tarrow once put it in describing the travail of a party like the PCI, is that establishing a new legitimacy for the party's political role entails delegitimizing the old one. The dangers involved in this process are formidable. It is particularly true for any party that has held a basically rigid ideological and hostile attitude toward the prevailing political culture. Such an outlook tends to engender a degree of militancy and commitment to change in its leaders and many of its followers. It also engenders profound distrust combined with fear among non-Communists within the polity.

The severity of this problem has not affected the position of the PCI, PCF, or PCE—the leading Eurocommunist parties—to the same degree. Nevertheless, they are all subject to it to some considerable extent. This factor also has contributed to their still differentiated but increasingly positive adoption of the Eurocommunist label. They used the term only sparingly at first because it seemed certain to antagonize Moscow and indirectly also to place a strain on their relations with East European regimes. But these fears have been gradually overcome as each party has become preoccupied with achieving greater domestic respectability. Eurocommunism has thus slowly acquired an identity of its own in the French, Italian, and Spanish parties. To all three of them it denotes not only resistance to Moscow's persistent hegemonic aspirations in laying down basic ideological guidelines, but also general agreement on certain broad principles of political and civil freedoms as well as political pluralism—less so, however, in the PCF—in the pursuit of socialism in their respective countries.[2]

The Waning Power of the Past

The following is not a description of how Eurocommunism evolved in the key West European Communist parties, not is it a step-by-step account of these parties' polemics with Moscow and, on occasion, with some of Moscow's stalwart East European followers. It might be useful, however, to delineate—if only provisionally—certain aspects of the perceptions key Eurocommunist parties have of the situation in Eastern Europe and the extent to which these perceptions have come to influence their relations with the regimes and other political forces in those countries.

At first glance the subject hardly seems worth discussing. The area in question is so clearly part of the Soviet domain that the issue reduces itself to one of dealing directly with the Soviet leadership itself. In many ways Moscow's involvement and influence indeed has significantly shaped the Eurocommunists' perception of and interaction with Eastern Europe. But power-political reasons alone hardly suffice in treating the issue. Soviet power and political behavior in Eastern Europe probably have contributed importantly to the rise of Eurocommunism in the first place, and they continue to pose problems whose resolution seems bound to affect relations between the Eurocommunists and the East Europeans.

This complex relationship between the Eurocommunists and Eastern Europe has not escaped scholarly attention, and some already see in the Eurocommunist phenomenon a challenge to the "very legitimacy [of the East European regimes] . . . offering the prospect of the Europeanization of world communism."[3] Whether this prophecy will come true remains to be seen. The course of events does point to the seriously disturbing effect that persistent Eurocommunist criticism of the undemocratic character of these regimes could have on their relationship. More problematic is the extent to which such criticism not only will encourage restive elements in these societies but will also contribute to systemic changes in them. Regardless of the small likelihood of this happening, there seems to be distinct apprehension in certain East European circles as well as in the Soviet Union. Apparently, there is much concern that such a development may have a kind of domino effect in the region, ultimately impinging on the active dissident elements in the Soviet Union. Not surprisingly, those primarily worried are the hardliners in the Soviet Union, followed closely by their supporters in Czechoslovakia and Bulgaria. All of these elements have for some time sounded the tocsin against the dangers of Eurocommunism.[4]

We cannot forget in this context that some of the sharpest blows to continued Soviet ideological preeminence in the Communist movement resulted not only from Josip Tito's successful resistance to Stalin and from the far more important Sino-Soviet dispute, but also from the repeated Soviet interventions in Eastern Europe. For a time, the Cold War helped the leadership in the key Eurocommunist parties to rationalize for themselves and to defend to a basically docile membership the repressive character of the East European regimes and the need for a Soviet-like system in building socialism. Such reasoning, however, suffered an irreparable loss of credibility once Stalin was denounced at the Twentieth CPSU Congress. The cumulative effects, therefore, of that event combined with the bloody suppression of the Hungarian revolution, capped by the invasion of Czechoslovakia in 1968, were bound to take their toll. Moreover, with the waning of the Cold War, the Soviet intervention in Czechoslovakia served to fan the long-simmering differences between Moscow and most West European Communist parties. In the process, the parties' critical attitude towards Moscow-style Communism was also strengthened, as were autonomist tendencies within the parties.

To an important degree, the backlash against the invasion of Czechoslovakia has been the mainspring for the current behavior of the PCF, PCI, and PCE in their continued rejection of the Soviet action and the resultant developments in that country. To a greater or lesser degree, their attitude also has found an echo in many smaller West European Communist parties who are also striving to escape their own political ghetto. For somewhat different reasons, but no less importantly, both the Yugoslavs and the Romanians also have taken up the cudgels for Eurocommunism. In part, they have done this to buttress autonomist trends in the movement that will help to reinforce their own particular path of socialist development. Yugoslav or Romanian support in this instance, however, is not primarily designed to advance their domestic credibility but rather to checkmate Moscow's hegemonic aspirations. That is why these regimes joined hands with Eurocommunists at the 1976 Berlin Communist conference and pressed so hard for the adoption of the final communique, which eschews all the traditional code words denoting Soviet preeminence in ideological and organizational matters.[5]

It is clear that the independent-minded Romanians and Yugoslavs supported the Eurocommunist parties at the Berlin conference for very pragmatic and limited reasons. Their support of each other could not and did not affect other aspects of their very different situations. Romania and Yugoslavia have only limited sympathy and little inclination for introducing into their own societies practices that conform more closely to the Western-type democratic principles that have become the mainstay of Eurocommunist criticism of the Soviet and East European systems. On the other hand, the shock effect that the Soviet intervention in Czechoslovakia had on the Eurocommunist parties was enhanced precisely because it foreclosed a development that they regarded as a harbinger for their own future: the possibility that social transformation could be accomplished without undermining essential civil and political rights.

Hence, the conviction that the architects of the Prague Spring were developing an alternative to the traditional Soviet model for building socialism, consonant with the needs of parties operating in an advanced industrialized environment, continues to militate against any reconciliation between the Eurocommunists and the current Czech regime. To put it somewhat differently, for parties like the PCI and the PCE, the short-circuiting of the Czech experiment set back their hopes of benefiting from a political evolution that gradually might have extended over the entire East European area and might have favored their own domestic fortunes as well. The forced cessation of the Czech experiment threatened to damage the domestic prospects of such parties. It is no wonder, therefore, that the brutal suppression of the Prague Spring almost forced these parties to defend the possibility of "socialism with a human face" and also compelled them to remain critically insistent on its applicability in Eastern Europe.[6]

Approaching the Precipice

The recent post-mortem by the PCI on Czechoslovakia indicates that domestic political and ideological factors have become inextricably intertwined in the rising Eurocommunist criticism of the state of civil and political rights in Eastern Europe and the Soviet Union. The Eurocommunist parties' need to maintain political credibility at home requires them to continue expressing concern about the absence of these rights. The echo of their anxiety reverberates not only in Eastern Europe and beyond but also in the parties' own ranks, where its repercussions may be hard to control. Moreover, attempts to contain the consequences of this development are bound to exact a price from each party in terms of its domestic future and its relation with the East Europeans, as well as the Soviets, that party leaders will have difficulty avoiding the cost.

To some extent this dilemma is the result of a changing international political climate that has encouraged the French, Italian, and Spanish Communists to improve their domestic positions. The situation in Eastern Europe and Moscow's own behavior also have had their impact, beginning with the dethronement of Stalin and the *annus terribilis* of 1956. As early as the 1960s, even a party as dogmatic as the PCF occasionally criticized East Germany's cultural orthodoxy, the distribution of antisemitic literature in the Ukraine, and the Soviet trial of the writers Andrei Sinyavsky and Yulii Daniel.[7] Later on the pace accelerated when several Eurocommunist parties were critical of the Polish government's handling of the 1970 food riots; they also began to open the pages of their party journals to factual reports about the treatment of dissidents in Eastern Europe and finally to the dissidents themselves.[8]

The extent to which the party press and other channels of communication have been opened to protesting and dissident views from Eastern Europe has varied from party to party. The Italians probably have gone the farthest. The PCI has printed the works of prominent Polish and Czech dissidents in its publishing houses and invited a prominent Soviet dissident, Roy Medvedev, to become a contributor to *Rinascità*, the PCI monthly theoretical journal.[9] In the past the French and Spanish parties have been more reticent about publishing dissenters' views. Nevertheless, both the PCI daily, *L'Unità,* and the PCF daily, *L'Humanité,* were suspended at times from selling their papers in Eastern Europe because of their coverage of the dissident scene. And since its legalization in 1977, the PCE has opened its paper to key Czech and East German dissidents and published interviews with F. Kriegel, T. Janouch, and W. Biermann. Finally, other considerations aside from pointing to the worst offenses against human rights in Eastern Europe seem to have dictated the direction of Eurocommunist criticism.

The Hungarians, for example, have generally received scant, if any, attention. The Yugoslavs and Romanians are left out altogether. These three parties either have refused to join actively in the Soviet-supported attack on Eurocommunists or have been directly aligned with them in their fight against Soviet domination throughout the preparation for the 1976 Communist summit. This probably accounts for the omission.[10]

The Eurocommunists may have growing difficulties sustaining this variegated approach to the East European scene. Their actions have provoked reactions that militate against the establishment of a finely differentiated relationship between those in Eastern Europe who are basically more favorably inclined towards Eurocommunism and those who regard it essentially with undisguised hostility. To appreciate why the Eurocommunists may encounter growing problems in this area, it must be recalled that one of the characteristics of all Communist parties is that power and ideology are always closely related. Hence, any challenge with ideological overtones is perceived immediately as a threat to a party's or regime's power structure.

It is this vulnerability that has turned the Eurocommunist criticism into a particularly grave matter aggravated by the earmarks it has of an ostensible intervention into the internal affairs of the East Europeans. The latter seems especially designed to arouse the ire of even the friends of the Eurocommunists because it smacks of a practice often associated with Moscow in the past. Eurocommunist support of rising reformist currents in certain East European countries was brought on by increasing economic difficulties and disillusion with an ideological and cultural dogmatism that was reminiscent of Stalin's time. Thus, it ran the danger that these regimes would regard it as both provocative and an incitement to subversion. Under these conditions, the question arises whether a moderate Communist regime, like the Hungarian or even the pro-Eurocommunist Romanians, would sit idly by if the legitimacy of the East Germans, Czechs, or Poles came under attack.[11]

The preceding account offers just a small sample of the many communications that have appeared in the Eurocommunist press in recent years. These have, in many cases, served to strain relations between the Eurocommunists and certain East European regimes. This is not intended to suggest, however, that a collision between the East European ruling parties and the Eurocommunists of Western Europe is imminent. Such a course would not serve the interests of either group. Nevertheless, the ideological content of many of the criticisms leveled by the Eurocommunists against the East Europeans, as well as the Soviet Union, raises problems about the nature of their continued relationship. Circumstances increasingly find the Hungarians, Romanians, and sometimes even the Poles caught up in a polemic that primarily involves the Eurocommunists and the Soviets, with the East Europeans relegated to the role of apprehensive observers. Furthermore, current developments seem to be taking the direction of ever increasing diversity without unity, in contradistinction to Palmiro Togliatti's elusive formula of "unity in diversity and autonomy."

The Rediscovery of Ends and Means

The seemingly endless discourse between the Eurocommunists and the East Europeans involves considerably more than just the demands of their respective domestic situations, or questions regarding the restructuring of party relationships in the Communist movement. In the latter instance, a number of East Europeans are rather sympathetic to opposing Moscow's hegemonic role. The main issue, however, concerns a more fundamental reassessment of Soviet-style socialism. This debate has gradually shifted its ideological focus from insisting on the right to pursue different paths in achieving socialism to questioning the methods employed in its pursuit. In effect, this approach gives renewed emphasis to the view that the deformities that socialism has experienced in Eastern Europe and the Soviet Union may be inherent in their systems, rather than a temporary aberration.

The criticism is not new. Togliatti advanced it in 1956 only to be shouted down almost immediately. Its reappearance in considerably amplified form attests to the unresolved, if not insoluble, nature of the problem. One finds it this time in Santiago Carrillo's question about the socialist nature of the present Soviet system and his suggestion that its structure may itself be "a restraint to the development of an authentic workers' democracy."[12] Moreover, such statements no longer are repudiated the moment they are made. In fact, the PCI and the PCF, although not in entire agreement with the Spanish Communist leader, still found it necessary to come to his support, as did the Yugoslavs and the Romanians. How far the last two are prepared to go in their demonstration of solidarity of Carrillo will depend partly on their perception of the impact of his strictures on their own systems.

It is particularly striking that Carrillo's criticism, which implied a basic reassessment of Soviet-style socialism, also has begun to be taken up by the PCF. In spite of its often abrasive encounters with the Soviet leadership in recent years and its belated joining of the Eurocommunist camp at the 1976 European Communist party summit, the PCF has not been notable for its readiness to scrutinize the Soviet past. It has preferred to make do with explanations that merely noted errors, deviations, and distortions. With Maurice Thorez dead for over a decade, the PCF leadership stubbornly maintained the fiction that it did not know about Nikita Khrushchev's revelations of Stalin's misdeeds. Finally, twenty years after the Secret Speech, an embarrassing revelation forced it to admit that it had lied about this. That also explains why the party may find itself embarked on an accelerated course of seeking to overcome its compromised past. Domestic circumstances, no doubt, play an important role in this development, reinforcing elements within the party that are striving to effect a change in its outlook. The latest and possibly most revealing sign that the PCF is continuing to examine and reassess its position towards Soviet-style socialism is a recently published book, *L'URSS et Nous* (The USSR and Us),[13] ordered by the party leadership for the next party congress. Has the result been the usual whitewash or does it go beyond the customary platitudes? The book received high-level party endorsement, and considerable publicity surrounded its publication: its somewhat prolix preface was reprinted in full in *L'Humanité*.[14] Nevertheless, it does not seem as hard-hitting as Carrillo's piece. For instance, some of the old encomia about the importance of the Soviet role in containing imperialism are still present.[15] At the same time, however, the book's introduction is not the usual tract expected in a publication of this sort.

Some important questions are raised regarding the PCF's past "naive" adoption of "Stalin's simplified and dogmatic 'Leninism.'" This discussion eventually leads up to the obvious but still sensitive issue of whether the concept of "Marxism-Leninism" is still a useful one in light of the increasingly diversified experience of the various Communist parties. The book's preface suggests that it is "no outrage" to ask this question, which lends additional credence to repeated rumors that the PCF is about to follow the example of the Spanish and the Japanese Communist parties and drop "Leninism" from its official theses at the forthcoming party congress.

The book's introduction also makes some greatly overdue but cursory admissions regarding the party's long suppression of Khrushchev's Secret Speech. However, these do include the first public, albeit hesitant, criticism of the way Thorez handled the situation:

> We may think that Maurice Thorez and the party leadership hesitated in the face of revelations they believed could create confusion among the militants and strike against the prestige of the Soviet Union. Was this not in one sense lacking confidence in the party's ability . . . and also in the strength of the truth told to the masses by the party?[16]

All this leads finally to the possibly most delicate problem, which the writer of the preface and the authors of the book profess not to want to evade: Is the USSR socialist? What are the internal conflicts? Is terror implicit in the system? Has a new exploiter class been formed? What are the principles of Soviet foreign policy? Is there an economic or political crisis in the Soviet Union?

One should not be too surprised if the book fails to answer these questions in a definitive fashion. But it is apparent from the questions that the party leadership seems more intent than before to treat these issues more objectively than in the past. There is also more than a hint of criticism of the East European and Soviet systems. This stance may be influenced by the PCF's recently expressed and somewhat fulsome affirmations for civil and political liberties. For once the difficulty of separating political and economic democracy is questioned openly: "the former cannot have shortcomings when everything is supposed to be going marvellously for the latter."[17]

The Reassertion of Principles

In view of these core issues that have fueled Eurocommunist criticism of the violations of human and political rights in Eastern Europe and the Soviet Union, the possibility for a widened and ideologically sharpened debate was bound to grow stronger. In addition, the frequency of incidents involving dissidents or human rights advocates, like the Charter 77 supporters in Czechoslovakia, has made it more difficult to avoid new and acerbic exchanges. Finally, as the momentum of this acrimonious dialogue has increased, the ideological gap between the two sides has widened as each attack has sparked a counter-attack.[18]

At its congress in April 1978, the PCE decided to drop "Leninism" from its program as a determining principle.[19] Carrillo then proclaimed the party an "authentic Eurocommunist party."[20] This announcement met with a resounding rebuff from the Soviets, the East Germans, and the Czechs. The chief Soviet delegate at the PCE congress stated bluntly that "Eurocommunism does not exist because there is only one communism, scientific communism, Marxist-Leninist communism."[21] And *Pravda* featured the reaction of one of Eurocommunism's most embittered enemies, Czech party secretary Jan Fojtik. Fojtik scoffed at the PCE decision to drop "Leninism" from its party theses and railed that it is "impossible to renounce Leninism while at the same time declaring loyalty to Marxism. . . . There is nothing more absurd."[22]

Is this escalatory cycle of invectives an inevitable by-product of the defensive reactions on both sides as the tenor of their attacks on one another increases? Perhaps. Or are some Eurocommunists moving towards a more general proposition of linking socialism and essential aspects of Western-style democracy as a prerequisite to both greater domestic success and the articulation of a general principle for the attainment of socialism everywhere?

There have been occasions during the last few years when certain Eurocommunists felt challenged enough to regard their "Westernization" or "de-Leninization" of the socialist model as having applicability beyond their own situation. Moreover, as suggested earlier, the moral support they provided to dissidents and reformist elements in a number of East European countries created a climate of mutuality. This, in turn, reawakened hopes that the Eurocommunist model could alleviate, if not undo, the damage caused by the aborted Prague Spring. The overwhelming desire, therefore, to come to grips with the Czech debacle has tended to collide with disavowals of seeking to challenge Moscow, let alone, of desiring to create a rival Communist center. In addition, there is an unmistakable ring of universality in some Eurocommunist statements aiming to define the nature of a socialist system. This element persists even though it flies in the face of all realistic expectations, given the situation in Eastern Europe, not to speak of the attitude of the Soviet Union.

Would the Soviets acquiesce to such changes? Not very likely, opined Carrillo three years ago. Yet he seemed certain that a model of West European pluralistic socialism would be attractive to Eastern Europe, were it no longer subject to the Soviet Union and able to experiment with a quite different political structure.[23] Lombardo Radice, the well-known PCI intellectual, has also voiced similar views. Radice not only regarded it as "inevitable" that the socialist opposition in Eastern Europe should link itself, at least ideologically, with Eurocommunism, but also as "equally" inevitable that this development should become "a political problem" for the ruling Communist elites in Eastern Europe.[24]

Even the customarily more cautious and circumspect PCI leader, Enrico Berlinguer, managed to slip some "universalist" claims for Eurocommunism into his address at the sixtieth anniversary celebration of the Bolshevik Revolution in Moscow. Reviewing the post-World War II experiences of the PCI, Berlinguer noted that his party, like other Communist parties in capitalist Europe, has come to accept democracy not only as "the only ground on which the class enemy is compelled to retreat, but . . . also as the historic, *universal* value on which the unique socialist society is founded." He then went on to define this new socialist society as one "which will guarantee all personal and collective, civic and religious freedoms, the non-ideological nature of the state, and the possibility of the coexistence of different parties and pluralism in public, cultural, and ideological life."[25]

Whether it sometimes threatens the legitimacy of the established East European regimes or, conversely, seems to help them to emerge from what appears to be a growing ideological and political impasse, Eurocommunism has manifested universalist tendencies. The logic of this development partly derives from a certain ideological void regarded as intolerable by Communist parties and partly from Moscow's inability to fill it.[26] Soviet-style socialism is the product of too many distortions and has caused too much damage to warrant resurrection. This much seems obvious not only to the Eurocommunists but also to many on the other side of the geopolitical border. But that is as far as it goes. Any wider claim for Eurocommunism seems bound to alienate even those in Eastern Europe who are generally sympathetic to the more limited demands by the Eurocommunists for autonomy and noninterference in their internal party affairs.

It seems inevitable, in this context, that any general prescription by Eurocommunists for effecting systemic changes can only come into conflict with those very restraints invoked by ruling but restive Communist parties intent on shoring up their "national" roads to socialism. This position, as will be recalled, underpinned the collaboration of the forces that resisted Soviet dictates at the 1976 European

Communist party summit. That is precisely why the Romanians regarded Eurocommunism not as an ideological heresy but as a way of implementing socialist principles in accordance with the particular conditions existing in developed countries. Bucharest's ostensibly permissive attitude, therefore, also could accept the PCE's dropping of "Leninism" from its party theses since this was not a matter of principle. A party has the right to "call itself what it considers appropriate," for what counts "is the scientific content of the theory by which it is guided, the correctness of its political line, and its faithfulness to basic principles of socialism and to the requirements of life."[27] Such Leninist "pragmatism," however, gives way to irritation with the Eurocommunists when they assert that certain linkages between political and economic democracy are essential to any "genuine" socialist system.[28]

The Hungarians also thought Eurocommunist prescriptions for socialism smelled of an ethnocentric snobbery that implied that existing socialism was Asiatic, uncultured, negative, and unacceptable.[29] Ferenc Varnai, the senior Hungarian party official who made this assertion, expressed skepticism that Eurocommunism offered a way to achieve socialism successfully. At the same time, however, he allowed that such an outcome might be possible inasmuch as the Eurocommunists not only operated in more developed countries but had also been able to learn from the experiences, positive or negative, of the socialist countries. Nevertheless, Varnai still considered it unreasonable that the East European regimes should be held responsible for following an example that the Eurocommunists had invented.

Prospects

Eurocommunist norms, in the last analysis, have come to permeate the complex interplay among the Eurocommunists and even among those regimes in Eastern Europe who, for a number of reasons, have made common cause with them in resisting Soviet hegemonic aspirations. To the extent, therefore, that Moscow remains the principal obstacle in their quest for greater autonomy, both sides will continue to need each other. But as the preceding account suggests, this symbiotic relationship increasingly is beset by diverse perceptions and often different concerns of the parties involved in this uneasy collaboration.

In the near future the Eurocommunists will be under constant pressure from their supporters in Eastern Europe to temper their criticism of Soviet-style socialism and to avoid emphasizing the universalist aspects of Eurocommunism. As far as the East Europeans are concerned, limiting themselves to advocating a different approach suitable for their situation has its advantages. It gives the Eurocommunists the opportunity to respond to their own domestic need for a critical detachment from Moscow, but spares the East Europeans from having to take sides. Seen from that vantage point, a Eurocommunist stance stressing "autonomy" and "noninterference" would help to reinforce the sort of independence the Hungarians, Poles, Romanians, and possibly others crave. Conceivably, this approach could in time erode Moscow's more restricted interpretation of "separate roads" to socialism that still points to Soviet socialism as the only destination.

Will it be possible for the Eurocommunists, irrespective of their own very different situations, to avoid criticizing Moscow in ways that might compel the East Europeans to join the Soviets in resisting Eurocommunist universalist pretensions? On this score much will depend on the domestic fortunes of the PCE, PCF, and PCI. With their domestic legitimacy still under a cloud, however, it is hard to see how these parties can soon stop articulating their concern over the still lagging liberalization in Eastern Europe, where they have little or no influence. What is more, the limited prospects for early systemic changes in that area leave little room for either the Eurocommunists or the East Europeans to maneuver and thus provide no real respite from continuing confrontations.

The view that no early breakthrough seems likely to improve an uneasy relationship between the Eurocommunists and the East Europeans assumes that Moscow will maintain its preeminent role in Eastern Europe and that no basic change will occur in the domestic situation of the three Eurocommunist parties. Short of a disastrous decline in Soviet power, it seems unlikely that Eastern Europe will experience a significant diminution in Moscow's efforts to resist further attacks on the ideological and political cohesion of the area. On the other hand, the already shaky relationship could deteriorate markedly were one of the three Eurocommunist parties to attain power, or, as is more likely, formally join the government of its country.

Such an event might serve to complicate matters considerably. What seems unlikely, however, is that any Eurocommunist domestic success will enhance its influence in Eastern Europe. In the first place, any party in that position still would have to reassure its own polity by not abandoning its critical attitude towards East European as well as Soviet socialism. Secondly, as members of a government, Communists could find themselves committed to policies objectionable to Eastern Europe or even the Soviet Union. Differences over such issues would no longer be party squabbles but rather would assume the character of foreign policy disputes. As Richard Lowenthal has pointed out in analyzing Moscow's relations with the Eurocommunists, such disputes involving ideological issues seem more difficult to resolve precisely because they legitimate official positions wherever ruling Communist parties are concerned.[30] This has clearly been the case, for example, in the conflicts among Moscow, the Yugoslavs, and the Chinese.

With some qualifications, a similar situation is likely to arise with the Eurocommunists in the event that they gain substantial governmental influence. Hence the chances of a major schism between Eurocommunists and the East Europeans would be greatly enhanced, particularly so long as the Soviets continue to set the basic tone of the relationship between them. Whether the actual course of events will move in that direction remains conjectural, but the ingredients for such a development are clearly present.

NOTES

1. The three West European Communist leaders, in separate statements, reaffirmed their adherence to the principles of political and civil freedoms and political pluralism but disavowed any intention of seeking to engage in "anti-Sovietism." Those assembled in Sofia limited themselves to criticizing "anti-communist campaigns . . . trying to distort the content of the domestic and foreign policy of the socialist countries." Foreign Broadcast Information Service (FBIS), *Daily Report, Eastern Europe*, March 4, 1977, pp. AA 3–4.

2. In the aftermath of the March 1977 French, Italian, and Spanish summit in Madrid, Spanish Communist leader Santiago Carrillo noted that "Eurocommunism is a reality." *Cambio 16* (Madrid), March 14–20, 1977.

Jean Kanapa, French Communist party Politburo member, though still quibbling about the term "Eurocommunist," because it excluded Communist parties in other industrialized countries with similar aims, noted that these parties have developed similar approaches in spite of their different situations, all outlining a new socialist perspective "which is strongly marked by a common concern for democracy." Jean Kanapa, "French Communism's New Policy," *Foreign Affairs*, 55 (January 1977), p. 284.

The well-known Italian Communist commentator Giuseppe Boffa wrote on the twenty-fifth anniversary of Stalin's death that "Eurocommunism . . . is an alternative to Stalinism which originated in quite another context. Its significance lies in the realization of the necessary link between democracy and socialism . . . to resolve a new problem . . . rejecting both the path of leadership from above and that of disintegration. For these reasons Eurocommunism's consolidation can provide one of the greatest contributions to real historical progress beyond Stalinist ideas . . . and *not only in our own countries*. *L'Unità*, March 5, 1978, p. 1. Emphasis added.

3. Charles Gati, "The Europeanization of Communism," *Foreign Affairs*, 55 (April 1977), pp. 550–554.

4. That the phenomenon of Eurocommunism coincided historically with broader aspects of East-West relations seeking, among other things, a lowering of cultural and human barriers exemplified by the 1975 Helsinki summit and the signing of the Final Act has only complicated the problem. As a result, Eurocommunists have felt compelled, and also have taken advantage of the Helsinki conference, to point increasingly to Soviet and East European failures in the human rights field and to disassociate themselves from these practices. In turn, Soviet leaders like Mikhail Suslov have branded such attacks, as well as Eurocommunist support for Western-type political and civil freedoms, as "slanderous" of "real socialism" and attempts to "wash out the revolutionary essence of Marxist-Leninist teaching and substitute bourgeois liberalism for Marxism." *Pravda*, March 18, 1976. Another ideological stalwart, Bulgarian party head Todor Zhivkov, attacked Eurocommunism as a bourgeois tool aiming to subvert the Communist movement. Todor Zhivkov, "Unity in the Communist Movement," *World Marxist Review*, 19 (December 1976), pp. 3ff. Not to be outdone, Vasil Bilak, a senior Czech party leader, has seen deep conspiratorial links between Czech dissidents and the Eurocommunists. *Rude Pravo*, I (April 29, 1977), pp 26–33.

5. The final communique dropped "proletarian internationalism" and "single communist strategy" and replaced it with "voluntary cooperation and solidarity." Equally important for the Romanians and the Yugoslavs, no less than for the Eurocommunists, was the communique's explicit recognition that no universal (read Moscow-inspired) model of socialism existed and that parties had a "free choice of different roads in the struggle for social change, and each country has the right to choose for itself its political, economic, social, and legal system. *Neues Deutschland*, June 30/July 1, 1976, quoted in FBIS, *Daily Report, USSR*, pp. I 26–33.

6. The Italian Communist party held a three-day meeting on "Czechoslovakia in 1968" at the Gramsci Institute in July 1968. The meeting undertook an exhaustive analysis of the party's position ten years after the event. Senior party leaders at that conference confirmed the view that the Czech experience of 1968 had indeed corresponded to the kind of socialist democracy that important West European Communist parties had been developing since the Twentieth CPSU Congress. Moreover, other Communist parties' resistance to this judgment only demonstrated the need for a new form of "internationalism" already propounded by Palmiro Togliatti. FBIS, *Daily Report, Western Europe*, July 20, 1978, pp. L 3 ff.

7. See Jiri Valenta, "Eurocommunism and Eastern Europe," *Problems of Communism* (March–April 1978), p. 44.

8. Ibid., p. 46. See also Joan B. Urban, "The Impact of Eurocommunism on the Socialist Community," in *Innovations in Communist Systems*, ed. by A. Gyorgy and J. A. Kuhlmann (Boulder, Colo.: Westview Press, 1978), pp. 115–142.

9. Valenta, "Eurocommunism," p. 46 notes that the work of Polish theoretician, W. Brus, was picked up by *Riuniti* (an Italian Communist publishing house), as were pieces by Alexander Dubcek and the late Josef Smrkovsky (chairman of Czech National Assembly under Dubcek). The same printing house also recently published former Czech Foreign Minister Jiri Hajek's book on the Prague Spring.

10. The case of Romania and Yugoslavia seems obvious enough. But Hungary, though basically aligned with the Soviets, also has developed a more

nuanced position towards the Eurocommunists. Janos Kadar has made a considerable effort to avoid being classed with the hardliners on this issue. When Todor Zhivkov attacked the Eurocommunists in December 1976 in the *World Marxist Review*, Kadar publicly disassociated himself from the attack. *International Herald Tribune*, December 9, 1976.

11. A case in point is when the Italian Communists printed a letter from a Czech supporter of the "new course" praising the party's democracy as "authentic" and suggesting that it provided support for all those who regarded further progress of socialist society as a necessary condition for overcoming existing deformations. The letter appeared in *L'Unità*, June 18, 1976. Similarly, the exiled East German balladeer Wolf Biermann observed in an interview that the West European Communist parties had encouraged East German dissidents to become "more daring . . . and more clear-sighted." *Le Monde*, November 21–22, 1976.

12. Santiago Carrillo, *"Eurocommunismo" y Estado* (Barcelona: Editorial Crítica, 1977), p. 208.

13. Francis Cohen, *"L'URSS et Nous"* (Paris: Editions Sociales, 1978).

14. *L'Humanité*, September 4, 1978, pp. 7–8.

15. Ibid.

16. Ibid.

17. Ibid.

18. The interesting role that the Italian Communist party has played in this context can only be alluded to here. The Italians, never comfortable in confrontational situations, not only have striven to couch their criticism in less strident terms but also have engaged in efforts to maintain contact with all sides, including Moscow. While this tactic on the part of the party leadership has given the impression of carrying water on both shoulders, it also has saved the party from becoming the butt of the fierce onslaughts that the Spanish Communist party experienced at the hands of the Soviets and their principal East European supporters.

19. *Mundo Obrero*, April 23, 1978.

20. *Le Monde*, April 21, 1978.

21. V. Afanesiev, editor-in-chief of *Pravda*, quoted in *Le Monde*, April 25, 1978.

22. See Ken Devlin, *Radio Free Europe Background Report* (April 25, 1978).

23. Interview in *Il Manifesto*, November 1, 1975.

24. Interview in *La Stampa*, December 8, 1976.

25. FBIS, *Daily Report, USSR*, November 3, 1977, p. 9. Emphasis added.

26. Carrillo discusses the degree to which external influence can also help in the shaping of the socialist state inasmuch as "the progress of the socialist movement in the developed capitalist countries can help the Soviet society and communists to eliminate this type of state, and to make progress in transforming themselves into an authentic state of the workers' democracy. This is an historical necessity . . . and would totally destroy much of the bourgeois propaganda. Hence, it is all the more regrettable that in 1968, the Czech comrades were not allowed to continue their experiment. Carrillo, *"Eurocommunism" y Estado*, p. 218.

27. Constantin Florea, "The RCP's Stand on New Phenomena and Trends in The Communist and Workers Movement," *Era Socialista*, (1978), quoted in FBIS, *Daily Report, Eastern Europe*, October 18, 1978, pp H 1 ff.

28. "The RCP believes that certain aspects of the reality in socialist countries may obviously be criticized; however, one can hardly understand why certain communist parties make official statements against certain acts and events in these [East European] countries, since such positions serve neither the respective parties nor the socialist countries and the policy of international detente and cooperation." Ibid.

29. Ferenc Varnai, editor of *Nepszabadsag*, in an interview with Frane Barbieri in *La Stampa*, June 15, 1978, p. 3.

30. Richard Lowenthal, "Moscow and the 'Eurocommunists,'" *Problems of Communism*, XXVII (July–August 1978), pp. 38–49.

Part Three •

EUROCOMMUNISM AND
THE WORLD

CHAPTER XIII

The Effects of Eurocommunism on NATO

Robert E. Osgood

The Possible Effects of Eurocommunism on United States Interests in NATO

The significance of Eurocommunism for American security interests can be explored by examining the effects that Eurocommunism in power might exert in NATO and by suggesting some American policy implications that follow.

There are three major American interests in NATO. First is the maintenance of an organized allied military force that will deter Soviet aggression against Western Europe, provide American allies in Europe with a confident sense of security, and successfully cope with a military encounter if deterrence should fail. The second interest is the maintenance of a harmonious international order among the allies, based on a mutually satisfactory balance of military strength and contributions, particularly with respect to the relationship of West Germany to its European allies and the relationship of the European allies to the United States. Third is the maintenance of democratic institutions and processes in allied countries as the moral and political basis of collective defense.

The possible effects of Eurocommunism on these three interests are of several kinds: (1) The effect on allied defense contributions and policies where Communists are in positions of influence. (2) The effect on the response or anticipated response of these allies to Soviet aggression against members of NATO and adjacent countries, such as Yugoslavia, and to crises short of war. (3) The effect on the U.S. military role in NATO, particularly on U.S. troops in Europe and American use of naval and air bases. (4) The effect on U.S. military and economic support of allies with Communists in their governments. (5) The effect on the military balance and political cohesion among all the allies. (6) The direct effect on Soviet policy toward the West through the impact on Soviet policies and actions and on the quality of allied relations with the Soviet Union. (7) The indirect effect on Soviet foreign relations through the impact on relations between the East European Communist governments and the Soviet Union. (8) The effect on democratic institutions and processes in allied countries with Communists in their governments.

Of all these ways in which Eurocommunism might affect United States interests in NATO, the most important are those affecting the American position in Europe and the way the Soviet Union perceives that position.

The State of NATO

The effects that Eurocommunism may exert on American interests in NATO depend very much on the structure of power in NATO, the conditions of NATO's internal cohesion and external strength, and NATO's general state of health.

NATO is always said to be in "disarray." No wonder, since it is a peacetime alliance among a number of democratic countries with divergent as well as convergent interests, and it calls for continual budgetary sacrifices and interallied accommodations for the sake of military security when the prospect of Soviet aggression usually seems remote and hypothetical. Yet NATO has managed to survive with remarkable strength and cohesion through great changes in East-West relations, interallied relations, and domestic political and economic conditions. And it has continued to serve—through what mixture of luck and effort one cannot know—the military and political purposes for which the North Atlantic Treaty and its organization were created. It could not have done so if its member governments and their constituents had not regarded NATO as vital to their national security and to cooperative and orderly relations with each other. On the face of things, therefore, one must pronounce NATO fundamentally healthy.

What are the conditions of NATO's strength and cohesion? If one looks for them in its present structure of power, they are primarily: (1) The credibility to Soviet leaders, but also to allied governments and parliaments, of American will and ability to make Soviet aggression unprofitable and allied resistance worthwhile; (2) a capability for effective forward defense against a less-than-massive attack based on American military leadership and strategic nuclear parity, U.S. troops in Europe, exclusive American control of nuclear weapons, and a preponderant German nonnuclear contribution; (3) the assured constraint, in the eyes of its allies, of West Germany's military and political influence, through its integration in a NATO under American leadership.

These conditions of NATO's strength and cohesion are quite different from and, in the last two respects, directly contrary to, those contemplated when the alliance was formed in 1949. Nevertheless, for reasons deeply embedded in the history of American-Soviet-West European postwar relations, they have come to seem so critically important that any threat to them would be a threat to the stability and effectiveness of the alliance. Yet because these conditions are, by their nature, never guaranteed but are continually subject to challenge in a hostile international environment, NATO is always in one degree or another threatened.

The current threat to NATO, as most see it, lies not, as in past periods, in the lively prospect of Soviet aggression, the defiance of NATO strategy and American "hegemony" by France, intense controversies among allies over military strategy or East-West diplomacy, issues concerning the control of nuclear weapons, or doubts about the maintenance of adequate American troops in Europe. Indeed, there has seldom been a greater sense of security and harmony in NATO. The threat lies, presumably, in the steady growth of the USSR/Warsaw Pact's military strength in comparison to NATO's and its increased capacity for a short-warning attack, the constant undertone of suspicion in Western Europe that the United States will respond to Soviet weapons or arms control positions in ways that "decouple" American strategic nuclear weapons from a theater war, the diminished and uncertain ties of Greece and Turkey to NATO and the corrosive effect of their dispute with each other, the danger of Soviet intervention in Yugoslavia following the death of Josip Tito, and, more remotely, the prospect of Communist and leftist parties obtaining dominant positions of power in Italy and France.

This analysis assesses the nature, magnitude, and significance of the last-mentioned threat, bearing in mind its relationship to the others. This relationship depends, in part, on the roles in NATO of allied countries with influential Communist parties and the likely effects of these parties on those roles.

The French and Italian Contributions to NATO

In order to speculate about the effects of Eurocommunism on American interests in NATO, one must first evaluate the contributions to these interests that are made by allied countries in which Eurocommunism is strongest. The most direct effects of Eurocommunism in power will be exerted through their impact on these contributions. France and Italy are the major members of the alliance with important Communist parties.

The importance of France to the security of the allies lies principally in its possession of major military forces, which would probably become engaged if an attack on NATO's central front seemed like a territorial threat to West Germany; in its geographical position, which, in any case, provides a military sanctuary and a staging and supply base for allied forces; and in its possession of one of the major allied naval forces. French tactical and long-range nuclear weapons, although not committed to respond to attacks outside France, provide some additional deterrence against a major attack on West Germany by adding a factor of uncertainty to Soviet calculations.

President Charles de Gaulle's withdrawal of France from NATO's integrated military command in 1966 enhances France's freedom to abstain from intervening in a war involving NATO members. Significantly, however, de Gaulle also reaffirmed France's commitment to the basic mutual security guarantee in NATO, and his insistence on France's military autonomy did not prevent him from taking measures to coordinate French military plans with those of NATO and its member states or from participating in collective technological developments (such as NADGE, the aerial detection system) and joint land and sea military exercises.

Since de Gaulle's departure from office, the failure of French hopes for a European defense coalition to materialize, the concern to keep American forces deployed in Germany, and the growing anxiety about the Soviet military build-up have led his successors to develop various forms of military collaboration with West Germany, the United States, and the NATO command; to abandon General Charles Ailleret's formulation of a *stratégie tous azimuts;* and to identify French security with an "enlarged sanctuary" including all of Western Europe and its "immediate approaches." Although France decided not to deploy its battlefield nuclear missile, the Pluton, in Germany, which would have required close Franco-German coordination of strategy and force plans, President Valéry Giscard d'Estaing and Chancellor Helmut Schmidt have fostered an expanded working military relationship within a broad Franco-German entente.

Italy's principal contribution to NATO's security lies not in the forces it provides, which are useful principally for the defense of Italy, but in the fact that it provides air and sea bases and other facilities to American forces for the protection of NATO's southern flank. The importance of this contribution is enhanced by the withdrawal of French naval forces from NATO's command and by limitations that Greece and Turkey have placed on American use of their territory.

There are some 12,000 American military personnel on nine bases in Italy. American units include a major tactical air command; two mobile fighting units; several Army bases, which accommodate storage, logistics communications, and command facilities; and U.S. troops, which, in cooperation with Italian troops, guard tactical nuclear warheads for missiles and artillery. Most importantly, Italy provides home ports for the U.S. Sixth Fleet, together with storage bases and repair, maintenance and training facilities, and bases vital to surveillance of Soviet shipping and antisubmarine warfare operations. If these bases and facilities were not available to the United States in Italy, partial substitutes might be sought in Spain (particularly at Rota) but only, perhaps, in the face of some political resistance in Spain and among the European allies. Even as a member of NATO, however, Spain would not provide Italy's unique geographical position for monitoring surface and submarine traffic across the Mediterranean.

The importance of France and Italy to NATO's security transcends their military contributions. Their membership in the alliance keeps NATO from resembling and essentially functioning as a German-American military alliance. Therefore, they preserve the multinational military framework that contains Germany both militarily and politically, and they provide indispensable political support to the cohesion of the entire alliance.

Eurocommunist parties in power might affect the French and Italian contributions to NATO in various ways, including withholding cooperation altogether. In order to survey the range of possible effects, we must try to anticipate the policies that the French Communist party (PCF) and the Italian Communist party (PCI) would pursue.

Eurocommunist Policies toward NATO

The influence of Eurocommunist parties on NATO is in part a function of their influence on national policies, which is likely to change in unpredictable ways. For the time being (writing in early 1979), only the PCI is sufficiently strong to have significant influence on foreign policy, and that influence is largely latent or indirect. But for the sake of contingent analysis rather than prediction, let us assume that the PCF and PCI gain power, through positions in their governments, that is equal to or greater than the power of non-Communist parties but

short of dominance.[1] What policies affecting NATO would they pursue? The answer must be contingent and speculative, since these
policies will be shaped by the interplay of a number of factors: long-
range ideological and strategic goals, the expediencies of getting and
holding domestic power, the requirements of party cohesion, the
strength of other parties and the nature of Communist participation in
power, the extent of East-West tension or détente, Soviet behavior in
Eastern Europe, and the reaction and anticipated reaction of the
United States and other allies to Eurocommunist power and policies.
These factors have led to a substantial convergence of PCF and PCI
policies since 1975, but each party continues to reflect differences of
national interest no less significant than those among non-Communist
parties.

Whatever net effect the combination of these factors may exert,
one is certainly not warranted in extrapolating from the experience of
East European Communist parties that also asserted their commitment to democratic procedures and national independence before
seizing power after World War II. The NATO countries are not subject to occupation by the Red Army. They are not part of the Soviet
international economic system. Eurocommunist parties have infinitely
greater latitude in pursuing policies that diverge from Soviet
prescriptions, and they need to exercise this latitude in order to get
and keep power in their different national settings. Without dismissing
the real possibility that Eurocommunist parties—especially the PCI
with its long tradition of democratic participation and national
independence—may adhere to their traditions partly by conviction
and habit, one can find in the imperatives of power sufficient reasons
for fundamental differences between their policies and those of the
East European Communist parties. These differences have developed
only in the last two decades and particularly since the Czechoslova-
kian crisis of 1968, but they have developed for important international and domestic reasons that preclude the reversion of Eurocommunist parties to their Stalinist past.

To be sure, neither the PCF nor the PCI is likely to become just
another leftist democratic party with no ties to the CPSU or other
international Communist parties. Both are committed to the Communist mission and vision of reality. In their outlook all political life is
based on class conflict, which must result eventually in the defeat of
capitalism and the triumph of Communism, represented by the Communist parties. In pursuit of this mission and vision, Eurocommunists
think of themselves as members of an international movement from
which they gain ideological, political, and, indirectly, economic
support.

Nevertheless, Eurocommunists know that their party must be strategically correct and tactically wise in its pursuit of political power, which alone permits attainment of their ultimate goals. Therefore, the PCF and PCI, in adjusting to the environments in which they seek power, have renounced the "dictatorship of the proletariat"— and they did so before the Soviet Union followed suit in its constitutional revision.[2] They have also embraced democratic pluralism, free elections, and Western liberties, although they continue to govern themselves by "democratic centralism." Reconciled to the necessity of gaining power through coalition with non-Communist parties, they are also anxious to avoid assuming full power and responsibility prematurely, lest they provoke a backlash or precipitate a right-wing reaction, as happened in Chile, before they have consolidated their power.

In their relationship with the CPSU, the PCF (since Georges Marchais' split with Leonid Brezhnev in 1976) and the PCI are governed by the need to protect their independence and verify their nationalist claims in the eyes of the electorate. Thus, they reject the formulation of "proletarian internationalism," with its implication of automatic loyalty to the CPSU, but continue to signify their special ties to the Soviet Union and all Communist parties by substituting the formula of "international solidarity." This position enables them to retain tactical flexibility in their national settings and to oppose some excesses of bloc dominance and even condemn Soviet domestic repression without challenging the imperative of basic solidarity with the most powerful Communist state.

In terms of avoiding domestic political costs, these parties can best afford to follow the Soviet line in foreign policy on Third World issues. Here the correspondence with Moscow's views was almost perfect before the 1978 split among Communist parties over Cuban intervention in Africa. On Atlantic and European issues, however, they must establish their credentials as Western-oriented parties, avoid any implication that they are lackeys of the Kremlin, and not stray too far from the national consensus or at least traditional leftist positions. Some Eurocommunists—in Italy, at least—may have come to see the European Economic Community (EEC) and NATO as useful instruments of national security and even of protection against Soviet interference.[3] However, they find it very difficult to go beyond accepting to positively supporting a military alliance whose central purpose is to contain the principal Communist state. At the same time, both parties must, and consistently do, oppose American "hegemony" and look for ways to reduce American influence in the alliance if they are not incompatible with domestic political realities.

Once strongly opposed to both the EEC and NATO as levers of international capitalism and American hegemony, the PCF and PCI have recently come to accept them,[4] although they wish eventually to transform the former and dissolve the latter. They wish to transform EEC into a Communist-dominated group with expanded political and economic ties to the East. This, they say, will break down the present blocs and supplant them with a broader European framework in which West European countries can assume something like the neutralist or *equidistanza* stance that the PCI (and most of the Italian left) sought after World War II. Pending this transformation of Europe, however, both Eurocommunist parties have come to accept NATO as part of the existing equilibrium, which provides the basis for consolidating détente—the next best thing to the dissolution of the blocs.

From the PCI's standpoint, acceptance of NATO, which gives Italy not only security but a major-power role it would not otherwise enjoy, is a prerequisite for the existence of the *compromeso storico*. Nevertheless, the PCI also looks upon NATO as an instrument of American dominance in Europe and of interference in Italy's domestic affairs. It cannot, without qualification, embrace an organization that makes Italy an American military base aimed against the Soviet Union. Nor can it readily support increased defense expenditures and other measures to meet NATO (as distinct from purely Italian) goals, even if this would enhance its domestic credibility as a defender of the West.

The PCF, while avowing its acceptance of France's membership in the alliance, is seemingly more Gaullist than was de Gaulle. Once fervently opposed to French nuclear weapons, the PCF endorsed the *force nucleaire stratégique* in 1977 as part of its bid for popular support and as a kind of surrogate for alliance ties. Presenting the nuclear force as the guarantor of military independence from East and West, it criticized the government's abandonment of the strategy of *tous azimuts* and its concessions to the strategy of flexible response and forward defense and charged that recent measures of military collaboration with NATO and its members threatened the reintegration of France into NATO's military command.

The PCF looks toward arms control agreements, nonaggression pacts, and other treaties with the Soviet Union to erode further the remnants of the Cold War. It evidently believes that France best serves its own interests by acting as a militarily unfettered state dedicated to an East-West accommodation. Such accord will remove the practical necessity of aiming French forces against the Soviet Union and open the road toward new political ties with the East and the Third World. Meanwhile, it wants France to avoid any commitment to the forward defense of West Germany; to concentrate its military efforts on the strategic nuclear force, with no predesignated targets; and, above all, to reject military collaboration with the United States, West Germany, and NATO. Despite concessions to the pro-European bias of the Socialist party, the PCF is fundamentally opposed to any West European cooperation, whether through the EEC or NATO, with a political or military dimension.[5]

The Eurocommunists' acceptance of NATO in Italy and, even more so, in France may indeed arise more from the requirements of currying political support in order to gain a share in government than from firm and lasting convictions about national security interests and needs. However, this does not necessarily mean that, upon gaining power, these parties would repudiate the alliance. Public opinion, political bargains, American and allied reactions, and other considerations would probably make such a drastic course inadvisable. But it does mean that they are inclined to avoid or minimize defense outlays, strategic positions, and more direct forms of collaboration that appear to serve NATO, or bilateral efforts with the United States to contain the Soviet Union, as opposed to defense efforts that can be represented as purely national. The PCF, unlike the PCI, can readily downplay collaboration with the alliance, since France does not participate in NATO's military command, and opposition to American hegemony is more broadly popular as a nationalist posture. One might therefore expect the PCF in power to try at least to terminate the measures of NATO collaboration that have developed in the last decade and to abrogate all strategic and defense policies conspicuously based on the premise that the Soviet Union might constitute a military threat.

Both parties will find downplaying the alliance and security issues easier if East-West tensions are at a low level. If national fears of Soviet power and behavior become intense, on the other hand, even the PCF would find it difficult to pursue a neutral posture except at the expense of its electoral ambitions.

The persistence of American-Soviet détente at a fairly low level of tension is virtually a prerequisite for PCI internal power and external influence. Unless the PCI should thoroughly establish its predominance after a long period of rule, it cannot afford to remain indifferent to a widely perceived Soviet threat. Such a threat may be the one thing that would enable the Christian Democrats to regain the popular appeal they have lost.

Assuming the persistence of détente, the PCI in a coalition government would surely be cautious about abandoning its membership in NATO. Until it was solidly entrenched as a legitimate representative of Italy's national interests, it could not afford to confirm the suspicions and charges that its basic loyalty lies with Moscow. Nor could it appeal to the kind of Gaullism and anti-Americanism that the PCF finds natural, for that would not be consistent with its conception or with the popular conception of Italy's role in Europe.

On the other hand, the PCI might be happy to take Italy out of NATO (that is, the military organization, not the alliance) if the onus could be placed on the United States or its allies. But the onus would have to be unmistakable, resulting from some kind of blatant foreign interference expressed in official criticisms, the refusal of economic aid, credits or loans on political grounds, the encouragement of capital flight, or heavy-handed covert action. Unlike the PCF, the PCI under these conditions might seek in Italy's European allies a political and even military surrogate for the American connection.

In any case, as long as apprehensions of Soviet power and intentions are low, one might expect the PCI to work cautiously toward restricting the status of U.S. forces in Italy, the emplacement of nuclear weapons (now under joint American and Italian custody but exclusive American control) on Italian soil, and American access to bases and facilities. It can hardly wish to do less in this direction than the Turks did, although it may not find a suitable pretext. On the other hand, defense and security issues are not likely to be at the top of the PCI's agenda. Unless the PCI were to dominate Italian defense and foreign policy positions, a prospect it currently rejects, it will probably assume a low posture on such questions while concentrating on arms control, denuclearization, and possibly disengagement schemes, in which it can lean toward Soviet positions at no domestic political risk.

The ultimate test of the effect of the PCF and PCI on NATO would be their reaction to a Soviet or Soviet-supported aggression against the NATO area. Eurocommunists generally evade questions about this contingency by asserting that Soviet aggression is unthinkable and affirming the necessity of détente. The only military threats cited in PCF documents have been attributed to the United States and West Germany.[6] Yet insistent questioning by the press since 1976 has elicited scattered concessions by PCF and PCI spokesmen that they would oppose aggression from the East if it should occur. Perhaps neither party documents nor the forced answers to hypothetical questions are reliable forecasts of the response to Soviet aggression that Eurocommunists would advocate if they shared government responsibility.

The logic of their political position and strategy in France and Italy suggests that these two parties would support their country's obligations under the North Atlantic Treaty in response to an unambiguous

armed Soviet aggression on the central front, while hoping to confine
its military role to defense of the homeland. To act otherwise would
be to abdicate their popular national standing. In cases of proxy attack and encounters on the flanks of NATO, they would also have to
find compelling extenuating circumstances in order to refuse cooperation without jeopardizing their base of political support. The threat of
Soviet intervention in Yugoslavia is a case in point. Although the PCI
has argued for reducing Italian forces on the northeast boundary lest
they be provocative to Yugoslavia and the Warsaw Pact (despite the
fact that they are a sign of Italy's military cooperation in defense of
Yugoslavia), it could hardly deny the United States use of NATO
facilities to provide aid short of direct military involvement. Having
so conspicuously criticized the Soviet Union for intervening in
Czechoslovakia, it would surely condemn the Soviets for a com-
parably clear violation of Yugoslavian sovereignty. Yet in the event
that Yugoslavia actually came under Soviet influence as a member of
the Warsaw Pact, and if after time détente resumed, the PCI might
revert to its basic preference for *equidistanza*. Again, it would have to
weigh this preference against Christian Democrat pressure, popular
Italian sentiment, and the positions of the United States and West
European countries.

One should also consider the possibility that the Soviet Union
might become involved in a military encounter that threatened Western Europe in which it could not count on the support of Poland and
Romania, for example, an attack on Yugoslavia or an intervention in
East Germany that spilled over into the West. In this event,
Eurocommunist parties might lend important support to overt or
covert negotiations with East European Communist parties designed
to dissociate their governments from Soviet operations.

The security threats toward which the response of Eurocommunists
in power would be more hesitant or negative, however, are posed by
crises in which diplomatic and military maneuvers were to take place
under the prospect of war, Soviet intentions were ambiguous, and
limited hostile actions might enjoy the pretense of legitimacy. In these
situations Eurocommunists would be inclined to resist official and
popular pressure for action and to keep their governments neutral,
while supporting diplomatic concessions to terminate the crisis. They
would be particularly resistant to the support of West Germany in
such crises and might be quick to condemn American support as
provocative.

If the exigencies of getting and keeping power can be expected to
exert a dominant influence on PCF and PCI policies in the near future, what are the prospects that in the fullness of time their experi-

ence of successfully holding power in a multiparty system might transform their strategies of foreign policy? Might this experience either embolden them to revert to policies more congruent with the needs of international Communism as interpreted by the Soviet Union, or might it lead them to think of themselves for all practical purposes as national leftist parties with only faint ideological ties to the socialist commonwealth? As long as the basic East-West antagonism persists in Europe and non-Communist parties are not demoralized or intimidated by Soviet strength, the first kind of transformation seems exceedingly unlikely. The independent road of Eurocommunist parties is the result of a long evolution from Stalinism to polycentrism and a progressive adaptation to democratic national environments, which clearly differentiates them from the national Communist parties in the Soviet bloc. The second kind of transformation is more likely, but for Eurocommunist parties to abandon "international solidarity" presupposes their abandonment of the ideological basis of the party's internal discipline and political identity. This is not something likely to follow from political success. It may only occur, perhaps, if a revival of Soviet repression in Eastern Europe and Soviet pressure against Western Europe were to compel the Eurocommunists to break completely with the CPSU.

The Spanish Communist Party

The Spanish Communist party (PCE) is far less influential in Spain than is the PCI in Italy or PCF in France. Supported largely by the labor movement, the PCE seems unable to get more than 10 percent of the popular vote, which earns it no more than 6 percent of the seats in the Congress of Deputies. In contrast, the PCF garners 20 percent and the PCI over 30 percent of the popular vote, and both have substantial representation in their parliaments. What domestic influence the PCE can achieve will depend on its persuasiveness as a vocal minority among opposition parties.

The importance of the PCE to American interests springs not from its domestic power but from its prominence among Eurocommunist parties by virtue of Secretary General Santiago Carrillo's defiance of Moscow and Moscow's subsequent public chastisement of him, its close relations with the PCF, the PCI, and the ruling Communist parties of Romania and Yugoslavia, and its generally favorable attitude toward NATO.

Once notorious for its subordination to Moscow, the PCE under Carrillo's leadership began departing from the positions of its pro-

Soviet faction and developing alliances with non-Communist forces even before the invasion of Czechoslovakia. In 1977 Carrillo, in publications (particularly his book *Eurocommunism and the State*) and in press interviews, began defining more clearly the PCE's departure from Moscow's line in foreign affairs as well as in its basic political and ideological stance. Its support for both the European community and a European defense community goes farther than the PCI or PCF toward endorsing a West European bloc that would be an alternative to either Soviet or American dominance. Pending the creation of this bloc, however, it supports U.S. bases in Spain but opposes Spain's entry into NATO, although it promises to accept this event if the Spanish parliament were to vote for it.

Under Carrillo the PCE has been more outspoken than either the PCF or PCI in rejecting Soviet leadership of the Communist movement and criticizing the East European as well as Soviet regimes for their lack of democracy and their transgression of human rights. The Soviet condemnation (in *New Times,* June 16, 1977) of Carrillo's defiance as contrary to the interests of peace and socialism in Europe—possibly intended as a warning to the PCI—did far more to enhance the PCE's reputation in both East and West European countries than any political influence it could possibly gain inside Spain.

The Interaction of Eastern and Western Communist Parties

The effects of Eurocommunism on American interests in NATO may be transmitted not only directly through the policies of Communist parties in power but also indirectly through the interaction of Western and Eastern national Communist parties as it affects Soviet policy and action.

Increasingly, since the Soviet suppression of liberalization in Czechoslovakia in 1968, the Eurocommunist parties have openly called for the expression of political liberties, the respect for human rights, and the assertion of independence from Soviet control in foreign policies in Eastern Europe while criticizing Soviet oppression and hegemony there. East European dissidents and reformers, in turn, have encouraged this kind of Eurocommunist intervention. The effects have been greatest, both in private support and official opposition and anxiety, in Czechoslovakia, Poland, and East Germany. Although only a marginal influence compared to indigenous factors, Eurocommunist intervention has apparently helped to moderate political oppression in some East European countries, promoted some Soviet concessions to the independence of East European Communist parties,[7] and generally strengthened the hands of internal reformers and of governments asserting their independence from Moscow.

The Soviet Union, in its relations with East European governments, evidently tolerates either a considerable measure of national autonomy in foreign policy, as in Romania, or a considerable measure of liberalization of domestic policies, as in Hungary and Poland, as long as Communist parties are firmly in control of their governments. But if Communist parties seem to be infected with an alien political virus or are in danger of losing control of the country, Moscow might again intervene to restore order as it did in Czechoslovakia.

From the Soviet standpoint, either acquiescence or suppression in response to the movement toward autonomy or liberalization in East European countries carries costs and risks. The effects of acquiescence or suppression on East-West relations and on Eurocommunist parties might have implications for American security interests. Soviet acquiescence to internal liberalization and external autonomy may encourage a degree of Western influence and national independence and legitimize a degree of Communist pluralism that, in Soviet eyes, will jeopardize the assurance of friendly and cooperative governments in its East European security zone, generate destabilizing schisms in the East European countries, and even disturb the domestic order in the Soviet Union itself. Soviet acceptance of such developments tends to enhance a source of political deterrence against Soviet military pressures or adventures westward and helps to consolidate a genuine East-West détente.

On the other hand, if the Soviets decide to suppress such developments, they will destroy détente—at least for a while—and risk provoking greater dissidence in Eastern Europe. Suppression would also affect Eurocommunist parties. It would drive them further away from CPSU influence, possibly unite them in an anti-Soviet faction, and deprive Moscow of its claims to be head of a socialist commonwealth transcending the orbit of its imperial control. Of course, if Moscow fears the loss of its security belt in Eastern Europe, it will not decide on action or inaction because of the effect on Eurocommunism. In less drastic situations, however, Moscow's anticipation of the adverse effects of suppression on Eurocommunist parties and, hence, indirectly on American-Soviet relations may be a marginal deterrent.

In the event of Soviet armed suppression, the Western allies might benefit somewhat from the diminished appeal of pro-Soviet positions in their countries and from the embarrassment of Communist parties. These benefits, however, would have to be weighed against the adverse effects of increased East-West tension on arms control and

other measures that purport to enhance Western security at a moderated level of defense effort, not to mention the vicarious political loss
from the suppression of East European liberties and independence.

It follows that, from the standpoint of American security interests
in NATO, one must hope that the liberalizing effects of Eurocommunism on East European governments will strengthen their independence from Moscow without provoking Soviet suppression. Implicit in this position is the ability of West European governments to
cope with the somewhat enhanced opportunities for Eurocommunist
power and influence in an atmosphere of deepening détente. Implicit
also, ironically, is the possibility that the very existence of Eurocommunist parties that have not severed all their ties to CPSU or united
against Soviet leadership constitutes some deterrence against new
Soviet "Czechoslovakias" or Soviet aggression against Yugoslavia.

American and West European Influence on
Eurocommunism

In acquiring and managing power, Eurocommunists will be sensitive to their relations with the United States and the European allies
as well as to their relations with political parties and the electorates in
their own countries. Having obtained prominent positions in their
governments, they would value the continuation of normal relations
with the United States as proof of their legitimacy. They might also
try to exploit the disruption of normal relations as a sign of American
hegemony and interference if the United States seemed to bear the
onus. The way the United States responded to appeals for economic
and financial aid—the implied linkages between aid and security
policies or the explicit economic conditions—would be matters of
particular concern, especially in Italy, where relations with the United
States have been such an important element in foreign policy and
domestic affairs since World War II. Equally important, and more
likely to be the subject of bargaining, would be the policies or anticipated policies of the EEC and West European governments.

That this sensitivity to external relations with allies would enable
the United States and other governments to apply effective *quid pro
quo*s to the foreign policies of the PCF or PCI in power is doubtful,
but the implicit linkage would be the unavoidable consequence of
French and Italian participation in a Western-oriented international
economic system and security community for which they have no
substitute. Generally, this linkage would exert a moderating effect on
Eurocommunist security policies.

Would Eurocommunist Power Undermine the Moral Base of Alliance?

The most direct effect that Eurocommunism might exert on American interests in NATO would arise if Communist accession to governmental power destroyed the character of the alliance as a community of democratic countries. Can nations who pledged in the North Atlantic Treaty that "they are determined to safeguard the freedom, common heritage and civilization of their peoples, founded on the principles of democracy, individual liberty, and the rule of Law" maintain the moral base of their alliance with countries that share government with Communists committed to an antithetical political order? Consider the Eurocommunists' declared commitment to an ideology that subordinates democratic processes and liberal values to the achievement of messianic goals; the notorious tactical flexibility of Marxist-Leninist parties; the postwar years of slavish fidelity to Moscow's foreign policy line, broken only recently by the expediencies of seeking power in democratic systems; and the persistence of a rigid, antidemocratic discipline in the enforcement of party decisions on policy. The record, to put it mildly, does not inspire confidence in the Communist parties' long-term dedication to liberal political values and democratic processes. If they successfully obtained considerable power, the Eurocommunists might find the need for tactical concessions to democratic pluralism less compelling. The danger is not so much that a Communist party in formal power would institute an East European-style coup or even that it would decline to observe the rules of the democratic game if voted out of office, but rather than it would use its power to infiltrate and subvert education, the media, and other institutions that are the lifeblood of a pluralistic democracy, and bring under Communist discipline the police, internal security forces, and the armed services.

On the other hand, one does not have to believe in conversion to be reasonably hopeful that Eurocommunists in power would continue to be constrained by the exigencies of democratic bargaining and compromise, that other parites and the electorate's basic commitment to representative government would be strong enough to prevent one-party government or the installation of democratic centralism on a national scale, and that national objectives would take precedence over the interests of the socialist commonwealth in the conduct of foreign relations. Furthermore, the record of European Communist parties in coalition governments and in control of numerous urban governments is one of responsible adherence to democratic rules of the game. Indeed, the PCI's exemplary parliamentary behavior and

creditable municipal record has tended to strengthen and legitimate
the basic institutions of Italian democracy.

This hopeful prospect may be beside the point, however, if the
United States and other European allies, rightly or wrongly, were to
believe that the accession of the PCF or PCI to formal power would
undermine the moral basis for continued collaboration. Henry Kissinger has argued that a Eurocommunist party in power would "totally transform" the "character of the Atlantic relationship" even if
the party were to split with Moscow and the United States were to
support it on pragmatic grounds:

> While the United States can never be indifferent to the extension of
> Soviet hegemony to Western Europe, the permanent stationing of
> American forces in Europe could hardly be maintained for the ob-
> ject of defending some communist governments against other com-
> munist governments. Such a deployment could be justified only on
> the crudest balance of power grounds that would be incompatible
> with American tradition and American public sentiment.[8]

This judgement seems extreme under the conditions of coalition
government in which Eurocommunist parties would come to power. It
could be correct, however, if one postulates that the Eurocommunists' acquisition of a formal share of government in France or
Italy would lead to a Communist-dominated government, no matter
what independence from Moscow that government might display. In
this case the alliance might become essentially a United States-West
German alliance, as the other allies lapsed into indifference or neutralism. Faced with something less than this worst case, however, one
might expect American pragmatism to respond to the many practical
incentives to keep allied democratic governments with Communist
components alive and healthy rather than condemn them to suffer the
full consequences of political sin. But realistically one might also expect, even under the best of circumstances, an added degree of congressional opposition to financial and economic aid to such governments or even to budgetary outlays for maintaining American troops
or strengthening NATO directly.

Net Assessment of Eurocommunist Impact

As the basis for drawing policy implications, a net assessment of
the likely effects of Eurocommunism accession to formal power in
France and Italy on American interests in NATO means anticipating
neither the worst nor the best possible outcome. This, in turn,

presupposes the basic health and popularity of the alliance in member nations, the continued vitality of democratic values and procedures in countries sharing power with Communist parties, and pervasive constraints against one-party Communist dominance. But it does not presuppose the Eurocommunists' abandonment of their animus toward U.S. troops and bases and their determination to erode American leadership in NATO's military strategy, command, weapons procurement, and the like. It does not presuppose their unqualified acceptance of defense measures and strategic policies oriented toward the containment of Soviet aggression or their conversion from Communists who think of themselves as participants in a socialist commonwealth and value international Communist solidarity, however loosely organized, to Communists in purely national democratic parties indistinguishable in their motives and modes of operation from non-Communist leftist parties.

On these premises, and assuming an atmosphere of détente, one must expect Communist parties in power to aggravate the problem of eliciting measures of military collaboration that go beyond minimal national self-defense, while favoring schemes of arms control, nonaggression, and disengagement as alternatives to defense outlays. Although the PCI might feel constrained to continue granting American access to bases and facilities in Italy, the PCF would try to negate all the forms of collaboration with the United States and NATO that have recently developed. It would also cease the tentative military cooperation with West Germany and the commitment to forward defense, while dismantling the general Franco-German entente. Neither party would be in a position to block allied countermeasures against unambiguous Soviet or Soviet-supported military attacks against NATO territory or Yugoslavia, but both might throw their weight against collective opposition to hostile moves in crises short of war.

One could derive some consolation from the prospect that the Soviet concern to keep Eurocommunists in the commonwealth, together with the Eurocommunists' appeal to East European independence, would somewhat enhance the deterrence of Soviet military action in the East or against the West. This deterrent, however, would be achieved at the risk of Eurocommunists acquiring and wielding power for ends that are fundamentally inconsistent with containment and perhaps with Western liberal values. In any event, formal Eurocommunist power would be likely to compound the problem of eliciting support in the United States and Western Europe for budgetary and other measures necessary to sustain the military, political, and economic underpinnings of NATO's strength and cohesion.

Therefore, the United States has more to lose than to gain from

Eurocommunists' accession to formal power, but the losses are neither so certain nor great as necessarily to exert a drastic effect on American interests in NATO. The seriousness of this effect depends, in part, on the American response to Eurocommunist power or the anticipation of it.

Policy Implications

From a policy standpoint, the Eurocommunists' acquisition of formal power in France or Italy should be viewed as a serious setback, but not a disastrous blow, to American interests in NATO. What would seem to be called for, therefore, is a cautious damage-limiting strategy based on presenting the Communist parties with the least pretext and opportunity for acquiring power in the government and, whether or not they acquire it, lending maximum support through normal channels to the forces of democracy, domestic political and economic health, and commitment to the alliance.

The principal direct policy implications of this net assessment arise in three areas: (1) how to deal with the prospect of the PCF or PCI coming to power; (2) how to deal with the NATO security issue if the PCI should come to power; and (3) how to deal with the issues of foreign assistance to Italy if the PCI shares governmental power.

One must start with the recognition that the United States and its allies have only a little influence that can be effectively used to affect the prospect of the PCF or PCI coming to power. For this prospect mostly depends on the efficacy and unity or inefficacy and disorganization of the non-Communist political forces in coping with economic and social problems and their success or failure in winning the respect and hope of the people. The difficulties of governing effectively, however, are deep-seated—especially in Italy—and in their international economic sources go far beyond the capacity of any single government to remedy.

What marginal influence the United States does have in impeding Communist accession to power must be exercised with great discretion, since the implication of punitive or overbearing interference in domestic politics could be readily exploited by Communists. At the same time, Europe still has a profound sense of American power— otherwise the United States would not be so vulnerable to excessive expectations—and a widespread disposition to value American friendship. This sentiment is especially deep-rooted in Italy. The United States, therefore, would probably do best to follow a combined course: cooperation with other nations in solving common problems, such as those pertaining to energy and economic stability, and a clear official position—whatever the delicate modalities of presentation may be—against relying on Communist parties to assure prosperity and security. Whereas heavy-handed opposition to Communist accession to power would backfire, an attitude of indifference or, worse still, of conspicuous reconciliation to accession would demoralize many moderates and be exploited by Communists.

PCI participation in government—even if its members do not hold the defense and foreign ministries—would raise the question of whether to admit and how to deal with Communists in NATO committees that provide access to sensitive information. Objectively, in terms of the risk that vital military secrets would reach Moscow, it would not make a crucial difference whether PCI members participated in such committees. Whether or not one assumes that the PCI would run the political risk of being caught sponsoring espionage, one must assume that, outside the supreme allied command in Europe, there are already some espionage agents among the 250 Italians and other representatives in NATO's international staffs. The United States already operates on the assumption that it cannot guarantee the security of some of its own classified information in NATO's staffs. Moreover, there are PCI members on the defense committee of the Western European Union. Anyway, Moscow has other ways of getting essential information about Western defense plans.

Nevertheless, there is a widespread feeling among NATO officials and allied governments that they cannot simply view with indifference the prospect of Communists freely participating in the conduct of international security affairs. To do so would be to signal all NATO governments and employees that NATO has no secrets worth protecting. The effect on American participation, in this view, might be particularly devastating to the efficacy and morale of NATO: one can well imagine a vocal congressional objection to sharing secrets with Communists. Given this attitude, the practical question of how to restrict the participation of PCI members in NATO would arise if the PCI were formally a partner in government.

The solution of this security question in Italy would be a much larger and more awkward problem than it was in Iceland, which has no representatives in sensitive military positions, or in Portugal. Portugal took itself out of the Nuclear Planning Group when Communists entered the government and found ways to exclude Communists from sensitive meetings and files. Italy, however, has a far greater number of representatives in NATO's staffs, as well as nuclear weapons on its soil. The easiest solution would be for the Christian Democrats to make an agreement with the PCI that would enforce the necessary restrictions. If, however, the other members of NATO or the Secretary General were to impose such restrictions unilaterally either against Communists or against all Italians, that would strain relations with the Italian government and possibly provide the PCI with a pretext for restricting American forces in Italy or taking Italy out of NATO altogether. On balance, the value of avoiding this kind of confrontation, even at some expense in security of information, would seem to outweigh the value of formally protecting NATO's internal security if a formula agreeable to member governments can be found.

Of course, there would be no way of avoiding such a confrontation, short of complete inaction, if the PCI were clearly the majority party and held the defense ministry. In that case, if the PCI still wished to keep Italy in NATO, NATO members would have to make a basic judgement as to whether the PCI had been sufficiently transformed into a Western-oriented national party for Italy to remain a loyal member of NATO or whether the time had come to expel the country (or possibly the government but not the country) from NATO because the purposes of the organization and the party were incompatible. By the time this hypothetical and unlikely event took place, it is to be hoped that the non-Communist parties, encouraged by the anxiety of the American and other allied governments, would have enough evidence to make this judgement wisely by compelling the PCI to take responsibility for clear positions on the critical defense and NATO issues.

The issue of whether and, if so, on what conditions to extend economic assistance to Italy under coalition government would also pose a dilemma for the United States and its European allies. If aid were not extended, whether on political or economic grounds, the economic situation in Italy would probably deteriorate. Whether or not the PCI was able to capitalize politically on the American rejection of aid, Western interests would surely suffer from Italy's economic collapse. If the United States were to resort to punitive economic sanctions and deliberately discourage investment and encourage the flight of capital (it is hard to imagine the European allies joining in these measures), it would surely enhance the opportunity of the PCI to exploit the resulting economic disruption. If punitive measures, economic collapse, and civil strife were to unseat or appear to unseat the Communists, the United States might find itself in the equally disadvantageous position of sponsoring and bolstering a right-wing regime, which, although loyal to NATO, would be a political pariah in Western Europe. Moreover, it is doubtful that an unreformed right-wing government could restore the Italian economy without the assistance of the PCI. Consequently, the United States would bear the double onus of trying to sustain a deteriorating economy and a reactionary government.

On the other hand, if aid and credit were extended without some reliable assurances of economic and bureaucratic reform, it probably would not help save the Italian economy, and the PCI might point to unconditional aid as further evidence of its legitimacy. In any case, the PCI's key role in restoring the Italian economy suggests that the United States and its allies can hardly escape the ironic logic of helping the PCI establish its political power if they give aid without political conditions.

This dilemma may be soluble if the Christian Democratic party plays a constructive and politically advantageous role in restoring the economy, if the Christian Democrats and the PCI agree to accept reasonable and effective economic conditions on foreign assistance, and if the United States and its European allies combine to give foreign assistance, without political conditions. But this solution implies some extraordinary statesmanship and a good deal of luck. In the United States, the prospect of helping a government dependent on a party suspected of hostility to American security interests and democratic principles implies a high degree of congressional sophistication and restraint.

In the end, the most important consequence of PCI accession to formal power is likely to be the American reaction. The latent anti-Communism and the rising uneasiness with détente in Congress and the country at large, not to mention the views of organized Italo-American sentiment, are liable to have major impact on this response. The reaction in the United States could be explosive and anything but conducive to the politically sophisticated and finely modulated response that the situation would require, particularly if it occurred in a presidential election year. For the U.S. government has done nothing to prepare critical segments of congressional and public opinion for this event, other than to somewhat relax restrictions against visiting Eurocommunists. Indeed, the executive branch may well regard this task as impossible, since even to study the issue inside the government, let alone decide upon a concerted policy, might raise the implication of official anticipation or acceptance of the event. Consequently, this issue of PCI accession to formal power is the kind of issue upon which a popular base of understanding will depend very largely on the intelligent concern and initiative of those in Congress or outside the government who care most about the future of the North Atlantic Alliance.

NOTES

1. In reality, the PCF's split with the Socialists, which ruined whatever chance it had to come into office in a leftist coalition in the March 1978 elections, virtually eliminates the prospect of the PCF entering the government for a long time, particularly in light of the fact that its portion of the vote in the Fifth Republic has remained at about 20 percent in recent years, which is less than during the Fourth. The PCI, on the other hand, is already a major governing force in every region and most large cities, as well as in the central government. It has virtual veto power over national legislation, consolidated by an agreement with the Christian Democrats to vote for it in parliament in return for consultation on all aspects of government policy. Its possession of major ministerial posts would not drastically increase its influence, except in the unlikely case that they included defense and foreign affairs, and might actually reduce its flexibility and appeal or complicate its problem of maintaining internal cohesion. In any event, the decline of the PCI vote in the local elections of May 1978 (9.1 percent from its popular vote in the 1976 general elections) does not bode well for its entrance into the government. The prospect of either party becoming dominant seems too remote to be worth considering, barring the complete collapse of domestic political systems under overwhelming economic and social crises and failure of the United States and the EEC to come to the rescue.

2. In 1964 the PCI, under Palmiro Togliatti, although still considering itself a Marxist-Leninist party, renounced violence as the means to power and substituted "working class hegemony" for "dictatorship of the proletariat," according to Antonio Gramsci's formulation. The PCF abandoned the phrase in 1976 as part of its drive to enter the government in coalition with the Socialists.

3. Enrico Berlinguer, when asked whether he considered NATO a useful shield against Soviet interference in Italian affairs, said, "I want Italy to remain in NATO *also* for this and not only because our withdrawal would upset the international equilibrium. I feel safer being on this side (the other being the Warsaw Pact), although also here I feel efforts to limit our autonomy." *Corriere della Sera,* June 15, 1976.

4. The PCI ceased opposing EEC in 1962 and NATO after 1972. The PCF, until 1965 the most Stalinist of Eurocommunist parties, was somewhat slower to endorse these institutions and, even afterward, continued to oppose the supranational aspects of EEC and American dominance of NATO. Only with the PCI-PCF rapprochement of November 1975 and the PCF's coalition with the Socialist party did the PCF begin openly condemning Soviet oppression, championing personal liberties and human rights in Eastern Europe, and insisting on its independence from Moscow.

5. Thus, as late as March 1978, Secretary General Georges Marchais declared that "France ought to practice a policy founded on the rejection of alignment—of any alignment with anyone whatsoever." Interview in *Le Monde,* March 3, 1968.

6. See, for example, the statement of official PCF defense policy in Jean Marrane, *L'Armée de la France democratique* (Paris: Editions sociales, 1977).

7. At the June 1976 conference of Communist parties in Berlin, Eurocommunists were instrumental in moving the Soviet Union to formally renounce its leading role in the international Communist movement, accept the right of

each Communist party to pursue an independent road to socialism, and acknowledge the possibility of a peaceful democratic transition to socialism in the advanced capitalist countries.

8. Transcript of remarks by Henry A. Kissinger, "Communist Parties in Western Europe: Challenge to the West," delivered at the Woodrow Wilson International Center for Scholars, Washington, D.C., June 9, 1977.

CHAPTER XIV

Chinese Perceptions
and Relations
with Eurocommunism

Parris H. Chang

In the 1950s China was a member of the Soviet-led socialist camp, and China and the Soviet Union formed an alliance against their common enemies, the United States and Japan. The sharp and open Sino-Soviet conflict since the 1960s has irrevocably shattered the monolithic unity of the Communist bloc of Stalin's days and ushered in far-reaching changes in both the world Communist movement and the international system. According to Teng Hsiao-p'ing's speech, the socialist camp is "no longer in existence," and the "Western imperialist bloc, too, is disintegrating."[1] Instead of a bipolar world, Peking sees a new division of the world into three parts: The United States and the Soviet Union make up the first world; the developing countries in Asia, Africa, Latin America, and other regions make up the third world; and the developed countries (those of Western Europe, Japan, Canada, and Australia) between the two make up the second world. Whereas Peking frequently brackets the two superpowers in the first world in rhetoric, in practice Peking treats the Soviet Union as China's principal and most dangerous enemy, and is striving to forge a tacit alliance with the United States, Japan, and Western Europe against the Soviet Union and its allies.

This essay proposes to study China's attitude toward Eurocommunism. The first section deals with the Chinese Communists' rejection of Titoism, which represents one form of Eurocommunism, that is independent, national Communism, and offers an explanation for it. Section two analyzes how the Sino-Soviet conflict accelerates the emergence of polycentrism in the world Communist movement, which in turn prepared the ground for many other forms of Eurocommunism. Inasmuch as China's relations with Eurocommunist parties are shaped by China's perception of Western Europe and her overall policy toward the region, section three is devoted to an examination of that policy. Finally, section four examines the interactions between Peking and the Eurocommunist parties in the 1970s and analyzes why the relations have not blossomed.

The Two-Camp Theory and Rejection of Titoism

Until the late 1950s Chinese Communists had uncritically accepted Lenin's theory of a bipolar world divided into two diametrically opposing camps, socialist and imperialist, and had sought alliance with the Soviet Union against the imperialists. As far back as 1926, for example, Mao Tse-tung stated that "the present world situation is such that the two major forces, revolution and counter-revolution, are locked in final struggle." This two-camp world view was forcefully articulated by Mao in his 1940 essay "On New Democracy" in which he wrote:

> Once the conflict between the socialist Soviet Union and the imperialist powers grows sharper, China will have to take her stand on one side or the other. This is an inevitable trend. . . . The whole world will be swept into one or the other of these two fronts, and "neutrality" will then be merely a deceptive term.[2]

Mao also asserted that "all the imperialist powers in the world are our enemies," and that China cannot possibly gain her independence "without the assistance of the land of socialism and the international proletariat." As he put it, "refuse Soviet assistance, and the revolution will fail."[3]

Viewing the world through the Communist ideological lens, Mao thus considered the United States and other Western nations as enemies and hostile to his cause and an alliance with the socialist camp as necessary to the success of revolution in China. Such assumptions were to condition Peking's foreign policy in the 1950s. On June 30, 1949, three months before the establishment of the Communist regime in China, Mao enunciated the celebrated "lean to one side" policy of alliance with the Soviet Union and declared in the treatise entitled "On People's Democratic Dictatorship": "Internationally, we belong to the side of the anti-imperialist front headed by the Soviet Union, and so we can turn only to this side for genuine and friendly help, not to the side of the imperialist front."[4]

Of course, Chinese leaders did not make the decision to ally with the Soviet Union on ideological grounds alone; the decision was forced on them also by China's international milieu, especially American hostility toward the Chinese Communists and other strategic considerations. Under those circumstances, the Moscow "connection" would seem the only alternative. In February 1950 the Sino-Soviet alliance was embodied officially in a thirty-year Treaty of Friendship, Alliance and Mutual Assistance—a relationship that Peking believed would enable China not only to obtain Soviet material and technical assistance for China's economic and military construction at home but also to enhance China's national security in the face of American threat and to achieve other foreign policy goals, such as world Communist revolution.

Inasmuch as the Chinese Communists were committed to the goal of world revolution, and the monolithic unity of the socialist camp was seen as important for the promotion of this goal, they were opposed to actions of other fraternal parties that appeared to weaken the unity of the camp. Thus, not surprisingly, in 1948 the Chinese strongly backed the attack of the Cominform on Josip Tito, who had led his party and Yugoslavia out of the socialist camp. Tito was accused of betrayal of basic viewpoints of Marxism-Leninism, of falling into the mire of bourgeois nationalism, and of faked neutralism. As Liu Shao-ch'i, leading Chinese Communist party (CCP) theoretician, wrote:

> If one is not in the imperialist camp, assisting American imperialism and its agents to enslave the world or one's own people, then one must be in the anti-imperialist camp. . . . To refrain from lining up on one side or the other and to keep neutral is impossible. . . . So-called neutralism . . . is nothing but deception, intentional or otherwise.[5]

Officials of Yugoslavia were understandably disappointed by the Chinese Communist's attitude, which they construed as renouncing the principle of equality among Communist parties.[6] In retrospect, Tito's departure from the Soviet-led socialist camp and defiance of Moscow's leadership can be seen as the first manifestation of Eurocommunism, if it is defined both as a "tendency" for each party to assert independence from domination by the center or leader of the world Communist movement, equality in interparty relations and autonomy of each party to pursue its own path of socialist revolution and socialist construction in accordance with local circumstances, and as a "policy" aimed at the creation or preservation of the tendency toward independence.[7] Although Tito's assertion of independence did have an impact on Eastern Europe, as suggested by the purges of "potential Titoists" in other European parties, overall national Communism appeared to be far ahead of its time and could not flourish under the conditions then prevailing in the international milieu. At that time, insofar as the international Communist movement was concerned, Stalin was the "Godfather" of the Communist world and the Soviet Union was the only source of final authority. The CCP, which was to emerge on the world scene as the ruling party of a huge nation in 1949, was the only other Communist party possessing many of the prerequisites for independent authority, but it chose to uphold Moscow's leadership.

For considerations of ideology and national interests, the CCP sided with Moscow once more in 1950 to suppress the tendency of Titoism in the Japanese Communist party (JCP). During 1946–49, the JCP adopted a strategy of nonviolent political action and pursued a "parliamentary path" and a broad united front, including important elements of the bourgeoisie. It was making considerable headway. In the 1949 election, for example, it won close to 3 million or 9.6 percent of the votes and captured thirty-five seats in the House of Representatives. Its party membership consisted of more than 100,000—equal to any political party in Japan. Then in January 1950 the Cominform launched a scathing attack on the JCP's approach to effecting peaceful transition to socialism, accusing the JCP leader Sanzo Nosaka of being antidemocratic, antisocialist, antipatriotic, and anti-Japanese, and directed the JCP to make a radical shift to armed revolution.[8]

For a brief period the mainstream JCP leaders, led by Kyuichi Tokuda and Nosaka, defied Moscow by refuting the criticisms of the Cominform article. They strongly defended the JCP program as the "Japanization" of Marxism-Leninism, that is, an attempt to adapt Marxist theories creatively to the needs and special conditions of Japanese society.[9] As Tokuda and Nosaka spent several years in Yenan and were close to Mao and other CCP leaders, they may have counted on Peking's support to withstand Moscow's pressure. If they indeed had entertained such a hope, they were quickly disillusioned. On January 17 Peking's *Jen-min Jih-pao* published an editorial backing the position of Moscow and criticizing Nosaka's nonviolent parliamentary strategy as erroneous. Bowing to these criticisms of successful revolutionary parties, the JCP complied with Moscow's call for violence and began to organize riots and prepare for armed struggle. The new tactics soon proved disastrous—leaders of the JCP were banned from public life by the Japanese government and forced underground for several years, and the JCP, having alienated the people by its violent tactics, lost all of its thirty-five seats in the House of Representatives in the 1952 election.

It is true that Tito's challenge to Moscow and the JCP's attempt at defiance were kept in check. Nonetheless, they were significant in the sense that they already raised, if only in embryonic form, major issues which were to confront the international Communist movement from the late 1950s on and that confront Eurocommunism today (insofar as Eurocommunism stands for independence from Moscow). These issues include such questions as independent roads to Communism, the locus of world Communist leadership and ideological authority, the correct strategy of global revolution, and the avoidance of "big-power chauvinism" in intra-bloc relations.

It should be noted that, on these and other issues, the stand of the CCP has never been consistent and that at different times it has taken whatever position would best serve its interests. Thus, while the CCP supported Moscow to expel Yugoslavia from the Cominform and to dictate a violent revolutionary strategy to the JCP, it asserted its autonomy and independence and refused to concede to Moscow, then subsequently, the right to make decisions for the world Communist movement. It is quite well known that the Chinese Communists long took pride in their own road to power, wanted a leading role in the global Communist movement, and claimed the Chinese revolution to be a model for all developing areas. Hence, no sooner had the CCP come to power than it began to assert its leadership role in the world Communist movement. In November 1949, Liu stated before the trade union conference of Asian and Australasian countries in Peking:

> The road taken by the Chinese people in defeating imperialism and in founding the Chinese People's Republic is the road that should be taken by the peoples of many colonial and semicolonial countries in their fight for national independence and people's democracy. . . . This is the essential road on which the Chinese people marched to achieve victory in their country. This road is the road of Mao Tsetung. It can also be the basic road for liberation of peoples of other colonial and semicolonial countries, where similar conditions exist.[10]

In the autumn of 1951 on the occasion of the thirtieth anniversary of the founding of the party, Lu Ting-yi, head of the propaganda department of the Central Committee, reiterated Liu's statement of the Maoist strategy and added several new embellishments. "Mao Tsetung's theory of the Chinese revolution," he said,

> is a new development of Marxism-Leninism in the revolutions of the colonial and semicolonial countries and especially in the Chinese revolution. Mao Tse-tung's theory of the Chinese revolution has significance not only for China and Asia—it is of universal

significance for the World Communist movement. It is indeed a new
contribution to the treasury of Marxism-Leninism.

Lu added, somewhat extravagantly, that "the classic type of revolution in imperialist countries is the October Revolution. The classic type of revolution in colonial and semicolonial countries is the Chinese revolution."[11]

However extraordinary was Peking's claim of the relevance of the Chinese Revolution for countries of Asia, which Moscow understandably resisted, Peking and Moscow did reach some sort of compromise on the question in 1952 and avoided the conflict in the Sino-Soviet relations and the schism in the international Communist movement of a decade thereafter. In any case, the Chinese claim underlied the fact that the CCP, as the ruling part of a huge nation, with an independent power base, massive popular support, and a tradition of independent existence, possessed the necessary capital to assert its leadership role and challenge Moscow's ideological authority over the global Communist movement. The Chinese temporized in the early 1950s as the great *vozhd* Stalin, who was admired highly even by Mao, was still alive, and Peking was heavily dependent on Moscow for national security and economic assistance. After Stalin died, and particularly when the Chinese Communists perceived Nikita Khrushchev's de-Stalinization and policy of détente with the West as detrimental to their national interest, they would begin to challenge Moscow's leadership.

The Sino-Soviet Conflict and the Emergence of Polycentrism

Students of international Communism generally agree that the Sino-Soviet rivalry has accelerated the tendency toward polycentrism in the world Communist movement. In this section we will examine exactly how this process was set in motion. Polycentrism, carried to its logical conclusion, is, of course, national Communism; and national Communism is one feature of Eurocommunism.

The causes of the Sino-Soviet conflict and how it developed over time have been analyzed and documented by many superb studies.[12] Suffice it to note here that the absence of an institutional mechanism to settle fraternal disagreements and the inability to create one led to further deterioration, rather than to a solution of the conflict. Efforts were indeed made to patch up the differences between Peking and Moscow and to bring about the unity of the bloc. The 1957 and 1960 Moscow meetings were such unavailing attempts.

The first meeting, which tried to solve the problems caused by de-Stalinization, came after the 1956 upheaval in Eastern Europe. The Chinese, who in 1956 and early 1957 had placed stress on the need to avoid "great power chauvinism" and to build socialism in accord with national peculiarities, urged Moscow to take a more moderate and flexible attitude toward Poland and toward other fraternal parties. In 1957 they reversed themselves suddenly—much to the disappointment of Wladyslaw Gomulka, Palmiro Togliatti, Janos Kadar and others who wanted more freedom in pursuing their own liberal domestic policies. At the November 1957 conference, Mao shifted to a hard line in favor of Communist conformity. He stressed Moscow's leading role in the bloc, emphasized the importance of following the Soviet experience, and minimized the role of national characteristics. As Mao had insisted, the conference declaration included a strong passage on Soviet leadership, but Gomulka and Togliatti were conspicuously silent on Soviet leadership of the camp in their post-conference statements. The Yugoslav delegation refused to sign the declaration, as it contained the statement on the need for subordination to Moscow.[13] Mao's call for a new intra-bloc relationship, much like the CCP's support for Yugoslavia's expulsion in 1948, was designed to strengthen the unity of the bloc and to apply maximum political and military pressure on the West. The strategy failed to receive support from both the East Europeans and the Russians.

The 1960 Moscow conference, convened after a sharp clash at Bucharest between Russians and the Chinese, likewise failed to bring about bloc unity. The conference managed to issue a declaration, but it contained incompatible ideological formulas that could only lead to a continuation of polemics, with both sides stressing their own parts of the document. It is not accidental that the statement no longer contained the 1957 formula of "the socialist camp headed by the Soviet Union." Liu Shao-ch'i, head of China's delegation, had announced a new formula to 12,000 Russians in the Lenin Stadium in Moscow: "The CCP and the CPSU are the two biggest parties in the international Communist movement, China and the Soviet Union are the two largest countries in the socialist camp."[14]

In the years following the conference, the interparty dispute deteriorated further as the Sino-Soviet polemics came into the open and increasingly affected all the Communist parties of the world. For example, while other Communist parties sided with the CPSU and attacked the CCP, Peking hit back against such prominent Italian and French exponents of the Moscow point of view as Togliatti and Maurice Thorez. On December 31, 1962 and March 4, 1963, the *People's Daily* and *Red Flag* unleashed bristling attacks on Togliatti and the Italian Communist party (PCI). Togliatti was sharply criticized for attempting to substitute class collaboration for class struggle, "structural reform" for proletarian revolution, and for other revisionist ideas. On February 27, 1963, in a *People's Daily* article entitled "Whence the Differences?—A Reply to Thorez and Other Comrades," Thorez and the Moscow-oriented French Communist party (PCF) were severely castigated by Peking for joining the anti-China chorus and for slavishly following the Soviet line. Indeed, the PCF was then a most staunch follower of the CPSU, ever so faithfully and subserviently parroting the Moscow line, and Thorez was particularly energetic and outdid leaders of other pro-Moscow Communist parties in assailing the CCP, levelling attacks at the Albanians, the North Koreans, and other Asian parties friendly toward the CCP. Hence, Peking's attack on Thorez and the PCF was probably for a different reason than the Chinese attack on Togliatti.

By the fall of 1963 the Sino-Soviet conflict had reached a point of no return, which also marked the beginning of the disintegration of the bloc. The publication of the twenty-five-point Chinese program on the international Communist movement in June 1963 was a clarion call to independence from Moscow and an outright challenge to the ideological authority and leadership of the CPSU in international Communism. Peking actually went so far as to defend the formation of secessionist parties, thus raising the banner of revolt and "revolution" against a mere "pretender." The conclusion of the Test Ban Treaty in July 1963 by the United States, Great Britain, and the USSR, to which Peking strongly objected even before it was signed, was seen by the Chinese as an act of Soviet-American collusion aimed primarily at them and as the end, for all practical purposes, of the Sino-Soviet military alliance.[15]

By the end of this period the Rubicon had been crossed. Realizing that Peking could no longer be kept in line, Moscow now actively lobbied among fraternal parties to convene an international conference to excommunicate the CCP from the world Communist movement. Meanwhile, to counter this Soviet design, Peking not only mounted an intensified campaign to enlist support throughout the Communist movement, it also encouraged pro-Chinese factions within parties and promoted the formation of new secessionist parties and splinter groups in Europe, the Americas, Asia, and Africa.

In Europe, for example, many pro-Chinese factionalist publications appeared, supported by direct, massive Chinese subsidies. Among them were the international monthly *Revolution* (July 1963), based in Paris and *La Voix du Peuple* (September 1963), the "Periodical of Belgian Communists."[16] Also through Chinese intervention, a seces-

sionist Belgian Communist party was formed in December 1963 under
the leadership of Jacques Grippa, a fiery veteran who had been expelled from the Central Committee of the orthodox party one year
before. Grippa's followers were not numerous and their antirevisionist rebellion was not particularly successful in its challenge
to the orthodox Belgian Communist party (which had a numerical
superiority of about eight or nine to one), but the Belgian split did
serve several useful purposes for Peking. In the first place, Grippa's
party served as a bridgehead in Europe for the Chinese to establish
ties with other antirevisionist groups. Moreover, as Kevin Devlin correctly pointed out, a full-fledged secessionist party in Western
Europe, recognized as such by the pro-Chinese parties, reinforced
Peking's claim "to offer a global, and not merely regional, alternative
to Moscow's diminished leadership of the world movement."[17]

During 1963 and 1964, Peking was also involved in supporting secessionist factions in the Spanish Communist party (PCE) and in
financing antiparty publications in Spain. This was revealed by an article in the PCE organ *Mundo Obrero,* which was reprinted in *Pravda*
in June 1964.[18] The article revealed that the PCE had sent a letter to
the CCP complaining of China's involvement in the factional activities, but to no avail. In the summer of 1964 a new antiparty publication, *El Communista,* appeared. It described itself as "the organ of
the Federación Centro de los communistas marxistas-leninistas." An
editorial in the first issue claimed that:

> In Spain, nuclei of Marxist-Leninist Communists have been formed
> and are forming. Our periodical . . . is the organ of the nuclei of the
> Center Federation. . . . In the present circumstances, the duty of
> Spanish Marxist-Leninists is to move towards the break with the
> anti-party, liquidationist and revisionist group headed by [Sec-
> retary-General] D. Santiago Carrillo.[19]

In October 1964 three factional groups of "antirevisionists" inside
and outside Spain were brought together. They were the Communist
party of Spain, the "Proletario," and the Communist Revolutionary
Opposition of Spain, which published the journals *Mundo Obrero
Revolucionario, Proletario,* and *La Chispa.* Their joint communique
stated that they had "proceeded to rebuild the Communist Party of
Spain on the basis of . . . Marxism-Leninism," and that their joint
organization would be entitled *Vanguardia Obrera.*

By the late 1960s pro-Peking secessionist parties or splinter groups
had been set up in virtually every West European country, Asia, and
Latin America. Most of them continued to exist through 1979. Although numerically insignificant, they published polemical journals

(subsidized by Peking), propogated Peking's line, and gave the impression that the support for China within the Communist movement was global in scope.[20] Moreover, Peking's encouragement of secession has not been confined to nonruling Communist parties—it has attempted to subvert and divide some ruling parties in Eastern Europe. For example, a pro-Chinese Polish Communist party under Kazimierz Mijal, and an obscure "New Unity" Communist party of Germany have existed in exile in Albania and West Berlin, respectively, but their followers are probably negligible.

The Chinese were not alone in promoting factionalism in the world Communist movement, for Moscow also resorted to the same tactic to split the pro-Peking parties. An outstanding example was Moscow's support for Yoshio Shiga, a veteran Japanese Communist leader. In December 1964, shortly after returning from a visit to Moscow, Shiga and his followers established a new party called the Japanese Communist party (Voice of Japan) to challenge what they called the "Japanese Communist party (Yoyogi faction)" led by Kenji Miyamoto. Moscow called the Shiga group true Marxist-Leninists of Japan and castigated the Yoyogi group as Chinese puppets.[21] Apparently Moscow also attempted to factionalize the pro-Peking Communist party of Indonesia (PKI). Criticizing the Russians, the PKI leader D.N. Aidit charged that "the modern revisionists are . . . resorting to the establishment of new and phony parties not only in Japan but elsewhere in the world."[22]

In their competition with the Russians to promote the formation of secessionist parties, the Chinese were clearly on the offensive. They had more to gain, for the leaderships of most of the nonruling parties were on the side of Moscow, and any factionalist activities within their parties could only be at Moscow's expense. This consideration may have reinforced Khrushchev's determination to call a preparatory meeting for a general conference of world Communist parties to read the CCP out of the movement. Moscow suggested such a conference in late 1963, but steps to convene it were postponed repeatedly. The CCP and pro-Chinese Communist parties naturally declared in advance that they would refuse to attend, but many other parties that were not friendly to the CCP were also critical of the idea of the conference. Despite Khrushchev's urging, the Italian, Yugoslav, British, Dutch, Norwegian, Australian, Belgian, and other Communist parties continued to drag their feet, and even the Poles and Hungarians expressed strong reservations.

In the face of such objections, Moscow beat a retreat and assured its allies that the meeting was called not to "condemn anybody or to excommunicate anybody from the Communist movement."[23] Despite such assurances, most pro-Moscow Communist parties were equivocal. However, the crushing blow to the concept of the conference as envisaged by Moscow was subsequently dealt by the posthumous publication of Togliatti's "testament" in the summer of 1964. In it the deceased PCI leader criticized the Soviet handling of Chinese tactics, expressed dissatisfaction with the slow pace of de-Stalinization in the USSR and East Europe, and asserted the independence of the parties and strongly defended the Italian strategy of peaceful transition to socialism. Togliatti's emphasis on the autonomy of the parties severely undermined Soviet attempts to rally their supporters. This "testament" became a catalyst for critical Communist attitudes regarding the conference, and it focused reservations and reinforced doubts among Moscow's reluctant allies.[24]

Khrushchev had intended to convene a so-called Preparatory Conference in December 1964, but it had to be put off when he was ousted two months before by his rivals in the CPSU. Even though the new Soviet leaders continued to push the conference, it never took place. Many parties that were much closer to the Soviet point of view in the Sino-Soviet conflict were by then keenly jealous of their autonomy. They would take part in the conference only if there would be no renewal of Moscow-centered international discipline, no excommunication, and no binding majority decisions. Moscow's difficulties in getting even the largely pro-Soviet parties to agree to a world conference boycotted by the Chinese served to illustrate just how far the decline of its authority had gone.

These emerging relationships within the Communist world were, to be sure, not altogether China's doing. The Italians had developed a sense of critical detachment from the Soviet model and had asserted their independence in the 1950s. Khrushchev's early reforms and the settlement following the 1956 de-Stalinization crisis, for example, granted increased autonomy to various East European regimes. This newly-acquired autonomy enabled the rulers of the former Soviet satellites to pursue policies in accord with local peculiarities, to identify themselves with national interests, and to build bases of popular support which, in turn, sustained them and emboldened them to stand up occasionally to the Soviets. At the same time, the Sino-Soviet dispute was a critical factor that accelerated the autonomy of the Communist parties, speeded up the disintegration of the Russian-controlled Communist movement, and greatly fostered diversity and divergencies in the Communist world.

The bitter factional struggle between Peking and Moscow for the allegiance of the Communist parties throughout the world so severely disrupted, factionalized, and split the movement that the Humpty-

Dumpty of single-centered world Communism could not be put together again. Moreover, the two rivals clashed over many crucial issues of domestic policy and the strategy of world revolution. Out of
this dispute emerged two sharply different doctrines, and the small
parties were able to pick and choose between them and increasingly
go their own way. Some parties and factions more or less fully
adopted the Chinese point of view—among them the Koreans, the
Japanese, the Indonesians, large sections of the Communist parties of
India and Ceylon, important minorities in a number of Latin-
American parties, the Albanian Communists, and a number of smaller
minority groups in Western Europe. Some, such as the Romanians
and the Vietnamese, chose to play off Peking against Moscow. The
large majority of the Communist parties still supported Moscow
against the Chinese, but they were able (and more inclined) to assert
their independence, and they would no longer uphold the Soviet
Union as the unique model and its changing leaders as the infallible
guides to the correct "Communist" policy.

China's Opening to Europe

China's overall strategy for Europe shapes to a large extent her
relations with the Eurocommunist parties. Thus, before China's relations with various Eurocommunist parties are examined, China's policy toward Europe in the last decade must be reviewed.

For the past three decades, China's relationship with Europe has
fluctuated. Soon after the founding of the People's Republic of China,
Peking established relations with Moscow's East European satellites,
the Scandinavian countries, Switzerland, Holland, and the United
Kingdom. In the winter months of 1956–57, Peking forcefully intervened in Moscow's handling of the East European unrest, thus demonstrating China's growing influence in the backyard of the Soviet
Union. This trend was halted, however, in the ensuing decade as the
Sino-Soviet conflict evolved and most of the East European regimes
sided with Moscow. Peking found a new ally in Albania, it maintained
cordial state and party relations with the Romanians, and it promoted
the pro-Peking Communist secessionist parties or factions in Western
Europe, but official relations between the CCP and other East and
West European Communist parties were cut off in the early 1960s.

At the same time China displayed little interest in Western Europe.
It maintained low-key relations with only about half a dozen non-
Communist European states up to the mid-1960s. The French recog-
nition of the People's Republic in 1964 was the only bright spot in

China's otherwise unsuccessful diplomatic activity in Europe. Before China could capitalize on the new links with France, however, the Great Proletarian Cultural Revolution (GPCR) erupted in 1966 and China's foreign relations were plunged in total chaos. When the GPCR was at its peak of violence and disorder in 1967, all of China's ambassadors and key diplomatic officials, except those in Cairo, were called home to undergo ideological rectification. In the same year, Red Guard mobs burned the British Embassy in Peking and harassed the embassies and diplomats of many other countries.

The Soviet invasion of Czechoslovakia in August 1968 was a turning point in China's European diplomacy and global strategy. Unlike its endorsement of the Soviet intervention in Hungary in November 1956, Peking denounced more severely than other governments the Soviet occupation of Czechoslovakia, which Peking saw as Moscow's attempt to secure its European flank in preparation for the coming conflict with China. Moreover, Moscow's enunciation of the Brezhnev Doctrine to rationalize Soviet intervention in other socialist states particularly alarmed Peking, for the Soviets could invoke the same principle to invade China. The bloody Sino-Soviet border clashes in the spring and summer of 1969 only increased Chinese fears that the Russians would do just that.

Amid the war scare, China quickly moved to restore order to her diplomacy. It is significant that in 1969, after the upheaval of the GPCR, Chinese ambassadors were first returned to Albania and France; those posted in Romania, Sweden, and Finland returned just after those to China's Asian neighbors and well before the ambassadors to the Soviet Union and other countries of Eastern Europe. In addition to mending ties with the West European states, Peking sought to create disturbances in the Soviet Union's backyard by inciting nationalist resentment against the Russians. For example, Chinese propaganda supported the resistance of the people of Czechoslovakia against "social-imperialism." Chinese diplomats also told the Poles that their eastern border was an iniquity and criticized Muscovite "colonialism" for preventing German reunification—but with little success in loosening Moscow's grip on Eastern Europe.

The Chinese adopted a new approach in the Balkans—they not only toned down their attack on Yugoslav revisionism, but they also encouraged closer collaboration among Albania, Yugoslavia, and Romania. After the 1968 Czech invasion, according to the Albanians, Peking went so far as to urge Albania to "conclude a military alliance with Yugoslavia and Rumania" to counter Soviet invasion threats.[25] Such a military alliance never materialized, most probably because of Albanian hostility toward Yugoslavia. Nonetheless, Peking did strengthen political, economic, and military ties with Romania and gave considerable support to Romania's policy of independence from the Soviet domination. China also improved relations with Yugoslavia (as evidenced by Yugoslav Foreign Minister Mirko Tepavac's visit to China in June 1971), although the rapprochement was gradual and was confined to government-to-government relations in the early 1970s.

In the early 1970s, as part of a new strategy to cope with the Soviet threat, Peking also stepped up its diplomatic drive in Europe. China established diplomatic relations with Italy in 1970, with Austria, Turkey, Belgium, Iceland, and Cyprus in 1971, and with Malta, West Germany, Luxembourg, Spain, and Greece (under a military junta) in the following year. Thus, by the end of 1972, China had embraced all of the European states of the NATO alliance, with the exception of Portugal. Peking's eagerness to strengthen state-to-state relations coincided with a perceptible decline in its interest in and support for the Marxist-Leninist splinter groups (which gradually turned to Tirana for leadership).[26] The expansion of China's relations with Europe formed part of the country's new global strategy that sought to forge an international united front against Soviet "social imperialism" in the wake of the Soviet invasion of Czechoslovakia and in the face of newly perceived Soviet military threat to China. The central element of this global strategy was to "play the American card," namely, to use the United States and its allies as counterweight against the Soviets. This was first expressed in the dramatic rapprochement with the United States in 1971–72 and President Richard Nixon's visit to China in February 1972.

The strategic thinking behind the new approach was spelled out in an article in *Hungch'i* (Red Flag) in August 1971 devoted to a study of Mao's 1940 essay "On Policy." The article stressed the importance of clearly distinguishing "who is the principal enemy, who is the secondary enemy, and who is the temporary ally or indirect ally." One basic strategic principle laid down by Mao was "to exploit contradictions, win over the majority, oppose the minority and crush them one by one," according to the article. Thus, instead of fighting the United States and Soviet Union at the same time, China would distinguish between the principal and secondary enemies, "pull together and manipulate all conflicts, gaps, contradictions in the enemy camps, and use them against today's principal enemy."[27]

In line with this global strategy, Peking assigned Western Europe a new role in Chinese foreign policy. Western Europe would serve as a partner in China's international anti-Soviet united front operation and provide an additional political and military counterweight to divert Moscow's pressure and to deter a possible Soviet attack on China.[28]

The more the Soviets had to worry about a build-up of hostile strength on their European flank, the less energy and capability they could devote to their eastern border with China. To serve China's purposes, a united and a militarily and economically strong Western Europe would be essential. Hence Peking strongly supported the expansion of the European Economic Community and the extension of its free trade zone, hailed Western Europe's efforts at integration, and became an ardent champion of European security.

For example, when West German Foreign Minister Karl Scheel visited China in October 1972, the Chinese leaders deplored the "abnormal situation" in Germany, criticized outside interference, and endorsed German reunification. They seized every occasion to stress the Soviet hegemonic ambition and to express China's support for Europe's efforts to assert its independence from the pressures of the two superpowers. As Chou En-lai put it to French President Georges Pompidou in Peking in September 1973:

> We . . . support the people of Europe in uniting themselves to safeguard their sovereignty and independence. We are for the view that the cause of European unity, if it is carried out well, will contribute to the improvement of the situation in Europe and the whole world.[29]

In the same vein, Peking has actively promoted Europe's military preparedness and a strong NATO alliance. Despite its expressions of encouragement of independence and sovereignty of European nations and its criticisms of contention and collusion in Europe between the two superpowers, which allegedly threaten the vital interests of Western Europe, China does not favor an American withdrawal from Western Europe. On the contrary, Peking accepts the dependence of Europe on the United States. It openly supports a strong American role in NATO and often voices concern for the decline in the American commitment to defense spending and to the defense of Western Europe.

Thus, China's repeated criticism of the West's policy of détente with the Soviet Union should come as no surprise. Western visitors to China in the first half of the 1970s, including President Gerald Ford in December 1975, were sternly lectured by Chinese leaders on the danger of détente. The Chinese were understandably apprehensive that détente, the strategic arms limitation agreement, and the Helsinki European security accord could lull the United States and Western Europe into a false sense of security, which in turn could lead to an erosion of Western military power. At the worst, Peking saw détente as a malicious design by the West to "urge the Soviet revisionists eastward'' so as to "divert the peril" from itself.[30] Thus, Peking coupled its attack upon superpower domination with a blunt warning that the West European nations could ignore the threat of Soviet aggression only at their risk. It urged every West European leader to keep the military strength of the region high and to forego precipitous détente with the totally untrustworthy Soviets.

From time to time there are reports—denied by all the parties concerned—that China has offered to collaborate with France and Italy on nuclear weapons, and a Western columnist has concluded that "Peking is more favorable than Washington to the long-range goal of a European nuclear force, based on the existing atomic weapons of Britain and France."[31] There is no question that China favors a united and strong Western Europe that would not only be a reliable counterweight to the Soviet threat to China, but would in the long run play an independent role vis-à-vis the United States. In a multipolar world, the Chinese hope that Western Europe would play its own role alongside Japan and the United States, and in doing so would give China greater room for maneuver and help China redress her balance in relation to all these powers.

Peking's positive attitude toward Western Europe has political as well as economic motivations. In the 1970s the EEC was China's second largest trade partner, next only to Japan.[32] Since Mao's death and the purge of radical leaders in 1976, the post-Mao leadership has embarked on an ambitious drive for modernization and has turned to Japan, Western Europe, and the United States for assistance in the next stage of China's industrial revolution. Already Peking has clearly signalled its interest in long-range economic relations and is actively seeking large-scale Western aid in capital and technology. China is also in the process of sending thousands of students to Western Europe, Japan, and the United States to receive advanced training.

Moreover, Peking also desires to capitalize on advanced Western military technology for the modernization of China's outdated weapons systems. Already China has bought the Rolls-Royce Spey engine from Britain to use to power a new delta-winged combat plane. In recent years high-ranking Chinese military and civilian officials have visited England, France, Switzerland, Belgium, Denmark, and West Germany in search of arms. Included in China's "shopping list" are British Harrier "jump jets," the new Chieftain tank, and the Jaguar fighter-bomber; the French MILAN antitank missile and Mirage 2000 jet; and the German Leopard tank and 120-mm smooth-bore gun (which the Pentagon selected to arm the newest American battle tank). China has tried to link arms purchases with other trade contracts, and Washington has changed its stance on the allies' transfer of arms to China. This makes it more likely that, despite Moscow's warnings against arming China, Peking may still be able to acquire some of these weapons systems from various West European nations.

China and Eurocommunism

In the past three decades, Chinese Communist attitudes toward Eurocommunism have changed frequently. According to Jiri Valenta, various manifestations of Eurocommunism (which either means independence from the USSR or stands for a type of democratic and pluralistic socialism) had occurred in Tito's Yugoslavia (1948–49 and after 1952), in Czechoslovakia (1946–1948 and in 1968), in Hungary and Poland (1956), and in Albania and Romania (since the 1960s).[33] The Chinese reactions to these developments were highly inconsistent and opportunistic.

As pointed out earlier, the Chinese Communists supported Moscow's expulsion of Yugoslavia from the Cominform in 1948 and sided with the Russians again in 1950 to insist that the JCP follow a violent revolutionary strategy, thereby upholding unity and Soviet leadership in the Communist movement. In 1956 and 1957, China shifted its earlier position and urged toleration of diversity in the socialist bloc, evidenced by Chou's visit to the Soviet Union, Poland, and Hungary in January 1957 as a mediator in the wake of the Polish and Hungarian developments and his support of Poland in its attempt to obtain greater autonomy from Moscow. In the early stages of the Hungarian uprising in 1956, Peking also displayed sympathy toward Hungary and criticized the Soviet "big-power chauvinism," but its position changed quickly and it backed (if not actually pressed for) Moscow's suppression of the Hungarian "counterrevolution" in November 1956 when the Nagy regime sought to withdraw from the Warsaw Pact. By the fall of 1957, Peking actively espoused a hard line and campaigned for conformity in the bloc and Moscow's leading role in it.

As the Sino-Soviet dispute widened in the early 1960s, however, and as Albania broke relations with the Soviet Union in December 1961, China tried to strengthen Albania by siding with this tiny Balkan Communist state and publicly backing its independence from Moscow. Similarly, Peking maintained good relations with and displayed support for Romania, which refused to take sides in the Sino-Soviet dispute. Meanwhile Peking continued to launch virulent attacks on the revisionist Yugoslavia, despite the fact that Yugoslavia, not unlike Albania and Romania, was striving for independence from the Soviet domination. If the Yugoslav revisionism was objectionable to Peking,

Czechoslovakia's pluralistic and democratic socialism was even more so, hence the Chinese condemned both the Soviet invasion of Czechoslovakia in 1968 and the revisionist Dubcek regime.

In retrospect, the Sino-Soviet polemics, the CCP's challenge to Soviet ideological primacy and leadership in the international Communist movement, and Peking's promotion of the pro-Chinese factions and secessionist parties in the 1960s facilitated and gave impetus to polycentrism in the Communist world, which in turn speeded up the emergence of Eurocommunism. In spite of its role as a catalyst, Peking has remained aloof and has contributed little to the growth of the Eurocommunist movement that began a new epoch in the aftermath of the 1968 Prague Spring. It is indeed surprising that Peking has not embraced the Eurocommunist parties, given that such parties as the PCE, PCF, and PCI were previously pro-Moscow and they have, since the early 1970s, increasingly asserted their independence and moved away from the Soviet bloc. It is even more surprising when one considers that the PCE, PCI, and PCF have taken initiatives on several occasions to approach the CCP.

Among the West European Communist parties, the PCE, under the leadership of Santiago Carrillo, was the first to attempt to reopen the relations with the CCP, which had been severed in the heat of the Sino-Soviet polemics in the early 1960s. Carrillo, one of Moscow's harshest Communist critics, was confronted with opposition from a pro-Soviet dissident faction in 1969 and 1970. He was also under heavy pressure from Moscow and was interested in broadening the PCE's base of support within the world Communist movement in order to increase his party's autonomy from Moscow. The goals of the PCE received solid backing of the Romanian Communist party. Romanian President Nicolae Ceausescu, who visited China in June 1971, was apparently instrumental in arranging the first contacts between the PCE and the CCP. While visiting Romania in August 1971, Carrillo issued a statement claiming that the PCE had achieved "positive results" in its efforts to reestablish relations with the CCP.[34] In the following month the PCE made a bold move to demonstrate its new autonomy from Moscow by sending a top delegation led by Carrillo and four other high-ranking leaders to Peking. This marked the first and only time since the early 1960s that the CCP had accepted a delegation from a "revisionist" nonruling Communist party that had previously sided with Moscow in the Sino-Soviet dispute. The PCE delegation was unable to meet with any higher CCP official than Keng Piao, director of the CCP International Liaison Department (in charge of relations with foreign Communist parties), and the visit did not produce a joint communique, as major differences between the CCP and the PCE persisted.[35] The PCE appeared to view the visit as a major step toward independence from Moscow and prominently publicized the affair.

Peking sought to play down the Carrillo mission, however, and in a few lines under "News Briefs" in the *Peking Review* (December 3, 1971, p. 26) curtly stated that "The Spanish Communist Party led by Santiago Carrillo, General Secretary of the Party, visited China at the invitation of the Chinese People's Association for Friendship with Foreign Countries." It is possible to argue that the Chinese from the outset agreed to the visit of the PCE delegation reluctantly in deference to the request of Ceausescu, who enjoyed their high esteem and who was serving as a middleman between Peking and Washington, without really being interested in a rapprochement. Thus, the efforts of the PCE notwithstanding, the attempt to normalize relations with the CCP was unsuccessful. A message of the PCI to the Chinese, carried by Carrillo, seeking "meetings with leaders of the CCP, in Italy or in China" was also ignored.[36] Peking has since continued to snub the PCE, and has not exchanged fraternal greetings at party holidays. To add insult to injury, Peking continues to associate itself with various PCE splinter groups.[37]

China's refusal to reopen relations with PCE and other West European Communist parties has been motivated by several factors. Whereas their assertion of independence from Moscow pleases the Chinese, their renunciation of violent revolution and the dictatorship of the proletariat, and their endorsement of Western humanism and plural democracy do not. "Revisionism" is a factor, but not the most important one, however. Since the early 1970s the main thrust of Chinese foreign policy has been to forge a global anti-Soviet united front, including the United States (despite verbal attacks on American imperialism). Hence, Peking's top priority has been to strengthen state-to-state relations. Peking's objectives in Western Europe have been to strengthen the EEC and NATO and to foster tensions between Western Europe and the Warsaw pact in order to divert Soviet pressures from China. Although not all Eurocommunist parties are opposed to strengthening the EEC and NATO and all espouse policies diametrically at odds with Soviet aims (the PCE is pro-EEC and favors U.S. bases in Spain, the PCF is anti-NATO but supports a strong, independent French nuclear force, and the PCI is pro-NATO and pro-EEC), somehow Peking distrusts them. In an interview with Agence France Press, for example, Teng Hsiao-p'ing said that China "would not like to see the Communist Parties of France, Italy and Spain come to power or even to participate in government." They would carry out "a policy of appeasement" toward the Soviet

Union.[38] Hence, Peking has refrained from reestablishing relations with them.[39]

Peking's support for capitalist Europe has been criticized on many occasions by the West European Communist parties. For example, a speech by the Chinese ambassador in Oslo praising the EEC was ridiculed as "nonsense" by the Norwegian Communist journal *Friheten*. "China did a disservice to West European socialism by backing so fulsomely an ultra-capitalist project," the magazine added.[40] When Teng visited France in May 1975 and openly supported the EEC and the NATO alliance, he drew sharp fire from the French Communists. George Marchais, leader of the PCF, was quoted by the *New York Times* (May 15, 1975) when, among other things, he castigated the CCP for "abandonment of Marxism-Leninism" and for supporting "an aggressive Europe of monopolies." Over the years, the PCF was the most vocal of the West European Communist parties in criticizing Peking's European policy. At the Twenty-second PCF Congress in February 1976, for example, Marchais denounced the "profoundly reactionary . . . senseless and dangerous" policies of China, while stressing the party's new independence of Moscow and criticizing Soviet repression.[41]

The East Berlin summit of twenty-nine European Communist parties in June 1976 was an important watershed for Eurocommunism. The Western parties won major concessions from the CPSU and its loyal East European allies. The conference document formally proclaimed equality and autonomy of all parties, noninterference in internal affairs, and respect for free choice of different roads to socialism. It also discarded the concept of proletarian internationalism and contained no criticism of the Chinese and no praise of the Soviets. Thus, it is surprising that the Peking media have kept silent on the Berlin conference and on the differences between Moscow and the West European parties.

There are clear indications, nevertheless, that the Chinese Communists have been watching the emergence of Eurocommunism closely and that it presents both hopes and fears to Peking. For example, Chinese diplomats in Europe and pro-Peking publications in Hong Kong have commented with glee on the disarray of the Soviet bloc and the further weakening of the Soviet position and have expressed the hope that the success of Eurocommunism would enable the East European parties to achieve greater independence from the Soviet Union.[42] The Chinese were also seriously worried that if the Communists come to power in Western Europe, the coherence of the EEC and NATO would be undermined.

In short, Peking has viewed the growing strength of some Western

Communist parties with mixed feelings. The implicit warning (or bluff) by Secretary of State Henry Kissinger in 1975–76 that the United States might pull out of NATO or substantially reduce support for it if Communists joined the governments of NATO nations caused considerable anxiety in the Chinese leadership—for without American participation, NATO would have no teeth, and China would not be able to rely on this chief bulwark against the Soviet hegemony. As if to present the best face of the undersirable situation and to dissuade Kissinger from taking an extreme step, Peking put forth a new line in the summer of 1976. Chiao Kuan-hua, then China's foreign minister, was heard to muse that the presence of Communists in a West European government need not be viewed with too much apprehension, and he reportedly cited France as a country that successfully coped with this problem in the past.[43] To admit to such reasoning the Chinese must have given some credence to Enrico Belinguer's statements that Italy would stay in the EEC and NATO should the PCI come to power, and to the PCE's support for U.S. bases in Spain and for Spanish entry into the EEC. Yet, to have Communists join West European governments is the last thing Peking wants to see. Hence, in order to avoid aiding their cause, it has refrained from associating with the Eurocommunist parties and from praising their struggle for independence.

Given such a policy, it is not difficult to understand why Peking rejected the condolence messages sent by all the West European parties (together with CPSU and other pro-Moscow East European parties) on the occasion of Mao Tse-tung's death in September 1976. As a matter of fact, both the PCI organ L'Unità and the PCF journal L'Humanité devoted four pages to paying tribute to what Marchais called "one of the greatest figures in history," and the messages of condolences clearly indicated the intent of the two parties to improve relations with the CCP. Nonetheless, they were ignored by Peking. In spite of this snub, the reaction of the PCF and the PCI was surprisingly restrained. Jean Kanapa, an official of the PCF, said this would not change the PCF's "deep rooted conviction that, no matter how grave our divergences may be, they should not result in a deterioration of relations . . . and that in future another form of relations between our Parties can be established—relaxed, comprehensive, and friendly." There is good reason to believe, as suggested by Kevin Devlin, that the gestures of the PCF and the PCI to Peking were motivated more by a desire to affirm their independence from Moscow than by a genuine hope of renewing relations with the CCP.[44]

On their part, the Chinese have continued to criticize the Eurocommunist parties as revisionist and have shown no willingness to resume party relations with them—rather, their attitudes toward Eurocommunism have remained largely unchanged in spite of the removal of the radical "Gang of Four" from power in October 1976. This is amply demonstrated by the remarks of Chinese Vice Minister Yu Chan in an interview with *El País* of Madrid in December 1977:

> The parties advocating Eurocommunism want to be independent and are opposed to the Soviet Union and to hegemonism in relations among parties. We consider that this is positive. However, the means which they propose for achieving socialism are not correct. The Eurocommunist parties no longer talk about making a proletarian revolution or establishing the dictatorship of the proletariat. They want, in short, to maintain capitalism intact. How can socialism be achieved in this way? Because of all this, we do not maintain relations with these parties and do not agree with their stances with respect to the means of achieving socialism, which— we believe—are revisionist.[45]

Though Peking opposes Eurocommunist parties on the ground that they are "revisionist," it does not have difficulty reconciling its hatred of revisionism with its friendly attitude toward the proto-revisionists—the Yugoslavs! The Sino-Yugoslav rapprochement made considerable headway in 1977. Party-to-party relations were reestablished and Tito, who used to be denounced bitterly in the Chinese press as the arch-revisionist of the Communist world, was given a hero's welcome in Peking.

The improvement of the Peking-Belgrade relations was also marked by the disappearance of articles in the Chinese press criticizing Yugoslav revisionism and the publication of many favorable press reports on Yugoslav achievements in socialist construction. Quite a few such articles praised highly Yugoslavia's system of self-management and dwelt at length on its operation, and Chinese delegations that visited Yugoslavia reportedly displayed keen interest in the system and asked detailed questions about it.[46] Does Peking seriously consider adopting some aspects of the Yugoslav self-management system for China's economy, as has been suggested? Or are the Chinese merely polite in a period of the Sino-Yugoslav "honeymoon" and say nice things about the self-management system in which the Yugoslavs have taken a great pride? There seems to be a combination of both elements. Even should Peking in the future decide against adopting the Yugoslav system (which involves broad participation by the workers in the economic decision-making process, hence at variance with the trend in the post-Mao China to elevate the role and strengthen the power of such managerial personnel as factory directors in economic production), Belgrade would still feel greatly honored by the praise the Chinese showered on its unique system. It is said that Yugoslavia's self-management system has never before been taken very seriously by Communists outside of Yugoslavia, and that for a Communist giant like China to affirm it must have enhanced immeasurably the internal image and legitimacy of the Yugoslav Communists.[47]

This is not to say that the Sino-Yugoslav rapprochement has been based solely on the ideological considerations. Unquestionably, the repudiation of the Maoist radicalism and the espousal of a pragmatic line at home by the post-Mao leadership has facilitated Peking's acceptance of the Yugoslav brand of socialism. A much more important and decisive factor is the common interest Peking and Belgrade share in opposing the Soviet "hegemonism." By "playing the China card," Belgrade seeks to reassert Yugoslavia's independence from Moscow and enlist China's endorsement in order to broaden the base of support for the nonalignment movement.[48]

The Chinese also see a community of interests with Yugoslavia and Romania—countries which consider their sovereignty threatened by the Soviet Union. Although some foreign policy differences remain between China and Yugoslavia, the differences are outweighed by their perception of common threat. This understanding underlies CCP Chairman Hua Kuo-feng's historic visit to Romania and Yugoslavia in August 1978 in which he unleashed sharp attacks on Soviet "hegemonism," praised the Romanians and Yugoslavs for their struggle to maintain independence from the Soviets, and expressed support for Tito's nonaligned movement. In this anti-Soviet drive, China was seeking at a minimum to bolster the independence of these two Balkan states and deny Moscow's control over human and natural resources there and was hoping at a maximum to promote a new anti-Soviet movement throughout Eastern Europe so as to weaken Soviet control over their Western flank.[49]

The improvement of the Peking-Belgrade ties also coincided with the breakup in the Sino-Albanian alliance. Since the early 1970s Albania had become disaffected by China's rapprochement with the United States and changes in Chinese global strategy, and trouble between the two former allies had simmered for some time. On July 8, 1977 their conflict became public when the Albanian party organ, *Zeri I Popullit*, published a lengthy editorial that denounced Peking's "three worlds theory" and its practice of adopting the principle "my enemy's enemy is my friend" in Chinese foreign policy as "opportunistic and anti-Marxist."[50] The Albanian ire was apparently prompted by the announcement that Peking had invited Tito to visit China in August. Tito's revisionism has been anathema in Tirana, and the Albanian leadership under Enver Hoxha has refused to compromise over ideological issues even for the sake of taking an anti-Moscow common stand. Thus, on the eve of Tito's arrival in Peking, the Albanians reissued and distributed among the foreign embassies in Peking a 1963 speech by Hoxha entitled "Khrushchev Kneels before Tito."[51]

The Chinese responded to the Albanian criticisms by reproducing statements by foreign Marxist-Leninists friendly to China. The first of these was the republication in the *People's Daily* (July 26, 1977) of an attack by Petros Stagos (a leader of the Greek Revolutionary Communist Movement) on "revisionism, dogmatism, splitism and opportunism which may be leftist in words." Moreover, Peking also applied economic sanctions against Tirana by substantially cutting back Chinese aid (which had been declining for several years) in 1977. As the Sino-Albanian dispute escalated further, the Chinese Ministry of Foreign Affairs presented a note to the Albanian Embassy on July 7, 1978 announcing the cessation of its economic and military aid and the repatriation of 513 Chinese economic and military experts from Albania, thereby breaking seventeen years of "unbreakable friendship."

It can be argued that, if the Chinese can abandon the Albanian Marxist purists and patch up relations with the Yugoslav revisionists, they should have no difficulty overcoming ideological differences with Eurocommunist parties. Indeed, there are signs that Peking has been rethinking its links with the large West European parties. Reportedly, the Romanians and the Yugoslavs explicitly raised the issue of relations between the CCP and West European Communist parties during Hua's trip to Bucharest and Belgrade and urged a normalization of these relations which, they argued, would be to everyone's advantage and would appear as a logical extension of the present Chinese domestic and foreign policies.[52]

Perhaps, as a result, Peking seems to be softening its attitude toward West European Communist parties. An indication of such change was given a few weeks after Chairman Hua returned to China from Eastern Europe when a PCF member, Mr. Dumont, chief editor of *L'Echo du Centre–La Marseillaise*, was allowed to visit China as a member of the French provincial press delegation. This seemingly trivial matter would be of no interest, except that in January 1978 the special envoy of *L'Humanité* was not granted a visa to accompany French Premier Raymond Barre on his visit to China.[53] In his meeting with the delegation of French journalists on October 1, 1978, Vice Foreign Minister Yu admitted that various Western Communist parties "demonstrate a certain independence in relations to Moscow" and are particularly opposed to the CPSU's "hegemonist practices" in interparty relations. He characterized this as "a favorable state of affairs." According to Yu, the Chinese and West European Communist parties "are divided by disagreement of an ideological nature, particularly with regard to the dictatorship of the proletariat," therefore, it is "very difficult to establish relations with these parties," but that China continues to take care not to respond to their attacks. Questioned about Dumont's visit to China, Yu explained: "For the time being we cannot talk of normalizing relations with these parties. But if they come in their journalists' capacity, PCF journalists will be welcome."[54]

This appears to be the extent to which Peking is prepared to go in dealing with the Eurocommunist parties in the late 1970s. Despite Dumont's visit, China's media continues to shower publicity on the "Marxist-Leninist Communist Party of France" led by its Secretary-General Jacques Juguet and to ignore the PCF totally.[55] Nor does the PCI have better luck. On October 6, 1978, Berlinguer told Agence France Press that the PCI favored resuming contracts with the CCP, but nothing has resulted from his latest signal to Peking. While Peking's interest in the Communist splinter movement has declined substantially since the early 1970s, it continues to espouse various splinter groups in the PCI, the PCE, and other West European parties (for whose allegiance there is competition with Tirana) and gives them spurious legitimacy through publicity in the *New China News Agency* dispatches and in the *Peking Review*.[56]

Concluding Remarks

Ideology alone does not dictate Chinese attitude toward Eurocommunism, and other factors, such as national security, anti-Soviet strategy, and domestic economic considerations, often appear to be more decisive in shaping that attitude, especially since the 1960s. Hence the Chinese Communist reactions toward Eurocommunism have been highly inconsistent, opportunistic, and utilitarian.

The changes in the Peking-Belgrade relations clearly underly this point. In the wake of Tito's visit to China in September 1977 and Hua's visit to Yugoslavia in August 1978, China has openly embraced Yugoslav socialism. Insofar as Belgrade would resist Moscow's "hegemonism" and cooperate with Peking in its anti-Soviet game, Yugoslavia would be regarded as a good socialist country.

At the same time, China has "dumped" its former ally Albania, largely on utilitarian considerations. Although Albania continues to display hostility toward the Soviets, China finds the value of an alliance with a tiny Communist state markedly diminished in its new global strategy that stresses state-to-state diplomacy. Albania simply has little to contibute. Moreover, Albania has been a heavy economic burden for China (Albania has received over 10 billion yuan in Chinese aid) and would further drain China's much needed resources. Furthermore, Tirana's espousal of an "isolationist" line, its opposition to the West and Yugoslavia, in addition to the Soviets, and its scathing attacks on China's collaboration with American imperialism and Yugoslav revisionism severely angers Peking. For these reasons, the Chinese do not hesitate to abandon the Albanians.

Notwithstanding the changes in Peking's attitude toward Belgrade and Tirana (which symbolize both the diminishing weight of ideology and pragmatism in China's external behavior), Peking has been slow to normalize relations with the West European Communist parties, partly on the ideological ground that they are utterly revisionist for wanting to abandon the dictatorship of the proletariat. The Chinese, like the Romanians and Yugoslavs, insist on the dominance of the Communist party in the life of the state, while the Eurocommunists do not. This significant ideological difference, which has already caused some troubles in Romanian-Eurocommunist relations, may account partly for Peking's reluctance to reopen relations with the Eurocommunists.

This does not mean, however, that the deadlock would stay for good. Judging from the ever increasing pragmatic tendencies in China's domestic and external policies, there are good reasons to believe that before long Peking will restore relations with some of the more independent-minded Eurocommunist parties, especially the PCI, which has maintained distance from Moscow. There are already indications of such a development. On May 21, 1978, in a meeting with Vittorino Colombo, the Italian Minister of Transport and Merchant Navy, who is a Christian Democrat, Vice-Premier Teng Hsiao-p'ing did not mention the danger of Eurocommunist parties sharing political power and credited Togliatti, who was previously considered very pro-Soviet by Peking, as the first to defend the principle of polycentrism.[57] On October 4, 1979, the *People's Daily* published the full text of the congratulatory message sent by the PCI on the occasion of the thirtieth anniversary of the people's republic. In the same month, two reporters of the *People's Daily* visited Italy for twelve days at the invitation of the PCI organ *L'Unità*; they published a highly favorable account of the PCI and quoted approvingly the remarks by the PCI leader Berlinguer in the interview that "the workers and farmers of Italy and the cadres and members of the PCI cherish friendship and admiration for Chinese people and the Chinese Communist Party."[58]

When Hua Kuo-feng, CCP Chairman and State Council Premier, visited Italy in November 1979, he had a cordial meeting with Berlinguer.

In addition to these positive signs, concrete steps have been undertaken to pave the way for the CCP-PCI reconciliation. The visit to China by an official delegation of the Italian Communist Youth League headed by the league secretary general in December 1979 is one such step. According to a Chinese source in Peking, Berlinguer and a PCI delegation have been invited and have accepted an invitation to visit China at "an opportune moment" in 1980;[59] most likely the occasion of Berlinguer's visit would formalize the restoration of CCP-PCI relations. The reconciliation between the CCP and the PCI would also be conducive to the reopening of the relations between Peking and the PCE. On the other hand, Peking still sees the PCF as basically anti-Chinese and pro-Soviet;[60] hence, as long as the PCF is perceived to be too submissive to Moscow, Peking will continue to refuse to deal with it.

NOTES

I wish to thank David Burke, Hank Carde, and Jiri Valenta for providing me much valuable source material. I am particularly grateful for their many helpful criticisms and suggestions for revisions of an earlier version of the chapter.

1. See Teng Hsiao-p'ing's speech to the United Nations in April 1974, *Peking Review*, no. 16 (April, 19, 1974).

2. Mao Tse-tung, "On New Democracy," in *Selected Works of Mao Tse-Tung* (Peking: Foreign Languages Press, 1967), vol. II, p. 364.

3. Ibid., vol. II, p. 355.

4. Ibid., vol. 4, p. 47.

5. Liu Shao-ch'i, *On Internationalism and Nationalism*, 2nd ed. (Peking: Foreign Languages Press, 1952), pp. 26–27.

6. One reason given by Vladimir Dedijer, a former colleague of Josip Tito, for China's support of Moscow was that "The Chinese were in the middle of an offensive against Chiang Kai-shek, who was getting all possible assistance from the United States. Perhaps taking our part would have strained relations with the Soviet Union at a crucial period in their revolution." Reportedly, in 1956 Chinese officials explained their 1948 decision to support Moscow in these words: "We were hard pressed, in the midst of a blockade, surrounded on all sides, and to be quite honest we did not know enough about the whole matter." See Vladimir Dedijer, *The Battle Stalin Lost: Memoirs of Yugoslavia 1948–1953* (New York: Viking Press, 1970), pp. 183, 185.

7. Compare Jiri Valenta, "Eurocommunism and Eastern Europe," *Problems of Communism* (March-April 1978), p. 42. This conceptualization is based on Vernon Asaturian's definition of Eurocommunism given in chapter one.

8. See Robert A. Scalapino, *The Japanese Communist Movement, 1920–1966* (Berkeley: University of California Press, 1967), pp. 60–62.

9. Ibid., p. 63.

10. Cited in Donald S. Zagoria, "Some Comparisons between the Russian and Chinese Models," in A. Doak Barnett, ed., *Communist Strategies in Asia* (New York: Praeger, 1963), p. 17.

11. Lu Ting-yi, "The World Significance of the Chinese Democratic United Front," *Current Background* (Hong Kong), no. 89 (July 5, 1951).

12. To cite a few examples: Donald S. Zagoria, *The Sino-Soviet Conflict 1956–1961* (Princeton: Princeton University Press, 1962); William E. Griffith, *The Sino-Soviet Rift* (Cambridge: MIT Press, 1964); Richard Lowenthal, *World Communism—The Disintegration of a Secular Faith* (New York, 1964); Klaus Mehnert, *Peking and Moscow* (New York: Frederick A. Praeger, 1963); and Harold Hinton, *The Bear at the Gate* (Washington: American Enterprise Institute for Public Policy Research, 1971).

13. Zagoria, *The Sino-Soviet Conflict*, p. 147.

14. Quoted in Mehnert, *Peking and Moscow*, p. 35.

15. A. Doak Barnett, "Peking and the Asian Power Balance," *Problems of Communism* (July-August 1976), p. 38.

16. Other pro-Chinese publications in Europe included *Die Rote Fahne* (Austria), *Vanguard* (Great Britain), *Bulletin d'Information Marxiste-Léniniste* (France), *Rode Vlag* (Holland), *Nuova Unità* (Italy), and *Mundo Obrero Revolucionario* (Spain).

17. Kevin Devlin, "Schism and Secession," *Survey*, no. 54 (January 1965), p. 38. In early 1968 Peking abandoned Grippa's BCP and transferred its moral and material support to another splinter group, the Marxist-Leninist Communist party of Belgium as Grippa came out in support of Liu Shao-ch'i. See Joseph C. Kun, "Peking and World Communism," *Problems of Communism* (November-December 1974), p. 40.

18. Devlin, "Schism and Secession," p. 40.

19. Quoted in *Pravda*, June 30, 1964. Devlin, "Schism and Secession," p. 41.

20. My incomplete list has more than forty pro-Peking factional groups or secessionist parties, which include Spanish Workers' Revolutionary organization, Spanish Communist party CP (M-L), Marxist-Leninist Communist Party of France, Italian Marxist-Leninist Communist party, and the Communist party of Portugal (M-L).

21. Scalapino, *Japanese Communist Movement*, pp. 171, 303.

22. *New China News Agency*, September 12, 1964.

23. *Pravda*, September 12, 1964.

24. For Palmiro Togliatti's "testament," see Dan N. Jacobs, *From Marx to Mao and Marchais: Documents on the Development of Communist Variations* (New York: Longman, 1979), pp. 231–250.

25. Foreign Broadcast Information Service (FBIS), *Daily Report, USSR*, August 15, 1978, p. D 2.

26. For a detailed account of this point, see Kun, "Peking and World Communism," pp. 41–43.

27. "A Powerful Weapon to Unite People and Defeat Enemies," *Hungch'i*, no. 9 (August 2, 1971), p. 13.

28. The Chinese view of the role of Western Europe in China's global policy was expressed through many talks between Chinese leaders (including Mao and Chou En-lai) and visiting West European dignitaries during 1972–

1974, and incorporated into a new ideological formulation on China's global diplomacy—known as the "tripartite world" theory—which was presented to the world by Teng Hsiao-ping in a speech to the United Nations. See *Peking Review*, no. 16 (April 19, 1974).

29. *People's Daily*, September 12, 1973.

30. *Peking Review*, nos. 35–36 (September 7, 1973). The remark was made by Chou En-lai.

31. C. L. Sulzberger, "From China with Love," *New York Times*, February 4, 1973.

32. In 1977, for example, the total volume of trade between China and Western Europe (including Spain, Portugal, Greece, and Malta) was 2,395 million dollars, while between China and Japan it was 3,509 million dollars; in 1976, the former was 2,675 million dollars and the latter was 3,052 million dollars. Central Intelligence Agency, National Foreign Assessment Center, *China: International Trade, 1977–78* (Washington, 1978).

33. Valenta, "Eurocommunism and Eastern Europe," p. 42.

34. Eusebio M. Mujal-Leon, "Spanish Communism in the 1970's," *Problems of Communism* (March-April 1975), p. 49.

35. This is indicated by a *New China News Agency* dispatch of November 17, 1971, which reported that Keng Piao received the PCE delegation and had "a frank conversation" in which the two sides "expressed their respective stands and views"—a Chinese formula reflecting dissension. The report is quoted in Kun, "Peking and World Communism," p. 41.

36. Kevin Devlin, "The Challenge of Eurocommunism," *Problems of Communism* (January-February 1977), p. 19.

37. Up to 1977, the CCP had openly associated with the PCE (M-L), the Labor Party of Spain, and the Spanish Workers' Revolutionary Organization and reported their activities in the Chinese media.

38. *Morning Star*, October 24, 1977.

39. Likewise, Peking has not reconciled relations with the JCP, which has increasingly taken on the characteristics of Eurocommunist parties. As with Europe, Peking stressed state-to-state relations with Japan; it values highly good ties with the "capitalist powerholders" and favors a strong American-Japanese defense relationship, in sharp contrast to the stand taken by the JCP.

40. Dick Wilson, "China and the European Community," *China Quarterly*, no. 56 (October-December 1973), p. 654.

41. Devlin, "Challenge of Eurocommunism," p. 19.

42. See Chi Hsin [pen name of a Communist writing group], "Whither the Eurocommunist Parties?" *The Seventies*, no. 79 (August 1976), pp. 59–63, and Edith Lenart, "Silence From An Interested Party," *Far Eastern Economic Review* (August 27, 1976), pp. 10–11.

43. David Bonavia, "Peking's Warsaw Wedge," *Far Eastern Economic Review* (August 27, 1976), p. 11.

44. Devlin, "Challenge of Eurocommunism," p. 20.

45. FBIS, *Daily Report, People's Republic of China*, January 12, 1978, p. A.

46. See, for example, "Report from Yugoslavia: The Podravka Agro-Industrial Complex," *Peking Review*, no. 9 (March 3, 1978), pp. 25–27; "A Visit to the Sarajevo Energoinvest," ibid., no. 12 (March 24, 1978), pp.

41–42; and "Yugoslavia: Achievements in Socialist Construction," ibid., no. 35 (September 1, 1978), pp. 15, 25.

47. Paul W. Dahlquist, "The Politics of Balance in Tito's Yugoslavia," (M.A. Thesis, Naval Postgraduate School, 1979), pp. 236–37.

48. Ibid., especially the section on "The China Card" in ch. 5.

49. Compare Vernon Aspaturian, "Has Eastern Europe Become a Liability to the Soviet Union?" in Charles Gati, ed., *The International Politics of Eastern Europe* (New York: Praeger Publishers, 1976), p. 21.

50. Dessa Trevisan, "Harsh Albanian Attack Signals the End of Special Link with China," *Times* (London), July 9, 1977.

51. "Quarterly Chronicle and Documentation," *China Quarterly*, no. 72 (December 1977), p. 898.

52. Alain Jacob, "Peking Seems to be Softening its Attitude toward Western Communist Parties," *Le Monde*, October 4, 1978, as translated in FBIS, *Daily Report, People's Republic of China*, October 6, 1978, p. A 11.

53. Ibid.

54. Ibid.

55. On October 10, 1978, New China News Agency reported from Paris that Juquet has just returned from a trip to Cambodia and quoted in length his attack on Vietnamese design to invade Cambodia. Other reports on the French Marxist-Leninist Communist party can be found in *Peking Review*, no. 1 (January 6, 1978), p. 4; no. 8 (February 24, 1978), p. 28; and no. 14 (April 17, 1978), p. 22.

56. On the Italian Unified Communist party, see ibid., No. 31 (August 4, 1978), p. 23; on the Party of Socialist Revolution of Italy, see ibid., no. 23 (June 9, 1978), p. 24; on the Spanish Workers' Revolutionary Organization, see ibid., no. 1 (January 6, 1978), p. 28; no. 13 (March 31, 1978), p. 22; no. 31 (August 4, 1978), p. 21; and no. 38 (September 24, 1978), p. 24.

57. *Times* (London), May 27, 1978.

58. *People's Daily*, November 23, 1979.

59. My interview with a Chinese official on Soviet affairs in Peking on December 26, 1979.

60. Whereas Italian and Spanish Communists have strongly condemned the Soviet invasion of Afghanistan, the French Communists have come out in support of the Russian action, declaring the Soviet invasion as perfectly justified because of Afghanistan's sovereign right to call on its allies to fight against "foreign elements." See the dispatch by Edward Girardet, *Christian Science Monitor*, January 8, 1980.

CHAPTER XV

Japan: Euro-Nippo-Communism

Peter Berton

In a recent Japanese election campaign, four women representing the major political parties were discussing the issues on a television panel. All of them except one were dressed in customary Western-style clothes. The only one who wore the traditional kimono was a representative of the Japanese Communist party (JCP). This use of the symbol of traditional Japan is typical of the JCP's conscious effort to change the party's image of an essentially alien and violent group. Without such a change the JCP stands no chance of becoming a viable political force in present-day democratic Japan.

Introduction

After its founding in 1922, the Communist party was seen in Japan as a small, illegal, alien, conspiratorial, and violent group that took its orders from Moscow and that was bent on destroying traditional Japanese institutions and values. One might argue, of course, that the political environment in prewar Japan, especially during the domination of the military in the 1930s, was hardly conducive to meaningful political change even by peaceful, parliamentary methods. But the fact remains that the JCP was a small conspiratorial revolutionary group hounded by an efficient police apparatus. By the eve of Japan's defeat in 1945, the party had long ceased to function. Most of its supporters had either recanted and defected, or had rotted in jail; a few escaped persecution by fleeing abroad.[1]

How did the party operate in the postwar period, when Japan emerged as one of the world's most advanced industrial countries and a stable parliamentary democracy? The record is mixed. The JCP went through several stages before it embarked on a not always successful campaign to create the image of an independent, nationalist party that accepts the parliamentary road to power. These policies sound remarkably like those pursued by the Eurocommunist parties in Western Europe. Indeed, a Soviet analyst has objected to the term "Eurocommunism" as too narrow, specifically listing Japan as an advanced capitalist country outside Europe.[2]

What is, then, the putative relationship between the evolution of "Eurocommunist" ideas in Western Europe and in Japan? What are the linkages between the JCP and the Eurocommunist parties? This chapter will explore the evolution of the present line of the JCP, including its electoral record, and the party's relations with the Soviet Union and the Eurocommunist parties. The final section will analyze the metamorphosis of the JCP with particular reference to the impact of West European Eurocommunism.

If Eurocommunism connotes primarily a commitment to compete in the host country's parliamentary system, then the JCP started on the "Eurocommunist" path in 1946, when prewar leaders who returned from exile or were freed from jail by the Americans began to transform their small conspiratorial group into a "lovable" Communist party ostensibly committed to peaceful competition in the postwar Japanese democratic environment created by the occupation and bolstered by the new constitution. But the JCP was not very popular despite its impeccable record of opposition to Japanese militarism and the war. Its greatest electoral success came in 1949, when it attracted 3 million votes (about 10 percent of the total cast) and captured 35 seats in the 466-member lower house.

What of that characteristic of Eurocommunist parties that favors independent policies and refuses to acknowledge the existence of a Communist center whose directives are binding on all parties? The first postwar JCP experiment with parliamentarism came during a period when a number of Communist parties (especially in Asia) were engaged in violent tactics and when the Soviet line was being harshly enunciated by Andrey Zhdanov as the "theory of two camps." So in a sense the JCP was pursuing an independent policy. But was it prepared to defy a direct order from Moscow? While their circumstances are not at all analogous, Josip Tito and the Yugoslav Communists said no. The Japanese Communists backed down.

In January 1950, shortly after the JCP achieved its greatest electoral success, the Cominform issued a blistering attack against the party's peaceful parliamentary tactics, urging it to adopt a radical line at all costs. The Soviet leadership had its own reasons for insisting on this policy change, which ignored the real interests of the JCP. The Japanese leaders accepted the Moscow *diktat* (seconded and reinforced by Peking). After the outbreak of the Korean War, it reverted to sabotage and illegal underground activity. The JCP was back in the fold, its premature "Eurocommunist" experiment at an end.

The JCP paid dearly for following foreign advice. Not only were the top party leaders purged by the occupation authorities, but the damage to the image of the party among the Japanese voting public was immediate and catastrophic. In the next general election in 1952, the JCP lost all 35 of its seats in the National Diet. Although this violent period in the history of the JCP was short (Stalin died soon after, and the Korean conflict came to an end), it took the party ten years to get back on an independent track and over twenty years (1972) before it could again garner 10 percent of the vote and win three dozen seats in the lower house.

The Miyamoto Line: Toward a Growing Convergence with Eurocommunism?

Since the mid-1950s the JCP's development and policies have borne the imprint of its undisputed leader—Miyamoto Kenji,[3] seventy years old in 1979. A graduate of Tokyo Imperial University, the most prestigious institution of higher learning in Japan, he was a prominent literary critic in his twenties and, along with his famous late wife Yuriko, a noted member of the "Proletarian School" of literature. Miyamoto picked up the pieces in the aftermath of the radical-line debacle. He steered party fortunes through consolidation and the establishment of "a new people's democratic revolutionary policy," which led to rapid growth in JCP membership, electoral successes, attempts to form united fronts with other opposition parties, and an independent stance in the international Communist movement.

Veteran leader eighty-six-year-old Nosaka Sanzo, originator of the "lovable" party tactics, cooperated as party chairman with Miyamoto, the secretary general, and came to play an increasingly ceremonial role. A charter member of the British Communist party, Nosaka spent many years in exile in the 1930s and 1940s: first at the Comintern headquarters in Moscow as the Japanese delegate, and then in Yenan with Mao Tse-tung trying to indoctrinate Japanese prisoners of war. A prison mate of Miyamoto's, Moscow-trained Hakamada Satomi (seventy-five years old), served for many years as vice-chairman of the Standing Committee of the Presidium until his expulsion from the JCP in 1978. But over the past decade Miyamoto's closest assistants have been the Ueda brothers: Ueda Koichiro (fifty-two years old) and his younger brother Fuwa Tetsuzo (born Ueda Kenjiro), both graduates of the elitist Tokyo University. Fuwa (forty-nine years old), for many years director of the Party Secretariat, is also acting chairman of the Presidium. A bright organizer with a theoretical bent who has spent his entire life in the party, Fuwa is the author of many JCP documents that try to refurbish Marxist-Leninist theory by making it palatable to the Japanese electorate. Recently he has turned his attention to relations with the Eurocommunist parties. The party is fortunate to have vigorous younger men among its top leaders. With Fuwa as anointed crown prince, the JCP is likely to continue its soft line after Miyamoto's departure.

The dramatic growth of party membership is one measure of Miyamoto's organizing skill. From 20,000 members in 1955 (down from some 100,000 in the late 1940s before the Cominform criticism and radicalization), the JCP grew to 150,000 members in 1963 and about 300,000 in 1966. Membership dropped in the wake of the quarrel with China, then rose much more slowly, tapering off at a little less than 400,000.[4] This figure is more than the membership of all other Japanese opposition parties combined, making the JCP the third largest non-ruling Communist party in the world.

Another measure of party growth is the circulation of its various publications—its financial lifeline. The JCP derives over 90 percent of its budget of over $50 million from the sale of newspapers, periodicals, and books (membership dues constitute only 5 percent). The party organ *Akahata* (Red Flag) comes out in daily and Sunday editions. While JCP claims should probably be discounted, the circulation of the daily is reported to have risen in the past ten years from 300,000 to 700,000, and that of the Sunday edition from one to two-and-a-half million, surpassing the circulation of the newspaper of any other non-ruling Communist party. In fact, Miyamoto bragged that his colleagues in the French Communist party (PCF) and the Italian Communist party (PCI) were astounded when they learned about the three million *Akahata* readership.[5] The party goal is four million readers and half a million members.

Electoral Record. The most important elections in Japan are those for the 511 seats in the House of Representatives, the lower but more powerful house of the National Diet. In the last five elections to the lower house (1963 to December 1976), the total vote for JCP candidates rose steadily from 1.6 million (or 4 percent of the total votes) in 1963 to 5.5 million (10.5 percent) in 1972 and to 5.9 million (10.4 percent) in 1976. The number of Communist Dietmen in the same five elections rose from 5 (1 percent) in 1963 to 14 (almost 3 percent) in 1969 and to 38 (7.7 percent) in 1972, falling to 17 (3.3 percent) in 1976. Thus while the total JCP vote continued to rise, and the JCP percentage of the total vote showed only a one-tenth of 1 percent drop from 1972 to 1976, the JCP lower house contingent was more than halved from 38 to 17.[6]

Although elections to the upper house are less important than those to the House of Representatives, a similar trend is evident. In the 1968 House of Councillors elections, the JCP elected 7 members (out of 250), increased its delegation to 10 in the 1971 elections (the figure rose to 11 through a by-election victory in 1973), doubled its number of seats to 20 in 1974, and fell to 16 in July 1977.

The JCP has also vigorously contested elections at the subnational level: (1) elections of prefectural governors and mayors of cities, towns, and villages, and (2) elections to prefectural, municipal, and village assemblies.

Party history was made in 1967 when a Communist was elected mayor of Shiokiri in Nagano Prefecture, but in general the JCP has participated in broad left-wing coalitions to elect "progressives" as governors or mayors of the major cities, the election of Governor Minobe of Tokyo in 1967 being the most important. In subsequent years all six of the largest cities came under non-conservative control. But as the "progressives" became intrenched in city government, the united front of the opposition parties collapsed; some elections became three-cornered affairs with one conservative and two "progressive" candidates. Thus, in the past decade the JCP backed some candidates in an election alliance with other opposition parties, and some candidates alone. In 1974 and 1975 it succeeded in electing the governors of Kyoto and Osaka against two other candidates in each case. In April 1978, however, the party lost the Kyoto and Yokohama elections, and in April 1979 Tokyo and Osaka. The tide has clearly turned against the JCP and other opposition parties.[7]

Communist representation in local assemblies rose from 700 in 1960 to 1,700 in 1970 and to over 3,000 (out of 70,000 seats) in recent elections. In a number of key areas, like the Tokyo Municipal Assembly, however, the JCP representation rose in three consecutive elections, but, paralleling the national trend, dropped by half in 1977.

Evolution of Policy. How does one characterize Miyamoto's policies in the post-radical period, 1955 to the present (1979)? Were they influenced by the Soviet, Chinese, Eurocommunist, or other models? Have they changed over time? And if so, what factors were responsible—domestic, external, or intra-Communist?

Overall, Miyamoto's policies can be characterized as a continuous soft line when compared with the hard, radical line of the prewar and 1950–1955 periods. But during the past twenty years or so, one notices an evolution from an almost grudging acceptance of parliamentary tactics to an appreciation of the transformation of postwar, especially post-occupation, Japan into an advanced industrial (in many respects even post-industrial) democratic society, where neither the Soviet nor the Chinese but only the Eurocommunist model has any relevance.

For convenience let us consider the evolution of the Miyamoto line over three periods: (1) 1955–1961, consolidation of power and rejection of Togliatti's structural reform theories; (2) 1961–1968, growth, rejection of the Soviet and Chinese models, and declaration of independence; and (3) 1968 to the present (1979), nationalism and growing convergence with Eurocommunism.

Consolidation, 1955–1961. This was a complex and controversial period in JCP history. A number of young cadres returned from their refuge in Peking and the Party emerged from its radical episode with two competing factions. Eventually Miyamoto switched from the "Internationalist" to the "Mainstream" faction in a successful bid to become secretary general. But the JCP was not the only party in turmoil. The international Communist movement itself was undergoing a metamorphosis that began with Nikita Khrushchev's de-Stalinization speech at the Twentieth Congress of the CPSU in early 1956. This was followed by Palmiro Togliatti's "polycentrism" and structural reform theories, the Polish and Hungarian revolts, further Yugoslav shifts to the right—all leading to the break between Moscow and Peking which shook up the entire movement.

The JCP was much affected by the epochal changes in international Communism. Many Communists and socialists alike were attracted to Togliatti's position. Others saw the principal enemy in "U.S. imperialism"; they believed in a kind of "national liberation" on the Chinese model with at least the option of violent action, although most agreed that under present Japanese circumstances a radical, violent line was counterproductive. These personal rivalries, factional struggles, and foreign influences were resolved after a fashion at the Eighth JCP Congress in July 1961 with the expulsion of the advocates of structural reform and the victory of Miyamoto and his allies.[8] West European ideas were thus rebuffed and "U.S. imperialism" (along with Japanese monopoly capitalism) was proclaimed as the principal enemy (clearly a Chinese position in opposition to Soviet "peaceful coexistence" and détente). At the same time, the party cautiously returned to the peaceful parliamentary tactics of Nosaka's "lovable" party, advocating a "united national democratic front" in a National Diet considered to be an important "tool" of the people. In the international Communist arena, the JCP, although clearly sympathetic with the Chinese position, was hewing cautiously to a neutral line and endorsing the ambiguous 1960 Moscow Statement, while enshrining in the party program "the camp of socialism headed by the USSR."

Rejection of the Soviet and Chinese models, 1961–1968. This was a traumatic period for the JCP leadership, who first had to take sides and then had to break umbilical ties both to Moscow and to Peking. It was also a period of mass expulsions and threats posed to the party by splinter groups favoring the CPSU and the Chinese Communist party (CCP). It is a measure of Miyamoto's political talent that he kept the party together, while presiding over the period of its greatest growth in membership, which toward the end of the period translated itself into dramatic gains at the polls. Two JCP congresses, in 1964 and 1966, consolidated Miyamoto's power, reiterated the policy of pursuing peaceful parliamentary tactics, and proclaimed the party's independence from outside influence and control. At the same time, *Akahata* reprinted Chinese articles on people's war and violent revolution, including Lin Piao's famous 1965 manifesto; the violent revolutionary formula was considered unacceptable only "under present circumstances." The JCP's relations during this period were heavily tilted toward Asian Communist parties, with very few personal ties to the parties of Western Europe.

Nationalism and the Eurocommunist Model, 1968 to the Present (1979). The Soviet invasion of Czechoslovakia graphically demonstrated to the JCP leadership the need to emulate the PCI in drawing away from the Soviet Union and in pursuing a more peaceful, parliamentary road to power.

In July 1969 a member of the Standing Committee of the JCP Presidium declared that, if the party came to power, it would permit the free functioning of opposition parties, unless they resorted to unlawful means. This statement, made in an election year, may have been intended simply to improve the Party image, but the same criticism of one-party dictatorship showed up the following year in an official party program submitted to the Eleventh JCP Congress. (To create an image of an "open" party, the congress for the first time was thrown open to the public and the press.)[9] In its next two congresses, in 1973 and 1976, the JCP continued to advance its autonomy and independence on the one hand, and its commitment to peaceful change on the other.

To stress the relevance for Japan of the West European model (and thus the irrelevance of the Soviet and Chinese models), the JCP, in commemoration of its fiftieth anniversary in July 1972, staged an International Conference on Theory devoted to the problems encountered by Communist parties in advanced capitalist countries. The Italian, French, Spanish, British, West German, and Australian parties sent delegates. The topics discussed included parliamentary and constitutional experiences; united front tactics; methods for making the transition from capitalism to socialism in a democratic setting, including structural reforms; and the question of terminology, such as the proper rendering of the term "dictatorship of the proletariat" in various languages.[10] In fact, at the Twelfth JCP Congress the following year, the JCP dropped the Japanese word *dokusai* (dictatorship) in favor of *shikken* (regency or exercise of power) in translating "dictatorship of the proletariat," and at the Thirteenth JCP Congress in July 1976 the "dictatorship of the proletariat" was dropped altogether in favor of "working class power."[11] "Marxism-Leninism" itself suffered the fate of "dictatorship of the proletariat." At the 1970 Eleventh JCP Congress, rules were amended to make Marxism-Leninism only a "theoretical basis" and not a "guide to action."[12] The term was given the *coup de grâce* six years later at the Thirteenth JCP Congress when references to Marxism-Leninism were either eliminated completely or replaced by "scientific socialism" in the party's program and constitution. The Central Committee tried to explain that, while the terms were essentially synonymous, it was almost a century since Marx and Engels were active and more than half a century since the death of Lenin, and therefore that "scientific socialism" comprised more than just the theories of Marx, Engels, and Lenin. Furthermore, aware that Marx and Engels were less controversial in Japan than Lenin, the party cleverly dissociated itself from the latter (and in the process from Russia and by implication from China), at the same time stressing Japan's position as an advanced industrial country:

> In particular, the name of Marxism-Leninism greatly reflects the theoretical development by Lenin, who applied this doctrine to the reality at that time to make the first socialist revolution successful in Russia and who led the early activities of the Comintern. In our country, however, it should be taken into consideration that a creative development of scientific socialism is being searched for as the revolutionary movement in a highly developed capitalist country under historical conditions different from the revolutionary movement at the time when Lenin was active and developed his theory.[13]

Repeated declarations of independence by the JCP were formalized officially in 1973 at the Twelfth JCP Congress by amending the basic party program of 1961 to eliminate the reference to the USSR in the phrase "the camp of socialism *headed by the USSR*" [emphasis added]. The JCP also tried to dissociate itself from student violence by branding such activities as Trotskyist. Miyamoto even declared that violence, along with sex, drugs, and gambling, was one of the "four sins."[14]

Along with eliminating this or that offending term, the JCP sought to promote the image of a party devoted to the preservation and expansion of freedoms in Japan. This was necessary partly to erase the totalitarian image of Communism and partly to counteract the Liberal Democratic party (LDP) slogan of "Defend the Free Society." In a June 1974 speech supporting JCP candidates for the upcoming House of Councillors election in Hokkaido, Miyamoto said that, "in contrast to the LDP, however, we think of the question of freedom more seriously and more extensively," and went on to outline three freedoms: the freedom of existence, civil-political freedom, and the freedom of the nation.[15] A member of the Presidium took special pains to say that religion was not an "opiate" but a comfort to people in trouble.[16]

In the spring of 1976, Fuwa published a nine-part essay on "Scientific Socialism and the Question of Dictatura—A study of Marx and Engels" in which he stressed "the institutions of a democratic state, with the Diet as an organ of supreme authority of the country in name and reality" (previously the Diet was termed only a "tool" of the people). He went on at great length to spell out "the plural party system to guarantee the freedom of activities to every political party," the "system of the change of power by elections," and a host of freedoms using such terms as "guarantee," "total guarantee," and "perfect guarantee."[17]

Fuwa's essay was followed by a draft of the far-reaching "Manifesto of Freedom and Democracy," which was adopted and published at the Ninth Central Committee Plenum on June 2, 1976. After a period of intense party discussion, the document was officially adopted on July 30 at the Thirteenth Extraordinary Party Congress. The Manifesto consists of four sections: "Deteriorating Crisis of Freedom and Democracy," "Japanese Democracy, Past and Present," "Question of Scientific Socialism and Freedom," and "For Established, Developed and Flourishing Freedom and Democracy." It mentions approvingly the American Declaration of Independence and the French Declaration of the Rights of Man. The third section ends with this eloquent declaration of JCP independence:

> The Communist Party of Japan reiterates that it will make no model of the experiences of any foreign countries, such as the Soviet Union and the People's Republic of China. As a consistent defender of freedom and democracy of the people, it will correctly inherit the original stand of scientific socialism; it will seek a creative development of socialism under the condition of a highly developed capitalist country, Japan; and it will continue to pursue a unique way to an independent democratic Japan and a socialist Japan, hand in hand with the people.[18]

Publication of Fuwa's essay and the Manifesto followed the Berlinguer-Marchais summit in November 1975 (given much publicity and approval in the Japanese Communist press), the Twenty-second French Communist party (PCF) Congress in February 1976, where the PCF discarded the term "dictatorship of the proletariat," and the visits to Tokyo of Santiago Carrillo and Georges Marchais in March and April 1976. This raises the question of whether the JCP was influenced in its policies by the Eurocommunist parties. While it is impossible to discount the impact of these events, the more proximate cause was probably the desperate need on the part of the JCP to stem the deterioration of its own domestic position in anticipation of general elections. The party was dealt a big blow in the press and in the Diet by the official reopening of the "lynching case"—the accusation that back in the 1930s Miyamoto had taken part in the murder of a JCP member who was thought to be a police spy.[19] If Miyamoto was guilty of murder, he had been serving time before and during World War II as an ordinary criminal and not as a political prisoner eligible to be released by order of the American occupation. This bad publicity was obviously not helpful to the JCP in an election year.

The elections to the lower house in December 1976 and to the upper house in July 1977 reversed the upward trend of JCP representation, and halved the party's delegation in the National Diet. Space limitations preclude a detailing here of reasons for the party's electoral successes in the late 1960s and early 1970s, and for the more recent reverses,[20] but a few major factors should be mentioned. The adoption of an independent, nationalist, and Eurocommunist line after 1968 has helped the party to grow and, more important, to capture a segment of the floating and protest votes. The JCP has also been effective on the local level—especially in urban areas—in helping citizens to cope with the complexities of daily living and to deal with local authorities.[21]

Paradoxically, the very success of the JCP has sown the seeds for subsequent failure. So long as the JCP was an insignificant political force, it attracted the floating and protest votes and competed with other opposition parties for votes on the left. But as soon as it was perceived as a potential force (it emerged in 1972 as the second largest opposition party in the lower house, and for a while it *was* the largest opposition party in the Tokyo Municipal Assembly), uncommitted voters became more careful about casting their vote and the other opposition parties often made agreements not to split the anti-JCP vote on the left.

The inability of the JCP to promote and become a member of a united front of all so-called "progressive" opposition parties is another factor in the party's weakness. (In this area the JCP would like to emulate the success of the PCF.) Its failure is not for lack of trying. Indeed, at every recent party congress, considerable attention has been paid to the concept of a "progressive united front," especially with the Socialist party and a future "democratic coalition government."[22]

Yet another important factor in the JCP's recent electoral reverses is the move of the Democratic Socialist party and the Komeito to the center, accompanied by a similar trend on the part of the Japanese voting public. (Public opinion polls for the last two decades have consistently shown that larger and larger segments of the Japanese people consider themselves part of the middle class, the latest figure being around 90 percent.) This trend erodes the traditional support of the "progressive" parties, especially those, like the JCP, perceived to be on the extreme left.

While the JCP's strident defense of democracy and freedom was largely a reaction to domestic developments and the growing "Communist allergy" of the Japanese public, it has fed suspicions about the party's motives.[23] This "Communist allergy," coupled with attacks by the mass media in recent years, has forced the JCP to the defensive. In fact, its fourteenth congress in October 1977 concerned itself with the "anti-Communist counteroffensive," and the Fifth Central Committee Plenum in September 1978 likewise stressed the need to fight "against various kinds of anti-Communist poison."[24]

Recent public opinion polls substantiate the low popularity of the JCP and the erosion of its support in the past two years. One such monthly poll shows that support for the JCP has fluctuated over the past four years between 0.9 and 3.13 percent (somewhat comparable to the range for the Democratic Socialist party of 1.1 to 3.4 percent, and a little less than the Komeito range of 2.6 to 4.9 percent); support for the Socialist party varied from 8 to 12 percent, and for the Liberal-Democratic party from 22 to 33 percent. (It is significant that people who support no political party constitute upward of one-quarter of those polled, reaching over 36 percent in late 1978.) Although support for the JCP in 1975 and 1976 fluctuated from 1.6 to 3.1 percent, it was down in 1977 to between 1.3 and 2.7 percent, and in 1978 it fluctuated between 0.9 and 2.3 percent.[25]

It is probable that media attacks on the JCP have been effective in turning the Japanese electorate further away from the party. In 1976 attention centered on the validity of the party's commitment to democracy and on Miyamoto personally.[26] These points were underscored by the latest and potentially the most damaging party purge — the expulsion of Hakamada Satomi, vice-chairman of the Standing

Committee of the Presidium and Miyamoto's erstwhile right-hand man. Hakamada openly characterized Miyamoto's rule in the JCP as "despotic," and directly linked him to the "lynching" case to which Hakamada was a witness.[27] Furthermore, even the JCP membership does not evaluate the leadership of the party very highly.[28]

Aside from launching a counteroffensive against anti-Communist forces, how did the party react to these electoral setbacks? One measure was the revamping of study texts for all levels of membership. For several years the party deemphasized Marx, Engels, and other Communist classics and stressed indigenous JCP documents. The Fourteenth JCP Congress in October 1977 went even further. The list for new members now contains only JCP documents, and only the highest listed level contains a substantial number of non-Japanese materials (about one-third).[29] Significantly, these materials omit the writings of Mao Tse-tung, Stalin, Tito, Fidel Castro, and even Togliatti. The JCP is stressing its Japanese heritage, but its borrowings betray its real policy of favoring Lenin over Togliatti. Two quotations, one from a Japanese and the other from an American analyst of the JCP, sum up the matter: The JCP under Miyamoto can be characterized as following a "structural reform line without structural reform theory," and as pursuing "iron discipline" with a "smiling image."

Relations with the Soviet Union

Relations with Moscow are of primary concern to all Communist parties. As an Asian party, however, the JCP has also been heavily influenced by Peking. It was, therefore, natural that the Japanese party would be affected by disagreements between the CPSU and the CCP; and in the late 1950s Miyamoto and his allies, like the leaders of many Communist parties, were dismayed by the emerging dispute between the two Communist giants. The first reaction was to keep the dispute quiet, minimize its seriousness, and hope for an early reconciliation. (The JCP was not, however, one of the several ruling and nonruling parties that tried mediation.) When the split degenerated into open polemics in 1963, the JCP along with several Asian parties, including the North Korean and North Vietnamese, swung to the Chinese side.

One issue in Sino-Soviet dispute was particularly decisive for the JCP: the signing by the Soviet Union of the partial nuclear test-ban treaty with the United States and Great Britain in August 1963. This move was bitterly opposed by China, which was still a year away from developing its atomic bomb, a weapon that under the terms of the new treaty could not be tested in the atmosphere. The issue produced a split in the JCP leadership; one of the top leaders, Shiga Yoshio, as a member of the National Diet voted for the treaty in defiance of party instructions. He took Moscow's side in the dispute against Peking, which on this issue had the support of most of the JCP leadership. (Many pro-Soviet JCP leaders had been purged in 1961.)

Of course, this was not the only issue between the JCP and the CPSU. In its opposition to "U.S. imperialism" the JCP was closer to the Chinese view on the broader questions of peace and peaceful coexistence. The titles of sections in the JCP definitive statement "On the Intrinsic Nature of N. S. Khrushchev's Peaceful Co-existence Line" give an idea of the scope of its criticism of the CPSU: (1) "Who have praised N. S. Khrushchev?"; (2) "Capitulationism which has submitted to nuclear threat"; (3) "Peaceful co-existence substituted by following in the wake of the United States"; and (4) "Illusion about 'peaceful' imperialism."[30]

Bilateral talks in Moscow in March 1964 between Leonid Brezhnev and Moscow-trained Hakamada failed to resolve the differences between the two parties. Shortly thereafter Shiga and his pro-Moscow followers were expelled from the party, whereupon they formed a rival organization called the Japanese Communist party—The Voice of Japan (Nihon Kyosanto—Nihon no Koe). Subsequent Soviet support of this group, as well as of other anti-JCP splinter organizations in the student and anti-nuclear weapons movements—and even, comically, of a rival Japanese-Soviet friendship society—became a thorny issue between the JCP and the CPSU that has contributed over the years to the estrangement of the two parties.[31] The Ninth JCP Congress in November 1964 formally endorsed a basically anti-Soviet, pro-China line.

After the break with the CPSU, the JCP refused to take part in the preparatory conferences for a summit of Communist parties (eventually held in June 1969), which Moscow desperately tried to convene in order to isolate and condemn Peking and to retain control of the international Communist movement.[32] For the next fifteen years relations between the two parties fluctuated from none at all to mutual attempts at reconciliation.

One measure of the climate of relations between Communist parties is attendance and speeches made at party congresses and other important congregations, such as anniversaries of coming to power. The JCP, under Chinese pressure, refused to send a delegation to the Twenty-third Congress of the CPSU held in March 1966. After some preliminary negotiations in Moscow, two JCP delegates attended the Twenty-fourth CPSU Congress held in 1971, but no one represented the JCP at the Twenty-fifth Congress of the CPSU in 1976. Correspondingly, no Soviet delegates were present at any of the JCP congresses from the tenth in 1966 through the fourteenth, held in 1977. The Soviet Ambassador in Tokyo, Oleg Troyanovsky, however, was invited to attend the celebration of the JCP's fiftieth anniversary in July 1972, and Ambassador Dimitry Polyansky attended the fifty-fifth anniversary celebrations in 1977.[33]

Another measure of the climate of JCP-CPSU relations is Soviet attendance at annual meetings of the JCP-supported Japan Council against Atomic and Hydrogen Bombs (Gensuikyo), which are held in August to commemorate the atomic bombings of Hiroshima and Nagasaki. A related measure is Soviet attendance at the rival Congress for the Prohibition of Atomic and Hydrogen Bombs (Gensuikin), which split off from the older Gensuikyo in 1965 over the nuclear testing issue and which was founded and controlled by the Japanese Socialist party (JSP). As the JCP leaned toward Peking or insisted on an independent line, the Soviet Union moved toward the Socialist party and its affiliated organizations. In 1966, for example, many Soviet and East European delegates attended the Socialist-backed Gensuikin convention. In 1967, in an attempt to reconcile with the JCP, the Soviets sent delegates to neither congress, and in 1968 they attempted to send delegates to both. When the JCP leadership in Gensuikyo protested in the latter case, the Soviets withdrew from both meetings. Of course, Soviet support of the Socialist party introduces a foreign element in JCP-JSP rivalry. While Soviet support of the JCP potentially weakens the Communists, it also indirectly strengthens their image as an independent party.

The past dozen years have seen several attempts to normalize JCP-CPSU relations, including Miyamoto's meetings with Suslov in Tokyo in January 1968 and with Suslov and Brezhnev in Moscow in September 1971. By and large the initiatives for reconciliation came from the CPSU. Examples are the 1968 attempts by the Soviets to talk the JCP into attending the planned Moscow summit of Communist parties, which the Japanese eventually boycotted, and in March 1971 to send delegates to the Twenty-fourth CPSU Congress, which the Japanese attended.[34]

An analysis of the issues between the parties shows a significant shift away from JCP criticism of the CPSU's ideology and its attempts to dominate the international Communist movement and to interfere in the internal affairs of other Communist parties (including support of pro-Moscow splinter groups). At the same time, criticism of the Soviet Union as a state and defense of Japan's national interest vis-à-vis the Soviet Union has grown. In all instances, however, the target of JCP criticism—whether the CPSU as a party or the USSR as a state—is accused of great-power chauvinism toward other parties or states.

The two major JCP criticisms of the Soviet Union as a state focus on the Soviet-inspired invasion of Czechoslovakia by the Warsaw Pact countries in 1968 and the expulsion of Aleksandr Solzhenitsyn in 1974. On both issues the JCP lined up with many of the West European parties. And, of course, an anti-Soviet stand was critically needed on the Japanese domestic political scene.

The JCP viewed the Prague Spring with great interest. In mid-July 1968 the party came out in support of Alexander Dubcek and against any intervention by other Communist countries. Yet when the Soviet invasion occurred a month later, the JCP, in contrast to most West European Communist parties, did not respond immediately. Four days later, however, the JCP officially condemned the intervention, and it has continued to criticize the Soviet Union for the action as well as for the subsequent "legitimation" of the occupation and the so-called Brezhnev Doctrine of limited sovereignty. Although the JCP also criticized the Czechoslovaks for revisionism, the outright condemnation of the Soviet action in Czechoslovakia abruptly ended the first attempt at reconciliation between the JCP and the CPSU since the break in 1964.

The Solzhenitsyn affair presented the JCP with two difficulties: (1) the conservative LDP and other parties seized on it in an election year as an example of the suppression of freedom not only in the Soviet Union, but also in Japan should the Communists come to power; and (2) in contrast to the invasion of Czechoslovakia, which was clearly an international event, the expulsion of Solzhenitsyn was an internal Soviet affair—thus the JCP would violate its long-held position that Communist parties should respect "non-interference in each others' internal affairs" if it criticized the Soviet Union for the action.

Nonetheless, complaining that reactionary forces took advantage of the Solzhenitsyn affair and "embarked on an anti-Communist propaganda campaign on a world wide scale," and placing special stress on the allegation that under socialism freedom of speech and expression would be lost, the JCP argued that "the Solzhenitsyn affair has thus become an international issue as well as an important domestic issue of our country."[35] Party spokesmen added that it "is a problem different in nature from the interference in internal affairs and the infringement upon the sovereignty of a foreign country . . . it is not a Soviet affair exclusively."[36]

Having thus established the Solzhenitsyn affair as fair game for criticism by the JCP, the party stated condescendingly that "the infringement upon democratic liberties and fundamental human rights during the Stalin era is indeed a well-known fact of history."[37] A member of the Standing Committee of the JCP Presidium noted that publication of Solzhenitsyn's literary works was not permitted inside the Soviet Union and that "we cannot but have serious concerns over this as a problem in which freedom of speech and expression is involved."[38] The JCP also sarcastically responded to "certain people overseas" who had alleged that the JCP had "joined in the current of 'anti-Sovietism' of reactionary forces" because *Akahata* had "failed to make reports about the Soviet people's 'indignation' at the literary works of Solzhenitsyn:"

> Nobody can believe that the reading public [in the Soviet Union] have had their indignation roused as they read the contents of Solzhenitsyn's works; for his literary works except for some earliest ones have not been published in the Soviet Union, to say nothing of his controversial latest piece, *The Gulag Archipelago*, and so the people of the Soviet Union have had no opportunity to read them.[39]

Having attacked the Soviet Union for its anti-democratic policies, the JCP tried to reassure the Japanese public that the party "has not acted as an apologist for the Soviet government" and that, should the JCP participate in a future government, "political democracy including freedom of speech and expression and plural-party system will genuinely flourish," and the JCP "shall not make a model of any particular phenomenon in the present socialist countries in this respect."[40] At a press conference on February 21, Miyamoto himself declared:

> In Japan there will be no such a way of doing things, never; besides, such a way of doing things is not an inevitable product or method of socialism and communism.[41]

Possibly connected with the strident JCP criticism of the Solzhenitsyn affair was the CPSU counterattack through the Communist party of Argentina, which published an article highly critical of the Twelfth JCP Congress (held in 1973) in the March 1974 issue of its official theoretical and political organ *Nueva Era*. This article was "reprinted" in the CPSU Central Committee journal "Party Life" (*Partiinaia zhizn*, No. 10, May 1974), but *Akahata* brought out some facts that pointed toward initial Russian authorship or sponsorship of the Argentine criticism.[42]

The JCP also joined the West European Communist parties in defense of Santiago Carrillo when his book *"Eurocommunism" and the State* was attacked in the June 24, 1977 issue of the Moscow *New*

Times. But the JCP was not among the parties that immediately dissented from Soviet opinion, precipitating the follow-up *New Times* article of July 8. In fact, the JCP published the relevant attacks and counterattacks in the August 1 issue of its documentary *Sekai seiji shiryo* (Documents on World Politics) and officially but belatedly commented in an article entitled "'Eurocommunism' and the Interventionist Attitude of the Soviet Union" in *Akahata* on August 30. The article factually presented Carrillo's arguments, questioned Soviet motives, and reiterated the party's basic position on autonomy, its own road to socialism, and Soviet interference in JCP affairs. Here are a few samples:

> In spite of Carrillo's clearly stated aims, the Soviet Union, in defiance of logic, set about finding "purposes" of their own invention and attributing them to Carrillo, putting up their own "aunt sallies" and then knocking them down. . . .
> This attack, which defies reason, seems very strange to everyone, and the bases of the attack are even stranger. To penetrating observers the Soviet accusations are without substance. . . .
> What, then, is the real purpose of the Soviets' groundless, arbitrary denunciation of Carrillo? The answer to this is easy. It claims that it, the Soviet Union, is "true, scientific communism." So it denounces and uses various pretexts to attack trends toward the independent search for revolutionary lines and perspectives that do not necessarily take the "Soviet" model as the pattern to be followed, opposing "rather widespread views" of the Communist parties in developed countries. . . . [43]

And, of course, the article maintains that no type of revolution made so far or development of socialism in any particular country can be a model for this.[44]

The JCP also seized upon the Soviet statement that "the Soviet Communist Party has not organized and does not organize any campaigns against any fraternal parties," offering proof of continuous Soviet intervention in the affairs of the Japanese party and CPSU support of the Shiga "anti-Party factionalist group."

The *Akahata* article closed with a ringing statement of JCP's independent position:

> As it has done in the past, the Japanese Communist Party will continue to oppose any attempt to make the "touchstone" of scientific socialism and internationalism the question of whether a party follows the line and foreign policy of another specific country. It will oppose all evidences of the leading-party concept, and great power chauvinism. It stands for scientific socialism and the inde-

pendent line of its Party program. No foreign experiences will be taken as a model as the JCP opens up the prospect of an abundant future for democracy and socialism that suit Japanese conditions.[45]

Why did the JCP wait two months to respond to the Soviet attack on Carrillo? It is probable that domestic pressures rather than unwillingness to attack the CPSU were responsible for this delay. The party was involved in a crucial House of Councillors election campaign that was followed by an anguished post-mortem of the election results, and preparations were under way for the upcoming fourteenth congress in October.

Of greater importance politically is the JCP's growing defense of Japan's national interest vis-à-vis the USSR. The territorial issue of the northern islands has been the stumbling block in Soviet-Japanese peace treaty negotiations. Initially, the JCP supported the Soviet position, but by 1969 the party reversed its previous stand and came out for Soviet return of the northern territories to Japan. Here we should distinguish three positions: (1) the position of the Soviet government, which in 1956 promised to return the Habomai and Shikotan islands off the western coast of Hokkaido upon the conclusion of a peace treaty with Japan; (2) the position of the Japanese government, which will not sign a peace treaty unless the Soviet Union also returns the so-called Southern Kuriles, the Japanese government's designation for the two southernmost islands of Kunashiri and Etorofu, recognized as Japanese territory by Russia in the 1855 treaty with Japan; and (3) the present position of the JCP, which argues that the Soviet Union should return Habomai and Shikotan upon the conclusion of a peace treaty and all of the Kurile island chain (all the way to Kamchatka) upon the abrogation of Japan's security treaty with the United States. Needless to say, the Soviet Union is extremely sensitive on territorial issues, given extensive Soviet territorial gains in Europe during and after World War II and the huge Chinese claims. (The Soviets are particularly upset by continuous Chinese support of Japanese territorial claims against the Soviet Union, which started dramatically in 1964 with Mao Tse-tung in an interview with a visiting Japanese socialist delegation.)[46]

The JCP has also protested Soviet fishing in Japanese waters, Soviet bombing exercises in the vicinity of Japan, and Soviet high-handedness in fishery negotiations with Japan, especially after the USSR claimed a 200-mile economic zone.[47]

JCP leaders like Nosaka, Miyamoto, and Hakamada—all veterans of prewar days when the Comintern directed JCP affairs and who weathered the 1950 Cominform's open criticism of Nosaka and JCP policy—must no doubt be ambivalent in their attitude toward the Soviet Union, in asserting their independence, and in opposing the mother party (not unlike a grown child having to disagree with and challenge a parent). Yet to survive in the Japanese political environment and to prove to the Japanese electorate that the party is a genuinely Japanese political institution that is not taking orders from abroad (as in prewar days and in the early 1950s), the JCP must distance itself from Moscow or any other center of Communist authority.

Relations with Eurocommunist Parties

As noted above, by 1963 the JCP, along with North Korea, North Vietnam, and the Indonesian Communist party had swung toward Peking. But in early 1966 the Japanese and the Chinese parties fell out largely as a result of Mao's unsuccessful attempt to dictate to a visiting JCP delegation headed by Miyamoto.[48] Relations between the two parties were further aggravated by the radicalism and chaos of the Cultural Revolution. And, paradoxically enough, China's post-Cultural Revolution policy of opening to the West and Japan hurt the Japanese party, as Peking saw no great advantage in closer relations with the JCP and perhaps some advantages in dealings with the Japanese conservative government if it remained hostile to native Japanese Communists. The feud between the Communist parties of China and Japan continues.

As the JCP's relations with the CPSU and CCP deteriorated, its relations with other Communist parties became more active. And as the JCP moved toward an independent position in the Sino-Soviet dispute, it sought closer ties with parties that themselves tried to steer a neutral course or to maintain their independence from Moscow and Peking. Of course, it was also useful to develop and exploit ties with independent or nonaligned parties to convince the Japanese public of the JCP's own national character and independence from international Communist centers of authority. As early as April 1966, the JCP singled out Romania and North Korea as countries on an independent road to socialism. In the same year, a member of the JCP Presidium placed the Cuban revolution alongside the Russian and Chinese ones as revolutions that succeeded by excluding foreign influences. And the JCP's strident opposition to "U.S. imperialism" made the North Vietnamese party a natural ally.

The JCP's discovery of the usefulness of closer ties with West European Communist parties dates after the break with the CPSU and the CCP in the mid-1960s, and certainly later than the party's rather

close relations with North Korea, North Vietnam, and Romania. At
first the incentive was simply to search for new allies, especially
among the neutrals and independents in the wake of isolation from
both Moscow and Peking. Later, however, the party leadership
realized that forging closer associations with parties of the advanced
industrial countries of Western Europe—particularly the PCI, which
emphasizes a commitment to democracy—could be useful on the
domestic political scene. Of course, the JCP shares with the Communist parties of Western Europe a democratic political environment and a high level of economic, industrial, and technological
development.

As shown elsewhere, the JCP not only failed to adopt Togliatti's
structural reform ideas but in fact expelled protagonists of reform
from the party. The first identification with West European parties
came with the mutual condemnation of the Soviet invasion of
Czechoslovakia in 1968, which led to almost annual visits by
Eurocommunist leaders to Japan. While it is relatively easy to
chronicle the comings and goings of the Japanese and West European
Communist leaders, it is difficult to determine the impact of the
policies of the Communist parties in advanced industrialized societies
on one another.

The JCP has been giving prominent coverage to activities of the
West European parties—especially the various party congresses, the
November 1975 PCI-PCF talks, and the 1977 Madrid summit of the
Communist parties of Italy, France, and Spain—in *Akahata* and other
party publications. The JCP also supported these developments and
the positions of the Eurocommunist parties. Indeed, Japanese government analysts view the JCP line as basically a Eurocommunist
one, giving as evidence the series of joint statements and communiqués signed with the Spanish Communist party (PCE), PCF,
PCI, and Communist party of Great Britain (PCGB) in 1976 and
1977.[49] The Japanese media also link the JCP with Eurocommunism,
and a book on the JCP by the prestigious Asahi Newspapers Press has
a special appendix on the PCI and the PCF.[50]

At the same time, the JCP has made it clear that it defines "three
revolutionary forces for mankind's progress": the socialist countries,
working people's movements in capitalist countries, and national liberation struggles, and that no single force should consider itself the
decisive factor.[51]

The Italian Communist Party. The JCP's essentially negative reaction to Togliatti's structural reform theories and "polycentrism" has
been discussed in previous sections. Close relations between the
Japanese and Italian parties date only from the aftermath of the Soviet

invasion of Czechoslovakia and the visit of a high-level JCP delegation to Rome in October-November 1968. The PCI reciprocated by
sending a delegation to Tokyo a year later. Since that time the two
parties have exchanged visits, attended each other's congresses, and
gradually developed closer ties. In 1970 the PCI dispatched Emilio
Sereni to attend the JCP's Eleventh Congress. He entered Japan on a
tourist visa to visit Expo '70, but when he addressed the congress the
Japanese government ordered his deportation. The case (together
with that of the Australian Laurie Aarons) was taken to court, where
the government lost. But while the PCI delegations to Japan have
been generally mid-echelon affairs, the JCP traffic to Rome has been
at the highest level: Hakamada and Ueda in 1968, Miyamoto in 1971,
and Fuwa in 1977. When questioned about his European travel plans
in 1978 and whether his itinerary would include Rome, Miyamoto
pointedly replied that it was Enrico Berlinguer's turn to visit Tokyo.[52]

The two most recent JCP-PCI joint communiqués were issued at
the end of the visit to Tokyo by the editors of *L'Unità* and *Rinascità*
in September 1975, and after Fuwa's visit to Rome in January 1977.
An analysis of these two documents, and what is *not* in them illumi-
nates the relationship between the two parties. It is worth noting that
neither party has high-ranking leaders who can speak the other
party's national language. All conversations are conducted in French,
including the drafting of final communiqués, which are then translated
into Italian and Japanese.[53]

The two parties differ, of course, in their attitudes toward the
United States. The JCP is opposed to Japan's alliance with the United
States, while the PCI promises to continue Italy's membership in the
NATO alliance. In the 1975 communiqué two paragraphs allow each
party to "explain":

> 1. The characteristics of the situation in Asia after the victory of
> the peoples of the three countries of Indochina, and reinforcement
> of the scheme for military integration of the U.S., Japan and the
> "Republic of Korea" led by U.S. imperialism, and the struggle of
> the JCP for abrogation of the Japan-U.S. military alliance.
> 2. The situation in Europe and in the Mediterranean basin and
> the NATO problem, as well as the struggle of the PCI for disarma-
> ment, gradual and balanced dissolution of the two blocs in Europe,
> and for construction of a Europe to play an autonomous and demo-
> cratic role.

The parties also probably bargained for and wound up including references to the need "to further develop the struggles of the peoples in
respective areas against intervention and aggression of imperialist
forces, and to establish relations of coexistence between states."[54]
The *Akahata* editorial "The Significance of the Joint Communiqué

between the JCP and the CPI'' weakened the case for peaceful coexistence by stating that ''a genuine co-existence will be made possible only on the preconditions of national self-determination and independence of movement of peoples: this is an important matter of principle.''[55] The 1977 communiqué, by contrast, makes no reference to ''struggles'' or to the United States. Instead, a single paragraph stresses essentially the PCI line:

> The. peaceful co-existence of all countries, an end to the armaments race, a complete ban of nuclear weapons, dissolution of all military blocs and military alliances, and withdrawal of all foreign military bases constitute common important tasks of the peace[-loving] and progressive forces in all parts of the world.[56]

Another area of potential disagreement is the stance of the two parties vis-à-vis the Soviet Union, with the PCI trying not to antagonize the CPSU unnecessarily. Thus the 1975 communiqué mentions only that:

> The present international situation and that of the international Communist movement demand that the principle of independence and equality of each party should be established not only in word but also in deed in developing the activities of each party including the research for a proper way to socialism.[57]

Only the *Akahata* editorial makes obvious reference to the Soviet Union and China:

> No party can deny independence, equality and non-intervention in internal affairs of others. As a matter of fact, however, great-power chauvinist intervention and pressure are still to be liquidated.[58]

The 1977 communiqué blandly expresses agreement upon ''strict respect for independence and autonomy and complete equality of all parties, non-interference in internal affairs and respect for each Party's free choice,''[59] but it does not mention explicitly the CPSU or the CCP, or the two signatories' opposition to a ''center'' of the international Communist movement.

Both communiqués stress the two parties' commitment to democracy and pluralism, but there are significant differences between them. In 1975 both parties reaffirmed that:

> in the future socialist society envisaged by them, they will fully guarantee pluralism, freedom of speech, thought, and religion including the propagation thereof, and the freedom of cultural and artistic expression.[60]

In the 1977 document the parties go further:

The future socialist society for which both Parties are struggling should be based, within the framework of the genuine independence of the nation, on such principles as the complete establishment and guarantee of individual and collective freedom, the undenominationalism of the state, the expansion of the local communities, [the] possibility of a democratic alternation of government based on political pluralism and parliamentary democracy, complete freedom of expression of all philosophic, cultural and artistic views, freedom of religion, free activities and autonomy of trade unions and the independence of justice.[61]

But a comparison of the Japanese and Italian texts of the joint communiqué as it appeared in *Akahata* and *L'Unità* reveals a significant difference: in speaking of the "position of both Parties that a democratic advance to socialism will be made through a thorough democratic change of society enjoying the support of the people based on the defense and development of freedom," the Italian version states unequivocally that "this is a strategic conviction; not a tactical attitude." The Japanese text, however, reads that this is a "scientifically grounded principle of conviction," shying away from a clearcut, unambiguous statement. Because previous PCI communiqués with the French and Spanish parties contained similar wording, and because the JCP did not protest the Italian reading, we can assume that the JCP deliberately toned down its commitment to the defense of freedom and pluralism.[62] Perhaps the JCP is not fully committed in this crucial area.

The French Communist Party. That a Stalinist and until recently loyalist party like the PCF should have maintained correct relations with the JCP throughout its gyrations in ideology and alignment is surprising. In the Miyamoto period, the PCF regularly sent greetings to the JCP congresses beginning with the seventh in 1958, and in 1961 a PCF delegation to the Eighth JCP Congress was turned back by Japanese authorities at Haneda Airport in Tokyo. Bilateral talks began with the visit of Jean Kanapa to Tokyo in 1967, reciprocated by the Hakamada mission in October 1968. In spite of its disapproval of the Soviet invasion of Czechoslovakia, the French party did not feel independent enough at that time to include a condemnation of the invasion in its bland joint communiqué with the JCP.[63]

Besides visits to Japan in August 1971, PCF delegations attended the International Conference on Theory and the celebrations of JCP's fiftieth anniversary in 1972, and the Twelfth JCP Congress in 1973. Fuwa headed a delegation to Paris the same year, and Politburo member Paul Laurent and three others came to Tokyo in late 1975, in part to prepare for Marchais' visit. Accompanied by his wife and PCF functionaries, Marchais paid a week-long call in Japan that included a welcoming rally and talks with Miyamoto and other Japanese leaders. But the joint statement with Miyamoto is a strange document. It begins with the following sentence: "The talks we have had in April of 1976 in Tokyo and the conclusion we have reached in the talks were an event of great importance."[64] The statement then plunges into a discussion of social conditions in Japan and France. By way of contrast, the joint statement with Laurent makes reference to a welcome luncheon and "a fruitful exchange of views," while the talks are characterized as having been conducted in a "warm and friendly atmosphere, and positive conclusions [as having been] reached on a series of problems."[65] Perhaps Marchais rubbed his Japanese hosts the wrong way when he said, in his speech at a welcoming rally, that "it is necessary to fight. . . . The democratic way to socialism, which we propose to the French people, is a series of unyielding struggles, mass struggles." He ended his speech with "Long live proletarian internationalism."[66]

The joint statement stressed the importance of forming "broad and democratic united fronts" and stated that "profound democratic transformations which constitute the only and genuine alternative" to the deep crisis that had hit Japan and France will be achieved through "entente of the Communist and Socialist Parties" (for the JCP especially, more a wish than a reality). A parallel was drawn between the parties that made the "heaviest sacrifices under the Tenno [Emperor] absolutist system in Japan and under the Hitlerian occupation in France." And after paying lip service to pluralism and human rights in one short paragraph (with no special promise to turn over power once achieved) and analyzing the international situation, the joint statement ends with an affirmation of principles governing relations between the parties "working in the highly developed capitalist countries."[67] From the statement one would never know that the two parties belong to a larger international Communist movement (which was not mentioned), so that it was unnecessary to mention relations among Communist parties, and the controversial issue of a "center" could be avoided altogether. What a contrast with the Carrillo joint statement signed in Tokyo only ten days earlier!

The Spanish Communist Party. Although the PCE sent greetings to the JCP Eighth Congress in 1961, there was little communication between the two parties until August 1971, when Miyamoto met Carrillo on a visit to Bucharest. Years later Miyamoto recalled that on that occasion, when he described the JCP's postwar experience (presumably the Cominform-imposed radical line and the subsequent "self-reliant and independent line"), Carrillo "with deep emotion" said, "You saved the Party of Japan."[68] Subsequently, relations between the two parties have expanded to regular attendance at each other's congresses and other important occasions. Representatives of the PCE attended the International Conference on Theory and the celebrations of the JCP's fiftieth anniversary in 1972, and the party congresses (where the PCE was one of only six to nine parties represented at these meetings). More recently, the JCP came to the defense of Carrillo and his book *"Eurocommunism" and the State* after Soviet attacks in *New Times*.[69] In 1978 a PCE delegation attended the JCP youth organization congress, while a two-man Presidium-level delegation attended the Ninth Congress of the PCE.

But the highlight of JCP-PCE relations was Carrillo's visit to Tokyo in March 1976. Miyamoto revealed that this was not Carrillo's first visit to Japan: in 1940 he had spent a week in Japan on his way "to the American continent for a new task." Parallels were drawn between the despotic Tenno regime and prewar military-Fascist forces in Japan and the military and reactionary forces of the dictatorial Franco regime. The talks were reputedly held in "an atmosphere of militant solidarity and of very cordial comradeship," and there was a "full coincidence on a series of political and theoretical questions, which distinguish today the postures of those most important Communist Parties of the developed capitalist countries." The two parties "jointly emphasized that the problems of freedom and democracy are inseparable from the principles of scientific socialism and are not temporary tactical problems for the two Parties," and that they would "completely defend pluralism, including alternation of power according to the result of elections," and would respect human rights, "freedoms of assembly, speech, press and association [and] freedom of religion including propagation of religion." Furthermore, "in the socialist societies which the two Parties envisage, the states [will] never be allowed to fix a particular ideology as the state ideology, the 'authorized philosophy' nor to force the peoples to accept those ideologies." In a somewhat sharper statement, both parties stated that they "will not imitate any existing socialist countries as models."[70]

Other Parties in Advanced Capitalist Societies. To help celebrate the fiftieth anniversary of its founding, the JCP decided to stage an International Conference on Theory in July 1972 which would be devoted to problems of Communist parties in advanced capitalist societies. Invitations were issued to eleven parties to send their secretaries-general or Politburo-level delegates. The response was disappointing. Only the Italian, French, Spanish, British, and Australian parties sent delegates (the PCI and the PCF at the Central Committee level), while the West German Communist party sent a staff member of the Research Institute on Marxism and the delegate of the Communist party of the United States (CPUSA) to the celebrations sat in as an observer. As a result neither Miyamoto nor Fuwa attended (Ueda was the top JCP delegate), and the Conference ended without the customary communiqué.[71]

The West German and British parties have maintained correct relations with the JCP—they have sent greetings to JCP congresses, but not delegates (the Japanese government stopped barring entry to Communist gatherings after 1971). That relations with the CPGB have become closer of late, however, may be evidenced by the fact that a meeting between the two parties was held in Tokyo in January 1977. And while no special mention was made of the international Communist movement, and no disavowal of a "center," the joint communiqué spelled out "a principled conviction of the two parties" to "fully safeguard and further expand" all civil and political liberties, including "a multi-party system with freedom of political activity guaranteeing a democratic change of regime based on parliamentary democracy."[72]

Given the proximity of Australia and the growing economic ties between the two countries, it is not surprising that special relations should have developed with the Communist party down under. Hakamada, accompanied by the deputy-director of the JCP's International Relations Department, visited Australia in November 1969 to attend a meeting of the Australian party's National Committee and to reciprocate several visits to Tokyo by prominent Australian Communist leaders. Laurie Aarons, the national secretary, participated in the Eleventh JCP Congress on an Expo '70 tourist visa, and the Australians have attended subsequent JCP congresses and other important functions.

The JCP was invited for the first time to send a delegate to the CPUSA Congress in 1972, but Nosaka, who had lived in the United States, was refused a visa by the American government. A similar situation arose in 1975.

Conclusions

What is the ideological and tactical impact of Eurocommunism on the JCP? How can the JCP be related to Eurocommunism? Does it consider itself part of the Eurocommunist group of parties? Is it a more nationalist, reasonable, autonomous, and peaceful party eschewing violent revolution and dedicated to Western values of parliamentary democracy, not only on the road to power, but also after achieving power, presumably in coalition with other "progressive" parties under an essentially pluralistic multiparty system? Has it shown a capacity for governing at the local level within the present political system? Is it genuinely autonomous, opposed to the notion of a guiding center, or centers, in the international Communist movement; and does this translate into opposition to the policies of the CPSU and CCP, and also, importantly, to the foreign policies of the Soviet Union and China as nation-states? Are nationalist constraints more important in guiding its policies than its role within the international Communist system? And if the answer to some of these questions is yes, then to what degree and why?

In seeking answers, it is useful to ask related questions, such as: What degree of democracy does the party practice within its own organization? How does it deal, within its ranks, with advocates of alternative policies, both ideological and organizational? Has the party's commitment to so-called Eurocommunist principles been relatively recent or of long standing? Did it arise out of ideological transformation or electoral necessity? And what of the leadership? Is the party led by the old leaders dedicated to dogmatic Marxist-Leninist principles and servile toward Moscow and Peking, who have adapted to fresh ideas, or by more independent, liberal, and flexible new leaders?

The JCP, as noted, is ruled by a prewar leader who not only spent many years in jail and was allegedly involved in the murder of a police informer, but was also in the vanguard of advocating acceptance of the Cominform criticism of what might now be called the first "Eurocommunist" experiment in Japan. One could argue, of course, that Miyamoto jumped on the Cominform bandwagon as a tactic to gain power with the help of Moscow and Peking. Whatever the motive, his early career to the mid-1950s does not show much commitment to Western values or fierce independence from the *diktats* of the USSR and China.

Perhaps, then, he saw the folly of pursuing the imposed, suicidal radical line and was influenced by Togliatti's polycentrist notions toward adopting an independent autonomous stance and by the PCI's structural reform theories to pursue a nonrevolutionary line. But Miyamoto was no Togliatti. He exhibited little independent spirit, supported the 1957 Moscow Declaration's formulation of the Soviet Union as first among equals, and enshrined in the JCP program of 1961 the notion that the socialist camp was "headed by the USSR." This program was adopted at the Eighth JCP Congress dominated by Miyamoto and his faction. As for ideas of structural reform,

Miyamoto not only opposed them but managed to expel their advocates from the party. If anything, Miyamoto initially supported Peking in the Sino-Soviet dispute, a position that does not exactly show a predilection to moderation, considering Peking's strident policies at that time. Indeed, while Miyamoto probably began to realize that party growth and electoral success depended upon the adoption of an independent, autonomous, and nationalist line, the CPSU and later the CCP obliged him by attacking the JCP and his leadership and actively supporting his opponents in and out of the party. Of course, the Sino-Soviet split undermined the confidence of Miyamoto and other subservient Communist leaders around the world in the infallibility of the Communist center, provided divergent authoritative models, and made it easier for them to stand on their own.

But however it is explained, for the past decade Miyamoto has actively pursued an independent line for the JCP, in the process allying himself with other independent-minded parties. These have included Asian parties (in North Korea and, at that time, North Vietnam), maverick parties (in Romania and later Yugoslavia, once the object of harsh JCP criticism), and West European nonruling parties (in Italy, France, Spain, and Great Britain). This independent line and ties to other independents serve two purposes. They buttress party morale in a time of estrangement from the two Communist giants and resultant isolation in the movement. And the very pursuit of autonomy and independence in the international Communist movement is useful domestically, helping to soften the long-held Japanese public image of the JCP as a servile, alien political group.

Still, JCP allies in the struggle for independence in the international Communist movement are a mixed lot. They include champions of domestic repression as Kim Il Sung and Nicolae Ceausescu—not very helpful symbols in postwar democratic Japan. But the West European nonruling parties are made to order. They are parties that grew up in advanced capitalist countries of Western Europe, a part of the world with which Japan is identified. As Japan experienced phenomenal economic growth during the 1960s, emerging as the third largest economic unit in the world (and second among non-Communist countries), it became fashionable to classify Japan along with the United States and Western Europe as part of a tripolar non-Communist group. Note the emergence of the Trilateral Commission and Japan's active participation in the Organization for Economic Cooperation and Development—that club of rich Western nations—and in the economic summit meetings of heads of government of the most important industrial countries, which all happen to be Western democracies. So if the JCP can identify itself with Communist parties operating in countries that are both highly industrialized and democratic, it will have gone a long way toward increasing its legitimacy in the Japanese political system. Thus Miyamoto's implicit acceptance of the JCP as a Eurocommunist party. While acknowledging that the label "Eurocommunism" was an invention of non-Communists, he cites approvingly a French journalist's remark that the JCP preceded the West European parties in pursuing policies that have come to be associated with Eurocommunism and a report that PCE circles speak of "Euro-Nippo-Communism."[73]

But ties to increasingly independent Communist parties in Western Europe, ostensibly dedicated to the acceptance of democratic and parliamentary environments, are not enough. Miyamoto and especially his hand-picked protégé Fuwa, an intellectual with a theoretical bent, have in the last decade and especially in the past five to six years tried, on the one hand, to revise, reformulate, or simply retranslate the antidemocratic aspects of Marxist-Leninist terminology (including the very term "Marxism-Leninism," which has been replaced by "scientific socialism"). On the other hand, they have tried to develop a program of action for a Communist party in a democratic, advanced, industrial country like Japan, which guarantees a pluralistic society even after Communist participation in government. To this end, the JCP convened the International Conference on Theory to deal with the problems of Communist parties in advanced capitalist countries and has issued a lengthy "Manifesto on Freedom and Democracy." More important, the JCP has paralleled the efforts of the PCI (if not of all other Eurocommunist parties) in placing a heavy emphasis on local elections and in electing local executives in coalition with other "progressive" forces. In the urban areas the political trend has been away from the conservative LDP, and until very recently most major Japanese cities have been governed by "progressive" mayors. For the JCP this brings two advantages: first, it weakens the governing party, and, second, it legitimizes the Communist party as part of a governing coalition, at least on the local level. Combined with direct, practical aid to citizens in their daily lives, and especially in their relations with the government, the JCP is desperately trying to change its image as a revolutionary party and to prove itself a logical partner in a realistic alternative to the conservative government that has ruled Japan for most of the postwar period.

To help change its unfortunate image as an alien political group, the JCP vigorously promotes its autonomy within the international Communist movement. It has been very much helped in this effort on the domestic scene by its relative isolation within the international Communist movement owing to its quarrels with the CPSU and the CCP.

But the JCP does not stop here. It strives to promote Japanese national interests, especially vis-à-vis the Soviet Union and China. Of course, in its strident anti-Americanism, the party has portrayed itself as defending Japanese national interests against the United States, but this sounded hollow to the Japanese public, an echo of the anti-Americanism emanating from Moscow and Peking. Moreover, a good part of the Japanese electorate actually approved of Japan's ties with the United States, which clearly contributed so much to the nation's security and to its phenomenal economic growth and prosperity. It should also not be forgotten that the JCP operates in a democratic country that is basically pro-Western and anti-Communist. For example, in recent public opinion polls—if we exclude the roughly one-quarter of respondents who have no preference—between one-half and two-thirds of those polled would like to see Japan as part of the "Free World." Thirty to 40 percent opt for neutrality, and only 1 to 3 percent would like to see Japan in the "Communist camp." It is also significant that in the same polls, the Japanese consistently name Switzerland, the United States, France, Great Britain, and Germany as their most liked countries.[74]

It is only when the JCP attacks Soviet and Chinese policies toward Japan that its claim as a nationalist Japanese party becomes more credible. Thus, the party criticizes the government for giving in to Peking on the antihegemony clause and weakening Japan's independent position in the world. It uses Japan's territorial dispute with the Soviet Union to make two points. By demanding that the Soviet Union return the entire Kurile island chain to Japan, the party poses as a true defender of Japanese national interests and as a more nationalistic party than the conservative LDP and the Japanese government, which only claims the two southernmost Kurile islands.

Thus, while pursuing an independent line and enjoying its autonomy, the JCP is also trying to expand its ties and break out of its relative isolation in the international Communist movement. Similarly, it is trying to stem its relative isolation, arising from a growing anti-Communism, on the Japanese political scene. The quest for autonomy is the result of the dynamics in intra-Communist relations, but the party's policy of stressing parliamentary democracy is the product of the domestic environment. This second major policy component of Eurocommunism came about in two stages. The first stage from 1946 to 1950, that of "lovable" JCP tactics, was a native idea independent of West European developments. But this policy was not accompanied by impulses toward autonomy in the international Communist movement; when the word came from on high to "stop it," the party complied. The second stage, which came much later, meshed with the

West European parties' alleged commitment to democracy and pluralism. This time, the "lovable" party policy coincided with the JCP's autonomy and alienation from Communist "centers."

Is the JCP's current policy emphasizing parliamentary democracy and pluralism genuine, or is it only a tactic? The most damaging evidence against the sincerity of the party is that it is itself run dictatorially. The history of the JCP for the past twenty years is one of continuous purges—not only of ideological opponents. As in the Eurocommunist parties, dissent is not tolerated; democratic centralism is the rule. Perhaps the next generation of party regulars, raised on a diet of at least declaratory commitment to democracy and pluralism, can be a force toward democratization of the party and eventual acceptance of the parliamentary road to power and the principle of relinquishing power. But that is conjecture. Meanwhile, the Japanese voting public seems to agree with this negative assessment and questions the genuineness of the Communist party's commitment to democracy.

NOTES

I wish to thank the editors of this volume, as well as Professors Thomas Greene of the University of Southern California, Haruhiro Fukui of the University of California at Santa Barbara, and especially Paul Langer of the Rand Corporation for insightful comments and suggestions. Dr. Bae Yeon Won of the University of Southern California provided timely and helpful research assistance. Needless to say, final responsibility for this chapter is mine alone.

1. There are several good books on the Japanese Communist movement: Rodger Swearingen and Paul Langer, *Red Flag in Japan: International Communism in Action, 1919–1951* (Cambridge, Mass.: Harvard University Press, 1952); George M. Beckmann and Okubo Genji, *The Japanese Communist Party, 1922–1945* (Stanford: Stanford University Press, 1969); Robert A. Scalapino, *The Japanese Communist Movement, 1920–1966* (Berkeley: University of California Press, 1967); and Paul F. Langer, *Communism in Japan: A Case of Political Naturalization* (Stanford: Hoover Institution, 1972). The most recent study is Haruhiro Fukui, "The Japanese Communist Party: The Miyamoto Line and Its Problems," in Morton A. Kaplan, ed., *The Many Faces of Communism* (New York: Free Press, 1978). Also very useful is the section on Japan in the annual *Yearbook on International Communist Affairs*, Richard F. Staar, ed. (Stanford: Hoover Institution, 1967–); most of the recent contributions on the JCP were written by John K. Emmerson. *K.D.K. Information*, edited by Etsuo Kohtani and published monthly in mimeographed form in English since 1964 by the K.D.K. Institute in Tokyo, is particularly useful on the JCP's relations with the Soviet Union and China. Another invaluable source is *Koan joho* (Public Security Intelligence), a monthly edited and published in Tokyo since 1954 by *Shakai undo kenkyukai*. Although not officially a publication of the *Koan chosa cho*, the Japanese counterpart of the FBI, the material is largely prepared by government analysts.

Primary sources for the study of the JCP include its daily *Akahata* (Red Flag) and the theoretical monthly *Zen'ei* (Vanguard), as well as other publications of the party and its affiliated organizations. The JCP headquarters also issues from time to time the English-language, typewritten *Bulletin: Information for Abroad,* which contains translations of important party documents, statements, editorials, speeches, and the like.

2. "Contrary to the Interests of Peace and Socialism in Europe," *Novoe vremia,* no. 26 (June 24, 1977), p. 11.

3. I follow the Japanese style of giving the surname first.

4. Japanese government security agencies estimate that party membership figures are somewhat inflated. Party membership is augmented by membership in such front organizations as the youth (close to 200,000 members), women's, peace, antinuclear, friendship, and Afro-Asian solidarity movements.

5. *Shukan Asahi,* May 30, 1975, cited in *Yearbook on International Communist Affairs, 1976,* p. 304.

6. Elections for the lower house were held on October 7, 1979. Although the JCP increased its percentage of the total vote only marginally (10.42% from 10.38%), it managed to elect 39 members and thus recapture all the seats it had lost in 1976. (The party's popular vote actually declined from 5.9 to 5.6 million.) The Liberal Democratic party, the conservative party that has governed Japan since its formation in 1955, captured 248 seats in the 511-member House of Representatives. The Japan Socialist party (JSP), the largest opposition party, won only 107 seats (a drop of 16 from 1976). The JSP is a doctrinaire Marxist organization that cooperates with the Soviet Union and China and advocates unarmed neutrality for Japan. It is very different in character from the moderate socialist parties in Britain and West Germany. The Democratic Socialist party, a moderate offshoot of the JSP (since 1960) increased its representation from 29 to 35, and the Komeito (Clean Government party), the political arm of the mass lay Buddhist organization Soka Gakkai (Value Creation Society) won 57 seats.

7. For a detailed discussion of JCP urban politics, see Ellis S. Krauss, "The Urban Strategy and Policy of the Japan Communist Party: Kyoto," *Studies in Comparative Communism,* XII (Winter 1979).

8. A few splinter groups propagate these ideas and publish organs such as *Kozo kaikaku* (Structural Reform).

9. At the same time, Fuwa, in a series of articles in *Akahata* entitled "Lenin and Parliamentarism," argued that the JCP's "people's parliamentarism" was not inconsistent with Leninism. *Akahata,* September 18, 1970 and following issues.

10. See *Akahata,* July 15–22, 1972; *Yearbook on International Communist Affairs, 1973,* p. 487. For more details about the Conference, see the section "Other Parties in Advanced Capitalist Societies."

11. With a long explanation about Japanese equivalents of the Latin word *dictatura* and claims that "Marx and Engels themselves used the terms 'dictatorship of the proletariat' and 'the power of the working class' or the 'political rule of the working class' as terms of the same meaning. "*Akahata* Extra, June 7, 1976; *Bulletin,* no. 356 (July 1976), p. 28.

12. *Asahi,* July 7, 1970, morning edition, p. 2.

13. *Akahata* Extra, June 7, 1976; *Bulletin,* no. 356 (July 1976), p. 31.

14. *Akahata,* January 8 and 9, 1976.

15. *Akahata,* June 8, 1974; *Bulletin,* no. 315 (June 1974), p. 2ff.

16. *Akahata*, August 31, 1975, as cited in *Yearbook on International Communist Affairs, 1976*, pp. 308–309.

17. *Akahata*, April 27–May 8, 1976; *Bulletin*, no. 354 (July 1976), p. 74.

18. *Akahata*, July 31, 1976; *Bulletin*, no. 359 (October 1976), p. 17.

19. See the January 1976 issue of the popular mass-circulation magazine *Bungei Shunju*. Chairman Kasuga of the Democratic Socialist party made the accusation in the National Diet on January 27, 1976. For JCP refutations, see Fuwa's statement and other documents in *Akahata*, January 28–30, 1976, and *Bulletin*, no. 345 (February 1976).

On March 14, 1979 Councillor Tamaki of the LDP reopened the "lynching case" by lodging an official complaint to President Yasui of the House of Councillors that Miyamoto was not qualified to serve as Councillor. *K.D.K. Information* (April 1, 1979), pp. 6–7.

20. For a good discussion of these electoral reverses, see John F. Copper, "The Japanese Communist Party's Recent Electoral Defeats: A Signal of Decline?," *Asian Survey*, XIX (April 1979), pp. 353–365.

21. In a traditional new year interview, Miyamoto said that the party has assisted not only in solving tax problems, installment-sale fraud, and housing loan swindles, but in such personal matters as divorce and "finding a wife." *Akahata*, January 8, 1977, and *Bulletin*, no. 367 (April 1977), p. 15.

22. See the "Struggle for Life, Rights, Sovereignty and Peace for the Establishment of a Progressive United Front and Democratic Coalition Government" and "The Proposal of the Communist Party of Japan Concerning the Programme of a Democratic Coalition Government," *Akahata*, November 21, 1973; *Bulletin*, nos. 303 and 304 (November 1973).

23. In referring to the JCP, the Japanese press began to use such imported English terms as "sofuto rain" (soft line), "sumairu" (smile) propaganda, "camouflage" tactics, *imeji chenji, mainasu imeji*, and *imeji daun* (image change, minus image, and image down—the latter expressions apparently Japanese artifacts).

24. Report of the Central Committee to the Fourteenth Party Congress by Fuwa Tetsuzo, Chief of the Secretariat, October 17, 1977, *Akahata*, October 18, 1977; *Bulletin*, no. 390 (January 1978), p. 11. Also concluding remarks at the Fifth Central Committee Plenum by Presidium Chairman Miyamoto, *Akahata*, September 23, 1978; *Bulletin*, no. 407 (December 1978), p. 65.

25. Calculated from the *Jiji seron chosa tokuho* [Jiji Public Opinion Survey: A Special Report] (Tokyo: Jiji tsushin sha, 1975–1978). (Hereinafter cited as Jiji Public Opinion Survey.)

Another poll, conducted in May 1977 among 15,000 labor union members in the Kansai Area, shows a lack of JCP support even among Japan's proletariat: JSP was favored by 28 percent, DSP by 11, LDP by 5.5 percent, and the JCP only by 2.5 percent (a whopping 45 percent do not support any political party). Nobuo Tomita *et al.*, "Japanese Politics at a Crossroads: The 11th House of Councillors Election," *Bulletin of the Institute of Social Sciences, Meiji University* (Tokyo), 1 (No. 3, 1978), p. 17.

The fact, however, that many Japanese are reluctant to identify themselves publicly with the JCP weakens the validity of such polls.

26. The alleged "lynching" incident must have hurt Miyamoto substantially at the polls—he came in 41st out of 50 in the national constituency of the House of Councillors in July 1977.

27. See Hakamada's articles in the weekly *Shukan shincho:* the January 12, 1978 ("Miyamoto Kenji: A Comrade of Yesterday") and the February 2, 1978

issues. He also accused Nosaka of being an American agent.

For official and unofficial JCP statements on the expulsion of Hakamada and Miyamoto's interview with a *Yomiuri* reporter, see *Akahata,* January 4, 6, 1978, and *Yomiuri,* January 13, 1978; *Bulletin,* no. 391 (January 1978) and no. 397 (May 1978).

28. In public opinion polls, when party supporters were asked to give the reason why they supported the JCP, only 3 percent (the lowest category) said they did so because of party leadership, compared with over 35 percent listing ideology, and 29 percent saying the other parties were no good. Jiji Public Opinion Survey, October 1975.

29. Of these, nine are by Marx and Engels, eight are by Lenin, and two are Comintern documents. *Akahata,* January 1, 1978, and *Bulletin,* no. 399 (June 1978).

30. Originally published in *Akahata,* November 22, 1964; reprinted as a separate pamphlet by the Foreign Languages Press in Peking in 1965.

31. For a JCP account of these CPSU activities, see "On Interventions in and Subversive Activities against the Democratic Movements of Our Country and Our Party by the CPSU Leadership and the Institutions and Organizations Under Its Guidance," *Akahata,* June 22, 1965; *Bulletin,* no. 41 (June 1965); reprinted as a separate pamphlet by the Foreign Languages Press in Peking in 1965.

32. See, for example, "On the Meeting Convened in Moscow from March 1 by the CPSU Leadership," *Akahata,* April 13 and May 7, 1965; *Bulletin,* April and May 1965; reprinted as a separate pamphlet by the Foreign Languages Press in Peking in 1965.

33. Interestingly, the JCP refused to send a delegation to either the fiftieth (1967) or the sixtieth (1977) anniversary celebrations of the Russian Revolution, but they did participate in the celebration of the Lenin centennial in 1970 and in the fiftieth anniversary of the establishment of the USSR in 1972.

34. Perhaps another such initiative was taken by the Soviets in late 1978 to counter the visit of Teng Hsiao-p'ing to Japan. A *Pravda* article praised the JCP (N. Vladimirov, "The Vanguard Role of the JCP," *Pravda,* December 27, 1978), though it did not promise that the CPSU would cease its support of the Shiga group—a condition that the JCP considers a *sine qua non* for full reconciliation between the two parties.

Negotiations intensified in 1979, and when the Soviet side capitulated on the Shiga group support issue, the way was paved for a summit. (See *Akahata,* March 3, 1979 and *Bulletin,* no. 411 (April 1979), pp. 6–7; and the joint JCP-CPSU statement in Moscow, *Akahata,* April 15, 1979 and *Bulletin,* no. 411 (April 1979), pp. 1–2.) Following further preparatory meetings in both capitals, Miyamoto accompanied by five of his top lieutenants arrived in Moscow on December 15 (*Pravda,* December 16, 1979, p. 4). Following a week of negotiations with the Soviet delegation, which included Brezhnev and Suslov, a joint statement was issued on December 24 (*Pravda,* December 18, 1979, p. 1, article and photograph, and December 25, pp. 1, 4; *Japan Times,* December 25, 1979, p. 3). The document admitted disagreements between the two delegations, which "frankly" expressed their views, and confirmed the preliminary joint agreement regarding "past problems," although the Soviets managed to avoid mention of embarrassing details of that agreement. The Soviets also managed to avoid any reference to the territorial problems between the two neighboring countries, but it was admitted that the two parties will continue to exchange views regarding the peace treaty (which is essentially held up by the territorial dispute). The Japanese succeeded in including their proposals regarding fishery problems and the visitation of graves in the Soviet Union, which the CPSU delegation agreed to consider. The Japanese also successfully kept out from the document the term Marxism-Leninism. The two parties had no trouble in agreeing to lambast United States imperialism and without specifically mentioning China to condemn "the violation of borders and armed invasion into western and northern regions of Vietnam as open hegemonism." While these negotiations formally ended the long period of abnormal relations between the JCP and the CPSU, many differences still remain.

35. "Scientific Socialism and Freedom of Speech and Expression—Our Views Regarding the Solzhenitsyn Affair," *Akahata*, March 20, 1974, and *Bulletin*, no. 311 (April 1974), p. 2.

36. Ibid., p. 4.

37. Ibid., p. 2.

38. Kurahara Korehito on February 13, 1974, ibid., p. 11.

39. Ibid., pp. 7–8.

40. Ibid., pp. 2–3.

41. Ibid., p. 5.

42. "Our Refutation—To CPA's Criticism of Our Party and Its 'Version' in a CPSU's Magazine," *Akahata*, September 15, 1974, and *Bulletin*, no. 319 (September 1974).

The following day *Akahata* issued a lengthy review of CPSU interventions in JCP affairs dating back to 1963. "The Sweeping Away of the Products of Interventions—The Very Way for the Normalization of Relations—Interventions by N. S. Khrushchev and Others—and Present Day Problems—(Explanation)," *Akahata*, Spetember 16, 1974, and *Bulletin*, no. 320 (September 1974).

This bitter exchange is reminiscent of CPSU criticism of the JCP on the occasion of its fiftieth anniversary in 1972 in *Pravda* and two other Soviet publications, and of *Akahata's* lengthy response, "Intolerable Gross Distortions—On Three Soviet Articles Concerning Our Party's History," *Akahata*, December 17, 1972, and *Bulletin*, no. 284 (February 1973).

43. *Akahata*, August 30, 1977, and *Bulletin*, no. 379 (September 1977), pp. 3–4.

44. Ibid., p. 2.

45. Ibid., p. 7.

46. "Chairman Mao Tse-tung Tells the Delegation of the Japanese Socialist Party that the Kuriles Must be Returned to Japan," *Sekai shuho* (Tokyo), August 11, 1964; see also Peter Berton, "The Territorial Issue Between Russia and China," *Studies in Comparative Communism*, 2 (July/October 1969), pp. 135–136.

47. See "The Position of the Communist Party of Japan on the Kurile Islands Question (Explanation)," *Akahata*, September 17, 1974, and *Bulletin*, no. 321 (September 1974). "The Open Letter of the Japanese Communist Party to the Communist Party of the Soviet Union on Chishima (Kurile) Islands Issue," *Akahata*, May 28, 1977, and *Bulletin*, no. 371 (June 1977); and JCP refutations of the *Pravda* editorial of June 12, 1977, "Contrary to the Interests of Peace and Goodneighbourness," in *Akahata*, June 13, 1977, and *Bulletin*, no. 372 (June 1977); and *Akahata*, July 6, 1977 and *Bulletin*, no. 374 (July 1977).

See also "The Position of the Communist Party of Japan on the Fishery

Issue Between Japan and the Soviet Union" [Miyamoto's statement of April 16, 1977], *Bulletin*, no. 369 (May 1977).

48. For a detailed account, see C.L. Chiou and Tsiu-shuang Han, "Ideology and Politics in the 1966–1967 Split between the Communist Parties of China and Japan," *Studies in Comparative Communism*, XI (Winter 1978), pp. 361–387.

49. Akiyama Jun'ichi, "'Yurokomyunizumu' no rekishiteki kosatsu" [A historical study of "Eurocommunism"], Part 4: "'Eurocommunism' and the JCP," *Koan joho* [*Public Security Inteligence*], no. 301 (October 1978), p. 19.

50. Asahi Shimbunsha, comp., *Nihon Kyosanto* [Japan Communist Party], (Tokyo: Asahi, 1973). This book is a collection of sixty articles originally published in *Asahi* in installments from February to May 1973.

51. *Akahata* editorial, October 23, 1975, and *Bulletin*, no. 338 (November 1975), p. 6, upon the conclusion of talks with a PCF delegation in Tokyo.

52. Traditional new year interview, *Akahata*, January 1, 1978, and *Bulletin*, no. 394 (February 1978), p. 2.

53. Nishida Shin'ichiro, "Nichi-I ryo Kyosanto no kyodo seimei ni tsuite" [On the Joint Statement of the Two Communist Parties of Japan and Italy], *Koan joho*, No. 283 (April 1977), p. 16.

54. *Akahata*, September 30, 1975, and *Bulletin*, no. 337 (October 1975), p. 3. (Hereinafter cited as the 1975 Communiqué.)

55. *Akahata*, October 2, 1975, and *Bulletin*, no. 337 (October 1975), p. 5. (Hereinafter cited as the *Akahata* Editorial.)

56. *Akahata*, January 21, 1977, and *Bulletin*, no. 365 (March 1977), p. 3. (Hereinafter cited as the 1977 Communiqué.)

57. 1975 Communiqué, p. 3.

58. *Akahata* Editorial, p. 5.

59. 1977 Communiqué, p. 4.

60. 1975 Communiqué, p. 2.

61. 1977 Communiqué, pp. 2–3.

62. I am indebted to a Japanese government analyst, Nishida Shin'ichiro, for the comparison and analysis of the Japanese and Italian texts: Nishida Shin'ichiro, "Nichi-I ryo Kyosanto no kyodo seimei ni tsuite," p. 16.

63. Significantly, Miyamoto omitted the Kanapa and Hakamada missions when he recounted important French and Japanese contacts in his speech at a welcoming rally for Marchais, April 8, 1976. *Akahata*, April 10, 1976, and *Bulletin*, no. 352 (May 1976), p. 3.

64. Joint statement, Tokyo, April 10, 1976, *Akahata*, April 11, 1976, and *Bulletin*, no. 352 (May 1976), p. 34.

65. Joint communiqué of the JCP and the PCF, made public simultaneously in *Akahata* and *L'Humanité*, October 21, 1975; also *Bulletin*, no. 338 (November 1975), pp. 1–2.

66. Marchais' speech, April 8, 1976, *Akahata*, April 10, 1976, and *Bulletin*, no. 352 (May 1976), pp. 27 and 33.

67. Joint statement, Tokyo, April 10, 1976, *Akahata*, April 11, 1976, and *Bulletin*, no. 352 (May 1976), pp. 34–36.

68. Traditional new year interview, *Akahata*, January 1, 1976, and *Bulletin*, no. 348 (February 1976), p. 13.

69. *Akahata*, August 30, 1977, and *Bulletin*, no. 379 (September 1978).

70. Miyamoto's and Carrillo's speeches at the Rally to Welcome the PCE Delegation, March 30, 1976, and the Joint JCP-PCE Statement, *Akahata*, April 1, 1976, and *Bulletin*, no. 350 (May 1976), pp. 3, 24, 30–32.

71. *Akahata*, July 15–22, 1972; Nishida Shin'ichiro, "Nikkyo soritsu 50-shunen kinen wo meguru tokuchoteki doko" [Distinctive Trends in the JCP on the Occasion of the 50th Anniversary of Its Founding], *Koan Joho*, no. 226 (July 1972), p. 2.

Another International Symposium on Theory, focusing on the struggle in advanced capitalist countries, was held at the party's headquarters in Tokyo, July 16–18, 1979, to commemorate the fifty-seventh anniversary of the party's founding. The conference was attended by delegates from nine Communist parties (including the Swedish and Mexican parties). *Akahata*, July 14–19, 1979.

72. *Akahata*, January 29, 1977, and *Bulletin*, no. 366 (March 1977).

73. Traditional new year interview with the Editor-in-Chief of *Akahata*, T. Nirasawa, January 1, 1978, *Bulletin*, no. 394 (February 1978), p. 2.

74. Calculated from Jiji Public Opinion Survey, 1975–1978.

Contributors

VERNON V. ASPATURIAN is Evan Pugh Professor of Political Science and Director of the Slavic and Soviet Language and Area Center at the Pennsylvania State University. He is the author of *Process and Power in Soviet Foreign Policy*, *The Union Republics in Soviet Diplomacy*, and *The Soviet Union in the World Communist System*.

PETER BERTON is Professor of International Relations and Coordinator of the East Asian Regional Studies Program at the University of Southern California. He is editor of *Studies in Comparative Communism;* author of several books on Japanese, Chinese, and Soviet affairs; and most recently, co-translator (with Robert A. Scalapino) of *The Fateful Choice: Japan's Advance into Southeast Asia, 1939–1941.*

DAVID P. BURKE, Lieutenant Colonel, U.S. Air Force, is Assistant Professor and Coordinator of Western European and Canadian Studies at the Naval Postgraduate School, Monterey, California. He has published articles and contributed to books on the simulation of policy-making and nuclear war and on the policies of Canada and Romania.

PARRIS H. CHANG is Professor of Political Science at the Pennsylvania State University and author of *Radicals and Radical Ideology in China's Cultural Revolution* and *Power and Policy in China*.

STEPHEN F. COHEN is Professor of Politics and Director of Russian Studies at Princeton University. His books include *Bukharin and the Bolshevik Revolution: A Political Biography, 1888–1938; The Soviet Union since Stalin*, coedited with Alexander Rabinowitch and Robert Sharlet; *The Great Purge Trial*, coedited with Robert C. Tucker; and *Political Diary*.

MELVIN CROAN is Professor of Political Science and former Chairman of the Russian Studies Program at the University of Wisconsin-Madison. He has published many scholarly articles on German, Soviet, East European, and international communist politics and is author of *East Germany: The Soviet Connection*.

HERBERT S. DINERSTEIN is Andrew W. Mellon Professor of Soviet Studies at the John Hopkins University School of Advanced International Studies. He has written many articles and books on Soviet politics; his most recent work is *The Making of a Missile Crisis, October 1962*. Professor Dinerstein is preparing a book on the reordering of the international system between 1944 and 1949.

TROND GILBERG is Professor of Political Science and Associate Director of the Slavic and Soviet Language and Area Center at the Pennsylvania State University. He is author of *The Soviet Communist Party and Scandinavian Communism* and *Modernization in Romania since World War II*.

ANDRZEJ KORBONSKI is Professor and Chairman of the Department of Political Science at the University of California, Los Angeles. He is the author of *The Politics of Socialist Agriculture in Poland, 1945–1960* and has written on various aspects of East European politics and economics, and problems of East-West trade and East European integration.

PAUL R. MILCH is Associate Professor of Operations Research and Statistics at the Naval Postgraduate School in Monterey, California. Although most of his work has been in operations research, he has recently entered the field of international studies.

ROBERT E. OSGOOD is Christian A. Herter Professor of American Foreign Policy and former Dean of the Johns Hopkins University School of Advanced International Studies. His books include *Ideals and Self-Interest in America's Foreign Relations; Limited War; NATO: The Entangling Alliance;* and *Limited War Revisited.*

ROBIN ALISON REMINGTON is Professor of Political Science at the University of Missouri-Columbia and a research affiliate of the Massachusetts Institute of Technology Center for International Studies. Her publications include *Winter in Prague: Documents on Czechoslovak Communism in Crisis* and *The Warsaw Pact: Case Studies in Communist Conflict Resolution.*

JAN F. TRISKA is Professor of Political Science and International Relations at Stanford University. He is the author of many books and articles on Soviet foreign policy, politics in Eastern Europe, and international relations. His most recent book is *The World of Superpowers* (with Nobutaka Ike and Robert North).

JIRI VALENTA is Associate Professor and Coordinator of Soviet and East European Studies in the Department of National Security Affairs at the Naval Postgraduate School, Monterey, California. He is the author of *Soviet Intervention in Czechoslovakia, 1968: Anatomy of a Decision* and coeditor of *Communist States and Africa* (forthcoming). He has contributed articles to scholarly journals on Soviet foreign policy, national security, and comparative communism.

ERIC WILLENZ heads the U.S. State Department's external research program for Europe, both East and West, and is Adjunct Professor at the Johns Hopkins University School of Advanced International Studies. He is the author of several books in the field of communist studies.

Index

Ackermann, Anton, 143
Afghanistan, 104
Akahata, 329, 332, 341–342, 345; PCJ-PCI Communique, 346–348
Albania, 14, 16, 49, 185, 305; Communist Party, 74, 84, 303, 307
Althusser, Louis, 67
Andreotti, Giulio, 94
Anglo-American Alliance (World War II), 27–29
Angola, 104
Auriol, Vincent, 44
Australian Communist Party, 8, 13, 105, 351; policy positions summarized, 67, 79, 89, 255, 305
Austria, 29; Socialist Party, 103
Austrian Communist Party (ACP), 73, 75, 119; policy positions summarized, 76, 79, 89, 91
Austro-Hungarian Empire, 158–161, 245–246
Autonomism. *See entries for individual countries and communist parties; Eurocommunism*
Azcarate, Manuel, 115, 116, 172–173, 176, 177

Badoglio, Pietro, 27, 28
Bahro, Rudolf, 147–149
Balibar, Etienne, 67
Barbieri, Frane, 5
Behrens, Fritz, 144
Belgian Communist Party, 73, 75, 303–304; policy positions summarized, 67, 77, 79, 89, 91, 305
Benary, Arno, 144
Benes, Edward, 32, 40, 50, 162
Beria, Lavrenti, 143
Berlin Blockade, 51–52
Berlin Conference (1976), 5, 7, 72, 93, 94, 136, 150; and Eurocommunism, 74–76, 84, 88, 113, 134, 198, 207, 214, 217, 254, 261, 264–265, 315; final document, 7, 74, 81, 134, 257, 315; preparations for, 13, 74, 108, 189–190, 211, 259
Berlinguer, Enrico, 66, 89, 94, 121, 157, 220, 249, 264; and Berlin Conference, 75, 84; and Madrid Meeting, 94, 103; and NATO, 106, 119, 172, 316; and USSR, 73, 95, 107–108, 117, 119, 190. *See also* Italian Communist Party

Bibo, Istvan, 231
Bidault, Georges, 45
Biermann, Wolf, 91, 147, 149–150, 259
Bilak, Vasil: and Eurocommunism, 111, 158, 175
Biszku, Bela, 238–239
Bloch, Ernst, 144
Blum, Leon, 45
Bolivian Communist Party, 84
Bolshevik Revolution, 12, 28, 56, 60, 66, 80, 161, 202, 246, 264
Brandt, Willy, 131
Brazilian Communist Party, 84
Brezhnev, Leonid, 64, 81, 128, 153, 214, 338–339; and Eurocommunism, 108, 110–111, 234, 278; and *Westpolitik,* 147, 152. *See also* USSR
Brezhnev Doctrine, 217, 308, 340
Browder, Earl, 14, 36
Brus, Wlodzimierz, 130, 137
Brzezinski, Zbigniew, 5, 109, 175, 234
Bukharin, Nikolai Ivanovich, 56–71, 144; and Eurocommunism, 14, 66–69; and New Economic Policy (NEP), 58–60, 63; rehabilitation of, 56, 61–69; and Stalinism, 56–60, 62–66, 68–69
Bulgaria, 26, 49; Communist Party (BCP), 40–41, 188; and Eurocommunism, 14, 109, 111, 112, 136, 217, 256; and Macedonia, 38–39
Canadian Communist Party, 8, 13
Carillo, Santiago: and PRC, 313–314; and Eurocommunism, 4–21, 103, 105, 107, 121, 149, 157, 169, 171, 247, 263; and *Eurocommunism and the State,* 5–6, 8, 9, 112, 136, 157, 217, 226–227, 261, 284, 341–342, 350; on forerunners of Eurocommunism, 14–15, 162; and Marxism-Leninism, 8–12, 20, 104–105, 206, 207, 230; *New Times* attack on, 7–8, 112–114, 217, 284, 341–342, 350; and USSR, 12, 15, 20–21, 95, 114, 116–117, 190, 215, 261, 263–264, 283–284, 313. *See also* Spanish Communist Party
Carter, Jimmy, 5, 220
Catholic Church: in Czechoslovakia, 158; in Hungary, 239; and PCI, 35, 37; in Poland, 131
Ceausescu, Nicolae, 313; and autonomism, 73, 111, 187, 191, 194, 199;

"cult of personality" of, 182–183; and Eurocommunism, 111, 182, 194, 196, 198, 313; policy aims, 182–184, 192–196. See also Romania

Chaban-Delmas, Jacques, 117–118

Chervonenko, S., 117–118

China, People's Republic of (PRC), 116, 128, 227, 296–325; and Albania, 303, 307–308, 312, 318–319, 320–321; Communist Party (CCP), 11, 12, 84, 298–307, 312–316, 321–322; Cultural Revolution, 132, 186, 308, 344; and Eastern Europe, 307; and Eurocommunism, 78, 94, 297, 312–322; and EEC, 310, 311, 314–315; and PCF, 78, 302–303, 319–320, 322; and Hungary, 312; and PCI, 78, 302–303, 314, 320–322; and JCP, 299, 305, 312, 353; and NATO, 309, 310–311, 314–316; and Poland, 132, 308, 312; and Romania, 78, 94, 186, 199, 307–309, 312, 318; and Sino-Soviet split, 300, 302–307, 312, 313; and Soviet invasion of Czechoslovakia, 308–309, 312–313; and PCE, 78, 304, 313–315; and Two-Camp Theory, 297–299; and USSR, 84, 115, 296–322; and United States, 296, 297–298, 309–312; and Western Europe, 297, 307–312; and Yugoslavia, 78, 94, 208, 298, 302, 308–309, 312, 317–319, 320–321

Chou En-lai, 310, 312

Christian Democrats. See Federal Republic of Germany; Italy

Christianity, 13–14, 21, 34, 176

Churchill, Winston, 32, 34, 38

Cierna Meeting, 110

Cold War, 107, 116, 166, 256, 279

Cominform: founding of, 1947, 25, 45–46, 47, 49, 127, 165–166; and JCP, 77, 299, 327, 329, 343–344; and Yugoslavia, 46, 48, 49, 53, 165, 205–206, 298, 300

Comintern, 36, 53, 57, 202, 204, 212, 343; and CPCz, 160–163, 166; and KPP, 126, 128; and popular front period, 16, 27

Communism, 4, 5, 8, 16, 41, 125. See also entries for individual countries and communist parties; Eurocommunism, Marxism-Leninism; World Communist Movement

Communist Manifesto, 79

Communist Party of Czechoslovakia (CPCz): assumes power, 17–18, 49–50, 165–166; in coalition, 18, 32, 40, 49–50, 163, 164–165; and Comintern, 160–163, 166; and democratic socialism, 18, 161, 163–164; popular support for, 161–164; "specific road to socialism" of (1945–1947), 163–165, 170, 172; and Stalinism, 162, 166–167, 168, 173–174. See also Czechoslovakia; Dubcek; Prague Spring

Communist Party of Great Britain (CPGB), 73, 119, 328; and Eurocommunism, 67, 75, 76; policy positions summarized, 78, 89, 186, 305, 351

Communist Party of the Soviet Union (CPSU): Central Committee, 57, 60, 109; party structure of, 91; Politburo, 53, 57, 60, 109–110, 111, 113, 116; Twentieth Congress, 20, 61, 167, 226, 257, 258; Twenty-second Congress, 63, 64, 243; Twenty-fifth Congress, 72–73, 76, 110, 214, 338. See also USSR

Croatia, 14, 29, 32, 208, 216

Cuba, 104, 215, 278, 344

Cunhal, Alvaro, 189

Czech Lands, 158–159, 164, 169

Czechoslovakia, 25, 157–180, 239–240, 243; Austrian Empire period, 158–161; Catholic Church in, 158; "Charter 77" Group, 90, 105, 175, 263; democratic traditions of, 17–18, 158–160, 168; and destalinization, 167–168; and Eurocommunism, 13, 90, 108, 115, 136, 157, 173–177, 256, 263, 284; and Poland, 129, 131, 133, 166, 167, 170, 171; Protestantism in, 158, 164; Social Democratic Party, 160–161; Soviet invasion of, 1968, 64, 75, 77, 79, 105, 108, 119, 129, 172–173, 186, 210, 212, 284; and Stalinism, 166–167, 171, 173–174, 242; and USSR, 159, 164, 166, 175. See also Communist Party of Czechoslovakia; Dubcek; Prague Spring

Dahlem, Franz, 143

De Gasperi, Alcide, 45

De Gaulle, Charles, 28, 30, 107, 118; and NATO, 275, 279; and Poland, 132–133

Democratic Centralism (Marxist-Leninist), 9, 20, 95, 162, 206, 256

Denitch, Bogdan, 216

Dictatorship of the Proletariat (Marxist-Leninist), 72, 214; and CPCz, 166; and PCF, 86–87, 278; and PCE, 10, 104–105, 263; and USSR, 9, 165, 217, 278

Dimitrov, Georgi, 49

Djilas, Milovan, 14, 46, 49, 173, 217

Dolanc, Stane, 73

Dubcek, Alexander, 14, 111, 158, 163, 175; and Cierna Meeting, 110; and Prague Spring, 105, 168–169, 170–175, 187, 211, 240, 313

Duclos, Jacques, 36, 44, 46–47

East Germany. *See* German Democratic Republic

Eastern Europe, 13, 14, 18, 42, 134, 256; and Eurocommunism, 106, 111–112, 120, 124, 137–138, 143, 177, 254–270, 284–286. *See also entries for individual countries and communist parties*

Elleinstein, Jean, 67, 118, 120, 177, 190

Engels, Friederich, 12, 87, 160

Eritrea, 215

Ethiopia, 104, 215

Eurocommunism: and autonomism, 11, 53, 72–73, 94, 134, 137, 189, 190, 191, 203, 255, 264–265, 283; and Bukharin, 57, 66–69; as challenge to Soviet Communism, 6, 10–13, 72–73, 75, 79, 83–84, 88–92, 104–108, 115, 254–255, 264; characteristics of, 9–11, 15, 20, 24, 53, 72, 91, 94–95, 103, 105, 124–125, 157, 173, 181, 203, 255, 258, 287, 312, 327; and "Charter 77" Group, 90, 105, 175, 263; common interests with CPSU, 104, 107–108, 109–110, 278; Communist parties and, 3, 6, 7, 75, 103, 143, 182, 255; as a concept, 3–21, 24, 73, 103, 124–125, 143, 181, 202; contradictions in, 20–21; and democratic centralism, 20–21, 95, 287; and detente, 84, 107, 116; and East European dissent, 90, 91, 105–106, 115, 150, 177, 256, 258–260, 284–285; forerunners of, 12, 14–15, 24, 59, 143, 162, 171, 173, 203; history and origins of term, 3–5; interpretations of, 10, 12, 15–17, 20–21, 104, 124–125; and Madrid Meeting, 6, 254; and Marxism-Leninism, 6, 8–12, 19, 21, 104, 124, 137, 147, 177, 263, 287; missing historical model of, 17; and national liberation movements, 104, 109, 110; *New Times* attack on, 6–8, 112–114, 116, 217, 284, 341–342, 350; and NATO, 104, 106, 107, 110, 188, 272, 276–293; party structure of, 20–21, 87–88, 91, 278; and pluralism, 11, 21, 91, 103, 105, 110, 120, 135, 137, 157, 181, 203, 255, 287–288, 312, 327; and Polish Workers' Strike, 89; political future of, 21, 93–95, 120, 137–138, 177, 265, 267; and popular fronts, 12, 15–16, 53, 162; and Prague Spring, 12, 18, 65, 89, 112, 157–158, 168–176, 258; and proletarian internationalism, 72–95, 207, 278; and Sino-Soviet split, 20, 84; and Soviet dissent, 65–66, 90, 105–106, 115, 256; and Soviet invasion of Czechoslovakia, 79, 86, 89, 108, 171–174, 211, 257, 284, 345; and Stalinism, 16, 57, 66, 124, 177, 203, 260, 283; and Third World, 104, 108, 110, 278; and "United Europe" concept, 107; universalist aspects of, 11, 263, 265–266; and World Communist Movement, 6, 135, 254–255, 260, 313. *See also* Berlin Conference; countries and communist parties; West European Communism

Eurocommunism and the State. See Carillo, Santiago

Europe and the Communists, 6

European Communist Movement, 6–7, 13

European Communist Party Conference, 1976. *See* Berlin Conference

European Economic Community (EEC), 84, 278, 279, 311, 314–315

Fascism, 16, 30, 53

Fechner, Max, 144

Federal Republic of Germany (FRG), 25, 110, 188, 196; Christian Democrats, 52; Communist Party, 188; and GDR, 52, 141–142; and NATO, 107, 274–276, 279, 288–289; Social Democrats, 34, 52, 149, 150, 154

Fedorov, M., 112–113

Finland, 17–18, 19, 26, 41; Communist Party, 17–19, 32, 39–40, 49–50, 73, 75, 76, 88; and USSR, 39–40, 49

Fischer, Ernst, 119, 163

Fojtik, Jan, 158, 168, 175, 263

Ford, Gerald, 310

France, 25–26, 31, 34–36, 48, 86; and PRC, 307–308; force de frappe, 106; and NATO, 274–275, 276; and Poland, 132–133; political traditions of, 19, 30; Socialist Party, 67, 117–118; Third Republic, 37

Franco, Francisco, 20, 107, 190

French Communist Party (PCF), 6, 16, 18, 19, 32; and autonomism, 76, 185, 186, 188, 189–190, 315, 348; and PRC, 78, 302–303, 313–316, 319–320, 322; in coalition (1945–1947), 30, 35–36, 44–47, 163, 165; coalition policy (1970s), 88, 117–118, 190; electoral record, 49, 120, 181–182, 186, 190, 266, 283; and Eurocommunism, 3, 118, 176–177, 190, 278; and EEC, 279, 315; and French strikes of 1947, 44, 48; and human rights, 75, 76, 258, 262; and JCP, 348–349, 350–351, 353; and NATO, 106–107, 276, 279–283, 286, 289, 314; policy positions summarized, 75–76, 86, 277–278; postwar economic policy of, 35–36; rejects "dictatorship of the proletariat" concept, 76, 278, 335; and Romania, 188–190; and Secret Speech, 261–262; and Soviet invasion

of Czechoslovakia, 77, 79, 89, 132–133, 171, 211, 257, 348; *L'URSS et Nous,* 261–262; and USSR, 35, 46–49, 73, 75, 76, 86, 89, 95, 107, 117–118, 132–133, 189–190, 214, 261–262, 278–279, 281, 307, 348. *See also* Marchais; Thorez
Fuwa, Tetsuzo, 328–329, 348; and Scientific Socialism, 87, 334–335, 354

Garaudy, Roger, 168
Gati, Charles, 11, 143
German Communist Party (KPD), 28, 34–35, 47, 52, 143
Germany (before East-West Division), 28, 34, 43, 51–53, 143
German Democratic Republic (GDR), 50, 140–156, 170; and destalinization, 140, 144; dissent in, 91, 141, 144–145, 147–149; economic policies of, 140–141, 144–147; and Eurocommunism, 13, 91, 111–112, 115, 136, 141–146, 148–151, 153–154, 263, 284; and FRG, 141–142, 146–147, 149, 152; "German road to socialism" of, 143; and Helsinki Accords, 141; and "Manifesto of the Opposition," 149; national legitimacy of, 140–141, 145–146; 1953 Uprising, 140, 143–144; and *Ostpolitik,* 141–142, 146; and Stalinism, 140, 143; and Romania, 150–151; Socialist Unity Party (SED), 35, 52, 140–154; SED factional struggles, 143–145; and USSR, 141–156; and West, 140–142, 146, 150, 151; and *Westpolitik,* 147, 152; and Yugoslavia, 144, 150, 151
Gierek, Edward, 130, 131, 133, 244; and PCI, 113, 135
Ginzburg, Alexander, 115, 220
Giscard d'Estaing, Valery, 107, 117–118, 190, 234, 275
Gollan, John, 14
Gomulka, Wladyslaw, 89, 127–128, 130, 131, 133, 168, 170, 244, 302
Gottwald, Klement, 163–164, 166
Greece, 14, 20, 274, 276; Civil War, 31–32, 38, 43, 45, 49; Communist Party (KKE), 17–18, 19, 48, 89, 119
Grippa, Jacques, 304
Grlickov, Alexander, 213, 215
Grotewohl, Otto, 35

Hager, Kurt, 149
Hakamada, Satomi, 336, 338, 343, 346, 348, 351
Harich, Wolfgang, 144, 149
Havemann, Robert, 144, 147, 149
Hegedus, Andras, 240–241

Helsinki Accords, 141, 186, 189, 196, 215, 310
Honecker, Erich, 111, 147, 150, 153
Hoxha, Enver, 319
Hua Kuo-feng, 199, 318, 319, 320, 322
Humanite, L', 175, 259, 261, 316, 319
Hungary, 40, 159, 223–253; and autonomism, 234, 266; Catholic Church in, 239; Compromise of 1867, 245–246; dissent in, 239–243; domestic reforms in 235–240, 243–244; and Eurocommunism, 13, 111–112, 136, 226, 231–234, 245–247, 259–260, 265; foreign policy of, 233, 244–245; Hungarian Communist Party (HCP), 40–41, 223; Hungarian Revolution, 167, 208, 226, 228–231, 246, 312; Hungarian Socialist Workers' Party (HSWP), 89, 233–240, 245–246, 305; Hungarian Soviet Republic period (1918–1919), 223–224; *Hungaricus* pamphlets (1956), 229–230; New Economic Mechanism (NEM), 112, 134, 235–236, 245; Patriotic People's Front (PPF), 229, 236, 237–239; Petofi Circle, 228–229; and Poland, 128, 244; Smallholders Party, 224; and Soviet invasion of Czechoslovakia, 240–241; and Stalinism, 51, 224–228, 230–232, 239, 244; trade union movement in, 238; and USSR, 223–226, 231, 233–234, 244–247; and Yugoslavia, 245. *See also* Kadar; Nagy
Husak, Gustav, 152, 246

Icelandic Communist Party, 74, 84, 186, 215
International Communist Movement. *See* World Communist Movement
Italian Communist Party (PCI), 3, 6, 18–20, 32, 66–67, 167; and autonomism, 150, 185, 187, 189–190, 220, 306; and Catholic Church, 35, 37; and PRC, 78, 212, 302–303, 305, 313–316, 320–322; and Christian Democrats, 94, 106, 282; in coalition (1945–1947), 30, 35, 37–38, 40, 44–45, 47, 163, 165; coalition policy (1970s), 88, 94, 106, 287–288; and Czechoslovakia, 90, 259; electoral record, 83, 94, 106, 117, 120, 181, 266, 283; and EEC, 278, 279, 314, 315; and Hungary, 211; and JCP, 345–348, 350, 353; Leftist criticism of, 94; and NATO, 104, 106, 119, 172, 276, 279–283, 286, 289–293, 314, 316, 346; and pluralism, 172, 219–220, 264, 278, 345, 347–348; and Poland, 133, 135, 259; policy positions summarized, 67,

177, 219–220, 264, 277–278; and
Prague Spring, 171, 174, 176, 187, 211;
and Romania, 185–187, 212; and Soviet
invasion of Czechoslovakia, 79, 89,
133, 171–172, 187, 211, 220, 257–258;
and USSR, 35, 46–49, 66, 73, 75, 86,
95, 106, 119, 120–121, 214, 219–220,
261, 281–282, 344; and Yugoslavia, 77,
165, 207–208, 212, 216, 219–220, 282.
See also Berlinguer; Togliatti
Italy, 19, 20, 25, 27, 31, 37, 45, 48, 160,
186, 220; Christian Democrats, 37–38,
94, 282, 291, 293; and NATO, 275–276,
289–293
Izvestia, 60

Japan, 13, 326, 335; Liberal Democratic
Party, 334, 354; Socialist Party, 336,
339
Japanese Communist Party (JCP), 8, 73,
105, 326–362; and autonomism, 333,
339–344, 345, 347, 352, 354–355; and
PRC, 299, 305, 312, 322, 331, 337, 344,
352–353, 354; and Cominform, 77, 299,
327, 329, 343–344, 352, 355; coalition
policy, 335–336; and Diet, 331, 334,
335, 338; electoral record, 77, 299,
327–330, 335–336, 354; and Eurocommunism, 13, 75, 77, 255, 327, 335,
344–356; and *Eurocommunism and the
State,* 341–343, 350; and PCF, 348–
349, 350–351, 353; International Conference on Theory of (1972), 332–333,
350–351, 354; and PCI, 332, 345–348,
350–351, 353; Japanese response to,
329, 336, 355; liberalization of, 331–
337, 355–356; "lovable Communism,"
328, 331, 355–356; "Manifesto of
Freedom and Democracy" (1976),
334–335, 354; nationalism of, 337, 339,
355; party structure, 337, 352–353, 356;
and pluralism, 332, 334, 336, 341, 345,
347–348, 351, 356; policy positions
summarized, 77, 299, 351–352; rejects
"dictatorship of the proletariat" concept, 77, 333; Scientific Socialism, 23
*n*31, 77, 333, 334, 350, 354; and Sino-
Soviet split, 331, 337, 353; and Solzhenitsyn affair, 340–341; and Soviet
invasion of Czechoslovakia, 77, 89,
332, 340, 345–346; and PCE, 345,
349–350, 353; and USSR, 13, 77,
326–328, 333, 337–344, 352–353, 355;
and United States, 331, 344, 346, 355

Kadar, Janos, 168, 302; and Eurocom-
munism, 111, 112, 233, 235; and Hun-
garian Revolution aftermath, 231–232;
liberalization policies of, 233, 236–240,
241, 244, 245–247; and New Economic
Mechanism, 235–236; and Prague
Spring, 240–241. *See also* Hungary
Kadarky, A. A., 241
Kafka, Franz, 168
Kalecki, Michal, 130
Kallai, Gyula, 237
Kamenev, Lev, 62
Kanapa, Jean, 76, 89, 190, 234, 316, 348
Kardelj, Edvard, 217, 218
Katushev, Konstantin, 214
Kautsky, Karl, 14–15, 144
Kenedi, Janos, 243
Khrushchev, Nikita, 143, 145, 229, 305;
and destalinization, 61–64, 115, 140,
144, 301, 306, 331; downfall of, 62, 76,
185–186, 306; and Twentieth Party
Congress, 61, 62, 226, 261, 331; and
Yugoslavia, 207, 208, 217
Kissinger, Henry, 12, 17, 104, 234, 287,
316
Koestler, Arthur, 56
Kolakowski, Leszek, 130, 137, 168
Konrad, Gyorgy, 240
Kovacs, Bela, 224
Kosik, Karel, 168
Kreisky, Bruno, 103
Kriegel, Frantisek, 169, 259
Kun, Bela, 223

Lange, Oskar, 130
Laos, 84
Larin, Yuri (Bukharin's son), 61, 64, 65,
66–67
Larina, Anna Mikhailovna (Bukharin's
widow), 61, 63–64, 65
League of Communists of Yugoslavia
(LCY), 75, 203, 245; Eleventh Con-
gress, 218–219; internal policy debates
of, 215, 216–217; 1958 program, 208–
209, 216, 217, 218; recentralization of,
128, 204, 216; Sixth Congress, 206, 216;
Tenth Congress, 218. *See also* Tito;
Yugoslavia
Lenin, Vladimir, 8–9, 14, 87, 223, 226;
and Bukharin, 56–57, 65–66; and New
Economic Policy, 58–59, 225
Leninism. *See* Marxism-Leninism
Leonhard, Wolfgang, 146
Lister, Enrique, 119
Liu Shao-ch'i, 298, 302
Longo, Luigi, 170, 171, 220
Lowenthal, Richard, 267
Lu Ting-yi, 300–301
Lukacs, Gyorgy, 168, 229; *History and*

Class Consciousness, 241–242
Luxembourg, Rosa, 14

Macedonia, 38
McInnes, Neil, 87
Madrid Meeting (1977), 6, 94, 103, 254, 345
Maisky, Ivan, 34
Malenkov, Georgi, 43, 143
Mandelstam, Osip, 58
Mao Tse-tung, 12, 300–301, 302, 309, 316, 328, 343; Two-camp theory, 297–299
Maosim, 12, 300–301. *See also* China
Marchais, Georges, 182, 190, 247; and Madrid Meeting, 6, 94; and USSR, 73, 76, 95, 118, 189, 214, 278, 315. *See also* French Communist Party
Marcuse, Herbert, 241
Marek, Franz, 119, 168
Marshall Plan, 42, 43, 48, 50, 165
Marx, Karl, 8, 12, 168, 226; *Communist Manifesto,* 79, 87; *Economic and Philosophical Manuscripts,* 160; on Germany, 154
Marxism, 74, 160, 241–243; in the West, 15, 18–19
Marxism-Leninism, 6, 85–88, 192; and Eurocommunism, 8–12, 15, 19, 21, 177, 263; and GDR revisionism, 147–149; and Hungarian revisionism, 226–227, 228–231, 241–243; and JCP, 333–334, 337, 354; and "Masarykism," 160–161; and Polish revisionism, 128–129, 137. *See also* Carillo; Lenin; USSR
Masaryk, Tomas, 159, 160–161, 167, 168
Matteotti, Giacomo, 30
Mayer, Hans, 144
Medvedev, Roy: and Eurocommunism, 65–66, 109, 259
Mexican Communist Party, 84
Mihalovic, Draza, 26, 29
Mikolajczyk, Stanislow, 26
Mitterand, Francois, 117–118
Miyamoto, Kenji, 305, 339, 343; and JCP, 328–329, 331–337, 341, 345, 349, 350, 351
Mlynar, Zdenek, 111, 169, 175
Molnar, Erik, 242–243
Monolithic Unity, 9, 82–83, 298
Moro, Aldo, 106
Mundo Obrero, 174, 304
Mussolini, Benito, 20, 27, 28, 30

Nagy, Imre, 168, 231, 232; "New Course" of, 226, 239; *On Communism* treatise,

225–228, 246; and Hungarian Revolution, 226, 228, 229, 246; and USSR, 225
Nemes, Deszo, 89, 234
Nepszabadsag, 234, 236
Netherlands Communist Party, 75, 76, 79, 84, 89, 215, 305
New Times: attack on Carillo, 7–8, 112–114, 217, 284, 341–342, 350; Eurocommunism articles of, 7–8, 10, 114
New York Times, 240, 315
New Zealand Communist Party, 13
Nixon, Richard, 309
Non-aggression Pact, 16–17, 67, 162–163
North Atlantic Treaty Organization (NATO), 84, 272–295; and FRG, 107, 274, 275, 276, 279, 288, 289; and France, 274–275, 276; and PCF, 106–107, 276, 279–283, 286, 289; and PCI, 104, 106, 276, 279–283, 286, 289–293; and Italy, 275–276, 289–293; and PCE, 106, 283–284; and USSR, 106–107, 274; and United States, 106, 107, 110, 272, 293, 316
North Korea, 84, 303, 337, 344
Nosaka, Sanzo, 299, 328, 331, 343; and "lovable Communism," 328, 331
Norwegian Communist Party, 186

Oelssner, Fred, 145

Pajetta, Gian, 113
Palestine Liberation Organization, 104
Paraguay Communist Party, 84
Pasternak, Boris, 58
Pavelic, Ante, 32
Pavlov, Ivan, 58
Peking Review, 314, 320
Pelikan, Jiri, 111, 175
People's Daily, 302–303, 319, 321
Peruvian Communist Party, 84
Peyrefitte, Alain, 117–118
Pijade, Mosa, 205
Poland, 124–139, 170; *Armija Krajowa,* 28, 29; and autonomism, 134, 167–168, 266; Catholic Church in, 131; and PRC, 128, 132, 305; Committee of National Liberation, 127; Communism in, 127, 131, 132, 134, 137, 167–168; Communist Party (KPP), 46, 126–128; and Czechoslovakia, 166, 170, 171; destalinization, 128; dissent in, 129–130, 131, 133, 135–136, 137; domestic unrest in, 130–131, 136, 244; economic policies, 131, 134; and Eurocommunism, 13, 105, 112, 124–125, 127, 129–130, 132–136, 258, 260, 284;

foreign policy, 131; and PCF, 132–133, 135; and Hungary, 128, 133; and PCI, 133, 135; and Kuron-Modzelewski letter, 130; national front in, 25, 26; nationalism of, 125–126, 159; and pluralism, 135; political traditions of, 125–126; and Soviet invasion of Czechoslovakia, 129, 131, 133; and Stalinism, 127–128, 242; and USSR, 26, 28–29, 125–126, 131–136; United Workers' Party (PZPR), 28, 128, 130–133, 135–137; Workers' Defense Committee, 105, 135, 175; Workers' Party (PPR), 28–29, 40–41, 126–128, 165; Workers' Strike, 1970, 89, 130, 136, 258; and World War II, 25, 28–29, 126–127; and Yugoslavia, 132, 133

Polisario, 104

Pollitt, Harry, 14, 62

Polycentrism. *See* Togliatti; World Communist Movement

Pompidou, Georges, 107, 310

Ponomarev, Boris, 82, 109, 113, 116, 213

Portuguese Communist Party, 186, 189

Prague Spring, 64, 105, 186; Action Program, 169–170, 172, 211; and destalinization, 65, 169; and Eurocommunism, 12, 18, 59, 65, 89, 112, 157–158, 166, 168–176, 258; "Socialism with a Human Face," 64, 89, 170, 172, 173, 177, 211, 258; Soviet opposition to, 89, 105, 171. *See also* Czechoslovakia

Pravda, 57, 114, 119, 212, 263, 304

Proletarian Internationalism (Marxist-Leninist), 202, 214; and CPCz, 162; and Eurocommunism, 72–95, 111, 278; and USSR, 9, 217

Radice, Lombardo, 168, 264

Rakosi, Matyas, 166; and Stalinism, 224–226, 228, 230–232, 233, 239–244

Rankovic, Alexander, 210

Red Flag, 302–303, 309

Revel, Jean-Francois: and Eurocommunism, 5, 12, 15–16, 17, 20

Rinascita, 90, 174, 259

Rochet, Waldeck, 170, 171

Romania, 14, 16, 26, 181–201; and autonomism, 97, 111, 137, 184, 186, 191, 266; and PRC, 78, 94, 199, 305, 313, 318; Communist Party (PCR), 23 *n*31, 32, 40–41, 73, 75, 84, 182–199; "Declaration of Independence" (1963), 185, 186; dissent in, 196, 198; and domestic policy, 78, 137, 182, 191–199; and Eurocommunism, 78, 111, 113, 182–185, 188, 191, 196–199, 207, 259–261, 265, 321; foreign policy, 137, 186, 188; and PCF, 188–190; and GDR, 150, 151; and PCI, 185–187, 212; "Multilaterally Developed Society" of, 183–184, 197; nationalism of, 193, 195–196; and pluralism, 183, 192–193, 198; and Prague Spring, 187; and Sino-Soviet split, 185, 186–187, 307; and PCE, 186, 313; and USSR, 31, 38, 135, 197; and West, 192, 193–194, 196, 198; and Yugoslavia, 78, 186, 189, 212. *See also* Ceausescu

Rusinow, Denison, 217

Russian Revolution. *See* Bolshevik Revolution

Salazar, Antonio, 20

San Marino, 23 *n*28, 75

Schirdewan, Karl, 145

Schmidt, Helmut, 275

Scientific Socialism. *See* Japanese Communist Party

Shcharansky, Anatoly, 115, 220

Shiga, Yoshiro, 305, 338

Shragin, Boris, 60

Sik, Ota, 169, 175

Skilling, Gordon H., 158, 167

Slansky, Rudolf, 49

Slovakia, 49, 159, 164, 169

Slovenia, 14

Smeral, Bohumir, 160–161, 163

Socialist parties. *See entries for individual countries*

Solzhenitsyn, Alexander, 69, 340–341

Somalia, 104

Soviet Union. *See* Union of Soviet Socialist Republics

Spain, 15, 160, 186, 276

Spanish Communist Party (PCE), 3, 6, 16, 67, 73, 90, 167; and autonomism, 185–190; and PRC, 304, 313–314; and Czechoslovakia, 259; electoral record, 182, 190, 266, 283; and GDR, 259; and JCP, 345, 349–350; and NATO, 106, 283–284, 314, 316; policy positions summarized, 75, 86, 284; and Prague Spring, 170–171, 174, 176; rejects "dictatorship of the proletariat" concept, 10, 104–105, 263; and Romania, 186, 313; and Soviet invasion of Czechoslovakia, 77, 79, 89, 172, 211, 257–258; and USSR, 76, 89, 113–115, 172, 211. *See also* Azcarate; Carillo

Spriano, Paolo, 27, 66

Stalin, Joseph, 6, 12, 226, 241, 258, 296, 337; and Bukharin, 59–61, 65; and Czechoslovakia, 164–165; death of,

211, 225, 328; and European Communism, 26, 41–42, 51, 299; and Greek Civil War, 32, 49, 206; and New Economic Policy, 59–60; and Poland, 126; World War II policies of, 26, 29, 30; and Yugoslavia, 18, 26, 205–206

Stalinism, 6, 12, 76, 127, 230, 242; and Bukharin, 56–57, 60, 64–65, 68–69; characteristics of, 57, 60, 148; destalinization, 80, 124, 306. *See also entries for individual countries and communist parties*

Suslov, Mikhail, 339; and Eurocommunism, 73–74, 113, 116

Svitak, Ivan, 168

Swedish Communist Party (SKP), 73, 75; policy positions summarized, 76, 79, 81, 89, 186; schism in, 77, 119

Szabad Nep, 224, 228

Szelenyi, Ivan, 240

Tarrow, Sidney, 255

Teng Hsiao-p'ing, 296, 314–315, 321

Third World, 104, 108, 110, 125, 215, 278, 279

Thorez, Maurice, 12, 47; coalition policy, 16, 28, 44, 163; and USSR, 62, 80, 86, 261–262, 302–303

Times (London), 68

Tito, Josip Broz, 12, 20, 58, 94, 166, 210; and LCY, 216; and Partisans, 30–32; and Stalin, 18, 26, 32, 205–206, 256; Titoism, 12, 132, 146, 296; and USSR, 29–30, 50–51, 73, 75, 77, 132, 204, 207, 214, 216, 217, 245, 256, 300, 327. *See also* League of Communists of Yugoslavia; Yugoslavia

Togliatti, Palmiro, 12, 14, 67, 220; coalition policy, 27–28, 30, 44–45, 163; and Marxism-Leninism, 86, 230, 302–303; and polycentrism, 167, 185, 207–208, 211, 212, 260, 321, 331, 345, 351; "Final Testament" of, 80, 133, 306; and USSR, 47, 261

Tokuda, Kyuichi, 299

Trotsky, Lev, 56, 58, 62, 176

Truman, Harry, 43

Turkey, 14, 274, 276

Ueda, Koichiro, 328, 351

Ulbricht, Walter, 140, 153; downfall, 146; and Prague Spring, 147; and SED, 143–145

Union of Soviet Socialist Republics (USSR), 11, 16, 17, 33, 126, 227; and autonomism, 80–81; and Berlin Conference, 7, 74–75, 81, 214; and PRC, 84, 115, 186, 212, 213, 296–312; and

Cominform, 46; and Czechoslovakia, 159, 164, 166, 175; and destalinization, 57, 61–65, 115; dissent in, 65, 105–106, 109, 115, 220, 243, 256; and Eurocommunism, 5–8, 10, 13, 72, 75, 88–92, 95, 103–123, 176, 208, 215, 220, 253–256, 263, 265, 285–286; and Finland, 39–40, 49; and PCF, 35, 46–47, 48–49, 75–76, 89, 107, 117–118; and GDR, 141–156; German policy (1945–1949), 28, 34, 51–52, 143; and Hungary, 223–226, 231, 233–234, 244–247, 285; invasion of Czechoslovakia, 64, 75, 77, 80, 105, 108, 119, 129, 172–173, 220; and PCI, 48–49, 75, 95, 106, 117–119, 214, 220; and Marshall Plan, 42–43, 46, 165; NEP period, 58–60; and Poland, 26, 28–29, 125–126, 131–136, 212, 285; and Prague Spring, 89, 105, 170, 171; Purge Trials (1930s), 46, 56, 60; and Romania, 185, 197, 285; Soviet communism, 8–9, 20, 58, 67, 80, 85–88, 92–93, 260, 263; and PCE, 76, 89, 113–115, 116, 119; and Stalinism, 56–71; and United States, 33–34, 35, 42–43, 45, 107–110, 119–120, 165; and West European Communism (1945–1949), 24–54; and World Communist Movement, 15, 24–25, 33, 73, 79–81, 84, 91–92, 104, 115, 128, 135, 188–189, 202, 203, 205, 211–212, 285; and Yugoslavia, 26, 29–30, 35, 39, 51, 204–208, 211–219. *See also* Communist Party of the Soviet Union

Unita, L', 90, 111, 174, 259, 316, 321, 368

United Kingdom, 28, 29, 31, 34, 38, 67–68. *See also* Communist Party of Great Britain

United States: Communist Party, 8, 13; and Eurocommunism, 104, 110, 120, 219–220, 286, 289–293; and NATO, 104, 107, 110, 272–293, 316; postwar policy (1945–1949), 32–34, 42–43, 45, 51, 165; and USSR, 33–34, 35, 42–43, 45, 107, 165

Varga, Eugene, 33, 41, 43

Varnai, Ferenc, 265

Vietnam, 84, 104, 337, 344

Vieweg, Kurt, 144

Vyshinsky, Andrei, 61

Warsaw Pact, 13, 105, 137, 187, 226, 244, 245, 312, 340; and NATO, 106, 119, 274, 282, 314

West European Communism, 15, 36, 53; 1945–1949 period, 25–55; regional meetings of, 13, 78–79; and Twenty-

fifth CPSU Congress, 72–73; World War II period, 25–32. *See also* Berlin Conference; Eurocommunism
West Germany. *See* Federal Republic of Germany
Wollweber, Ernst, 145
World Communist Conference: 1957 (Moscow), 208, 212, 301, 302; 1960 (Bucharest), 185, 212, 301–302; 1969, 212–213, 338
World Communist Movement, 6, 73, 78, 160, 202, 254–255; and Eurocommunism, 6, 254–255, 260, 313; National Front period, 12, 25–32, 35; and polycentrism, 128, 185–186, 296, 301, 303, 312, 313; Popular Front period, 12, 15–16, 35, 53, 162; and Sino-Soviet split, 20, 80, 212, 256, 296, 301, 303–307, 313, 331. *See also* Union of Soviet Socialist Republics
World Federation of Trade Unions, 105
World Marxist Review, 89

Yugoslavia, 11, 25, 26, 29, 32, 38, 49, 73, 202–222, 227; and autonomism, 167, 204–209, 215; Belgrade Declaration, 207, 214; and PRC, 78, 94, 186, 208, 212, 298, 302, 305, 309, 312, 317–319; and Cominform, 46, 48, 49, 53, 80, 165, 205–206, 298, 300; Communist Party (CPY), 29, 32, 204–206; Conference on Socialism in the Contemporary World,

90, 215; Croatian Crisis, 208, 216; dissent in, 218, 240; domestic policies, 205, 215–216; Economic Reform of (1965), 209–210; and Eurocommunism, 13–14, 113, 203, 206, 209, 211, 214–215, 217–220, 245, 257, 259–261, 298; and GDR, 144, 150, 151; and Hungary, 245; and PCI, 77, 165, 207–208, 212, 219–220; and Khrushchev, 207, 208, 217; and Macedonia, 38–39; nationalities question in, 32, 210, 216, 245; and non-aligned movement, 214–215, 220; Partisan movement, 29–30, 32, 205, 219; and pluralism, 203–219; and Poland, 132; post-Tito era, 120, 203–204, 218, 245, 274; and Romania, 78, 186, 189, 212; self-managing socialism of, 206–207, 216, 218; and Soviet invasion of Czechoslovakia, 210–211; and USSR, 26, 29–30, 35, 39, 46, 51, 77, 132, 186, 204–208, 211–219, 327. *See also* Djilas; League of Yugoslav Communists; Tito

Zagladin, Vadim, 5–7, 82, 94, 95, 109, 113–114, 116
Zakharaidis, Nikas, 49
Zaradov, Konstantin, 110
Zhdanov, Andrei, 165, 327
Zhivkov, Todor, 109, 111, 233
Zinoviev, Grigory, 62